THE BRITISH LEFT AND INDIA

OXFORD HISTORICAL MONOGRAPHS

The British Left and India

*Metropolitan Anti-Imperialism,
1885–1947*

NICHOLAS OWEN

OXFORD
UNIVERSITY PRESS

*This book has been printed digitally and produced in a standard specification
in order to ensure its continuing availability*

OXFORD
UNIVERSITY PRESS

Great Clarendon Street, Oxford OX2 6DP
United Kingdom

Oxford University Press is a department of the University of Oxford.
It furthers the University's objective of excellence in research, scholarship,
and education by publishing worldwide. Oxford is a registered trade mark of
Oxford University Press in the UK and in certain other countries

© Nicholas Owen 2007

The moral rights of the author have been asserted

First published 2007
Reprinted 2012

British Library Cataloguing in Publication Data
Data available

Library of Congress Cataloging in Publication Data
Data available

ISBN 978-0-19-923301-4

For my parents

Acknowledgements

Material in Crown Copyright is reproduced under the permission guidelines of the National Archives and the Office of Public Sector Information. I am grateful to the following for permission to reproduce unpublished material for which they hold or administer the copyright.

University of Hull: Ammon Papers; The Master and Fellows of University College, Oxford: Attlee Papers; The Bodleian Library: Dawson Diary; The Theosophical Society: Besant Papers; Sardar Patel Memorial Trust: Minute Book, British Committee of Congress; William Ready Division of Archives and Research Collections, McMaster University: Catlin Papers; The Warden and Fellows of Nuffield College, Oxford: Cripps Papers, Fabian Society Papers; The National Archives, Kew: Cripps Papers, J. Ramsay MacDonald Correspondence and Diary; Gandhi Smarak Nidhi: Gandhi Papers; Lord Gorell: Gorell Diary; Friends House, London: Indian Conciliation Group, Agatha Harrison Papers, Alexander Papers; The Master and Fellows of Trinity College, Cambridge: Montagu Diary and Pethick-Lawrence Papers; The Nehru Memorial Museum and Library: Motilal and Jawaharlal Nehru Correspondence; the All-India Congress Committee: the V. K. Krishna Menon Papers; The Michael Ayrton Estate: Nevinson Diary; Churchill Archives Centre, Churchill College, Cambridge: Noel-Baker Papers, Attlee Papers; Labour History Archive and Study Centre: Papers of the Labour Party and the Communist Party of Great Britain; London School of Economics and Political Science: Passfield Papers; Borthwick Institute for Archives, University of York: Pole Papers; The British Library: R. P. Dutt Papers; The National Archives of India: Sastri Papers, Khaparde Diary, Jayakar Papers; Oriental and India Office Collections, British Library: Seal Papers; Modern Records Centre, University of Warwick: Trades Union Congress Papers; Special Collections, University of Sussex: Woolf Papers.

Material from the Ramsay MacDonald Diaries is reproduced accompanied by the following statement: 'The contents of these diaries were, in Ramsay MacDonald's words, "meant as notes to guide and revive memory as regards happenings and must on no account be published as they are." ' I am grateful to Ramsay MacDonald's granddaughter for permission to quote from them.

Every effort has been made to contact other copyright holders.

The research for this book was supported by the British Academy and the University of Oxford, to whom I am very grateful. Its publication has been greatly assisted by the efficiency of the editors and staff of Oxford University Press. There are many other people who deserve my gratitude for their help at various stages of the research, writing and presentation of my arguments. They include Paul Addison, Carl Bridge, Judith M. Brown, David Cannadine, Suhash Chakravarty, Peter Clarke, John Darwin, Partha S. Gupta, Stephen Howe, David Howell, Angela John, Sudipta Kaviraj, Wm. Roger Louis, D. A. Low, Ross McKibbin, Robin J. Moore, S. R. Mehrotra, Kenneth O. Morgan, Kevin Morgan, David Omissi, Tapan Raychaudhuri, Andew S. Thompson, E. P. Thompson, and Philip Williamson. They have saved me from many errors of fact and judgement, but none of them, of course, bears any responsibility for those that remain.

Contents

Abbreviations

AICC	Papers of the All-India Congress Committee, NMML.
AITUC	Papers of the All India Trades Union Congress, NMML.
CI	Papers of the Communist International, RGASPI.
CPGB	Communist Party of Great Britain Archive, LHASC.
CSN	Cabinet Secretaries' Notebooks.
CWLR	Nanda, B. R. (ed.), *Collected Works of Lala Lajpat Rai* (4v., New Delhi, 2003–).
CWMG	Gandhi, M. K., *The Collected Works of Mahatma Gandhi* (printed edition, 100v., 1958–88; e-book edition, 2000). References are given in the form *CWMG* E, followed by the e-book volume and document numbers.
CWSCB	Bose, Sisir Kumar and Bose, Sugata (eds.), *Netaji: Collected Works of Subhas Chandra Bose* (10v., Calcutta, 1980–).
DCI	Director of Criminal Intelligence.
DNC	Patwardhan, R. P. (ed.), *Dadabhai Naoroji Correspondence* (2v., Bombay, 1977).
GM	Gokhale Microfilm, OIOC.
HC	Halifax Collection (C152), OIOC.
HPA	Home Political A, NAI.
HPB	Home Political B, NAI.
HPD	Home Political Deposit, NAI.
ICG	Indian Conciliation Group Archive, Friends House, London.
IISH	International Institute of Social History, Amsterdam.
ILP	Independent Labour Party.
INC	Indian National Congress.
IPI	Indian Political Intelligence.
JC	Jayakar Collection, NAI.
KMF	V. K. Krishna Menon Microfilm, Centre for South Asian Studies, Cambridge.
KMP	V. K. Krishna Menon Papers, NMML.
LAI	League Against Imperialism.

LHASC	Labour History Archives and Study Centre, Manchester.
LPA	Labour Party Archive, LHASC.
LPACImpQ	Labour Party Advisory Committee on Imperial Questions.
LPACIntQ	Labour Party Advisory Committee on International Questions.
MC	Morley Collection (D573), OIOC.
MNC	Motilal Nehru Correspondence, NMML.
NA	National Archives, Kew.
NAC	National Administrative Committee (of ILP).
NAI	National Archives of India, New Delhi.
NEC	National Executive Committee (of Labour Party).
NLS	National Library of Scotland.
NMML	Nehru Memorial Museum and Library, New Delhi.
NNR	Native Newspaper Reports.
OIOC	Oriental and India Office Collections, British Library.
PLP	Parliamentary Labour Party.
RGASPI	Rossiiskii gosudarstvennyi arkhiv sotsial'nopoliticheskoi istorii, Moscow.
RP	Reading Viceregal Collection (E238), OIOC.
SC	Sastri Collection, NAI.
SCLR	Dhanki, Joginder Singh (ed.), *Perspectives on Indian National Movement: Selected Correspondence of Lala Lajpat Rai* (New Delhi, 1998).
SM	Sapru Microfilm, OIOC.
SWJN	Gopal, Sarvepelli (ed.), *Selected Works of Jawaharlal Nehru*, First Series (15v., New Delhi, 1972–82).
SWMN	Ravindra Kumar et al. (eds.), *Selected Works of Motilal Nehru* (7v., New Delhi, 1982–95).
TP	*India: The Transfer of Power, 1942–7* (12v., London, 1970–83).
TUC	Trades Union Congress.

Introduction

This book is the story of two interwoven quests: the search of the British left for a form of anti-colonial nationalism of which they could approve, and the search of Indian nationalists for a mode of agitation in Britain which did not offend their commitment to self-reliant struggle.

I have generally followed Stephen Howe's useful working definition of anti-colonialism, based in turn on that of Thomas Hodgkin, which sees two paired commitments as necessary: first, to the basic equality of European and non-European peoples and cultures and to the right of all nations to self-determination; and secondly to political action aimed at eradicating colonialism in one's own country as well as in others, and to international as well as national work.[1] Of course, defined strictly in this sense, there was very little anti-colonialism in Britain before the Second World War. Few of even the most radical critics of empire envisaged the immediate liberation of Britain's colonies.[2] But then nor, at least before 1929—or perhaps even 1942 if the demand is an immediate one—did the Indian National Congress, its main demands until that point being a greater share in government, responsible government, or home rule within the empire. An exacting definition of anti-imperialism would tend to make it harder to see the differences, important for this study, between those who wished to meet Congress demands and those who did not. It would also restrict the chronological coverage of the study, neglecting the important continuities between the struggles for the more limited Congress goals before the First World War

---

[1] Stephen Howe, *Anticolonialism in British Politics: The Left and the End of Empire, 1918–1964* (Oxford, 1993), 1–2.

[2] Bernard Porter, *Critics of Empire: British Radical Attitudes to Colonialism in Africa, 1895–1914* (London, 1968) and *The Absent-Minded Imperialists: Empire, Society, and Culture in Britain* (Oxford, 2004), 242–8; Howe, *Anticolonialism*, 31–4.

and the independence movement of the 1930s and 1940s. So while retaining the label of anti-imperialist proper for the small numbers of Britons committed to self-determination, the book also examines, and treats as part of the anti-imperialist movement, not just those formally committed, but also those who aspired to self-determination as an ideal, or espoused it either conditionally or in a utopian mode. I take this to include those who worked for self-government when this was what Congress demanded, or even for widening access to administrative posts when this was the principal Congress request. Plotting, on an anti-imperialist scale, the shifting positions of the British left, on the one hand, and Congress, on the other, is a necessary preliminary. But the primary task of the book is to define and explain the persistent gap between them. 'It is almost as if we spoke a different language', Nehru told Labour MPs in 1936. 'Why is there such a gulf between our two points of view—a gulf bigger than any conflict on specific points?'[3]

It has been clear from the earliest scholarly studies that the relationship between the British left and the Indian anti-imperialist movement was a troubled one, exhibiting a distinctive pattern of strengths and weaknesses. First attempts to analyse it argued that the principal difficulty was the dominance of the Labour Party and the trade unions and their tolerance of, or even commitment to, an empire which delivered economic benefits to the elites of the labour movement—the skilled workers of the labour aristocracy—in the form of higher wages, supported by the profits of imperial trade.[4] P. S. Gupta's *Imperialism and the British Labour Movement* (1975),[5] however, convincingly showed that such 'social imperialist' explanations failed to explain why the support that the British labour movement, even the 'aristocratic' elements of it, gave to projects of imperial expansion or exploitation was so limited. Further work on the economics of imperialism has confirmed how little

---

[3] Speech by Nehru at the House of Commons, 6 Feb. 1936, L/PJ/12/293, OIOC.
[4] Georges Fischer, *Le Parti Travailliste et la décolonisation de l'Inde* (Paris, 1966); V. G. Kiernan, 'India and the Labour Party', *New Left Review*, 42 (1967), 44–55; 'The British Labour Movement and Imperialism', *Bulletin of Society for the Study of Labour History*, 31 (Autumn 1975), 96–101; Ioan Davies, 'The Labour Commonwealth', *New Left Review*, 22 (1963), 75–94.
[5] Partha S. Gupta, *Imperialism and the British Labour Movement, 1918–1964* (London, 1975).

the working classes—Labour's principal constituencies—gained from empire.[6] Before 1914, at least, industrial, provincial 'Labour Britain' before the First World War, was economically, geographically and socially almost the mirror image of the 'Imperial Britain'—finance and service-oriented and based in south-east England. The true priorities of the empire's governors were made painfully clear in the interwar years, when employment at home was sacrificed to ensure that the Dominions and colonies remained solvent enough to pay their debts.[7] Britain's recession-hit workforce favoured the USA while it could, only taking advantage of the empire when this route was closed to them, and efforts to promote imperial migration met with hostility from the Labour Party and trade unions when they were proposed at the end of the First World War.[8] Nor did imperial trade make much difference. As is well known, the volume of trade with the empire, as a proportion of overseas trade as a whole, was significant but not overwhelming. Before 1914, hardly any staple imports from the empire bore a price advantage for British consumers. The interwar creation of imperial preferences had little to offer British working-class consumers except higher food prices than they might have paid in a free market. It was not until after 1945 that colonial imports, paid for in sterling rather than hard currency, gave some cheer to the ration-weary. But this can scarcely be invoked to explain the 'social imperialism' of earlier generations. During the 1930s, empire markets held up better than other foreign markets, buffering the industrial economy against recession. But it is not clear that they did so because they were *empire* markets. Even had other countries undertaken the expense of governing, developing and protecting the colonies, Britain might have had as great an export trade as she did at

[6] Lance E. Davis and Robert A. Huttenback, with the assistance of Susan Gray Davis, *Mammon and the Pursuit of Empire: The Political Economy of British Imperialism, 1860–1912* (Cambridge, 1986), 200.

[7] P. J. Cain and A. G. Hopkins, *British Imperialism*, vol.1, *Innovation and Expansion, 1688–1914* and vol.2 *Crisis and Deconstruction, 1914–1990* (London, 1993). For an exploration of the debate surrounding these books, see Raymond E. Dummett (ed.), *Gentlemanly Capitalism and British Imperialism: The New Debate on Empire* (London, 1999).

[8] Keith Williams, ' "A Way Out of our Troubles": The Politics of Empire Settlement, 1900–22' in Stephen Constantine (ed.), *Emigrants and Empire: British Settlement in the Dominions Between the Wars* (Manchester, 1990); N. H. Carrier and J. R. Jeffery, *External Migration: A Study of the Available Statistics, 1815–1950* (London, 1953); Kent Federowich, *Unfit for Heroes: Reconstruction and Soldier Settlement in the Empire Between the Wars* (Manchester, 1995).

lower cost.[9] Indeed, had the internal biases that supported empire not existed, capital might have been released for the domestic economy, sufficient perhaps to overcome the rigidities that preventing new industries from emerging, and old ones from modernising.[10] The British manual worker might, as J. A. Hobson suggested, have benefited from increased job opportunities, rising wages and the flow of new consumer goods as home demand expanded, as well as from the greater resources that the state, liberated from the necessity to protect investments overseas, might have spent on health, education and housing.

Many criticisms have been raised about imperial accountancy of this kind, especially concerning its employment of counterfactuals, the neglect of transactional costs and of the interconnections and mutual dependences of the imperial and non-imperial economies. Labour supported the empire, we might suspect, even in those activities from which it did not directly benefit, because it was hard to separate from Britain's world system, from which it did. Nevertheless, the economic interests of the working classes can only be used to explain the weakness of the left's anti-imperialism on the basis of two further assumptions: first, that the nature of the economic interests, and their likely futures, were clearly understood; and secondly that the parties and movements of the left were simply a vehicle for them. Neither of these assumptions is especially plausible. First, the gains and losses were contested and hard to predict. 'I know of people who can prove to me with pencil and paper that we should be just as well off, or perhaps better, if all our colonial possessions were lost to us; and I know others who can prove that if we had no colonies to exploit our standard of living would slump catastrophically', wrote George Orwell in 1946. 'And yet . . . this is obviously not an insoluble question. The figures that would settle it once and for all must exist if one knew where to look for them.'[11] But the figures would not have solved it, because their implications depended

---

[9] Patrick K. O'Brien, 'The Costs and Benefits of British Imperialism 1846–1914', *Past and Present*, 120 (Aug. 1988), 163–200.

[10] Sidney Pollard, 'Capital Exports, 1870–1914: Harmful or Beneficial?', *Economic History Review*, 38/4 (1985), 489–514 and his *Britain's Prime and Decline* (1989), ch. 2; W. P. Kennedy, *Industrial Structure, Capital Markets and the Origins of British Economic Decline* (Cambridge, 1987).

[11] George Orwell, 'Do Our Colonies Pay?', in Peter Davison (ed.), *The Complete Works of George Orwell* (20v., London, 1986–98), xviii, 141–4. Orwell himself, indeed, was guilty of confusion on this score. In *The Lion and the Unicorn*, he describes India's value to Britain as simply that of 'a few hundred thousand dividend-drawers'. A few pages later, we are told that 'the wealth of England' is 'drawn largely from Asia and Africa' and that trade-unionists' livelihoods thus depend on 'the sweating of Indian coolies'. Orwell,

on knowing whether this economic stake, once defined, might be safer under imperial rule or only once power was transferred to nationalists. This had made, for example, trade unionists *potential* allies of an Indian nationalism which could promise an end to cotton boycotts and levels of industrial cooperation unachievable under the *raj*, as well as *potential* allies of the *raj* in suppressing the challenge of an unregulated industrial competitor. Secondly, as Gupta has shown, imperial policy within the Labour Party was made less by the trade unions, the principal guardians of the economic interest, than by professional party officials and advisers, often ex-colonial civil servants.[12] In government, the dominant voices on matters of imperial political development tended to be those of such professionals, with the trade unionists confining their involvement to narrower and better understood questions of labour organisation in the colonies.[13]

Other explanations of the weaknesses of metropolitan anti-imperialism identify, to simplify somewhat, five other candidates: the apathy and ignorance of the left's political constituencies on questions of empire; its concern for the electoral consequences of adopting anti-imperialist positions; its reliance, in the absence of a proper theory of imperialism, on inherited radical liberal humanitarianism; its inability to challenge an all-encompassing ideological orientalism; and its vulnerability to the capacity of its opponents to co-opt their critics and turn their attacks into plans for imperial reconstruction.[14] Bernard Porter has shown how little interest Labour supporters were likely to take in imperial matters, a product of the perceived irrelevance of empire to their domestically oriented struggles and the unwillingness or inability of imperialists to build cross-class movements.[15] However, as Porter acknowledges, this did not necessarily prevent the political movements of the left from embracing anti-imperialist positions, which could perfectly happily sit

The Lion and the Unicorn, in Sonia Orwell and Ian Angus (eds.), *The Collected Essays, Journalism and Letters of George Orwell* (4v., Harmondsworth, 1970), ii, 106–7, 113.

[12] Gupta, *Imperialism*, 227–31 for tables on attendance. G. T. Garratt, *The Mugwumps and the Labour Party* (London, 1932).

[13] Leonard Woolf, *Beginning Again: An Autobiography of the years 1911–1918* (London, 1964), 226–31; *Downhill All the Way: An Autobiography of the years 1919–1939* (London, 1967), 221–39; *The Journey Not the Arrival Matters: An Autobiography of the years 1939–69* (London, 1969), 157–66.

[14] For a summary, see Nicholas Owen, 'Critics of Empire in Britain', in Judith M. Brown and Wm. Roger Louis (eds.), *The Oxford History of the British Empire, vol. IV, The Twentieth Century* (Oxford, 1999).

[15] Porter, *Absent-Minded Imperialists*, esp. 194–226.

atop grass-roots indifference, provided they did not claim too many resources or clash too badly with domestic priorities. Moreover, apathy and ignorance should not be conflated. The leadership of the British left was not ignorant about India. Of the party's five principal leaders from 1906 to 1947, four (Keir Hardie, Ramsay MacDonald, George Lansbury and C. R. Attlee) made India a specialism, three of them (Hardie, MacDonald and Attlee) made visits to India and two (Attlee and MacDonald) served lengthy terms on specialist commissions on India. This compared quite favourably with their political opponents. In 1924, indeed, MacDonald was the first British Prime Minister since Wellington to have visited India before taking office. Thus it is insufficient for our purposes to show that the average British worker was untroubled by imperial matters. We have instead to examine the dynamics of commitment within the informed political organisations of the left, to see why they found the task of building solidarities with the colonised difficult.

The electoral salience of anti-imperialism is hard to assess, given the lack of sufficiently finely-grained polling data. Received wisdom suggested that Indian issues raised little interest at the polls in most working-class constituencies, and even where the Indian market mattered for local employment, the electorate was normally fairly easily satisfied. Any Indian policy was defensible there, the Labour Secretary of State cheerfully admitted in 1930. They were 'a mixture of ignorance and idealism, always with racial prejudice ready to be excited, so that the ground is indeed clear for any argument'.[16] However, in the 1920s, Labour wished to expand its support into the progressive middle ground previously held by Liberals. In the 1920s, many ex-Liberals seem to have regarded the Labour Party as a clumsily-driven and grubby vehicle, in which modern progressives, for want of anything better, now had to travel. For these individuals, and more importantly for the voters to which they provided the link, India was a test of Labour's competence and capacity for liberal statesmanship. The most obvious way to do this was to employ some Liberal statesmen, and Labour readily sought and obtained the advice and support of ex-Liberals on Indian and colonial policy. Cabinet formation reflected the same strategy, with the foreign and imperial portfolios generally going to those with colonial governing experience or Liberal credentials. But the policy implications of these electoral factors were not simple. Statesmanship implied attention to

---

[16] Benn to Irwin, 20 June 1930, Irwin Papers, MSS/Eur/C152/6.

persistent imperial interests and to the expectations of traditional allies, and above all to the maintenance of order. At moments of crisis in Indian affairs, public disquiet could grow surprisingly quickly, throwing Labour unexpectedly on the defensive and distracting it from urgent tasks at home. This was especially worrying if an Indian crisis threatened to interlock with parallel disturbances elsewhere. But statesmanship did not necessarily rule out anti-imperialist work. On the contrary, maintaining the momentum of progress, timely concession and the ability to deal easily with former enemies were the key skills of the political leaders of an empire under stress, especially (as we shall see) in wartime. A close political relationship with anti-colonialists would turn out after 1945 to be no electoral liability at all. Thus the task of an explanation constructed in terms of electoral concerns is to explain why this was not so before 1945.

Part of such an explanation might be the capacity of the officials of the *raj* to prevent alliances with nationalists from being built or sustained in government. The Viceroy and other British officials in India, and perhaps in London too, were not merely servants of an elected government, but carried considerable authority in their own right, if only because their semi-public protests, or, worse, resignations, could damage a reputation for statesmanship. This neglected dimension is important in explaining why metropolitan anti-imperialism functioned very differently in power and in opposition. The authoritative accounts of the state and its disengagement from its Indian empire have generally had little to say about it, partly because it is usually assumed that government ministers left their party politics at the door.[17] This is probably not badly wrong as an assumption, but it raises the important question of how incoming Labour governments were parted from their own distinctive principles and approaches. Among the possible reasons are the existence of political conventions which inhibited criticism of officials; the binding effect of previous policy commitments; the restricted flow of independent, non-official information from India to Britain; and the opportunities for bureaucratic resistance afforded by a devolved and undemocratic structure of governance. Labour ministers were not always the trapped victims of these procedures and institutions, which they did their

---

[17] R. J. Moore, *The Crisis of Indian Unity 1917–1940* (Oxford, 1974); *Churchill, Cripps and India, 1939–1945* (Oxford, 1979); *Escape from Empire: The Attlee Government and the Indian Problem* (Oxford, 1983); *Making the New Commonwealth* (Oxford, 1987); D. A. Low, *Britain and Indian Nationalism: The Imprint of Ambiguity* (Cambridge, 1997).

best to challenge by the construction of rival networks of information and influence, but their constraining effect was real. I explore this in Chapters 5, 6 and 9.

The dominant intellectual influences on the left, it is argued, have also played a part in weakening metropolitan anti-imperialism. One view has been that the weakness of British Marxism and Leninism left the British left without a position from which to criticise imperialism for anything worse than inhumane practices. Another argues that such Leninism as there was suffered from crippling ambiguities, especially on the question of whether workers gained or lost from imperialism, and hence never produced in Britain the distinctive and unambiguous socialist position on imperialism that it did in Germany, Austria and Russia.[18] Fabianism had obvious affinities with a progressive imperialism which might develop India before power was transferred, and many socialists had concerns about transferring power to indigenous capitalists and their political allies. A more far-reaching explanation still, developed by post-colonial theorists, suggests that *all* those ideologies which might have developed an anti-imperial cutting edge, including liberalism, forms of socialism, including classical Marxism, failed to do so, because they were themselves the children of imperialism, and, until challenged by the colonised themselves, remained tainted by orientalist assumptions of colonial inferiority.[19] There is now a huge literature assessing the theoretical validity of these claims, especially as applied to Marxism.[20] My concern here, however, is their descriptive accuracy about actually existing metropolitan anti-imperialism. There was, Edward Said argues, 'scarcely any dissent, any departure, any demurral' from orientalist attitudes at the metropole. Indeed, he observes, 'sectors of the metropolitan cultures that have since become vanguards in the social contests of our time', such as the working class and women's movements, were 'uncomplaining members of this imperial consensus'.[21] In later work, notably *Culture and Imperialism*, Said admits some exceptions to this claim. However, he still argues that they have been 'historically hidden

[18] See Howe, *Anticolonialism*, 57–8.
[19] Edward Said, *Orientalism* (London, 1978); Edward Said, 'Orientalism Reconsidered', in Francis Barker et al., *Europe and its Others*, v.1 (Colchester, 1985); *Culture and Imperialism* (London, 1993).
[20] See in particular, Aijaz Ahmad, *In Theory: Classes, Nations, Literatures* (London, 1992); Benita Parry, *Postcolonial Studies: A Materialist Critique* (London, 2004).
[21] Edward Said, 'Secular Interpretation, the Geographical Element, and the Methodology of Imperialism', in Gyan Prakash (ed.), *After Colonialism: Imperial Histories and Postcolonial Displacements* (Princeton, 1995), 30–1.

in and by imperialism's consolidating vision' and that they only came to be articulated once 'native uprisings had gone too far to be ignored or defeated'.[22] At the metropole, oppositional energy sufficient to counter orientalist ideas was supplied not by the metropolitan parties, but by the colonised expatriates: 'figures who address the metropolis using the techniques, the discourses, the very weapons of scholarship and criticism once reserved for the European, now adopted for insurgency or revisionism at the very heart of the Western centre'.[23]

Orientalist depictions of India were certainly very common on the British left. Chapter 3, for example, will detail Ramsay MacDonald's amateur speculations on caste and religion, Keir Hardie's romanticisation of India's history, and the Webbs' use of racial categorisations which came straight from colonial ethnography. But orientalist ideas did not always lead to imperialism. Some of those who held them, such as Annie Besant and even Gandhi, reworked them in an 'affirmative' form, in which the history and traditions of India, for the *raj* a sufficient justification for foreign rule, grounded the claim that India enjoyed civilizational status equal to that of the west, and hence mobilised resistance to imperialism.[24] Moreover, racial stereotyping *per se* was increasingly regarded as crude and unscientific, though elements of it undoubtedly persisted throughout the period covered here, as racially-grounded claims were reworked into claims about the relative development of different civilisations.[25] The Indians scored only a little better on this scale, but where the racially inferior could never gain equality, the civilisationally inferior could catch up through westernisation. Thus claims of the latter kind, ethnocentric and paternalistic as they were, could validate a conditional anti-imperialism, favouring devolution and transfers of power to modern, westernising elites in the place of stultifying colonial rule, though at least as easily, a trusteeship-based imperialism for the present. Orientalist knowledge of India was by the 1930s being challenged, not merely by alternative histories and epistemologies produced by colonial expatriates, but also by western views of a new, modern India, created and galvanised by Congress, opposed by a feeble and regressive *raj*, but which once free was set to mimic the social and political development of the west.

[22] Said, *Culture and Imperialism*, 288, 291.
[23] Edward Said, 'Third World Intellectuals and Metropolitan Culture', *Raritan*, 9/3 (1990), 27–50.
[24] Richard G. Fox, *Gandhian Utopia: Experiments with Culture* (Boston, 1989).
[25] Alastair Bonnett, *Idea of the West: Culture, Politics and History* (London, 2004).

However, the fact that this newer set of ideas never successfully formed the basis of a common struggle with Indians, suggests that the problem was not so much the British left's adherence to any specific body of notions about India as the way in which it gathered its information and formed its alliances. At one point and not altogether consistently, Said describes orientalism as not a matter of holding a particular set of views, but of '*positional* superiority, which puts the Westerner in a whole series of possible relationships with the Orient, without ever losing him the relative upper hand'.[26] This is potentially a more powerful explanation, in which the difficulty of building solidarity results from the relative positions which the parties held in any debate, rather than the differences of view themselves.

Indeed, nothing stands out from Labour discussions of India more strongly than the constant effort of Labour leaders to explain Congress to their followers and to themselves in familiar, British terms. Despite the fact that Congress had been founded some fifteen years before their own party, Labour often saw it as a junior partner in need of education in the arts of political activism or of good government, seldom questioning whether tactics designed to advance the interests of uniquely class-conscious workers in an industrial society whose ruling classes generally eschewed repression were appropriate for the divided mix of classes and interests over which Congress presided. Before the First World War, as I show in Chapter 3, a procession of Labour's senior figures visited India, setting down their thoughts on the nature of healthy political development. The lessons they drew were quite varied, and were strongly coloured by their views of how the Labour cause had advanced at home. For Keir Hardie, the devolution of political power to village councils would ensure that the urban professionals who made up the Congress movement were brought face-to-face with the problems of the rural, labouring poor. Sidney and Beatrice Webb hoped to see cooperation between the 'natural aristocracy' of educated Indians and sympathetic British officials in local schemes of social improvement, through which Indians might acquire the skills to run a modern, interventionist state. Ramsay MacDonald regarded Congress as only at the first stage of its development, comparing its proposals to the narrow, class-bound demands of the mid-Victorian Liberal Party. Indian nationalism should, he argued, follow the same lines of political evolution as the movement for labour representation had at home. Congress, contrary to the views

[26] Said, *Orientalism*, 7.

of the officials of the *raj*, was a healthy development, but to develop further it had to participate in the local government that Morley had provided, to carve out a broader-based political support among Indian workers and peasants, reduce its dependence on middle-class activists, and campaign not merely for political independence but for social reform to raise the condition of India's impoverished masses. In the years after 1914, Labour scanned the subcontinent for signs of appropriate progress and the emergence of authentic nationalism: perhaps the emergence of a multi-party system divided along class lines, or the political recruitment of peasants and workers, or the development of schemes for practical socialism, or the evolution of party programmes that went beyond attacks on the *raj*. As Labour moved from oppositional movement to party of government after 1918, it became increasingly keen to push Congress down the same road to responsibility. But judged against these standards, Congress, in seemingly moving away from parliamentarism towards Gandhian non-cooperation, seemed to be going in reverse. Many British observers, especially in the trade unions, doubted whether it was truly interested in social reform. Its demands for independence seemed too closely entwined with the vested interests of the Indian middle classes and too bound up with impractical Gandhism to act as an instrument for genuine industrial and economic change. Indian unions seemed too prone to spontaneous and undisciplined outbreaks of labour unrest, their leadership provided by lawyers or even employers rather than workers, and their work characterised by political objectives that ranged too far beyond wage-bargaining. This could all be satisfactorily changed, given time and patience, but to those who had won acceptance for Labour through negotiation in the parliamentary arena and demonstrating their fitness to govern to local electorates, there could be no short cuts to political maturity. As late as 1943, Labour ministers worked on plans to undermine the Congress leadership and remould Indian nationalism into a more acceptable form (Chapter 9).

However, there were very good reasons why Congress and other Indian nationalists were unable to meet Labour's criteria. India lacked nearly all the structural underpinnings that would have made Labour's strategy appropriate. The emergence of British Labour had been greatly eased by the fact that it happened in a state with a liberal constitutional framework, in which trade unions and socialist societies could operate without serious restriction. Labour's leaders had come to see the state as a largely neutral force, committed to rule-following and publicly declared 'fairness' between classes, which could be captured by winning a parliamentary majority.[27] In India, by contrast, politics were very much more circumscribed. The *raj*, despite its liberal pretensions, was very ready to lock up nationalist agitators without trial, ban newspapers and proscribe hostile organisations. It was quite impossible for nationalists to see it as neutral, or to make capture of local legislative power the sole aim of its strategy. As the Indian Communist M. N. Roy acerbically pointed out: '[T]here cannot be parliamentarism in a country without a parliament.'[28] Labour had emerged almost entirely within pre-existing political structures, and only rarely needed to step outside them. Even when it did, it did so within the wider margins of acceptable dissent. Congress, since it sought to displace the *raj* from India, could not work wholly in the same fashion. It had to step, often and far, outside the plans of the *raj*. Moreover, the Indian nationalist struggle after 1920, as Gandhi and others conceived it, was not intended to mimic British political traditions. It rejected the mendicancy of the early Congress. Independence was to be won through the purification of Indian efforts, not learned at the feet of British sympathisers, no matter how well intentioned. This kind of struggle was dictated by the specificity of Indian conditions, and in particular by the need to rally the support of much wider groups than had been attracted by the westernized strategies used hitherto. But it was also quite new and it is hardly surprising that so many Labour figures misunderstood it. The inner workings of the 'dominant parties' that led anti-imperialist struggles were more complex than their own typologies allowed, and could only be poorly understood by those anxious to squash them into the moulds of western, and usually British, experience.

The problem, therefore, was akin to those identified in contemporary postcolonial theory as false universalisation and of the neglect of multiple routes to modernity.[29] The judgement and values of the British anti-imperialists were 'provincial', the product of a specific and localised historical experience, but falsely universalised as

---

[27] Ross McKibbin, 'Why was there no Marxism in Great Britain?' *The English Historical Review*, 391 (1984), 297–331.

[28] Sibnarayan Ray (ed.), *Selected Works of M. N. Roy* (3v., Oxford, 1987–90), ii, 520–8.

[29] S. N. Eisenstadt, 'Multiple Modernities', and Sudipta Kaviraj, 'Modernity and Politics in India', *Daedalus*, 129/1 (Winter 2000); Charles Taylor, 'Modernity and Difference' in Paul Gilroy et al., (eds.), *Without Guarantees: In Honour of Stuart Hall* (London, 2000), 363–74; Dipesh Chakrabarty, *Provincializing Europe: Postcolonial Thought and Historical Difference* (Princeton, 2000).

the paradigmatic or normative standard forms, against which Indian versions were found wanting. Labour's early twentieth-century leaders, like most of their contemporaries, were soaked in Victorian ideals of unilinear social progress. For them the rise of democracy and the emancipated working man were the highly desirable fruits of these ideals, and it was their duty to encourage them to emerge elsewhere. Labour's industrial struggle was thus, as befitted the world's first industrial nation, the model from which others might learn and India was judged for its ability to replicate this pattern of development. From this standpoint, there was but a single route to maturity. Few could see India's differences as other than deviations from proper, western norms of historical and political development. Its industrial workers were judged against the superior rationality, energy and technical expertise of their British counterparts. Its political leaders were judged by their capacity to foster western conceptions of modernity, progress and development.

This helps to explain a feature of the interaction which is hard to understand in terms of persistent economic interests or enduring apathies: the *repeated*, almost cyclical pattern of engagement and failure. When Labour leaders visited India, they hoped to identify signs of modernity that they recognised. They were not wholly disappointed, for Congress leaders showed them newspaper editorials modelled on *The Times* and printed appeals resembling Victorian petitions, and took them to public meetings where the procedure and platform oratory seemed slightly dated, but familiar. Yet like all such mimicry, it also seemed too imitative to be authentic. Other sightings—the unfamiliar modes of protest—such as caste sanctions, the use of religious appeals, and traditional forms of leadership, for example, seemed to have more popular resonance and deeper roots, but they also seemed immature and pre-modern (rather than *non*-modern). This pattern of projection, crisis and paralysis was to be repeated many times, as the movements of the western left stepped forward to engage with Indian nationalism. A number of possible responses might follow from this lack of fit: sometimes a sense of blockage, followed by withdrawal and disengagement (the apathy noted above); sometimes conditional support, provided only if things changed; sometimes efforts, more or less successful, to ignore one or other side of the picture. Postcolonial theorists, often persuaded that the psychological tensions of encountering such irresolvable contradictions led to a kind of anxious fracturing of identity, probably underestimate the degree to which distance damped them down: the most common response was simply retreat.

It is here that Labour's dilemma interlocked with that of Congress. Some of the early Congress leadership shared the view that there was only one route to modernity, and assisted in the work of making the case for home rule on the basis of it. But others did not, either because they believed that such a perspective undervalued Indian traditions, or because they did not think that a nationalist movement could be built on the basis of it. Others again varied their repertoire: to their British supporters and their fellow Indian professionals they appealed in the language of universal Victorian liberalism; to other, less westernized Indians in the language of Hindu tradition and other local idioms. The former appeal was not necessarily weak strategy, despite its imitative character. Opponents held that it could only lead at best to a perpetually deferred promise of equality and hence a permanent secondariness. But the early Congress was not just engaged in mimicry, but in using the leverage provided by commonly held values to demand consistency of treatment. Its occupancy of British liberal positions was designed not purely for the purposes of imitation, but in order to stretch them and reveal their limitations.[30] Such appeals gained in effect at the metropole from being framed in the language of their occupiers, and also from their proximity. The officials of the *raj* feared a united front of Indian nationalists and their British friends speaking the language of modernity more than a solely Indian movement which could be depicted as alien, hostile and regressive. Nevertheless, such a strategy was contested by those who wanted an indigenously-oriented and self-reliant struggle, which would sacrifice intelligibility in London for gains in support in India among those who had not been much troubled by the compatibility of their world view with the dominant ideologies of the west. Gandhi, who became the spokesman for this position, exposed the false position in which the otherwise effective early Congress had placed itself. Rather than representing themselves as imperial subjects of sufficient maturity to be granted self-government, Indians should grant themselves the status of equals.

This debate had implications for the relationship between Congress and its British sympathisers and supporters. This relationship could operate in a number of different modes. The early Congress used

---

[30] Sudipta Kaviraj, 'On State, Society and Discourse in India' in James Manor (ed.), *Rethinking Third World Politics* (London, 1991).

an agency arrangement, hiring a British journalist to act for them. However, this was short-lived, for reasons explored in Chapter 1, and was abandoned in favour of reliance upon voluntary, unpaid, British 'responsible public men', among them former civil servants of the *raj* and Liberal MPs, running an autonomous British Committee of the Indian National Congress. This method was, however, disliked in India for its mendicancy, and was countered in Britain by the rejectionist mode favoured by Vinayak Savarkar and the India House (discussed in Chapter 2) which tried to dispense with British supporters altogether in a version of nativist struggle. However, such rejectionist campaigning was very hard to achieve, partly because it was so much easier to resist. It was generally either ignored, or easily crushed by the *raj*, partly because it lacked British supporters to create space for its operations, but also, and more subtly, because it inverted, rather than displaced, the claims of the west.

Vicarious struggle at the metropole was thus unavoidable, so the problem, when Gandhi encountered it in 1909, became one of finding a mode of interaction with Britons which did not leave them in charge, or Indians deferring to them. Gandhi believed that it would not be right to reject the contribution of British supporters, but that if their priorities were not to distort the growth of *swaraj* (i.e. self-government, but also autonomy) they had to be dislodged from positions of authority. More widely, as Ashis Nandy has argued, Gandhian strategy sought to decentre Europe and topple it from the position of natural hegemon in any discussion, in an effort to reassert the basic equality of cultures and their mutual imbrication.[31] This explains the otherwise mysterious destruction of the British Committee in 1920. It was not, as is usually assumed, a failing organisation, but one which had to be destroyed because of the redundancy of the mode of interaction it represented (Chapter 4). 'I do not want you to determine the pace', Gandhi told an audience of British allies in Oxford in 1931. 'Consciously or unconsciously, you adopt the role of divinity. I want you to step down from that pedestal.'[32] Was there not much that England had yet to teach India, a Labour Party member had asked Gandhi: 'certain things for which she has a special gift' such as 'her political sense [and] her gift for

---

[31] Ashis Nandy, *The Intimate Enemy: Loss and Recovery of Self under Colonialism* (Delhi, 1983), 51, 100–1.
[32] Talk at Oxford, 24 Oct. 1931, *CWMG* E54/42. The source has 'form that pedestal' which I treated as an error.

evolving and managing democratic institutions?' 'I question this claim
to exclusive political sense that the English arrogate to themselves',
Gandhi had replied. 'There is much in British political institutions
that I admire. But. . . I do not believe that they are the paragon of
perfection . . . Whatever is worth adopting for India must come to her
through the process of assimilation, not forcible superimposition.'[33]
Many of Congress' British supporters were disconcerted by such claims,
as they were intended to be. Resistance will always be in certain
senses incomprehensible, at least at first, from the perspective of the
dominant. Gandhi neither succumbed to nor straightforwardly rejected
their authority. This would have been easier to meet either with
instruction or a shrugging indifference. Instead, he aimed to transform
it, and them in the process. This was why they generally preferred
Jawaharlal Nehru, with his demands for the consistent practice of
international socialism (oddly reminiscent of the pleas of the early
Congress for consistent liberalism): he asked less of them.

Each of the modes of interaction therefore required a different type
of response from the British left, whether the provision of guidance, as
in the days of the British Committee; distant sympathy (the rejectionist
preference of Savarkar); dependable, active support or mutual affiliation
to wider, internationalist bodies (Nehru's preference); or a kind of
critical solidarity in the search for truth (Gandhi). These are often elided
into a general notion of support, but they are really quite different
phenomena, varying according to the relative position of the parties
in relation to each other and to the *raj*, and the functions that each
undertakes. There was an important difference, for example, between
British supporters who saw their role as being not to side with either
the *raj* or its opponents, but to interpose, or negotiate, between them in
the hope of achieving conciliation, and those who became more directly
absorbed into the struggle on the side of the latter.

Only rarely before 1920, and almost never thereafter, did British
supporters seek positions of formal or even informal leadership. They
saw the necessity for this to be in Indian hands, although paradoxically
their exhortations to this effect often took the form of instruction. But
they did not disdain to act as advisers, adjudicators, intermediaries,
conciliators or defence counsel. Indeed, one type of support, at times
perhaps the dominant one offered by the British left, was a kind of
professional mediation, involving sincere feelings of sympathy for the

---

[33] 'Interviews to Foreign Visitors', undated but prob. early 1929, *CWMG*, E45/148.

Indians as victims of imperialism (though not usually *fellow*-victims), and the desire to intercede on their behalf, speaking for them and representing them to British audiences. It was guided more by an ethos of public service to those less fortunate than by one of common struggle.[34] Some effective anti-imperial work was undoubtedly done in this fashion, but it was structured unequally, seeking to alter the relationship between the Indians and the *raj* without much altering the relationship between the emancipating sympathiser and the emancipated Indian. The professional campaigners on Labour's Imperial Advisory Committee were drawn to the lawyers, writers and political organizers of Congress, whom they believed represented the same civilising force in Indian society as they themselves did in Britain. But they were reluctant to give them places on the Committee, instead preserving their own role as spokespersons for Indians and mediators of their interests to the British Government. It was their books and journalism which represented India to Britain and their parliamentary speeches which stated India's demands. The informal title 'Member for India', bestowed at Westminster on MPs who made India their specialism, was, for Josiah Wedgwood and Fenner Brockway as it had been for John Bright, Henry Fawcett and Charles Bradlaugh, a highly prized one, even though it involved a kind of appropriation.

Congress's strategic dilemma was, after 1920, translated into an organizational problem. Once authority was denied to them by Gandhi, British supporters lost a key incentive, for which no substitute was easily found. It is usually assumed that as Congress outgrew its early reliance on British leaders it shed them, as a multi-stage rocket jettisons its boosters. But self-reliant campaigning was not all easy to achieve, mainly because Gandhi's hope for self-generated movements of solidarity was disappointed. Congress moved through a series of attempts to organise its British work, none of them satisfactorily reconciling the need for self-reliant, India-centred activity with the need to persuade British allies and audiences of India's case for self-government. Support for Congress in Britain came to be a function of other commitments and objectives, communist, theosophical, pacifist, socialist, anti-fascist, etc. It was in essence parasitic, reliant on the hospitality offered by progressive movements of the left, but still vulnerable to their desire for status. This pattern of indirect engagement was not necessarily weak:

---

[34] For similar ideas, see Raymond Williams, 'The Bloomsbury Fraction' in his *Problems in Materialism and Culture* (London, 1980).

parasitic arrangements only arise at all if each party is getting some net benefit out of them. What mattered was the closeness of fit between these primary objectives and the anti-imperialism. When this was close, as it became briefly, and arguably misleadingly, over anti-fascism, then Congress was feted in London. But such enthusiasm was generally fragile, transitory and characterised by boom and bust, as competition between different elements of the left first distracted and then split the Indian nationalists (Chapter 8).

There was little inevitable about the scale of such disappointment. British and Indian concerns did not need to be identical to provide each other with mutual support, but only to mesh more effectively. The forms of struggle which might have avoided this trap altogether are not always easy to discern. The key elements were probably critical solidarity, a location alongside and not above or ahead of the colonised, a sharing of risk, and willingness to undertake what a later generation of theorists, notably Gayatri Spivak, has identified as the 'unlearning of privilege' or 'learning to learn from below'.[35] There are some isolated examples of such practices in the relationships between the British left and India, though they are isolated, and it is evident that it was hard for most to descend from the pedestal Gandhi had identified in 1931. Some recent historical studies have identified individual efforts to stretch threads of friendship across the barriers thrown up by imperialism in other settings.[36] There are some examples of transcendental personal friendships in this story too. Yet the unresolved problems in making such connections even at the personal level are very evident in such studies, let alone the difficulties of expanding them beyond the personal, into the larger public sphere of organised political action, with implications for the lessons which their authors might wish to draw from them. Does their rarity suggest that they are unreasonably demanding? Are they really relationships of equals, or does only one party to it hold a guarantee of support from the other? What scope is there for criticism or other expressions of conditionality in a solidaristic relationship?

[35] Gayatri Spivak, *The Postcolonial Critic: Interviews, Strategies, Dialogues* (New York, 1990), 121–2; Raymond Williams, *The Politics of Modernism* (London, 1989), 181.

[36] For example, E. P. Thompson, *Alien Homage: Edward Thompson and Rabrindranath Tagore* (New Delhi, 1998); Elleke Boehmer, *Empire, the National and the Postcolonial, 1890–1920* (Oxford, 2002); Leela Gandhi, *Affective Communities: Anticolonial Thought, Fin-de-siécle Radicalism and the Politics of Friendship* (Durham, NC, 2006).

Viewed in the longer perspective provided by such considerations, the work of the metropolitan anti-imperialists in the interwar years might be judged as provisional, but not deferred, work. Like much politically oppositional activity, anti-imperialism made necessarily crab-like progress, before triumphing, as C. L. R. James wrote, 'by whatever tortuous and broken roads, despite the stumbling and the falls'.[37] Gandhian techniques, for example, were self-consciously experimental, and failure was written into their design, though failure from which one learned. The tensions and disagreements between metropolitan anti-imperialists played out in the pages that follow might seem, from this perspective, no more than the unease through which any liberatory politics emerges, through which 'newness enters the world' and ideas productively 'travel' from one setting to another, or encounter the limits of their application.[38] Attractive though this vision is, it needs to be sharply distinguished from the simpler possibility of failure, and to be true to the lived experience of its subjects. What distinguishes the enabling tensions posited by postcolonial theory is their propensity for growth, and the test of them is what, if anything, is left at the end of the engagement.

Muslim India forms only a small part of this story, though the reasons for this are themselves revealing. Muslims did not organise representation in Britain on any significant scale after 1920. The founding of the Muslim League in 1907 to push for special provision for Muslims in the proposed council reforms prompted the formation of a London Branch in 1908, under the direction of the senior Indian Muslim lawyer in London, Syed Ameer Ali. The Indian leaders found it hard to control the London Branch, which was influenced by radically-minded students rather than the landowners who dominated the League in India. The London Branch wanted public agitation to counter the championing of Congress by the British Committee, rather than reliance on private lobbying. It also wanted separate Muslim electorates rather than the joint electoral colleges and reserved seats Morley had offered and which the Indian leaders were prepared to accept. This position drew them

---

[37] Quoted in David Scott, *Conscripts of Modernity: The Tragedy of Colonial Enlightenment* (Durham, NC, 2004), 25.

[38] These terms are taken respectively from Homi Bhabha, 'DissemiNation: Time Narrative and the Margins of the Modern Nation' and 'How Newness Enters the World', *The Location of Culture* (1994), 139–70, 212–35; Edward Said, 'Travelling Theory', *Raritan* 1/3, (Winter 1982), 41–67.

into an alliance with the Unionists and retired officials in Britain. Their campaign succeeded in obtaining at least the principle of separate electorates, partly due to Minto's endorsement of it, but also to Morley's desire not to give the Unionists an additional excuse to oppose his Bill. However, and surprisingly, this proved to be the peak of the London Branch's activity. In 1919, in the brief rapprochement brokered by Gandhi, London Muslims worked alongside Congress, and in the constitutional negotiations after 1929 they relied on British officials and on delegates from India to make their case.[39] Jinnah, despite his lengthy stay in London from 1930 to 1934 made no effort to organise a body to counter the claims of Krishna Menon's India League that Congress enjoyed the support of India's Muslims and only the communally-minded and reactionary elements stood aloof. Despite official anxiety that the Muslim case was not being adequately heard, it was not until the end of 1946 that a Muslim India Information Centre was set up in London and efforts were made to reconnect with Churchill and the Conservatives.[40]

This book is based mainly on archival sources, some newly available. From India, they include the records of the Indian National Congress; the correspondence and newspaper articles of many of its leaders, especially with their foreign supporters; the archive of the India League; and the papers of the Home (Political) Department of the Government of India. A particularly useful and almost wholly unused source was the Minute Books of the British Committee of the Indian National Congress, and I am especially grateful to Professor S. R. Mehrotra for his help in accessing them. In Britain, I have consulted the papers of the main organisations of the political left, especially the papers of the British Labour Party, the Independent Labour Party and the Communist Party of Great Britain; as well as many private paper collections, especially, again, those containing correspondence with Indian leaders. British official papers include the usual records of state and parliamentary activity, of the Cabinet and Prime Minister, and of the India Office, especially the Public and Judicial Department and the official and semi-official correspondence of Secretary of State and

---

[39] Muhammad Yusuf Abbasi, *London Muslim League (1908–1928): An Historical Study* (Islamabad, 1988).
[40] 'Question Whether the Muslim point of View should be represented in the U.K. in opposition to the activities of Krishna Menon' Home-Political File 1/1/42-Poll(I), NAI.

Viceroy. In the last few years, some of the records of Britain's security services have begun to be released, among them the records of Indian Political Intelligence, a secret part of the India Office, close to MI5, which monitored the activities of campaigners for Indian independence in Britain.[41] These records, often superior in extent and detail to the records kept by the organisations they were watching, need to be treated cautiously. They are, for example, often ignorant about alignments on the left and are unreliable guides to the motivations of Indian activists, which they usually treat in the most cynical fashion. Nevertheless, reports of what was said at meetings, and which groups allied with which, seem generally accurate where it has been possible to cross-check, so I have used them for this purpose. I have made limited use of the extensive but largely unexplored papers of the CPGB and the Communist Party of India in the archives of the Communist International in Moscow, though it is clear that these papers hold a great deal more that is relevant to the subject.

[41] The records of IPI are in L/PJ/12, OIOC and there is a summary of its work in L/PJ/12/662.

1

Liberal Anti-Imperialism: The Indian National Congress in Britain, 1885–1906

The British regime in India around 1906 is perhaps best characterised as a defensive autocracy, operating as a subordinate component of a larger imperial system. It had to make its watches 'keep time in two longitudes at once', as Maine had put it in 1875.[1] First, it had to make its policies intelligible and generally tolerable to a colonised society which, though unable to make its demands effective, needed nonetheless to be convinced of the authority and unassailability of the regime. This in turn required it to solicit co-operation, or at least tolerance, from the dominant groups in Indian society, through a mixture of persuasion and coercion. At the same time, and with respect to the same policies, it had to defend them to the British state at home, which would judge them according to its own conceptions of justice, reasonableness and effectiveness.[*] This meant reconciling them with broader imperial governing strategies, with the economic and strategic interests of the British Government and of its principal clients, and also too, the demands of the parliamentary position.

Whitehall's supremacy over Calcutta (and later Delhi) was firmly established by the last decade of the nineteenth century and was, if anything, reinforced during the Curzon and Minto Viceroyalties (1899–1905, 1905–10).[2] While the *raj* continued to enjoy autonomy

---

[*] I am grateful to Sudipta Kaviraj for suggesting this argument to me.

[1] Sir Henry Maine, quoted in Nick O'Brien, ' "Something Older than Law Itself", Sir Henry Maine, Niebuhr and "the Path not Chosen" ', *Journal of Legal History*, 26/3 (2005), 245. See also Sudipta Kaviraj, 'On State, Society and Discourse in India' in James Manor (ed.), *Rethinking Third World Politics* (London, 1991).

[2] Arnold P. Kaminsky, *The India Office, 1880–1910* (London, 1986), 124–51. See also Stanley A. Wolpert, *Morley and India, 1906–1910* (Berkeley and Los Angeles, 1967), Stephen E. Koss, *John Morley at the India Office, 1905–1910* (New Haven, 1969).

with regard to day-to-day decision-making, questions of constitutional reform and matters which touched upon wider imperial interests were increasingly managed from London. The Liberal Secretary of State John Morley repeatedly asserted the subordinate status of the Government of India, and in a series of battles with Minto, extended the dominance of the India Office into administration as well as policy. In the absence of responsible government in India itself, he argued, only accountability to London could prevent a position of autocracy.[3] In matters of immediate importance, however, the Secretary of State's powers were more theoretical than real. Parliament still reserved considerable powers under the 1858 Act, should it choose to use them, but there was much deference to the man on the spot. When, in May 1907, the Government of India sent a telegram demanding ordinance powers, for example, Morley's protests were relentlessly overborne. His Private Secretary, Arthur Hirtzel, wrote in his diary:

[Morley] was greatly perturbed . . . He read it twice carefully and then threw it down saying, 'No, I can't stand that. *I will not have that.*' I said I did not see how we here could measure the emergency. He said, 'Then it comes to this, that I am to have nothing to say, but am to let them do just as they like.' I said yes, it did amount to that for the next week or so, at all events: he could give them general advice and warning but he must leave particular action to them. At least then, he said, he must have proper information, and I agreed, and left him to draft [a] telegram. This, when done, began, 'I cannot of course take responsibility of disallowing Ordinance.' I demurred strongly to this. He said he had power to disallow it, why should he not remind them of it? I pressed on him that disallowance would be so extreme a measure that it was inadvisable even to allude to it, and at last he gave way . . .'[4]

Under the 1858 Act, the Secretary of State was required to carry out his duties 'in Council'; that is, advised by a special and largely irremovable Council of old India hands created to keep a watchful eye on any tendencies to give way to British liberal sentiment. Although the ability of the Council to block moves of which it disapproved had diminished by the turn of the century, it retained power until after the First World War in financial and legislative matters and significant authority in others. Within Whitehall, therefore, policymaking was heavily dominated by a closed network of Indian officials and British civil servants, insulated

---

[3] John Morley, 'British Democracy and Indian Government', *Nineteenth Century and After*, 69/408 (April 1911), 189–209.
[4] Hirtzel, Diary, 9 May 1907, MSS/Eur/D1090, OIOC.

from their colleagues in other departments. There was little movement of bureaucratic personnel between the India Office and the Home Civil Service. However, there were much stronger patterns of movement from posts in the Indian Civil Service to and, less frequently, from posts in the India Office, reinforcing expertise and loyalties. Indeed, there were well-established lines of private communication, serving common bureaucratic interests, between the India Office civil servants and officials in India which bypassed the Secretary of State altogether.[5] Within Whitehall, the India Office was not a powerful player when wider imperial questions were being debated. But it managed to maintain autonomy with respect to internal affairs in India. Before 1919, the India Office was also not subject to the same Treasury controls as other departments. Indeed, one of the main early demands of British Radicals was for the Secretary of State's salary to be placed on the Treasury estimates in order to provide grounds for greater parliamentary scrutiny. Although the Government of India was not averse to such a move, largely as a means of cutting its own costs, the India Office strongly resisted it on the grounds that it would enlarge the scope for parliamentary interference in Indian affairs.

Formal scrutiny of the day-to-day management of affairs in India therefore remained generally weak and ministers and officials enjoyed considerable freedom from parliamentary control.[6] Even after 1919, most of the establishment costs of the India Office remained outside the Treasury estimates, and it was not until 1937 that the Treasury managed to gain full control of its spending. This imperviousness to scrutiny was compounded by a departmental culture which regarded the intervention of party politics into the government of India as, in the words of one its longest serving senior officials, 'very objectionable [and] a real hindrance to business'.[7] This seemed to justify acts of quiet resistance to parliamentary scrutiny: the censoring of parliamentary returns, rigging of commission memberships, concealing evidence obtained from India, and so forth. An effective Parliamentary Branch became adept at blocking awkward questions and in keeping its finger on the pulse of House of Commons opinion so as to avoid clashes by private approaches to friendlier critics. When in 1894, the MP Herbert Paul had managed

---

[5] Koss, *John Morley,* 106.

[6] Donovan Williams, *The India Office, 1858–1869* (Hoshiapur, 1983) and Kaminsky, *India Office.*

[7] Goldey to Elgin, 3 May 1894, quoted in Kaminsky, *India Office,* 93.

unexpectedly to swing a close and poorly attended vote in the Commons in favour of an Indian examination to be held simultaneously with the London examination for the Indian Civil Service (one of the principal Congress demands), the Secretary of State dismissed it as a 'fatal mistake' and forwarded it to India liberally stamped with his own and the Council of India's objections.[8]

Within Parliament, the Government of India was indirectly questioned, via the Secretary of State, not by a powerful specialist committee, but by amateur backbenchers. Questions could obtain information, signal dissent within Parliament, test the parliamentary skills of ministers, or even force a clearer statement of policy when Indian administrators, mindful of their two clocks, preferred ambiguity. This kind of pressure, exerted also at times through the press as well as Parliament, could not always be readily deflected by Secretaries of State. Much of it was passed on to the Government of India to answer, and, in putting pressure on Viceroys and Governors to strengthen the Government's position in Parliament did, at times, push them to make concessions against their better judgement. At the same time, however, Ministers could seek refuge in deference to Westminster's distance from India. Indeed, it was a parliamentary convention at Westminster that while discussion of the broad lines of Indian policy was permissible, India's internal administration was not to be a matter of open party dispute. Rather as parents facing manipulative children try to preserve a united front, Britain's political parties were supposed to mask their differences, for fear of encouraging bad behaviour and weakening the authority of hard-pressed administrators to deal with it. MPs might therefore criticise each other for their handling of Indian matters, but were not expected to side with the Indians. The Liberals attempted to preserve the convention throughout the early years of Congress nationalism, Campbell-Bannerman declaring it 'a wise rule that we shall assuredly not be the first to break'.[9] Of course, Radical MPs and their Labour successors did break it, and after 1918 it became rather easier for them to do so. Nevertheless, a sense of the delicacy of the political operations of the Government of India was shared even by those who wished to see the work carried further and faster. As a consequence, they practised considerable self-restraint in challenging it. Unless there was

---

[8] Kaminsky, *India Office*, 163–4.
[9] Quoted in B. R. Nanda, *Gokhale: The Indian Moderates and the British Raj* (Princeton, 1977), 486–7.

clear evidence of official misbehaviour, breaches of the party truce were accordingly infrequent. One of the many ironies of this self-restraint was that it actually functioned more effectively when the Liberals (later Labour) were in power than it did when the Unionists governed. This was because, in the former case, the parliamentary powers of the Opposition were deployed in resisting rather than urging reform, and Government backbenchers were restrained by the party whips and their own loyalties from questioning too closely. Parliamentary manoeuvres were thus better at handling individual abuses, such as infringements of civil liberties, than at forcing the pace of constitutional and political reform, let alone at undermining the *raj* itself.

Nevertheless, parliamentary calculations still loomed large in the minds of the senior India Office officials and of the Government of India too. In their view, Parliament was an unpredictable and volatile arena, subject at times of stress to the irresponsible influence of eloquent mavericks, and liable to capture by metropolitan fads and interested lobbies. Although Parliament was not well informed about India, for MPs rarely travelled there, that was exactly the danger. Lack of familiarity with Indian specificities, the officials believed, meant lack of familiarity with the relevant differences. MPs whose whole political experience had been obtained in Britain might well miss the dangers of allowing modern, western forms of political activity in a traditional and complex society under alien rule. The India Office thus feared an ignorant and ill-attended debate more than an informed and well-attended one. Hardly anyone on the Liberal benches in 1906 argued in favour of self-government for India, and none of the handful who did thought it immediately achievable. But this did not make them complacent supporters of the status quo, and neither the India Office nor the Government of India made the mistake of regarding them as such. For many Liberals the glory of the empire lay in its potential to spread British political and constitutional values across the globe. This had important implications for the nature and effectiveness of their criticism. It meant that there were real restrictions on the licence to be given to authoritarian rule in India: Calcutta time must not deviate too much from London time, and in the long run must be brought closer. Justifications of empire had now to be made, at least in part, in terms of its capacity to foster liberal values. This point of view was far from universal, even among Liberals. At least before 1918, there was another, hardly less powerful strand of opinion, which stressed the distinctions between the actually or potentially self-governing components of the empire created by white imperial settlement and sustained by common racial identities, culture and values, and the dependent empire, formed by conquest, in which none of these things was felt. Such sentiments help to explain why India was largely left out of the plans for imperial federation being considered at the turn of the century.[10] But even some of those who took this view did not think India should be forever so excluded. Its development in this direction required a lengthy and controlled education in liberalism, which in turn implied opportunities for independent political organisation, campaigning, legal challenges and governing experience.

Thus, while the British *raj* was an autocracy determined to retain its hold on India, it was never quite able to disown liberal values. Increasingly after 1906, this dual orientation placed it in an almost permanent state of ambiguity.[11] Its liberalism was selective, intermittent and invariably hedged around more or less explicitly by the threat of repression or entrapment. But it nonetheless provided a crucial opportunity to exert influence. It was by seizing on these liberal pretensions, or departures from them, that the tables could, albeit briefly, be turned. This was easiest when the *raj* over-reached itself and employed clearly illiberal methods. This allowed critics to cast themselves as a patriotic opposition shocked by the employment of un-British techniques. Given the resourcefulness and adaptability of imperialists, such opportunities did not present themselves very often. But when they did, critics were sometimes able to seize the moral high ground.

The line of safe political development in India, in the judgement of the India Office and the Government of India, rested on a careful and dynamic process of balancing and rebalancing alliances, and of always holding in reserve (at times of concession) the possibility of coercion, and (at times of coercion), the possibility of a lighter touch. To have these finely grained decisions subject to correction from London, especially from an ill-informed Parliament was to risk misjudgement. Thus while officials did not fear Parliament's capacity to subject administrative routine to scrutiny, they did fear that a weak Secretary of State might,

[10] Miles Taylor, '"Imperium et Libertas?" Rethinking the Radical Critique of Imperialism in the Nineteenth Century', *Journal of Imperial and Commonwealth History*, 19 (1991), 1–23; S. R. Mehrotra, 'Imperial Federation and India, 1868–1917', *Journal of Commonwealth Political Studies*, 1/1 (1961), 29–40.

[11] See D. A. Low, *Britain and Indian Nationalism: The Imprint of Ambiguity* (Cambridge, 1997).

under the pressure of a frontier crisis or civil unrest, be driven to throw a
sop to his parliamentary critics which it would be impossible to ignore,
and which would upset the delicate political strategies being pursued
in India.

Above all, officials feared a linked-up agitation. In Minto's view,
the British regime in India was threatened less by a strong and direct
challenge from within India, than from a co-ordinated double blow
from agitators in India and radical critics at home. He feared that
agitators in India had discerned the inherent weakness of the dual
governing structure, and proposed to drive a wedge between its two
supports. He foresaw a coordinated campaign in which unrepresentative
Indian activists would persuade gullible British Liberals in London of
their grievances, thereby putting pressure on the Secretary of State to
overrule the Government of India. Such long-distance 'wire-pulling'
was doubly dangerous. First of all it was unpredictable. It was not
hard to start such a campaign, especially when there was already unrest
under way, since MPs had little idea of which grievances were true and
which were not, and there was no telling which ones they would choose
to believe. Secondly, such campaigns were potentially cyclical in their
impact, for any success they achieved undermined the prestige of the
British regime in India, disheartening officials and the 'loyal classes'
in India. Since Indians had little idea which MPs were representative,
and which were not, this would encourage further agitation, thereby
increasing still further the pressure at home. For this reason, Minto
was deeply hostile to those Radical MPs at home whom, he believed,
'[kept] the pot of disaffection boiling'.[12] His preferred solution was
greater autonomy for the Government of India, but recognising that
this was politically impossible, he relied on the Secretary of State
to stand firm against the wire-pullers, and also on a battery of new
powers, brought in after the renewal of political agitation in India in
1907, which, besides restricting the activities of the Indian movement,
were intended to limit the scope for wire-pulling from London. These
included press laws which controlled the reporting of Indian events in
Indian newspapers, and hence in London; the banning and seizure of
British radical publications entering India; the interception and political

---

[12] Minto to Edward VII, 9 Aug 1906, 6 Feb, 18 June and 20 Dec 1908, Minto Papers,
MS 12728; Minto to Prince of Wales, 6 June and 13 Dec 1906, Minto Papers, MS
12776; Minto to Bigge, 5 July 1910, Minto Papers, MS 12728; Minto to Morley, 1 Aug
1906, MC MSS/Eur/D573/9; Minto to Morley, 2 Jan 1907, MC MSS/Eur/D573/11;
Minto to Morley, 27 May 1908, MC MSS/Eur/D573/15.

use of mail between Indian nationalists and British supporters; the more intensive surveillance of visiting British Radicals and Socialists, and efforts to use informed opinion in London to discredit metropolitan critics.[13] These techniques were intended to prevent the seepage of metropolitan radical ideas into India, and, conversely, the irruption of unmediated Indian voices in Parliament. They were far from perfect, and sometimes came into conflict with Morley's preference for more liberal flows of information, a proposed ban on H. M. Hyndman's newspaper *Justice*, for example, being rejected at his insistence.[14] But Morley still felt obliged to do what he could to limit the possibility of a linked-up agitation. 'I have succeeded', he told Minto, 'in keeping back the information of any serious group at Westminster whose utterances and tactics in our public life would have provided powder and shot for revolutionaries in India'.[15]

For critics of the British regime in India to deliver the kind of double blow feared by Minto was thus no easy matter. Success depended upon the *independent* strength of their two campaigns: the ability of Indian nationalists to build an All-India movement capable of sustained and effective pressure on the administration and its interests, and of British activists to maintain well-informed lobbying campaigns which publicised and assisted these efforts. But just as crucial was the linkage *between* the two movements: their capacity to bring simultaneous, interlocking pressure to bear on the dual structure of the *raj*. Just as, without support in Britain, Indian campaigns against the British regime could be more readily and silently crushed, so metropolitan movements faltered without a ready supply of verifiable grievances from India.

What was needed for the campaigns to mesh effectively? The logistical requirements were considerable. As we shall see, money and the flow of reliable information were crucial. But these in turn rested on a more basic issue: the choice of organisational structure which defined the respective roles of Indian and British agitators. In defining the relationship between the two, there were a large number of theoretical possibilities, defined in terms of the degree of mutual recognition each afforded the other, the relative positions of the two sets of agitators in the hierarchy of mutual

---

[13] N. Gerald Barrier, *Banned: Controversial Literature and Political Control in British India 1907–1947* (New York, 1974); Robert Darnton, 'Literary Surveillance in the British Raj: The Contradictions of Liberal Imperialism', *Book History*, 4 (2001), 133–76.
[14] See L/PJ/6/817, OIOC, and note by Morley, 21 May 1910, L/PJ/6/1006, OIOC.
[15] Morley to Minto, 28 May 1908, MC MSS/Eur/D573/3.

decision-making, and, where this was unequal, the degree of autonomy afforded to the lower level, and the methods of supervision and
control employed by the superior level. The resulting spectrum of
roles for the metropolitan anti-imperialist thus ranged from that of
leader of the movement, commanding varying degrees of organisational or cultural authority; or, less obtrusively, its guide or mentor,
providing advice but not commands; through various forms of partnership and reciprocal support, perhaps involving mutual affiliation
to an overarching umbrella organisation. At the opposite end of the
spectrum lay the subordinate roles of ambassador, with a recognised
representative role, but no independent authority to make policy, beyond, perhaps, a limited licence to negotiate; appointed or contracted
agent, bound by more or less strict regulation into the organisation
of the nationalist movement at the periphery, but lacking independent latitude; or simple supporter, with neither a formal role in the
movement, nor warrant to speak on its behalf, but only the duty to
report, preferably in positive terms, its views and activities to local
audiences.

When, in 1888, the leaders of the Indian National Congress turned
their attention to the organisation of sustained political work in Britain,
their first preference was for an agency arrangement.[16] The purpose
of Congress, at this stage of its evolution, was petition, and its leaders, drawn overwhelmingly from the professional classes in India, were
used to employing London agents to negotiate the arcane worlds of
the City and the law courts. Their choice fell upon William Digby,
ex-editor of the *Madras Times*, an outspoken critic of administrative
failures in India, and, after his return to Britain in 1879, an advocate of
constitutional reform and guide to visiting Indian politicians.[17] Digby
enjoyed a useful set of political contacts as secretary of the National
Liberal Club and through acquaintances at the India Office.[18] He had
already indicated his willingness to raise Indian grievances on a paid
basis if elected to Parliament, which he had tried unsuccessfully to do in

[16] S. R. Mehrotra, *A History of the Indian National Congress, volume 1* (New Delhi, 1995), 92.

[17] See Briton Martin, *New India, 1885* (Berkeley and Los Angeles, 1969); Mira Matikkala, 'William Digby and the British Radical debate on India from the 1880s to the 1890s' (Cambridge, M. Phil., 2004).

[18] Henderson to Bradford, 16 Sept 1889, L/PS/8/3, OIOC; Wacha to Naoroji, 30 Nov 1888, *DNC*, i, 135–6.

1885.[19] In May 1888, he had set up an Indian Political and General Agency in London, with the intention of raising in the press and in Parliament private and public grievances from India.[20] Once appointed the Congress agent, Digby threw himself energetically into the work, publicising Congress petitions, and securing prominent supporters, among them the supreme catch of Charles Bradlaugh, who attended the 1889 Congress and agreed to introduce a parliamentary bill to provide elected legislative councils in India.[21]

Digby's Agency was thus an effective machine for linked-up agitation, but it was not cheap. 'Nothing for nothing, something for something, is the rule the whole world over', Digby had cheerfully announced at the start of his work.[22] The Agency cost £1,700 in 1888 and planned on spending £2,500 in 1889. Digby himself received £500 a year as Secretary, £100 as editor of the Congress journal *India*, and £400 a year for the use of his rooms and secretaries.[23] Bradlaugh too had to be paid. The MP W. S. Caine, in India at the end of 1888, had advised the Congress leaders that Bradlaugh 'will not work till he is "well briefed" '. 'That is to say', the Congress secretary D. E. Wacha explained, 'that he can advocate our cause if he is liberally remunerated'.[24]

However, it proved very difficult to extract the funds promised.[25] This was not because of the poverty of the Indian educated classes. On the contrary, there was plenty of money available for political campaigning, which in turn reflected the relatively affluent nature of the groups involved. In 1888, Congress had spent £20,000.[26] As a proportion of this sum, the money needed for the Agency was thus not particularly great, yet it was clearly resented. 'To pay even Rs.6 [8 shillings] a year is to them a heavy tax as if they do not spend perhaps sixty times as much a month on less useful objects or objects of no

---

[19] Digby to National Indian Association, 24 April 1885, cited in Mehrotra, *History*, 92; Martin, *New India*, 224; Wacha to Naoroji, 13 May 1885, *DNC*, i, 8–9.

[20] *India*, Feb 1890.

[21] *India*, 31 Oct and 5 Dec 1890; 'Work of the Indian Political Agency', in Bishen Narayan Dar (ed.), *India in England* (2v., Lucknow, 1889–90), ii, 143–50; Sir William Wedderburn, *Allan Octavian Hume, C. B.* (London, 1913), 87.

[22] Digby to Mehta (National Indian Association), 24 April 1885, quoted in Margot Morrow, 'The Origin and Early Years of the British Committee of the Indian National Congress' 1885–1907', (London, Ph.D., 1977), 30.

[23] Mehrotra, *History*, 99–100.

[24] Wacha to Naoroji, 23 Nov 1888, *DNC*, i, 131–4.

[25] Wacha to Naoroji, 1, 3 and 10 July, 7 and 8 Aug, 4 and 21 Sept 1888; 22 Feb and 23 July 1889, *DNC*, i, 100–3, 111–15, 123–6, 148, 177–9.

[26] Hume to Pall Mall Gazette, undated but 1889, in Dar, *India in England*, ii, 14–16.

use', complained Wacha, who was charged with trying to collect it.[27] Congress in its early years was not a centralised organisation but, as Anil Seal suggests, a 'ramshackle set of local linkages',[28] its structures and procedures reflecting divergent provincial interests and a desire to avoid issues which might arouse religious or social controversy. The flow of money in such a system reflected these localised priorities. Spending varied greatly from province to province, but went mostly on the independent provincial organisations (the Bombay Presidency Association, the Poona Sarvajanik Sabha, the Madras Mahajan Sabha, the Bengal Indian Association) which ran alongside Congress until the First World War. Money could be raised for specific local purposes, for single-issue campaigns and to help secure election to district boards and corporations, but there was little inclination to fund All-India work of any kind, even that of the central Congress organisation. Still less was there inclination to fund distant and uncontrolled activity in London, unless it was dedicated to specific private goals. Dadabhai Naoroji, for example, had himself found few Indians willing to support his bid to enter Parliament in 1887, probably because they believed he would not be controllable once elected.[29] Paying for overseas work was also affected by the facts that costs (printing, hiring halls, etc.) were higher in Britain than in India, and that the rupee–sterling exchange rate was in decline, such that rupees raised in India were in London worth only about half in 1894 what they had been worth in 1860.[30] Hence, although large sums were initially voted for the work of Digby, the Congress founder Allan O. Hume had continually to deploy his moral authority to extract them. '[I]f [you] cannot combine as to effect the raising, yearly, promptly and without my having to dun you for every Rupee, of the paltry sum of thirty or forty thousand Rupees required for that primary essential, the English Agency', wrote Hume in disgust, 'then it simply means that

---

[27] Wacha to Naoroji, 22 Oct 1898, *DNC*, ii, 656–9. I have converted pre-1913 rupee sums to sterling using the table of exchange rate data in Raymond W. Goldsmith, *The Financial Development of India, 1860–1977* (New Haven, 1983), 5–6. For later sums, I have used Government of India, *Report of the Operations of the Currency Department* (1913/14–1922/3), *Report of the Controller of Currency* (1923/4–1934/5) and Reserve Bank of India, *Report on Currency and Finance* (1935/6–1947/8), V/24/3442–61, OIOC.

[28] Anil Seal, *The Emergence of Indian Nationalism: Competition and Collaboration in the Later Nineteenth Century* (Cambridge, 1968), 277–8.

[29] Ibid. 283–4.   [30] Goldsmith, *Financial Development*, 5–6.

you and I have been wrong and our opponents, who declare us unfit for self-government, right.'[31]

Short of money to promote Congress in the manner that he had been employed to do, Digby relied on the sums he raised more easily from private work for Indian clients. This was used, in effect, to subsidise the work for Congress.[32] However, this had its drawbacks. Digby's principal client was the Maharaja of Kashmir. The Maharaja had been persuaded to hand his powers to a Council headed by his brother and other British appointees after the discovery of letters apparently written by him inciting the murder of the British Resident. Regretting this decision, he paid large sums to Digby and Motilal Ghose, editor of the *Amrita Bazar Patrika*, to raise his case in the press. Ghose's agent was sent by the Maharaja with jewels and other gifts to present to Bradlaugh in the hope of soliciting his help.[33] Bradlaugh refused such a straightforward attempt at bribery, but later agreed to raise the case as long as he was provided with a petition from ordinary Kashmiris.[34] Backed with the Maharaja's money, Ghose then proceeded to solicit signatures for such a petition, instructing his fellow editor Gopi Nath of the Lahore newspaper *Akhbar-I-Am* on the appropriate technique for creating Indian public opinion:

You must use Kashmiri papers in writing the petitions. Let there be twenty or twenty five copies of the petition and we shall send them to 20 or 25 Members. You know the rule is that every M.P. is bound to present to the House every petition sent to him. It will then produce a considerable effect if 20 Members were to present 20 petitions together. Every signatory will then have to sign his name twenty times on twenty pieces of paper. Induce as many signatories as possible . . . It were better if you could get the petitions written by others rather [than] by yourself. Let not the Government connect the petitions with you.[35]

[31] Hume to secretaries of Congress, 15 Sept 1889, Minute Book of the British Committee of the Indian National Congress (hereafter Minute Book), Sardar Patel Memorial Trust Library, New Delhi, v.1.
[32] 'Work of the Indian Political Agency', 14 June 1889, in Dar, *India in England*, 143–50.
[33] Reports of Resident of Kashmir, 16 and 18 Nov 1889, L/PS/8/3, OIOC.
[34] Ghose to Gopi Nath Gurtu, 9 Jan 1890, L/PS/8/3, OIOC.
[35] Ghose to Gopi Nath Gurtu, 21 Feb 1890, intercepted and copied, L/PS/8/3, OIOC. See also Ghose to illegible, 7 Jan 1890 and Ghose to Gopi Nath Gurtu, 4 Feb 1890, L/PS/8/3, OIOC.

Bradlaugh, possibly suspicious of such tactics, had insisted that his briefs had to be prepared not by Indians but by Digby.[36] There was, it turned out, quite a record of government failure with which to contend, and, since the Maharaja had repudiated the letters, the India Office made sure 'concrete and telling examples of mismanagement' became the focus of debate.[37] Worse still, the Maharaja soon got cold feet about the whole idea of a campaign in Parliament, telling the Resident that he resented Bradlaugh's 'interference in Kashmir affairs without . . . any authority or suggestion from himself'. When the Resident protested that exactly this had been done through intermediaries like Ghose, the Maharaja denied it, but not, the Resident reported, 'in any hearty or honest way'.[38] Bradlaugh made the best of the situation, succeeding, to the Government's evident irritation, in getting the India Office to disclose its correspondence over the affair.[39] But he was shown the secret papers in advance and they made a generally convincing and sorry tale, denting his case badly. When Parliament debated the question, he hardly disputed the scale of the misgovernment involved, but insisted that the Maharaja had not had the opportunity to clear his name over the charges of incitement to murder. This was a weak performance by Bradlaugh's standards. It was curious, as the Secretary of State observed in the debate, that 'the Radical Member for Northampton should be pleading in the House for the Divine right of an Oriental despot to deal with his people as he pleases'.[40]

From the Congress point of view, Bradlaugh's support for the Maharaja was embarrassing. Digby wrote defensively about Bradlaugh's right to take up any cases—even those of Maharajas—if there was a point of justice involved.[41] But whatever the highhandedness of the

---

[36] Paramananda Dutt (ed.), *Memoirs of Moti Lal Ghose* (Calcutta, 1935), 68–70; Ghose to Gopi Nath Gurtu and illegible, 7 and 9 Jan 1890, 10 Jan 1890, L/PS/8/3, OIOC.

[37] Note by Gorst, 12 Feb 1890, L/PS/8/3, OIOC.

[38] 'Extract from the Diary of the Resident of Kashmir, week ending 5 Aug 1890', enclosed in Lansdowne to Cross, 1 Sept 1890, Lansdowne Coll., MSS/Eur/D558/3.

[39] Lansdowne to Cross, 26 May, 23 June, 7 July 1890; Cross to Lansdowne, 20 June, 1 and 21 Aug 1890, Lansdowne Coll., MSS/Eur/D558/3.

[40] *Hansard*, 3 July 1890, 3rd ser., v.346, cols. 699–731; *Parliamentary Papers*, 1890, liv, 229–307.

[41] *India*, 25 July 1890 and 19 Dec 1890; William Digby, *Condemned Unheard: The Government of India and H.H. the Maharaja of Kashmir* (London, 1890); William Digby, 'Disinterested Work for India', in his *Indian Politics in England: The Story of an Indian Reform Bill in Parliament Told Week by Week with other matters of interest to Indian reformers* (Lucknow, 1890), 145–6.

imperial governors, the Maharaja and his government were a standing reproach to claims that Indians were capable of effective self-government. The dual role that Bradlaugh and Digby played threatened to drag the Congress name into the mire of such private litigation. Similar problems were emerging in their handling of petitions from India, which Bradlaugh had made a point of soliciting when in India in 1889. In 1890, 777 petitions were presented to Parliament, bearing nearly 400,000 signatures, and Bradlaugh asked 120 parliamentary questions.[42] The paperwork was handled by Digby on Bradlaugh's behalf: he drew up briefs, supplied parliamentary questions, checked the petitions that came in, and offered advice on which causes to take up. Bradlaugh and Digby denied the allegations that this was first and foremost a financial arrangement. '[H]e neither receives a penny from us, nor is there any arrangement he shall receive a penny', wrote Digby in 1889: it was 'all for love and nothing for reward'.[43] But this was not true for long. Bradlaugh demanded payment of three guineas a petition and by June 1890, there were eighty in a single week.[44] He also received secret help from Digby with his election expenses.[45]

Concerned about this clash of public and private interests, Hume insisted on a 'bossing and guiding' committee in London to supervise Digby's work for Congress.[46] This was the British Committee of Congress, an association of public men, mostly ex-officials of the Indian Civil Service, allied with some of the more westernised long-term Indian expatriates in London, including Dadabhai Naoroji and W. C. Bonnerjee. When it came to review its first set of accounts, the British Committee, through whose books Digby had been making the payments to Bradlaugh, resisted the suggestion that it should become a clearing house for Digby's private work for rich Indians.[47] It demanded a clearer distinction between Digby's Agency work and the work done for Congress, and tightened its procedures for raising Indian grievances

[42] *India*, 31 Oct 1890.
[43] William Digby, 'Mr Bradlaugh libelled', in Dar, *India in England*, ii, 16–17; Digby, *Indian Politics in England*.
[44] Bradlaugh to Digby, 7 June and 27 June 1890, Digby Coll., MSS/Eur/D767/7.
[45] Bradlaugh to Digby, 20 June and 25 July 1890, ibid.
[46] Hume to Indian Political Agency, 7 June 1889, quoted in Harish P.Kaushik, *Indian National Congress in England* (Delhi, 1991), 21.
[47] *India*, Feb 1890; British Committee of Congress Memorandum, 25 Sept 1890, in *The Bradlaugh Papers (Letters, Papers and Printed Items relating to the life of Charles Bradlaugh (1833–1891) now in the possession of the National Secular Society* (Microfilm, Bodleian Library, Oxford), doc. 1755.

in Britain.[48] Congress, too, publicly distanced itself from Digby's Agency in December 1890.[49] The final straw came in September 1892 when Digby's behaviour in a number of prominent private cases seemed to go too far. Bradlaugh was now dead, but Digby was still offering his services as a lobbyist on Indian questions, with his new principal parliamentary ally, W. S. Caine. In September 1891, he wrote to the Dewan of Mysore, on behalf of a merchant with a private claim against the former Maharaja. Digby suggested that he was 'desired both at the India Office and in the House of Commons' to urge the merchant's claim. 'I am reluctant to bring this matter before Parliament or to have it written about in the British newspapers', Digby wrote somewhat disingenuously. 'Many very unkind and untrue things would be said reflecting upon His Highness.'[50] This thinly veiled attempt to represent himself as the agent of the India Office and Parliament, however, gave the Government of India the excuse to discredit Digby publicly.[51] Congress, anxious not to be caught up in the scandal, dispensed with Digby's services, and Caine departed at around the same time.[52]

Digby's departure ended the agency arrangement. Hereafter, work for Congress in Britain was carried out by the British Committee itself, under its chairman, former ICS official, Sir William Wedderburn.[53]

---

[48] *India*, 23 Oct 1891.

[49] Wacha to Naoroji, 17 Jan 1891, *DNC*, ii, 233; Wacha to Digby, 9 May 1891, Digby Coll., MSS/Eur/D767/8.

[50] Digby to Dewan of Mysore, 4 Sep 1991, copy in L/PS/8/4, OIOC.

[51] Memorandum of a meeting between Lansdowne and Digby, 16 Dec 1892; Digby to Ardagh, 20, 21 and 28 Dec 1892; Ardagh to Digby, 20 Dec 1892, L/PS/8/5, OIOC.

[52] Mehrotra, *History*, 96.

[53] On the British Congress Committee, see S. K. Ratcliffe, *Sir William Wedderburn and the Indian Reform Movement* (London, 1923); Mary Cumpston, 'Some Early Indian Nationalists and Their Allies in the British Parliament, 1851–1906', *English Historical Review*, 76 (1961), 279–97; Edward C. Moulton, 'British Radicals and India in the Early Twentieth Century', in A. J. Morris (ed.), *Edwardian Radicalism* (London, 1974); 'Early Indian Nationalism: Henry Cotton and the British Positivist and Radical Connection, 1870–1915', *Journal of Indian History*, 60 (1982), 25–59; 'William Wedderburn and Early Indian Nationalism', in Kenneth Ballhatchet et al. (eds.), *Changing South Asia: Politics and Government* (Hong Kong, 1984); and 'The Early Congress and the British Radical Connection', in D. A. Low (ed.), *The Indian National Congress: Centenary Hindsights* (Oxford, 1988); Morrow, 'Origin and Early Years'; Kaushik, *Indian National Congress in England*; Mehrotra, *History*, 90–105; Jonathan Schneer, *London 1900: the Imperial Metropolis* (New Haven, 1989); Andrew S. Thompson, '*Thinking imperially?: Imperial Pressure Groups and the Idea of Empire in Late-Victorian and Edwardian Britain*' (Oxford, D.Phil., 1994).

Its purpose was to organise the activities of Congress sympathisers in Britain, to write and distribute Congress annual reports and literature, to raise Congress petitions through its Indian Parliamentary Committee (IPC), and to give an accurate account of Indian events through its journal *India*. Its allies, principally the Bombay moderates who controlled the Congress organisation, supplied evidence of Indian grievances and disquiet for the Committee to take up. There were several important differences about this way of working. The British Committee was effectively self-appointed and self-renewing, its new members chosen by existing ones, without input from India. To an important degree it was self-financing, amateur, and dominated by ex-officials, and its guiding ethos was unpaid, disinterested public service, rather than the pecuniary considerations of the agency arrangement. Where Bradlaugh had asked parliamentary questions for cash, the IPC was, as Wedderburn stressed, neither the Congress' agent, nor even committed to the Congress programme, but only promised 'to give a fair hearing to Indian grievances'.[54]

The main need of the Committee, like other anti-imperialist groups, was to attract the time, money and support of participants. Like other pressure groups, it encountered the dilemma of finding the right balance of incentives to do so.[55] When compared to other forms of progressive activism, public campaigns for India suffered from peculiar difficulties. First, the costs of serious activism were often high. Colonial issues were inherently time-consuming and complex, requiring detailed research and first-hand knowledge. It was hard to find balancing benefits. Most obviously this was because the campaigns of anti-imperialists, unlike many other progressive collective endeavours, sought primarily to benefit those other than the campaigners themselves. A successful outcome to a campaign for Indian constitutional reform or political advance would in most senses benefit the Indian people rather than the British activist. Anti-imperialism therefore required greater altruism of its British supporters than other, more self-interested causes. Furthermore, to the degree that colonial self-government would profit the metropole at all, its benefits would not be confined to those who had campaigned for it, but distributed much more widely. Campaign leaders therefore had to show to each potential recruit that his or her participation was a

---

[54] *India*, Oct 1894.

[55] This dilemma was set out in its classic form by Mancur Olson in *The Logic of Collective Action: Public Goods and the Theory of Groups* (Cambridge, Mass., 1965).

necessary and sufficient condition of receiving the benefits of a successful campaign. Otherwise, potential recruits tended to calculate that even if the campaign were to succeed, they would gain no more than if they had not participated.

Group leaders facing this dilemma tend to respond by distributing selective and participatory incentives (those received by campaigners alone, and only to the degree to which they participate). What selective incentives could be offered by the Committee? There were few material incentives beyond some travelling expenses, a library and a free newspaper, and the British Committee's leaders paid more into the Congress coffers than they ever took out.[56] In any case, material incentives, had they been important, were more generously available for other types of work, such as private lobbying which could offer tangible selective incentives (fees, trading concessions, government contracts, etc.) in return for participation. This was why Digby had cross-subsidised public work with money raised from private causes where donors were more easily found. But this had effectively been ruled out by the new disinterested procedures adopted by the British Committee.

The main incentives for participation were the intangible benefits derived from the sense of involvement in, and influence in, what they took to be a worthy cause. For such incentives to be effective, however, British supporters had to be made to feel that their part was a part worth playing. The constitutional position of the British Committee was never entirely clear. It was probably intended to be, in the last resort, a subordinate body, but with regard to activities in Britain, its authority was greater than that of the Congress in India.[57] In existence all year round, unlike the Congress itself, the Committee enjoyed a high degree of effective independence, issuing its own statements and seeking

[56] Naoroji estimated that Wedderburn had put £15,000 into Indian work by 1901, including the whole of his £1,000 annual Indian Civil Service pension (Naoroji to Gokhale, 27 Sept 1901, GM 11701) and Morrow calculates that around a quarter of the spending done by the Committee over the period 1894–1900 was self-financed (Morrow, 'Origin and Early Years', 79).

[57] Before 1899, Congress had working rules for debate but no real constitution. The constitution adopted in that year states that the British Committee 'shall represent there [i.e. in Britain] the interests of the Indian National Congress' and that its funding was to be determined and provided by Congress in India. The 1908 constitution treats the British Committee as one of the 'component parts of the Congress organisation'. *Report of the Fifteenth Indian National Congress Held at Lucknow, on the 27th, 28th, 29th and 30th December, 1899* (Bombay, 1890), xxviii–xxxi; *Report of the Proceedings of the Twenty-Third Indian National Congress Held at Madras on the 28th, 29th and 30th December 1908* (Bombay, 1909), appendix B, xix–xxx.

to deal with government ministers and officials on behalf of Congress. It saw itself as an intermediary placed between Congress and the British Government, lobbying officials, constructing political alliances, controlling the raising of disputes, and, much though the India Office disliked it, influencing the course of Indian nationalism.[58] At times, indeed, it even led the Indian movement, offering rulings on the choice of Presidents, debates, and settling factional rivalries when Congress was divided. Its members and their opinions were generally treated by Congress Indians with deference and respect. A few were chosen to preside over the annual sessions of Congress, partly in the belief that this would deter harassment from the authorities, but also because such figures were men of influence who would command respect and greater attendance.[59] Congress' deference and the provision of authority to the British Committee thus provided essential participatory incentives. The Indian Congress President Anandu Charlu, stated the nature of this exchange quite explicitly in trying to calm the irritation of some delegates at the Congress in 1901:

On the ground of enlightened regard for our own interests, we must give them [the British Committee] a free hand to decide which of our suggestions and how much of our suggestions they may judge fit to give effect to. This much is surely due from us if we are to be worthy of their generous and spontaneous exertions.[60]

This is not to suggest simplistically that the British Committee stifled the natural energies of Congress, restricting it to a cautious Westminster lobbying style of politics. On the contrary, as Moulton has shown, the British founders of Congress and later the British Committee often outstripped their Indian counterparts in radicalism and energy.[61] 'Sons of Ind, why sit thee idle?', wrote Hume in 1886:

> Wait ye for some Deva's aid?
> Buckle to, be up and doing!
> Nations by themselves are made!

This exhortation, however, cannot be taken just as a plea for self-reliance: it is also a lecture and a set of orders, in which the Indians are castigated,

---

[58] 'Note on the relations between Government and the Indian National Congress Movement', undated, L/PJ/6/762, OIOC.

[59] Congress was presided over by British supporters on six occasions before 1918. See Mehrotra, *History*, 74–7, for details.

[60] Report of Indian National Congress, 1901, in A. M. Zaidi (ed.), *Encyclopaedia of the Indian National Congress* (28v., 1976–94), iv, 38.

[61] Moulton, 'Early Congress', 36.

in later verses, as 'ye that grovel in the shade' and 'ye that crouch, supine, afraid'.[62] Hume quarrelled with the Congress leaders in 1888 when his suggestion that Congress ideas were influencing the Indian sepoy exposed the organisation to charges of subversion, and again in 1892 when he spoke of an incipient revolution in India. It was, the Indian leaders argued, one thing for a Briton to say this and quite another for an Indian to say it. Hume, not a whit embarrassed, condemned the Indians for their timidity.[63] Similar criticism was offered, as we shall see, in later years by other muscular radicals. Their demand for a more manly or independent stance, coming from freeborn Britons, reflected their more secure position and was, as such, an expression of their riskless dominance of the Congress organisation. Much the same problem of the relationship between the Indian and British components arose, therefore, whether the British Committee was going too fast or too slow.

The British Committee derived its authority less from its solidarity with and loyalty to Congress decision-making than to deference. Deferential relationships are not always inhibiting, however, and it would be wrong to imply that Indian nationalists invariably seethed at these efforts to dominate their movement from afar. For one thing, there were certain advantages to the new arrangement: it was cheaper than paying an agent, and unpaid, disinterested British amateurs were at least as likely to win the support of those groups in British society which might be persuaded to endorse the Congress view. British Liberals were anxious to hear Indian voices, especially if they spoke in the familiar tones of British liberalism. But in British public forums—parliamentary, political, press—the chances of Indians being heard were greatly improved if they were spoken for, or at least endorsed by, trusted British public figures. 'The more you get Europeans of influence on your side . . . the less will be the cry that your object is revolutionary and anti-British', said Naoroji.[64] But whereas agents will, even if employed to offer professional advice, ultimately defer to their employer, a mentor or father-figure of the kind that the British committee sought to be, and was at least initially *desired* to be, is in an altogether different and

[62] A. O. Hume, *The Old Man's Hope: A Tract for the Times* (Calcutta, 1886).

[63] Mehrotra, *History*, 195–9; Edward Moulton, 'Introduction' to William Wedderburn, *Allan Octavian Hume: Father of the Indian National Congress 1829–1912* (New Delhi, 2002), xcvi.

[64] Naoroji to Wacha, 29 Aug 1900, quoted in R. P. Masani, *Dadabhai Naoroji: The Grand Old Man of India* (London, 1939), 311.

unequal relationship with their protégé or charge. This was not always a position that Liberals desired to adopt, or that Indians always resented, but because the content of their message—Indian self-reliance—was at odds with it, the relationship, as Congress developed and matured, came to be seen as a false one.

In its first twenty years or so, however, Congress lacked the confidence to confront the British Committee. Perhaps the most telling sign of this was the way that criticism of it took place mostly in private: one has to look at the level of the Indian provincial newspaper to find it, rather than in the direct dealings between the Committee and the Congress officials. There we find complaints that the dominance of British leaders suggested a lack of native talent, and that the British Committee journal, *India*, was too costly.[65] Indeed, nothing symbolised the topsy-turvy character of London-led anti-imperialism better than *India*: a journal which ostensibly represented Indian sentiment, which was nonetheless edited and almost wholly written by British Liberals with little or no Indian experience with a view to influencing opinion in Britain, but which was dispatched in large numbers to often involuntary recipients in India to inform them what Indians thought and felt. But hardly anyone dared to say this directly to the Committee itself. Instead, the complaints were made in corners, in a manner matching the parent–child relationship between Congress and its British Committee. Hume came to be seen as an irascible but indispensable influence on Congress, and, as we shall see, reform of the Committee in its long twilight under Wedderburn's leadership proved impossible mainly because Indians felt they had to wait for him to die before they could bring themselves to demand changes.

These semi-silent frustrations ensured that the British Committee was no better able than Digby to extract funds from India. Receipts and spending are shown in Fig. 1.[66]

The first thing to note is how little money there was, despite the fact that there was plenty of money in India for other causes. As Morrow points out, the receipts of a single Delhi cow protection society in 1903 exceeded the sums sent from the whole of India to the British Committee.[67] In theory, the Committee's work was mostly supported by a slice of the delegates' fees for the annual Congress, a scheme designed

---

[65] The number of copies printed shrank from 10,000 in 1894 to 3,000 by 1907. Morrow, 'Origin and Early Years', 68.

[66] Data from *Mahratta*, 11 Jan 1920.   [67] Morrow, 'Origin and Early Years', 72.

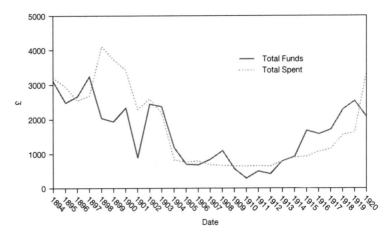

Fig. 1. Funds and Spending of the British Committee of the Indian National Congress, 1894–1920

to persuade unwilling Indians to pay for something they did not want—the British Committee—as a condition of getting something they did. However, passing the money on was the responsibility of forgetful or privately unsympathetic local organisers: in 1896, Tilak tried to prevent the money owed from Poona being sent at all and in 1899 the Lahore Committee also refused to hand over its surplus.[68] The graph shows that at least until 1910 there was a stepped decline in the sums made available for the British Committee, punctuated by injections of fresh funds followed in each case by a renewed decline to a new low. This reflects two overlapping trends: a sense of dwindling importance and frustration with the British Committee's work, counteracted from time to time by the ability of the Committee to extract funds at intervals by threatening to disband, or when a personal appearance was made at Congress by a veteran, for while Congress members found it very easy to default on their payments in private and when Congress was not in session, face to face pressure was harder to resist.[69] The best way, tellingly, in which funds could be extracted was by making donations a matter of competitive local ostentation. In 1889, for example, in the presence of Bradlaugh, Rs. 63,000 (£4,360) had been raised on

---

[68] Gokhale to Naoroji, 3 Sep 1896, GM 11704; Wacha to Gokhale, [illeg] Sept 1904, GM 11707.

[69] Wacha to Naoroji, 7 Feb 1903, *DNC*, ii, 821–2.

the spot. This was not a small sum: it was over twice what had been spent on the previous year's Congress.[70] Wacha described how 'the ball was set rolling by a distinguished Madras delegate coming forward and offering in hard cash Rs 2000 £138. The contagion spread. Every half a minute contributions of thousands and five hundreds were announced till at last small and large contributions swelled the whole amount to Rs 63,000.'[71]

In the 1890s, as Morrow has shown, the British Committee and the Indian movement repeatedly differed over issues of policy. They disagreed over Naoroji's claim, vital to the theory that India was exploited by imperialism, that money drained from India to pay for the pensions of the ICS and the dividends of British investors, most of the British Liberals maintaining that on balance British investment helped to develop India, and the real trouble was only that unsympathetic and alien administrators were in charge of the process. The British Committee opposed the opium trade in India, while Congress feared that the costs of abolition would fall mostly on India. The Committee's MPs were also almost all free-traders, on principled or constituency grounds, where the Indians thought that free trade was damaging nascent Indian industries and worsened the drain.[72] These differences of interest and view were quite natural. What made them problematic was that they were not the basis for *disagreements*. The unnatural organisational relationship made it impossible for them to be satisfactorily debated or for the Congress view to carry sufficient authority in London.

Increasingly towards the end of the 1890s, criticism was heard in India, if not in London. These irritations were fed by reports from London by critics of the British Committee, prominent among them the displaced team of Digby and Caine. Digby had been a thorn in the Committee's side ever since his removal in 1892, frequently attacking its failure to raise Indian grievances in a more direct and energetic fashion.[73] The Committee was, he argued, 'perfectly useless', an opinion echoed by Caine.[74] Caine also complained that Wedderburn was 'terribly weak in a crisis . . . and los[t] chance after chance in the House for want of

---

[70] Seal, *Emergence*, 285.
[71] Wacha to Naoroji, 3 Jan 1890 and 6 Jan 1893, *DNC*, i, 203–5, 315–17.
[72] Morrow, 'Origin and Early Years', esp. 52–9.
[73] Wacha to Naoroji, 6 July 1894, *DNC*, i, 398–9; *India*, Sep 1894.
[74] Wacha to Naoroji, 16, 24 and 30 Nov, and 15 Dec 1900, *DNC*, ii, 637–8, 666–7; Ghose to Digby, 6 Dec 1900, Digby Coll., MSS/Eur/D767/9.

good prompt action'.[75] The British Committee needed an infusion of new blood and strategic leadership.[76] Caine, a powerful campaigner and orator known in the Commons as the 'genial ruffian' naturally thought of himself. 'My fear is', Wacha warned the Committee, ' . . . that Caine wants to be the *supreme man* in matters of Congress and he thinks that so long as you, Hume and Sir W[illiam] W[edderburn] are there he is out'.[77] But even those close to Wedderburn were by now feeling nostalgic for the advocacy Congress had enjoyed under Bradlaugh.[78] In the *Bengalee* articles appeared, some by the Bengali nationalist Bipin Chandra Pal, who had worked with Caine on temperance questions in London,[79] damning Wedderburn's feeble leadership, calling for cutbacks on *India,* more Indians on the Committee, and for Caine to be installed as its new leader.[80] When an elected Indian Congress Committee (ICC) was set up in 1899 to manage the work of the Congress between the annual meetings, it was quick to try and pull back expenditure on *India* and the British Committee and Wacha had to fight hard to get a continued commitment to it.[81]

In 1900, practically all the parliamentary members of the British Committee either stood down or were carried off in the electoral rout of the Khaki Election. Caine, however, made it back into the Commons and with Digby's help set about trying to supplant the British Committee.[82] Digby looked forward to the 'recurrence of the grand days when Mr Charles Bradlaugh was India's champion in the House . . .', a position which would be 'all gain':

That Committee is the best which has on it one or two men who know their own minds, know the needs of the organization to be served, and who go their

[75] Caine to Gokhale, 1 and 30 Sept and 29 Oct 1897, GM 11698; *Bengalee,* 25 Sep 1897.

[76] Wacha to Naoroji, 6 Aug and 26 Nov 1898, *DNC,* ii, 637–8, 666–7; Caine to Gokhale, 30 Sept 1898, GM 11698; Goodridge to Gokhale, 18 May 1899, GM 11700.

[77] Wacha to Naoroji, 20 Aug and 10 Sept 1898, *DNC,* ii, 639–41, 644–5.

[78] Wacha to Naoroji, 23 July 1898, *DNC,* ii, 633–4.

[79] Morrow, 'Origin and Early Years', 59–60.

[80] *Bengalee,* 20 May 1899, 5 and 19 Aug 1899, 25 Nov 1899.

[81] Its first meeting, on 1–2 October 1900 agreed an annual expenditure of Rs. 12,000 [£795] for the British Committee and that *India* should be hived off and run independently, although this was reversed at the second meeting, which argued for the continuation of *India* and Rs. 30,000 [£1,988]. Wacha to Naoroji, 13 Oct, 3, 16 and 30 Nov, 15 Dec 1900, *DNC,* ii, 774–5, 778–9, 780–1, 783–6; *Mahratta,* 21 Oct and 30 Dec 1900.

[82] Caine to Mehta, undated, in *Hindu,* 13 Nov 1900.

way doing all they know, treating the Committee with respect but not with obedience . . . Better still is it when there is only an Agent who knows what his principals want . . . .[83]

Motilal Ghose, Digby's ally in the affair of the Maharaja of Kashmir, now emerged to recommend a revival of the old Agency arrangement.[84] It would be, he argued, cheaper, more energetic, and would more reliably speak for Congress. Digby was to be made Secretary once again of the reformed British Committee, ostensibly on the grounds that Caine would only accept the Presidency if he was.[85] Funding was to be secured, as in the days of Bradlaugh, through cash for questions: '[I]f you could manage through Mr Caine to ask questions, then we could secure supporters who would pay', Ghose told Digby.[86] There was also, as before, to be fundraising from the Indian princes. 'Don't ask him to join the Congress', Ghose told Digby of one likely princely mark, 'but advise him to do good to his country *privately* through our agency.'[87] The dispute had a provincial factional dimension too: Ghose hoped that a British Committee under Caine and Digby's leadership would bring Congress more under the influence of the Bengalis and away from the more moderate Bombay group of Naoroji, Wacha, Gokhale and Wedderburn.

This move was immediately and rightly taken as hostile by the British Committee.[88] It hit back using its best weapons: the authority of veteran leaders, and its financial independence. In 1893, it had bailed out the Committee with its own funds, and now it threatened to disband unless funds were forthcoming.[89] It gambled that no one in India wanted to assume financial responsibility for the money-losing *India*, so when the funds duly failed to appear in July 1901 it felt confident enough to offer to hand over *India* to 'persons of substance and trust duly authorised to assume the management'.[90] No offer was forthcoming,

[83] Digby, 'Anglo-Indian and Indo-English Topics', 26 Oct 1900, in *Hindu*, 12 Nov 1900.

[84] *Amrita Bazar Patrika* 28 Nov 1900; *Mahratta*, 25 Nov 1900.

[85] Ghose to Digby, 1 Aug 1903, Digby Coll., MSS/Eur/D767/9.

[86] Ghose to Digby, 24 Jan 1901, ibid.

[87] Ghose to Digby, 14 May 1902 and 23 July 1903, ibid.

[88] Mehrotra, *History*, 96; Minute Book v.5, 23 Oct 1901, 4 Mar 1902, 8 Apr 1902; Ghose to Digby, 24 Jan 1901, 22 Aug 1901, 9 Jan 1902, Digby Coll., MSS/Eur/D767/9.

[89] Hume and Wedderburn to Congress Committees 13 Oct 1899; Naoroji to Congress Committees, 3 Aug 1900, GM 11701; Minute Book, v.5, 31 July 1900; Wedderburn to Wacha, 24 Feb and 6 May 1901, and Wedderburn to Bonnerjee 6 June 1902, GM 11701; Mehrotra, *History*, 100–1.

[90] Minute Book, v. 5, 2 July 1901.

and the Committee took its offer to have been refused.[91] The future of
the Committee itself however, hung in the balance. Outside Bombay,
it was generally disliked, and in September 1901, the ICC voted to end
India and to infuse the British Committee with new blood.[92] Congress
leaders called for a properly accredited agent in London, working with
an Indianised Committee, campaigning more energetically in Britain
as a whole as Caine's temperance organisations did, and responsible
to Calcutta, rather than Bombay.[93] Fearful that the full Congress
might confirm this decision, the British Committee proposed a less
burdensome arrangement for its funding, to be guaranteed by Naoroji.
This was a powerful counterstroke, not least in being endorsed by the
Grand Old Man of Indian politics.[94] 'Certainly Mr Dadabhai has to be
satisfied in the matter', wrote *The Hindu*, through gritted teeth.[95] At
the December 1901 Congress, Ghose offered to publish *India* in India
for one-sixth of the cost, but a short-term deal was done to balance
the Committee's books and to save *India* on a reduced budget.[96] The
Bombay Moderates thereupon found procedural reasons to axe the
ICC, on the grounds of its evidently hostile attitude to the work in
London.[97]

The British Committee and its Indian allies were satisfied with
this outcome: 'the malcontents', Bonnerjee concluded, were 'few in
number and of no great influence'.[98] But, as often happened, they
missed the resentment that their high-handedness had aroused: 'You
have no idea how many ugly things were blurted out', Wacha had
warned Naoroji.[99] Ghose now called for the outright abolition of the
British Committee.[100] Elsewhere, the Congress secretaries resorted to

[91] Minute Book, v.5, 26 Sept 1901; Naoroji to Gokhale, 27 Sept 1901, GM 11701.
[92] Morrow, 'Origin and Early Years', 257; Wacha to Congress Committees, 1 June
1901, GM 11701; Wacha to Gokhale, 18 April and 11 June 1901, GM 11707; Report
of Indian National Congress 1901, in Zaidi, *Encyclopaedia*, iv, 39–42.
[93] *Native Opinion*, 16 Sept 1900, in B. L. Grover (ed.), *Curzon and Congress:
Curzonian Policies and the Great Debate (January 1899–March 1902)* (New Delhi,
1995), 391–2; *Mahratta*, 3 March 1901, 6 Oct 1901; *Amrita Bazar Patrika*, 19 June
1901, NNR Bengal, L/R/5/27, OIOC.
[94] Naoroji to Gokhale, 27 Aug, 29 Sep 1901 and 12 Oct 1902, GM 11701.
[95] *Hindu*, 21 Dec 1901.
[96] Zaidi, *Encyclopaedia*, iv, 255–6; Minute Book, v.5, 21 Jan 1902.
[97] Mehrotra, *History*, 162–3.   [98] Minute Book, v.5, 6 May 1902.
[99] Wacha to Naoroji, 16 Feb 1901, *DNC*, ii, 789–90.
[100] *Amrita Bazar Patrika*, reported in *Mahratta*, 19 Jan 1902 and *Tribune*, 4 Jan
1902; *Kayastha Samachar*, Jan 1902, in Grover, *Curzon and Congress*, 409; Morrow,
'Origin and Early Years', 264–5.

silent boycott, withholding the funds to which the British Committee was formally entitled. After the first year of the new arrangements, despite repeated requests to the provinces for payment, only one reply had been received, and that had been negative.[101] 'Every scheme has been tried and seems to have given no satisfaction', Wacha noted in anguish.[102] Naoroji renewed his support and guarantees and the Committee separated *India*, the main drain on its funds, from the rest of the work and issued shares in it, which were almost all bought by the Committee's members in Britain and its Moderate friends in India.[103] This reduced the financial burden on Congress, limited gripes about the poor quality of *India* and ensured that the main organ of Congress in Britain spoke clearly along Bombay Moderate lines. But this came at a price. The British Committee had, as it would continue to do, bought its way out of trouble without addressing the fundamental anomaly of its own position. The circulation of *India* fell and non-payment of Congress dues became rife.[104] In 1904, Madras refused to pay up until Gokhale made a special visit to insist on it. Benares in 1905 had to be threatened with a public legal action. Calcutta in 1906 only sent about half what was expected.[105] Caine and Digby, irritated by the defeat of their coup, continued to snipe at the Committee in the Indian press.[106] The result was weak organisation. The Committee employed no permanent lecturers or agents, published nothing except *India* and remained virtually unknown outside London. Grand plans for the 1905 election had to be abandoned for lack of funds.[107] Against it, the emerging Extremist wing of Congress, under Tilak, argued for their own conception of linked-up agitation: a properly funded permanent Congress office in England, run by Indians, with less lobbying of Anglo-Indian officials and civil servants and more public campaigning. It was telling that Tilak, in making

---

[101] Minute Book, v.5, 7 Oct 1902, 14 Oct 1902; Wacha to Naoroji, 28 Nov and 29 Dec 1902, in *DNC*, ii, 814–5, 817–18. Wedderburn to Bonnerjee, 6 June 1902, GM 11701.

[102] Wacha to Naoroji, 7, 14 and 28 Feb 1903, *DNC*, ii, 821–8.

[103] Morrow, 'Origin and Early Years', 266–7; Naoroji to Wedderburn, 12 Oct 1902, and Naoroji to Gokhale, 16 Oct 1902, GM 11701.

[104] Morrow, 'Origin and Early Years', 266; Minute Book, v.5, 19 Jan 1904.

[105] Wacha to Gokhale, [illeg] 1904, 13 and 17 Feb 1906; 16 and 28 Jan 1907, 4 March 1907, GM 11707.

[106] *India*, 7 Oct 1904.

[107] Minute Book v.5, 8 Dec 1903 and 5 Jan 1904; v.6, 24 Oct 1905; Symonds memorandum, undated but prob. May 1905, and Wedderburn to Congress Joint Secretaries, 1 May 1905, GM 11708. Morrow, 'Origins and Early Years', 86.

such a case to Naoroji in 1904, invoked the idea of a mission, but in reverse:

[I]f we wish to get any rights or privileges we must agitate in England in a missionary spirit. The Anglo-Indians here won't listen to what we say. The pressure must come from England and this is possible only if we . . . establish a permanent political mission . . . and work there persistently after the fashion of Christian missionaries in India or elsewhere . . . The only way to get privilege is to make it impossible for the English people to ignore our efforts.[108]

---

[108] Tilak to Naoroji, 6 Dec 1904, reprinted in H. D. Vidwans (ed.) *Letters of Lokamanya Tilak* (Poona, 1966), 252–4; Lajpat Rai to Verma, 3 Aug 1905, in *CWLR*, ii, 142–4.

2

Dilemmas of the Metropolitan Anti-Imperialist, 1906–1910

In 1906, a newly elected Liberal Government began to consider the case for political advance in India.[1] This chapter examines the two principal attempts by Indian nationalists in London to influence it. The first is the work of the British Committee, whose liberal and British-dominated approach was examined in the previous chapter. The second is the less familiar work of Shyamji Krishnavarma, Vinayak Savarkar and the political revolutionaries of India House. The chapter concludes by examining the beginnings of a third and radically different strategy, that of M. K. Gandhi.

The British Committee naturally welcomed the return of a Liberal Government. The minimal demands it made on its parliamentary members permitted a large number of new recruits to the IPC.[2] However, probably only a dozen at most were active, and, as before, Liberal MPs could be recruited for the Committee only when their own causes—temperance, social purity, anti-opium and so forth—had an Indian dimension. As before, rather fewer than half the members of the IPC actually voted for the Congress position on such questions.[3] Moreover, the Committee found it hard to persuade its fellow Liberals that India was fit for self-government within the empire, as Gokhale and Congress now demanded.

Wedderburn's strategy was to try and counter the conservative influence of the India Office by presenting Morley privately with the Moderate Congress case, especially through Gokhale. Public attacks on Morley, he insisted, would merely alienate anyone outside the

---

[1] Koss, *John Morley*; Wolpert, *Morley and India*; and Nanda, *Gokhale,* 221–319.
[2] Wedderburn predicted 100 recruits (Wedderburn to Gokhale, 16 Feb 1906, GM 11708) but 176 were noted in the Minute Book in May 1906 (v.6, 22 May 1906) and 192 claimed in *India,* 20 July 1906.
[3] Morrow, 'Origin and Early Years', 293–6.

Committee's immediate group of supporters.[4] In the debate on the King's Speech in February 1906, an amendment was moved urging greater attention to the demands of the Indian people, but it was not pushed to a division.[5] Morley's early pronouncements, which seemed to indicate some possibilities of political advance, were welcomed. In July 1906, following repression of Congress meetings in East Bengal and Assam, Keir Hardie moved an amendment on behalf of the IPC to put the Secretary of State's salary on the estimates, and 89 MPs voted for it.[6] This was, however, not designed to undermine Morley, but to strengthen the hands of his parliamentary supporters. By the end of the parliamentary session, Indians were becoming restive with this cautious and uncritical approach.

Wedderburn's strategy revealed a basic tension that was repeatedly to hamper anti-imperialist work: between linked-up agitation and sustaining a liberal in office. It depended for its success on Morley's liberal intentions and on the willingness of Indians to accept the very limited role it allowed them. Neither of these conditions fully applied. At its best, Wedderburn's approach provided the *opportunity* for Morley to resist conservative proposals from his officials or from India. Morley was not averse to using real or imagined parliamentary pressure as a means of pushing the Viceroy into political concessions.[7] But he had no desire to hand the initiative to the British Committee, and increasingly, his own techniques of management were employed against them.[8] Exactly what Morley wanted has been much disputed and is hard to extract from his contradictory pronouncements, but his priority seems to have been to ensure that the Government of India governed fairly and was properly accountable to London. He also wanted the expansion of the elected and representative element on the Indian Councils, and for it to have greater powers to question and challenge the executive, though it seems doubtful that he intended this to lead to responsible government.[9] This was, beyond agreement on first steps, a different view to that of Congress and most members of the British Committee, who wished to

---

[4] Wedderburn to Gokhale, 23 Aug 1906 and 6 Nov 1907, GM 11708.

[5] *Hansard*, 26 Feb 1906, 4th ser., v.152, cols.830–44.

[6] *Hansard*, 20 July 1906, 4th ser., v.161, cols.570–637.

[7] Morley to Minto, 22 June 1906, MC MSS/Eur/D573/1; Wolpert, *Morley and India*, 42.

[8] Morley to Minto, 8 Oct 1907, MC MSS/Eur/D573/2.

[9] R. J. Moore, 'John Morley's Acid Test: India, 1906–1910', *Pacific Affairs*, 40/3–4 (Autumn 1967—Winter 1967–8) 333–40; Koss, *John Morley*. But see also Wolpert, *Morley and India*, 130, 162–3.

see the gradual implementation of self-governing institutions, modelled on those of the Dominions. Morley's private comments regarding the British Committee, whose members he described in unflattering terms, bear this out.[10] Gokhale, therefore, far from Wedderburn's intention, was primarily used by Morley to restrain criticism from India, with the implicit threat that unrest would ensure the loss of the reforms altogether.[11]

Worse still, Wedderburn's strategy left little for Indians to do except to exercise patience and avoid criticism of the Liberal Government. It meant the temporary suspension of any form of linked-up agitation beyond the private petitioning of Indian moderates in London. The British Committee therefore cut itself off from the forces of movement in India. The partition of Bengal, which Morley had described in 1906 as a 'settled fact', was deeply unpalatable to the educated classes in eastern Bengal, who feared it would isolate them from career advancement in Calcutta and that Bengali Hindus would be swamped among larger numbers of Muslims and Assamese, and their counterparts in Calcutta who disliked the vivisection of the historical region, and the prospect of being lumped in with Bihar and Orissa. Along with other restrictions on elected councillors and university students in Calcutta partition had fuelled significant political unrest which had spread by 1907 to the Punjab and Maharashtra. The unexpected strength of the anti-partition movement in Bengal and responses to the deportation of Lajpat Rai in May 1907 had persuaded the so-called Extremist wing of Congress of the possibilities of a more militant approach. Arrests and detentions were no longer seen, as Gokhale and the Moderates had regarded them, as marks of failure, but badges of honour. The Extremists had serious reservations about the British Committee. Many if not all of them had decided against mendicancy, remonstrance and petition, and in favour of self-reliance; against following a British-defined colonial model rather than an Indian-defined Swaraj model; for national independence rather than a place within the empire; for methods of agitation based on traditional Indian strategies of non-cooperation and social boycott, rather than the broadening of democratic liberties through the expansion of precedents familiar to students of the British

[10] Kaminsky, *India Office*, 65–6. Morley to Minto, 18 May, 22 June 1906, MC MSS/Eur/D573/1; 27 Dec 1907, MC MSS/Eur/D573/2; 23 April 1908, MC MSS/Eur/D573/3.

[11] Hirtzel, Diary, 9 May 1906; Morley to Minto, 11 May 1906, MC MSS/Eur/ D573/1.

constitution; against appeal to the British sense of justice in favour of developing fellow-feeling with the Indian people and the creation of a mass organisation. They were distressed by the Committee's supine response to Morley's comments on Bengal and his unwillingness to attack methods of coercion in India.[12]

Having chosen to back moderation so strongly, the British Committee could not speak meaningfully for these movements, and was thus unable to use them credibly to pressure Morley. Instead, it made pleas for unity under Moderate leadership and tried to enforce them from afar. Wedderburn wrote to Tilak and Lajpat Rai to urge moderation while Morley was finding his feet.[13] When, at the end of 1906, Congress leaders in Calcutta, allied to the Tilakites, wished to elect Lajpat Rai as President of the coming session, Wedderburn refused to take sides,[14] and even suggested to the Moderates that they give the Tilakites 'a trial in the management and honours of the Congress', but attend in sufficient numbers to block them on questions of policy.[15] Wedderburn hoped that the Tilakites might supply the energy to revitalise Congress without wanting to take the leadership. But the implications of the strategy favoured by the Extremists for the work of the British Committee were clear enough: such a campaign would have its centre in India; it would be impossible to discuss with Morley; and it would have its own emissaries to send to London, rather than relying on the London Indians and their British allies.[16] The Congress Moderates therefore refused to take such a risk, and instead engineered the election of Naoroji as a holding manoeuvre. But Wedderburn's conviction that Morley must be

[12] NNR Bengal, 20 Feb and 1 March 1906, 9 July 1907, L/R/5/33, OIOC; NNR Bombay, 24 and 31 March 1906, L/R/5/161, OIOC; *NNR* Bombay, 12 Dec 1908, L/R/5/163, OIOC. Generally on this phase of agitation see Amales Tripathi, *The Extremist Challenge: India Between 1890 and 1910* (New Delhi, 1967); Daniel Argov, *Moderates and Extremists in the Indian Nationalist Movement* (Bombay, 1967); Gordon Johnson, *Provincial Politics and Indian Nationalism: Bombay and the Indian National Congress, 1880–1915* (Cambridge, 1973); Sumit Sarkar, *The Swadeshi Movement in Bengal, 1903–8* (New Delhi, 1973); Rajat Kanta Ray, 'Moderates, Extremists, and Revolutionaries: Bengal, 1900–1908', in Richard Sisson and Stanley Wolpert (eds.), *Congress and Indian Nationalism: The Pre-Independence Phase* (Delhi, 1988); Ranajit Guha, 'Discipline and Mobilize', in *Subaltern Studies VII* (Oxford, 1992).
[13] Wedderburn to Gokhale, 10 and 23 Aug 1906, GM 11708; Wedderburn to Lajpat Rai, 23 Aug 1906, *SCLR,* 18–19.
[14] Wedderburn to Gokhale, 30 July and 8 Aug 1906, GM 11708.
[15] Wedderburn to Gokhale, 8 Aug 1906.
[16] Wedderburn to Gokhale, 5 Dec 1907, GM 11708; *India,* 6 Dec 1907; Stanley A. Wolpert, *Tilak and Gokhale : Revolution and Reform in the Making of Modern India* (Berkeley and Los Angeles, 1962), 209.

supported became increasingly unsustainable.[17] At Surat at the end of 1907, the Extremists planned to end subsidies to the British Committee altogether, and only the collapse of the Congress in scenes of disorder on its second day prevented debate on it.

However, the possibilities of linked-up agitation did appeal to some supporters of the Committee. Chief among them was Sir Henry Cotton, former Chief Commissioner of Assam, who had joined the Committee on his retirement to England in 1902. Cotton had long favoured constitutional reform in India which would lead eventually to self-government.[18] At the end of 1904, he and Wedderburn had attended the Congress in India in the hope of a 'revival of the old spirit & a fresh start in usefulness'.[19] Cotton had been pleased by his reception there, and on his way back began to contemplate a reconstruction of the British Committee to enable it to provide proper support for the Bengal agitation. 'I despair of the British Committee', he told Gokhale. Under Wedderburn's leadership it had decayed into a collection of 'extinct volcanoes' while *India* was becoming 'feebler and feebler'.[20] Cotton therefore proposed that *India* be taken over by his son, Evan, a barrister recently returned from Calcutta.[21] This was resisted by Gokhale and Wedderburn, who feared Evan would 'sensationalise' the paper and abandon the 'sober moderation' which had, they believed, served Congress so well.[22] However, no rival candidate could be found, and Evan Cotton duly assumed the editorship in 1906. The editorials in *India* hardly became sensational, but they were noticeably more critical about Morley than Wedderburn liked, and reported in positive terms the development of swadeshi agitation in India. Simultaneously, Cotton *père* was returned to Parliament, which gave him a platform from which to assert leadership of the British Committee. When Morley declared partition settled, Cotton, assisted by a fellow MP C. J. O'Donnell, another ex-ICS official, wrote to Congress leaders in Bengal to urge them to press on with their agitation: '*mass meetings* by the *dozen* in *every* district . . . Morley will yet yield'. A Whig, they commented,

[17] Wedderburn to Gokhale, 2 May, 5 Sept, 2 Oct and 6 Nov 1907, GM 11708.
[18] Henry Cotton, *New India; or India in Transition* (London, 1885) and *Indian & Home Memories* (London, 1911); Moulton, 'Early Indian Nationalism'.
[19] Wedderburn to Gokhale, 28 April and 16 Aug 1904, GM 11708.
[20] H. J. S. Cotton to Gokhale, 18 Jan and 8 Sept 1905, GM 11699.
[21] H. J. S. Cotton to Wedderburn, 5 and 7 March 1905, GM 11707.
[22] Memorandum by Wedderburn, 3 March 1905, GM 11707, Gokhale to Nateshrao, 1 June 1906, GM 11700.

'does nothing unless pressed'.[23] Morley was furious to hear from the Viceroy about this communication, which probably prompted him to dig his heels in yet further, but the incident suggested the potential for linked-up agitation.[24]

In the autumn of 1907, tours of India by another Radical MP V. H. Rutherford, the journalist H. W. Nevinson and Independent Labour Party MP Keir Hardie threatened further strengthening of agitational links, bringing Congress parliamentary encouragement and the chance for publicity at home.[25] The visitors' impressions of India will be discussed in the next chapter, but for present purposes it is worth noting the way in which such visits revived official fears of long-distance wire-pulling. Dissenters within the ranks of the Europeans resident in India were always subject to criticism out of all proportion to their tiny numbers, partly because of the anxiety their crossing of the borders between Briton and Indian provoked, in challenging or destabilising hierarchies of racial prestige.[26] Hardie and Rutherford similarly threatened to create alternative solidarities in India, all the more dangerous because of the immunities and status they possessed as MPs. Hardie was quite cautious about encouraging a movement he did not fully understand, but his expenses and guidance were taken care of wholly by Congress, convincing officials that he was 'led by the nose by the Hindu agitators'.[27] They found instructions from Congress leaders that Hardie should be told that partition and the partiality of the *raj* towards the Muslims were the cause of the agitation there. In his first speeches in India, Hardie attacked the 'Russian methods' of the *raj*, promised the support of the Labour Party for parliamentary

[23] O'Donnell to Bannerjea, 2 March 1906, sent with Minto to Morley, 10 Sep 1906, MC MSS/Eur/D573/9.

[24] Morley even refused to shake O'Donnell's hand because of the incident. See Hirtzel Diary, 1 July 1907.

[25] Hardie to Gokhale, 9 July 1907, GM 11701. The following account is drawn from the following sources: Minto's Diary of Events, Minto Papers, MS 12609; Indian Tour Travel Jottings, dep 176, 2/1, J.Keir Hardie Papers; India Office file L/PJ/6/831, OIOC; the Government of India Criminal Intelligence Department reports in Government of India files HPD, Dec 1907, 23, and HPA, Feb 1908, 50–63.

[26] See Ann Laura Stoler, 'Cultivating Bourgeois Bodies and Racial Selves', in Catherine Hall (ed.), *Cultures of Empire: Colonizers in Britain and the Empire in the Nineteenth and Twentieth Centuries: A Reader* (Manchester, 2000), 87–8, 91.

[27] Le Mesurier to Risley, 12 Oct, 25 Oct and 12 Nov 1907; Risley to Lyall, 28 Nov 1907, L/PJ/6/831, OIOC; Minto to Lansdowne, 30 Nov 1907, and Minto to Hely-Hutchinson, 11 Jan 1908, Minto Papers, MS 12776; Minto to Edward VII, 6 Feb 1908, MS 12728; Minto to Fraser, 20 Oct 1907, MS 12767.

action to end them, and for extensions of self-government on Canadian lines.[28]

This was exactly the kind of linking-up, based on ignorance of Indian conditions, that officials feared. District officers blamed Hardie for the revival of agitation in eastern Bengal, since the protestors there were now claiming parliamentary support, or even that Hardie had been delegated by Parliament to investigate their condition.[29] When news of this reached London, creating a political storm, Morley cabled Minto he was ready 'to sanction whatever measures, no matter how strong, may seem advisable'.[30] As Hardie moved from Bengal towards the military cantonments of the Punjab, Minto issued instructions that he be prevented from speaking to 'inflammable populations' or to the troops.[31] 'I should like to pack him off and send him straight home', Minto told Morley, 'but can we find any legal ground for doing so?'[32] It turned out that Hardie could not be deported, but only arrested.[33] District officers were therefore warned that no action should be taken against him without the Government of India's approval.[34] An official who had not recognised Hardie's political importance and treated him offensively was censured and moved to another district.[35] Hardie met senior officials in Calcutta and proposed that he act as a confidential emissary between them and the Moderate leaders, trading renunciation of violence for promises of political concessions. But the Viceroy and his staff had no intention at all of permitting Hardie to adopt such a powerful role, and dismissed the proposal.[36]

On his return, however, Hardie was persuaded by Motilal Ghose to support a linked campaign by which the Indian movement would keep up its campaign of non-violent resistance against the *raj*, leaving political agitation in Britain to Britons who could better persuade

---

[28] Viceroy to Secretary of State, 7 Oct 1907, HPA, Feb 1908, 50.

[29] Le Mesurier to Risley, 25 Oct and 12 Nov 1907, L/PJ/6/831, OIOC.

[30] Morley to Minto, 3 Oct 1907, MC MSS/Eur/D573/2; Morley to Minto, 8 Oct 1908, MC MSS/Eur/D573/3; Morley to Haldane, 4 Oct 1907, Morley Papers (Bodleian), MS Eng c.7084.

[31] Dunlop-Smith to Risley, 11 Oct 1907, HPA, Feb 1908, 54.

[32] Memorandum by Minto, 5 Oct 1907, HPA, Feb 1908, 50.

[33] Hirtzel Diary, 15 and 17 Oct 1907; Morley to Minto, 8 and 17 Oct 1908, MC MSS/Eur/D573/3; Minto to Edward VII, 6 Feb 1908, Minto Papers, MS 12728.

[34] Secretary, Home Department, Government of India to Chief Secretary, Government of Eastern Bengal and Assam, 9 Oct 1907, HPA, Feb 1908, 51.

[35] Risley to Lyall, 28 Nov 1911, L/PJ/6/831, OIOC.

[36] Minto to Morley, 16 Oct 1907, MC MSS/Eur/573/13, Risley to Dunlop-Smith, 17 Oct 1907, and Hardie to Minto, 19 Oct 1907, Minto Papers MS 12767.

the press, public and parliament of the Indian case. By such means, Ghose wrote, 'the late Mr Bradlaugh was able to keep Indian wrongs constantly before the English public and make the whole Indian civil service tremble like an aspen leaf.'[37] The ILP accordingly gave an unequivocal welcome to Congress and Hardie became one of the key figures in a reinvigorated parliamentary grouping dedicated to a more confrontational approach in Parliament.[38] V. H. Rutherford also, on his return from India at the start of 1908, told Wedderburn that he too now intended to speak out 'without reserve'.[39] Cotton too now opposed Wedderburn's efforts to persuade Congress to give Morley any more time to prove himself.[40] The group refused to follow Wedderburn in welcoming Morley's statements, and abandoned private deputation for fierce Commons assaults.[41] 'No advocate . . . would open the case by denouncing and insulting the Judge', Wedderburn wrote sadly.[42]

There is little sign that these tactics made much impact on the Morley–Minto reforms which, after a weary parliamentary passage, were approved in May 1909. Where the Committee got what it wanted—on the appointment of unelected Indians to the Council of India and the Viceroy's executive, and more elected Indians to the legislative councils—it was because Morley believed it necessary to rally the Moderates. Where it did not—on the partition of Bengal, limited budgetary powers of the councils, special interest representation, separate electorates—it was largely because it was unable to persuade its fellow Liberals.[43] Part of the problem was that divisions over tactics did not coincide with divisions over policy: the ICS men who attacked Morley so vigorously still bore some of the traces of paternalism from their years in India: Cotton, despite his determination to resist the partition of Bengal was a socially conservative figure on political advance, and

---

[37] Ghose to Hardie, 21 and 28 May 1908, Francis Johnson Correspondence, 1908/207 and 1908/220.

[38] ILP, *Reports of Annual Conferences*, 1908, 66–7; 1910, 82–4; 1911, 18.

[39] Wedderburn to Gokhale, 30 Jan 1908, GM 11707; *Hansard*, 31 Jan 1908, 4th ser., v.183, cols.375–90.

[40] Wedderburn to Gokhale, 27 June, 6 Nov and 5 Dec 1907, GM 11708; Cotton to Wedderburn, 5 Dec 1907, enclosed in Wedderburn to Gokhale, 11 Dec 1907, GM 11708.

[41] Wedderburn to Gokhale, 31 Jan, 6, 14 and 28 Feb 1908, GM 11708; Moulton, 'British Radicals', 40–2.

[42] Wedderburn to Gokhale, 28 Feb 1908, GM 11708.

[43] Thompson, *'Thinking Imperially?'*.

favoured some of the same safeguards desired by Minto.[44] But in the main it was clear that parliamentary manoeuvres were never likely to defeat the Government as long as Unionists could be relied on to outvote the Radical critics of Morley's policies and the party whips to impose disciplinary sanctions on rebellion. Hence, though the critics undoubtedly wanted more, they tended to bow to Gokhale's view that the main thing in Parliament now was to support Morley and encourage him to stand firm against conservative revolts.[45]

Nevertheless, the India Office took their parliamentary critics much more seriously than they had Wedderburn's private lobbying, as is clear from Morley's correspondence and the voluminous files dealing with parliamentary questions.[46] Partly this was because ex-ICS men like Cotton and O'Donnell and even Rutherford and Hardie with their recent Indian experience, spoke with considerable authority and knew how the administration worked. In this context, indeed, Morley's comments on the idiocies of his parliamentary critics take on a different complexion. The key parliamentary weak spot was the Liberals' attachment to civil liberties. While few Liberal MPs outside the IPC (and not even all inside it) believed that India could be a Dominion, larger numbers could be persuaded that it should be *treated* like a Dominion, or at least Dominion-in-waiting. Even Morley felt this, frequently urging Minto that the spirit of free institutions might, or even must, precede their establishment.[47] In April 1907, despite nervousness on the part of Wedderburn, Cotton and others had attacked the deportation without trial of Lajpat Rai and Ajit Singh from the Punjab, putting Morley under pressure that he was forced to communicate to Minto, resulting in releases later in the year.[48] Koss suggests that this incident, about which Morley was misled by Minto, marked a turning point for him and thereafter he adopted a much more critical stance towards the man on the spot.[49] Measures introduced in 1908 to restrict the freedoms of the press and civil association, and rights to jury trial and

[44] Morrow, 'Origin and Early Years', 332.

[45] Clark to Hardie, 30 Dec 1908, Francis Johnson Correspondence, 1908/538; H. J. S. Cotton to Wedderburn, 11 Feb 1909, GM 11699; Morley to Minto, 11 and 25 Feb 1909, MC MSS/Eur/D573/4.

[46] Kaminsky, *India Office*, 160.

[47] Morley to Minto, 6 June 1906, MC MSS/Eur/D573/1.

[48] Hirtzel Diary, 30 May 1907; *The Times*, 18 Jun 1907; *India*, 26 July 1907; Morley to Minto, 7 June and 23 Aug 1907 MC MSS/Eur/D573/2; Wolpert, *Morley and India*, 111.

[49] Koss, *John Morley*, 101, 108, 152–72.

bail were similarly attacked by the British Committee, even though Gokhale and Wedderburn wanted only muted criticism.[50] When in December 1908 a group of nine Bengalis were summarily deported without trial there was a revolt: the British Committee was unsure how far to criticise an administration whose intentions they still trusted, so another organisation, the Indian Civil Rights Committee (ICRC) was established, led by the Liberal lawyer-MP Frederic Mackarness along-side Cotton, O'Donnell, Rutherford and Hardie.[51] In February 1909 Mackarness moved an amendment to the King's Speech criticising the deportations which attracted, despite a three-line whip, the support of 76 MPs. In May he secured the signatures of 146 MPs on a memo-randum to Asquith on the same topic.[52] Many Liberal MPs had been angered by Morley's unconvincing response to a deputation they had sent the previous month.[53] '[Y]ou will not be able to deport any more of your suspects—that is quite clear', Morley warned Minto.[54] Thus emboldened, Mackarness introduced a Private Member's Bill in June which provided that deportation had to be subject to proper warrant, with parliamentary approval. Although the Bill failed, the Government decided not to oppose the first reading, on the grounds it might be defeated.[55]

From one perspective these developments broadened a small but focussed drive for political concessions into a wide but diffuse call for humanitarian treatment of the *raj*'s victims. Certainly some critics from India saw it this way. Aurobindo Ghose, a longstanding critic of appeals to the British sense of justice, argued that Mackarness's efforts to bring deportations under parliamentary control simply empowered Liberal MPs who could then sit in judgement on the cases themselves, but did nothing for the victims of deportation. 'His amendments will not make [the Bills] less hateful', Aurobindo wrote. '[T]hey will only make them less calmly absurd. That is a gain to the Government, not to us or to justice.'[56] But the effect of the work of the ICRC was objectively very helpful to the Indian movement in creating the conditions in which

[50] Morley to Minto, 8 June 1908, quoted in Koss, *John Morley*, 158.

[51] G. P. Gooch, *Frederic Mackarness: A Brief Memoir* (London, 1922).

[52] *India*, 14 May 1909; H. E. A. Cotton to Gokhale, 20 May 1909, GM 11699; Morley to Minto 27 May, 24 June 20 and 22 Aug 1909, MC MSS/Eur/D573/4.

[53] H. E. A. Cotton to Gokhale, 8 April 1909, GM 11699.

[54] Morley to Minto, 5 May 1909, MC MSS/Eur/D573/4.

[55] Morley to Minto, 10 June 1909, MC MSS/Eur/D573/4.

[56] 'Mr Mackarness' Bill', *Karmayogin*, 3 July 1909; 'English Democracy Shown Up', *Bande Mataram*, 3 Nov 1907.

India nationalists could operate more freely. Mackarness provided a lawyer's variant of linked-up agitation, urging those Indian politicians with grievances to take officials to court, and if necessary to the Privy Council.[57] His arguments, Frederic Harrison told Morley regretfully, were 'impregnable as law & constitutional right'.[58] Unlike the British Committee, the ICRC was mostly indifferent to what Indians said: it merely insisted that they should be allowed to say it. Such a stance was easy to reconcile with liberal values, and hence better supported on the Liberal benches than the Congress programme itself. It was immune to pleas about the special needs of India, and hence more threatening to the *raj*. It was also, Aurobindo excepted, appealing to Indians, because it did no more than clear the space within which they might speak. Indeed, even Aurobindo might have been more grateful for it than he was, since he was one of its principal beneficiaries: Morley, mindful of ICRC pressure, refused to permit the Governor of Bengal to deport him, but insisted that he be properly tried, a procedure which, as the Governor predicted, duly collapsed for lack of sufficient evidence.[59] Its effectiveness was clear when in January 1910 Morley told Minto that 'the clock has struck' and the Bengali detenus must be released.[60] By this time, however, an election had intervened, and had carried off the mainstays of the ICRC: Rutherford, O'Donnell and Cotton as well as other Liberal supporters. Mackarness too felt obliged to withdraw from the campaign on his appointment to a judicial post the same year. When in July 1910 the ICRC survivors Hardie and Josiah Wedgwood moved a division on deportation, they got only 48 votes.[61]

The history of the British Committee shows the strengths and weaknesses of an anti-imperialism based on shared liberal ideals. It has been suggested with considerable force in recent years that such ideals were (and are) compromised by their exclusions. Uday Singh Mehta, for example, has argued that the originary documents of British liberalism

[57] Mackarness to Mitra, 22 March 1910, in *Bengalee*, 23 Aug 1910; Mackarness to Gokhale, 26 Jan and 17 March 1911, GM 11702.

[58] Harrison to Morley, 12 March 1909, Morley Papers (Bodleian), MS Eng d.3576.

[59] Koss, *John Morley*, 163.

[60] Morley to Minto, 27 Jan 1910, MC MSS/Eur/D573/5; Moulton, 'British Radicals', 36–42.

[61] *Hansard*, 26 July 1910, 5th ser., v.19, cols.2031–63.

made a distinction between those civilised peoples who might be admitted to a liberal society and those barbarians who could not.[62] '[B]arbarians', J. S. Mill famously wrote, 'had no rights as a nation, except a right to such treatment as may, at the earliest possible period, fit them for becoming one.'[63] Such liberalism, it is suggested, tended to serve imperial ends in the intellectual support its narrow conceptions of human flourishing and social progress provided for the project of a civilising mission, displacing older liberal theories, such as those associated with Smith, Burke and Bentham, in which the colonised were regarded as no less rational beings existing within a culturally different social order rather than failed or at best infant Europeans.[64]

However, this did not always prove as much of a bar to liberal anti-imperialism as might be thought. First, liberal theories were not wholly, but *selectively* supportive of imperialism, and not wholly, but *selectively* critical of indigenous political developments. The liberals of the British Committee did believe that India had become backward and that the lead in the task of its regeneration must be taken for the present by Europeans. But they believed that it had necessarily to be a shared project; that core liberal values could not be imposed by an alien power, but only inculcated through liberal modes of education and the provision of opportunities for free, rational enquiry, and for the expression and discussion of diverse points of view. They were also—as indeed Mill himself was, especially in his later years—sceptical about the motives of imperialists, and their willingness to develop the necessary institutions—constitutionally limited and accountable government, a

[62] See Bhikhu Parekh, 'Decolonizing Liberalism', in Alexandras Shtromas (ed.), *The End of 'Isms'? Reflections on the Fate of Ideological Politics* (Oxford, 1994); and 'Liberalism and Colonialism: A Critique of Locke and Mill', in Jan N. Pieterse and Bhikhu Parekh (eds.), *The Decolonization of Imagination: Culture, Knowledge and Power* (London, 1995); Lynn Zastoupil, *John Stuart Mill and India* (Stanford, Calif. 1994); Martin Moir, Douglas Peers, and Lynn Zastoupil (eds.), *J. S. Mill's Encounter With India* (Toronto, 1999); Uday Singh Mehta, *Liberalism and Empire: A Study in Nineteenth Century British Liberal Thought* (Chicago, 1999); criticised by Margaret Kohn and Daniel I. O'Neill, 'A Tale of Two Indias: Burke and Mill on Empire and Slavery in the West Indies and America', *Political Theory*, 32/4 (2005), 1–37.

[63] See Beate Jahn, 'Barbarian Thoughts: Imperialism in the Philosophy of John Stuart Mill', *Review of International Studies*, 31 (2005), 599–618.

[64] See David Armitage, *The Ideological Origins of the British Empire* (Cambridge, 2000); Jennifer Pitts, *A Turn to Empire: The Rise of Imperial Liberalism in Britain and France* (Princeton, 2005); Sankar Muthu, *Enlightenment Against Empire* (Princeton, 2003); Jeanne Morefield, *Covenants without Swords: Idealist Liberalism and the Spirit of Empire* (Princeton, 2004).

free press, the rule of law, widening educational opportunities—to enable this development to occur. This was why they insisted on the protection of civil liberties, and this form of space-clearing was genuinely valuable.

Moreover, it was important that the values of liberalism were shared by British and Indian activists. Indians influenced by liberalism such as Gokhale and Naoroji shared the British Committee's belief in India's degeneracy, especially its weak sense of public virtue and citizenship above the level of commitments to family and caste. This did not make them crude imitators of the west, for they believed that the values and projects of liberalism were not importantly western, but rather universal, ones, which had developed first in Europe, but in which India must naturally share. Since uncritical acceptance of liberalism as it had developed in the west threatened to obliterate the distinct strengths of the Indian nation altogether, their version of liberalism was both critical and syncretic, intended to combine western superiority in science, technology and government with Indian strengths: its spirituality, moral values and sociocentric traditions.[65]

The synthesis, however, was somewhat asymmetric. For it to move beyond a mere eclecticism involved a critical appraisal of both traditions, and only one was seriously criticised. It began from a position of weakness: the sense that liberal ideals posed more difficult questions for Indian traditions than *vice versa*, and hence in practice tended to collapse into endorsement of western positions. In India, this meant that it could only win support beyond the English-educated on the basis that Indians had much to learn and little to teach, a weakness that the Extremists were increasingly able to exploit. Moreover, while the nature of the synthesis formed the core of political discussion in Congress India, at every point of contact the debate made with British ideologies and organisations, it had to be veneered in western concepts, with little sign of any lessons for the west in India's political traditions. In order to gain a foothold in a more self-confident and self-justifying British political system, this form of presentation was probably inevitable and gave Indians such as Naoroji and Gokhale a legitimate if subordinate place as native informants, providing British sympathisers with facts about Indian history and culture, even economics.

---

[65] Bhikhu Parekh, *Colonialism, Tradition and Reform: An Analysis of Gandhi's Political Discourse* (New Delhi, 1989), 68–72; Partha Chatterjee, *Nationalist Thought and the Colonial World* (London, 1986).

On points concerning the interpretation or applicability of theories of liberal government, however, they neither sought nor obtained much authority. They felt confident enough to demand consistency between British liberal professions and imperial practices. But even this was often done deferentially: Rash Behari Ghose, for example, told Congress in 1907 that Morley forgot that 'we too may claim to have kindled our modest rush-lights at Burke and Mill's benignant lamps'.[66] No one felt confident enough, except in occasional outbursts of patriotism, to challenge openly the buried assumptions of British liberalism, or to claim the authority to rework its principles for themselves, let alone to stretch them, bring them to crisis, or reject them altogether, as others were later to do. In this sense, the liberalism of the British Committee was shared with Indians, but not commonly owned.

The organisational outgrowth of this relationship of deference was the British Committee itself, with its reliance on British sponsors to validate Congress grievances and guide its political strategy. This explained its successes, especially its work on civil liberties, which British liberals cared deeply about and enjoyed unquestioned authority, but also its failures: its inability to connect with emerging movements of Indo-centric struggle and self-reliance, and the hidden grumbling and footdragging this aroused in India. The Committee, Pal wrote bitterly (though for Indian eyes only) in 1905, 'vitiates the very root-springs of our own political life and activities, by leading our best and ablest men to view Indian questions through British Liberal spectacles'.[67]

Those like Pal who had helped to build the new movements in India thus sensed, if only imperfectly, the need to reverse these flows of authority and power. But this was not easily achieved. The principal attempt to do so was the brief flowering of revolutionary anti-imperialism at India House, Highgate, from 1906 to 1909. India House had been established by a disaffected ex-court official and businessman, Shyamji Krishnavarma, to house his Indian Home Rule Society, a rival organisation intended to contest the vicarious activity of the British Committee.[68]

---

[66] A. M. Zaidi (ed.), *Congress Presidential Addresses* (5v., New Delhi, 1985–9), ii, 341.

[67] *Indian Spectator*, 27 May 1905.

[68] Indulal Yajnik, *Shyamji Krishnavarma: Life and Times of an Indian Revolutionary* (Bombay, 1950); Arun Coomer Bose, *Indian Revolutionaries Abroad, 1905–1922: In the*

'No systematic attempt has . . . ever been made in this country *by Indians themselves* to enlighten the British public', Krishnavarma wrote.[69] The IHRS aimed to work without British membership: unlike the British Committee it was open to 'Indian gentlemen only'.[70] Students, the principal beneficiaries of Krishnavarma's largesse and also the most vocal opponents of the cautious approach of the British Committee, were quite prominent.[71] Krishnavarma also founded a weekly newspaper, *The Indian Sociologist*, to provide a counterweight to the moderate coverage provided by *India*. In it, he denounced Gokhale and the Moderates' plans for lobbying Morley as 'mere waste of money and labour'.[72] He disputed Gokhale's passive positioning within British liberalism, trying to reveal more clearly the contradictions between its philosophical claims and its response to Indian questions, forcing it to a point from which the only logical escape was the concession of India's right to self-government. The *Indian Sociologist* was full of quotations from British writers, principally Herbert Spencer, but also Mill and H. M. Hyndman, whose arguments were invoked to support claims of British exploitation in India, and of the right of those suffering under tyranny to rise up against it, even if necessary by assassination.[73] Krishnavarma also poured scorn on the ex-officials who ran the British Committee; beneficiaries through their ICS pensions, he argued, of the exploitation of India.[74] Wedderburn and the Committee refused to have anything to do with him, fearing damage to the Congress reputation for loyalty.[75]

Almost by accident, Krishnavarma had found a weak spot of the British Empire. It was created by the time-difference between the latitudes of Britain and India that I discussed in Chapter 1. Attachment to liberal values at home meant that even as repression was visited on Indians in India, there was much less restriction on their activities in England. The press was largely free to publish what it wanted, even *The Times* printing Krishnavarma's letters unedited. Political meetings on Indian questions were sometimes attended by India Office officials, but were not subject to the surveillance or bans deployed in India. In

Background of International Developments (Patna, 1971), 13–36; Tilak Raj Sareen, *Indian Revolutionary Movement Abroad (1905–1921)* (New Delhi, 1979), 1–36; V. N. Datta, *Madan Lal Dhingra and the Revolutionary Movement* (New Delhi, 1978).

[69] *Indian Sociologist*, Jan 1905, italics in original.   [70] Ibid., March 1905.
[71] Ibid., April 1906 and March 1907.   [72] Ibid., Feb 1908.
[73] Ibid., Sept 1908.   [74] Ibid., Sept and Dec 1905, March 1906.
[75] Ibid., April 1905; Gokhale to Rana, undated but prob. Jan 1906, GM 11708.

India, postal censorship had become a common nuisance for Extremists, but there was little of it in Britain. The movements of individuals also went remarkably unchecked before 1914: it was a comparatively easy matter for Indians to move to Britain. Educational institutions such as universities and the Inns of Court, which were the object of close scrutiny in India, were in Britain, if not exactly tolerant of Indian Extremists, resistant to efforts to police them or to restrict student discussion. From London, nationalist newspapers noted with satisfaction, students might return bearing 'the western love of independence and an extraordinary dislike of injustice'.[76] Even policing was light by comparison. Pal wrote in surprise how even when investigating a political murder the Metropolitan Police showed 'wondrous patience [and] . . . scrupulous regard for the sanctities of private relations and personal freedoms'.[77] More generally, there was strong cultural support for the idea of Britain as a haven for revolutionary exiles, and as open to all political opinions. The 'freer atmosphere of England', Tilak told Krishnavarma, 'gives you a scope which we can never hope to get here'.[78] Much of this was to change before long, but at the time it made England an attractive destination for Extremists as repression increased in India. By the end of 1908, Lajpat Rai, Pal, and Tilak's chief lieutenant Khaparde had all arrived in London.

However, the whole question of overseas work of this kind remained controversial. The Extremists wanted, Gokhale wrote acidly, 'to put six thousand miles between themselves and the administration they want to overthrow'.[79] Lajpat Rai and Pal argued that they were not seeking favours from the British, but to 'feed and strengthen' the 'feeble current' of British public sentiment and direct it against the *raj*.[80] However, Aurobindo Ghose continued to insist that Pal's work in Britain was 'hopeless and a waste of money and energy'. The British conscience was

[76] *Kesari*, 8 Sept 1908, NNR Bombay, 12 Sept 1908, L/R/5/163, OIOC; *Rashtramat*, 1 Aug 1908, NNR Bombay, L/R/5/163, OIOC.

[77] Bipin Chandra Pal, *Nationality and Empire: A Running Study of some Current Indian Problems* (Calcutta, 1916), 259–60.

[78] Tilak to Krishnavarma, 10 July 1905, in Vidwans, *Letters of Lokmanya Tilak*, 255–6; *India* (Pondicherry), 5 Nov 1908, NNR Madras, 12 Dec 1908, L/R/5/113, OIOC.

[79] Gokhale to Vamanrao, 2 Oct 1908, GM 11700.

[80] Lajpat Rai to Jaswant Rai, undated but Oct 1908, CWLR, iii, 153–5; *India* (Pondicherry), 10 Oct 1908, NNR Madras, 17 Oct 1908, L/R/5/113, OIOC; Pal,'The Situation', *Karmayogin*, 1/14, 9 Ashwin 1316 = 25 Sept 1909; *Karmayogin*, 1/15, 16 Ashwin, 1316 = 2 Oct 1909; 'Nationalist Work in England', *Karmayogin*, 1/16, 23 Ashwin 1316 = 9 Oct 1909; *India*, 10 Oct 1908, NNR Madras, 17 Oct 1908, L/R/5/113, OIOC; *Mahratta*, 1 Jan 1909, NNR Bombay, 9 Jan 1909, L/R/5/164, OIOC.

a fragile thing: 'very sensitive to breaches of principle by others, and very indignant when the same breaches of principle are questioned in its own conduct'.[81]

[H]owever correct the information we supply, the British public. . . will still prefer to put confidence in the mis-statements of their own countrymen rather than in the true statements of what they believe to be an inferior race indebted to them for any element of civilisation it may now possess.

'[T]here could not be a worse place than England, a worse time than the present and a worse audience than the British people', wrote Ghose. 'What is the prophet of self-help and dissociation doing in England?'[82]

At first, Krishnavarma did not undertake any active revolutionary work, or even much political organisation beyond the pages of the *Indian Sociologist.* His support for physical force tactics was intellectual before anything else: political violence was justified in the abstract and negatively, as a principle of liberal political theory, which British thinkers had permitted if tyrannies could not be toppled in other ways, and which they could not consistently or fairly deny to Indians similarly placed.[83] However, retired ICS men coming across copies of the *Indian Sociologist* or prompted from India, attacked Krishnavarma in the press and in Parliament. Their chief spokesman, Valentine Chirol of *The Times,* credited him quite wrongly with a determined and effective campaign of sedition.[84] Morley refused to take any action, but officials felt obliged to make enquiries, sending a detective to India House and questioning the printers of the *Indian Sociologist.* [85] Krishnavarma panicked and, unwarrantedly fearful that these activities were a prelude to attempts to close the paper and arrest him, decamped to Paris, never to return again to Britain or India.

[81] Ghose, 'Nationalist Work in England', *Karmayogin,* 1/16, 23 Ashwin 1316 = 9 Oct 1909.

[82] Aurobindo Ghose, 'Swaraj' and the Mussulmans, *Karmayogin,* 19 June 1909; *Vande Mataram,* 27 Dec 1908, NNR Bombay, 2 Jan 1909 L/PJ/5/164, OIOC; *Pudhari,* 10 Jan 1909, NNR Bombay, 16 Jan 1909, L/PJ/5/164, OIOC.

[83] *Indian Sociologist,* June 1906, Aug 1907; Peter Heehs, *The Bomb in Bengal: The Rise of Revolutionary Terrorism in India, 1900–1910* (New Delhi, 1994), 89; H. K. Korgeonkar: 'Information about the Revolutionary Party in London', Jan 1910, copy in L/PJ/6/986, OIOC; Hema Candra Kanungo, *Bamlaya biplaba praceshta* (Calcutta, 1928), 196–8.

[84] *The Times,* 20 Sept 1906, 17 May and 19 June 1907; *Hansard,* 30 July 1907, and 22 July 1908, 4th ser., v.179, col.758; v.193, cols.141–61; *Indian Sociologist,* 7 July 1907.

[85] Note by Morley, 16 Sept 1908 in L/PJ/6/891, OIOC. There is earlier discussion of the *Indian Sociologist* in files L/PJ/6/822 (July 1907) and L/PJ/6/871 (June 1908); *Indian Sociologist,* Aug 1907 and Sept 1907.

Much as officials and Chirol disliked hearing liberal arguments being made by an Indian, unendorsed by British sponsors, they had a powerful reply to make. Krishnavarma's methods and citation of British authorities were signs of inauthentic dependence on British thought, and a disconnection with Indian feeling.[86] 'The principal weakness of Indian Nationalism', G. K. Chesterton wrote, 'seems to be that it is not very Indian and not very National.' If an Indian appealed in the name of Indian values and traditions, however, Chesterton continued, 'I should call him an Indian Nationalist, or at least, an authentic Indian, and I think it would be very hard to answer him'.[87] This was misleading, for although Krishnavarma did admire Spencer and thought India could learn from him, his central point was not that India should adopt Spencer's ideas, but that those who claimed to support these ideas in Britain could not easily deny their applicability in India.[88] But after Krishnavarma's departure, India House fell under the control of just the kind of nationalist Chesterton had thought it hard to answer. This was Vinayak Savarkar, a law student and protégé of Tilak. Savarkar had considerable revolutionary form. As a student in Maharashtra he had founded a secret revolutionary organisation, the Abhinav Bharat, which had organised attacks on officials and undertaken paramilitary training.[89] While Krishnavarma believed in an appeal to British and European authorities, Savarkar thought there were sufficient materials in India's own past: not Mill, Spencer or Hyndman, but Shivaji and the 'martyrs' of the Indian Mutiny, or, as Savarkar renamed it, the First War of Indian Independence. The fiftieth anniversary of 1857, Savarkar defiantly argued, 'provided a subject on which we can talk to the English on equal terms'.[90] His history of 1857 used Indian as well as British sources, and reversed the usual way that it was remembered, with rebels recast as martyrs and pacification as atrocity. It was also written in Marathi, and only translated into English by one of Savarkar's associates so that it could be read to non-Marathi speaking Indians. An accompanying pamphlet *O Martyrs!*, repeated the injunction of death to foreigners, and, at

[86] Valentine Chirol, *Indian Unrest* (London, 1910), 146.

[87] *Illustrated London News*, 18 Sep 1909.   [88] *Indian Sociologist*, Dec 1908.

[89] Dhananjay Keer, *Veer Savarkar* (2nd ed., Bombay 1966), 23, 28–51 and Lise McKean, *Divine Enterprise: Gurus and the Hindu Nationalist Movement* (Chicago, 1996), 71–96.

[90] Savarkar newsletter, 10 June 1907, in V. D. Savarkar, *Samagra Savakara Vanmaya* (8v., Pune, 1963–5), iv, 50–4.

India House, vows of self-sacrifice for the cause were made by large numbers.[91]

Savarkar's India House was quite unlike any other anti-imperialist activity in Britain. It was almost wholly self-reliant, and did not seek to work through or even in collaboration with other British organisations. The flow of influences and ideas came from India to Britain, and not, as was the case with Gokhale and Krishnavarma, the other way around. Savarkar was not principally a follower of the scientific arguments for terrorism and assassination which Krishnavarma had derived from the work of western authorities. His borrowings were notably eclectic and unreverential, and quite devoid of mimicry. Though he took from Mazzini the argument that assassination was justified when no other means of liberation were available, his primary inspiration came from the revolutionary movement in Maharashtra.[92] At India House, readings from Mazzini were soon replaced by readings from religious scriptures such as the *Bhagavad Gita* and Savarkar's history of 1857. The former provided an ethical justification of violence: assassinations of those who were bleeding or imprisoning Mother India could be justified, and the historical accounts provided precedent: Hindu India had become weak under colonial occupation, and could only be reinvigorated through violent but inspirational acts of heroism. 'Mother Ganges', wrote Savarkar, 'who drank that day of the blood of Europeans, may drink her fill of it again.'[93]

Within a few months of Krishnavarma's departure, his IHRS was supplanted by Savarkar's Free India Society. Unlike Krishnavarma's wholly metropolitan organisation, the FIS was effectively the London end of the Abhinav Bharat and its function was to recruit and train revolutionary workers for armed struggle. Where the IHRS had a written constitution modelled on that of a Victorian public association, the FIS had a semi-religious oath of obedience to honour Mother India and to engage in a 'bloody and relentless war against the foreigner'.[94] Savarkar was struck by the way in which these tactics unsettled the British. As

[91] V. D. Savarkar, *Satrucya Sibiranta* (Mumbai, 1965), 156–65.

[92] Savarkar, *Satrucya Sibiranta*, 134–6; but see also Gita Srivastava, 'Savarkar and Mazzini', *Rassegna Storica del Risorgimento*, 71/3 (1984), 259–64; Enrico Fasana, 'Deshabhakta: The Leaders of the Italian Independence Movement in the Eyes of Marathi Nationalists', *Asian and African Studies*, 3/2 (1994), 152–75.

[93] V. D. Savarkar, *The Indian War of Independence (National Rising of 1857)* (4th ed., Bombay, 1946), 218.

[94] Chanjeri Rao, police statement, 1 Feb 1910, L/PJ/6/993, OIOC; Chaturbhuj's examination, 24–5 Jan 1911, is in L/PJ/6/1069, OIOC.

long as Indian students aped British manners no one troubled about
them, but when they dressed as Indians, fasted and read Indian texts,
the authorities panicked.[95] While Krishnavarma wanted Indians to visit
Britain in order to learn from the British love of liberty, Savarkar had
arrived with no intention of persuading the British about anything.[96]
Unlike Krishnavarma and Gokhale, he wrote almost nothing for British
audiences. His letters were written in Marathi for two newspapers in
Pune. The purpose of being in London, he claimed, was simply to learn
how to make bombs and to prepare for an armed revolt against the
British on return to India.[97] London was useful for this purpose: it was
an unsupervised meeting-place for intelligent young Indians from all
over the subcontinent who could be expected to achieve positions of
influence on their return. But it was otherwise inessential and he seems
quite genuinely to have seen his place as back in India. 'Duty', he told
his brother, 'consists in waging the struggle where the fight may be
going on.'[98]

Savarkar's view of British supporters was therefore rejectionist. Although Krishnavarma's associates attended the 1907 International
Socialist Congress at Hyndman's instigation, Savarakar was cynical
about linking up with socialists.[99] 'You can't get a piggy back on
persons like Hyndman', he told his readers. 'You must learn to stand
on your own two feet. Hyndman may have spoken with sincerity
and mean well, but the time has now come for you to throw away
the crutches and walk without their support. When you do that, not
only Mr Hyndman but the whole world will praise you'.[100] This
positioning, however, meant that Savarkar was an unknown figure
in Britain. He practised in London the dissociation which in India
had led Indian nationalists to refuse to associate with their occupiers.

---

[95] Savarkar, newsletter, 5 Sept 1908, *Samagra Savakara Vanmaya*, iv, 73–6.

[96] *Indian Sociologist*, May 1905; Savarkar, *Satrucya Sibiranta*, 20.

[97] Harindra Srivastava, *Five Stormy Years: Savarkar in London, June 1906-June 1911,
a Centenary Salute to Swatantrayaveer Vinayak Damodar Savarkar* (New Delhi, 1983), 4;
Rao, police statement; Korgeonkar, 'Information about the Revolutionary Party'.

[98] Savarkar to his brother, 11 Feb 1909, intercepted and translated by Government
of India, quoted in HPA, Aug 1909, 135–7.

[99] *VIIie Congrès socialiste international tenu à Stuttgart du 16 au 24 août 1907*
(Brussels, 1908) copy in INT 1008/130, Second International Papers, IISH, Amsterdam,
65, 323; John Riddell (ed.), *Lenin's Struggle for a Revolutionary International: Documents,
1907–1916* (New York, 1984), 9–15; *Indian Sociologist*, Aug and Sept 1907; DCI
Report, 21 Sept 1907, HPB, Oct 1907, 47.

[100] Savarkar newsletters, 20 Dec 1906 and 8 Feb 1907, *Samagra Savakara Vanmaya*,
iv, 19–23, 29–34.

British visitors were not generally welcome at India House, since they could not be trusted and were seen as a distraction. However, the 17-year-old David Garnett, later a Bloomsbury novelist, did visit India House as the guest of two Indian student friends, both very westernised. When with them, Garnett wrote later, 'I could forget they were Hindus and I was an Englishman, but at this meeting I felt alone'.[101] The structure and atmosphere of the meeting was quite unlike those of the British Committee of Congress, and was, for Garnett, a destabilising experience of solitude and incomprehension. There were devotional songs and readings by Savarkar which Garnett did not at first even detect as English. '[Savarkar's] accent, his mispronunciations, the strange rhythm of his staccato delivery had deceived me', Garnett later wrote. He seemed a man 'wrapped in visions', and unreachable.[102]

Members of the FIS underwent physical training and shooting practice at ranges in London—the latter would have been impossible in India—and attended lectures which explored the scope for an armed uprising in India, the structure of revolutionary organisations and bomb-making. The last of these was a practical enterprise too: there was an improvised chemistry laboratory at India House.[103] Literature, including vernacular translations of Savarkar's *O Martyrs!*, was sent to India. A manual on bomb-making was produced with the help of exiled Russian revolutionaries in Paris, and smuggled to India by students instructed to teach its contents to 100 recruits each before using their skills and risking arrest. The manual turned up in police raids of bomb-factories in Bengal in 1908 and was used in an attempt to assassinate an unpopular magistrate in Alipore.[104] There were also some attempts to link up with other nationalists, especially Egyptian and Irish groups.[105] However, these did not go much beyond friendly statements, largely because Savarkar was engaged in the construction of a small, cellular structure of dedicated activists, rather than a diffuse association of mutually affable supporters which might easily be infiltrated.

[101] David Garnett, *The Golden Echo* (3v., London, 1953–62), i, 144.
[102] Garnett, *Golden Echo*, i, 144–5, 149.
[103] J. C. Ker, *Political trouble in India, 1907–1917* (reprinted Calcutta, 1973), 161.
[104] DCI Report, 4 Sep 1909, HPB, Oct 1909, 110; Korgeonkar, 'Information about the Revolutionary Party'; Heehs, *Bomb in Bengal*.
[105] DCI Reports, 23 and 30 Jan 1909, HPB, Feb 1909, 8 and 10; 13 March 1909, HPB, April 1909, 105.

A rough sense of the composition of those who frequented India House can be found using intelligence records.[106] Seventy-two names are recorded as having attended meetings regularly. They came from all over India, with about a quarter each from Bengal and the Punjab and smaller but significant groups from Bombay-Maharashtra and Madras. They were almost all male, though one or two women attended meetings. Fully two-thirds were students, most of them studying for law examinations. The data on background and religion are not very complete, but suggest an elite composition—among them were the sons of millionaires, millowners, lawyers, officials and doctors—and the overwhelming dominance of Hindus. Nearly all those for whom age is available were in their twenties (the median age in 1909 was 26). Only a quarter had any previous record of political activity in India, and they were evenly divided between those who had expressed support for nationalism or *swadeshi* and those who had taken part in extremist or revolutionary activities. It seems, therefore, as autobiographical evidence also suggests, that most of those who attended India House had not arrived with any intention of revolutionary agitation, but were converted while in Britain.

This pattern of work and composition suggests some of the strengths and weaknesses of Savarkar's India House. There was emphasis on India-directed actions by the social elites, involving self-sacrifice which would inspire the masses to follow behind, but which did not require the building of a mass movement in advance.[107] The difficulty with this was the unwillingness of elites to make the self-sacrifice that was required. The students sent back to India with the bomb manual had met an unenviable fate. Implicated by an 'approver' (prosecution witness) who was later assassinated in jail, one was on the run, and the other sentenced to transportation to India's notoriously harsh prison on the Andaman Islands.[108] Volunteers for subsequent missions were understandably fewer. In February 1909, Savarkar persuaded Chaturbhuj Amin, the

---

[106] The following analysis is based on *Memorandum on the Anti-British Agitation Among Natives of India in England*, Part I Circular no 7 of 1909 (15 June 1909); Part II Circular 11 of 1909 (28 Oct 1909); Part III Circular 7 of 1910 (19 Sep 1910), R2/33/312, OIOC; and *Indian Agitators Abroad: containing short accounts of the more important Indian political agitators who have visited Europe and America in recent years, and their sympathisers* (Government of India, Criminal Intelligence Office, Simla, November 1911), IOR V/27/262/1, OIOC.

[107] Metropolitan Police report, 2 Sep 1908, L/PJ/6/890, OIOC.

[108] Heehs, *Bomb in Bengal*, 133–4, 139; Kanungo, *Bamlaya*, 196–208; Y. D. Phadke, *Portrait of a Revolutionary: Senapati Bapat* (Ahmedabad, 1981).

cook at India House, to carry 20 Browning pistols and ammunition back to India in return for money.[109] Later the same year, Chanjeri Rao, a sanitary inspector in his thirties who had come to Britain in search of professional qualifications, undertook a similar mission, also for money.[110] Savarkar also tried to persuade M. P. T. Acharya, an impoverished Madrassi, that he should sacrifice himself for the cause, but Acharya was canny enough to duck the call.[111] The fact that these individuals were all more or less financially dependent on Savarkar suggests the difficulties of finding recruits among the student body for revolutionary work. The reliance on students was an imaginative and lasting solution to the problems of finance that had hitherto restricted anti-imperialist work for India in Britain. Their families and government agencies which paid their scholarships unwittingly subsidised their anti-imperial work. But such elite groups were also naturally mindful of their own career prospects. Savarkar thought about 90 per cent of them secretly or openly believed in the inferiority of India and were not serious about political work.[112] One of Savarkar's associates, T. S. S. Rajan, commented bitterly that 'the intellectual or educated Indians. . . pushed their poorer brethren forward to do the dangerous work while they remained in security themselves'.[113] Yet Rajan himself, with a family in India to support on qualification, felt torn. 'Can we relinquish everything else just out of patriotism?', he later recalled. 'My mind was in turmoil.'[114] Like others, he carried on with his medical training as he attended India House meetings, with the intention of qualifying, returning to India and awaiting the call. In his own case, this was to lead to a successful career as a moderate Congress politician and Government Minister in Madras. The revolutionaries also struggled to make an impact on the wider community of London Indians, a strongly integrated and acclimatised, if not assimilated, body of Indians reluctant to jeopardise their position through acts which might be perceived as disloyal. The India House group took over the London Indian Society,

---

[109] Chaturbhuj examination.   [110] Rao, police statement.

[111] DCI Report, 17 July 1909, HPB, Aug 1909, 124; C. S. Subramanyam, *M. P. T. Acharya: His Life and Times* (Madras, 1995).

[112] Savarkar, *Satrucya Sibiranta*, 92; Savarkar newsletters, 12 April 1907 and 14 Aug 1908, *Samagra Savakara Vanmaya*, iv, 40–4, 70–1.

[113] DCI Report, 12 Feb 1910, HPB, Mar 1910, 3. See also DCI Report, 30 Oct 1909, HPB, Nov 1909, 19; M. P. T. Acharya, *Reminiscences of an Indian Revolutionary* (New Delhi, 1991), 84–5.

[114] T. S. S. Rajan, *Ninaivu Alaikal* (Madras, 1947). I am grateful to Professor G. Rangarajan for providing me with this text and a translation of it from Tamil.

the main association of London Indians set up by Naoroji in 1865, by packing the Annual General Meeting and displacing the old guard, 'a surprise and disappointment to those who thought we were entering the Club only to nod to them', as one later wrote.[115] But the gains were small: most of the ordinary members simply followed Naoroji himself out of the organisation, leaving it without funds.[116]

By 1909, the authorities had started to close down the space within which Savarkar aimed to operate. Up to this point, the policing of India House had been fairly ineffective. '[T]he ordinary square-toed English constable, even in the detective branch . . . [is] rather clumsy in tracing your wily Asiatics', Morley had admitted to Minto.[117] But Minto and his Council, anxious to seal this bolthole for the Extremists, asked in March 1909 for special measures to be taken in London to restrict the flow of seditious material and the suborning of students.[118] Although Morley remained reluctant to sanction this, policing was stepped up.[119] More threatening still was the threat of professional disbarment. Prompted by the India Office, the Inns of Court began proceedings to prevent Savarkar and a fellow Indian student from being called to the Bar.[120] This made it clear that definite professional sacrifice was required. By May, only two paying residents were left at India House, which Acharya described as a 'leper's home' unvisited by students for fear of the consequences.[121] Its days as a clandestine revolutionary base were numbered. Police reports spoke of 'distrust and disappointment'

---

[115] Acharya, *Reminscences*, 87. See *The Times*, 18 Sept 1906 for an earlier incident; also DCI Circular 7 of 1909; DCI Reports, 26 Dec 1908, HPB, Jan 1909, 112; 20 Feb 1909, HPB, April 1909, 104; 6 and 20 March 1909, HPB, April 1909, 103 and 107.

[116] DCI Reports, 29 May 1909 and 12 June 1909, HPB, June 1909, 123 and July 1909, 68.

[117] Morley to Minto, 4 June 1908, quoted in Richard J. Popplewell, *Intelligence and Imperial Defence: British Intelligence and the Defence of the Indian Empire, 1904–1924* (London, 1995), 129.

[118] *Proposal to check the manufacture of sedition in England*, HPA, March 1909, 148–50.

[119] *Hansard*, 11 March 1909, 5th ser., v.2, col.512; Savarkar newsletter, 9 April 1909, *Samagra Savakara Vanmaya*, iv, 96–100; Lajpat Rai to Gokhale, 23 Nov 1908, *CWLR* iii, 178; Popplewell, *Intelligence and Imperial Defence*, 130.

[120] *Refusal of the Benchers of Gray's Inn to admit V. D. Savarkar to the Bar and Proposal to Oppose the Application of Harman Singh for enrolment as an advocate of the Chief Court of the Punjab*, HPA, Aug 1909, 135–7.

[121] DCI Reports, 22 and 29 May 1909, HPB, June 1909, 121 and 123; 5 and 12 June 1909, HPB, July 1909, 66 and 68; Morley to the King, 3 July 1909, Morley Papers (Bodleian), Ms Eng. c.7084; G. N. S. Raghavan (ed.), *M. Asaf Ali's Memoirs: The Emergence of Modern India* (Delhi, 1994), 69; Acharya, *Reminscences*, 83, 87.

(17 April), 'marked abatement of activity' (24 April), '[growing] distrust and disunion' (15 May) with meetings 'very poorly attended' (29 May) and 'very quiet' (26 June). Savarkar was also irritated by Krishnavarma, whose peremptory demands from the safety of Paris for a change of leadership at India House were proving irksome.[122] It must have seemed preferable to arrest this decline with a dramatic act of defiance which would rally the revolutionaries both in Britain and India. This coincided with the willingness of an Indian student to undertake a revolutionary act, and on 1 July 1909, probably on Savarkar's instructions, Madan Lal Dhingra attended an India Office party for Indian students and assassinated Morley's aide-de-camp, Sir Curzon Wyllie.

Dhingra's action was a pure instance of the kind of anti-imperialism that Savarkar had been trying to develop in London. It achieved its immediate purpose in inspiring the demoralised activists, and Dhingra's otherwise unremarkable biography became a staple chapter in popular vernacular histories of the freedom struggle.[123] But for the Government of India this was too good a chance to miss. They insisted that the assassination simply showed the risks of permitting linked-up agitation to flourish, and successfully overrode Morley's objections to the measures they had proposed earlier in the year. Efforts to control student political activities were never easy: it was too controversial to restrict the rights of British Indian subjects to travel freely in the empire, even if their purpose in doing so was to undermine it. But efforts at censorship of materials were more successful, since they could more easily be identified as seditious, and the customs laws used to seize copies and the press laws to prevent republication.[124] Pal was an early victim of these new arrangements. A successful prosecution of his new British journal *Svaraj* in India destroyed its sales, forcing it to close down after only a few issues. Pal himself was reduced to penury and mental collapse in London.[125]

[122] DCI Reports, 17 April 1909, HPB, June 1909, 111; 24 April 1909, HPB, June 1909, 113; 15 May 1909, HPB, June 1909, 119; 22 May 1909, HPB, June 1909, 121; 3 and 17 July 1909, HPB, Aug 1909, 120 and 124; Korgeonkar, 'Information about the Revolutionary Party'.

[123] DCI Reports, 13 Nov and 3 May 1910, HPB, Aug 1910, 1, and Dec 1909, 47.

[124] *Proposed Interception . . . and Prohibition of the Entry into India . . . of 'Justice'*, HPA, June 1909, 36; Note by Morley, 15 June 1909; India Office to Government of India Home Department, 19 July 1909, L/PJ/6/942, OIOC; *Prevention of the importation into India of seditious and inflammatory pamphlets and newspapers published in England*, HPA, July 1910, 55.

[125] Pal to Khaparde, 21 April, 12 May, 9 June, 14, 21 and 28 July, 18 Aug 1911; Willis to Khaparde, 19 May, 17 June, 4 Aug 1911, in B. G. Kunte (ed.), *Source Material*

The FIS disintegrated amid allegations of spying, justified since a spy had been successfully placed inside the organization.[126] Accepting that it was impossible to police Britain as they did India, the authorities now sought to ensure that Indian agitators were subject to Indian rules, and enjoyed no benefit from the freer atmosphere of Britain. Pal was prosecuted not in Britain for his British publications, but on his return to India. Savarkar, rather than being prosecuted for conspiracy and sedition in Britain, where the laxer interpretation of the legislation and the more liberal tendencies of judges would have led to, at most, a sentence of two years, was extradited to India under the Fugitive Offenders Act, where the judges were more compliant. Instead of two years, Savarkar received two life sentences of transportation to the Andamans, to run sequentially rather than concurrently, with the expectation that he would be released in 1960. England, it was clear, was no longer a bolthole for Indian revolutionaries.[127]

The India House approach had thus been a very different form of engagement with liberal Britain. It did not appeal to liberal values as the British Committee did, but exploited them for the advantages they offered for revolutionary work. But this worked only as long as it remained secret. As soon as it was exposed to the authorities, the inadvertent tolerance that had been afforded to it was sharply withdrawn. Under these pressures, the India House group naturally

for a History of the Freedom Movement, vol. VII (Bombay, 1978), 160–9, 181–6; DCI Reports, 4 Oct 1909, HPB, Nov 1909, 32; 4 July 1910, HPB, Aug 1910, 19; 29 Nov 1910, HPB, Dec 1910, 10; 6 Dec 1910, HPB, Jan 1911, 17; 4 Jan 1911, HPB, Feb 1911, 1; 7 Feb 1911, HPB, March 1911, 1; 28 Feb 1911, HPB, March 1911, 4; 11 April 1911, HPB, June 1911, 1; 25 April 1911, HPB, June 1911, 3; 6 June 1911, HPB, July 1911, 1; Mukerjee and Mukerjee, *Pal*, 119; Khaparde Diary, 9 June 1910.

[126] DCI Reports, 7 Aug 1909, HPB, Sep 1909, 47; 30 Oct 1909, HPB, Nov 1909, 40; 13 Nov 1909, HPB, Dec 1909, 47; 27 Nov 1909, HPB, Dec 1909, 51; 12 March 1910, HPB, April 1910, 11; 16 April 1910, HPB, May 1910, 20; 23 April 1910, HPB, May 1910, 22; 10 May 1910, HPB, Aug 1910, 3; 17 May 1910, HPB, Aug 1910,5; 7 June 1910, HPB, Aug 1910, 11; 4 July 1910, HPB, Aug 1910, 19; 27 Sep 1910, HPB, Oct 1910, 7; 18 Oct 1910, HPB, Nov 1910, 21; 25 Oct 1910, HPB, Nov 1910, 23; 29 Nov 1910, HPB, Dec 1910, 10; 6 June 1911, HPB, July 1911, 1; Stevenson Moore to Ritchie, 19 Aug 1909; Memorandum by Quinn, 25 Nov 1912; Petrie to Hirtzel, 12 Dec 1912; Henry to Holderness, 26 Aug 1913, L/PS/8/67, OIOC; Amiya K. Samanta (ed.), *Terrorism in Bengal: A Collection of Documents on Terrorist Activities from 1905 to 1939* (6v., Calcutta, 1995), v, 400; Chattopadhyaya to Krishnavarma, 11 April 1910, quoted in Nirode K. Barooah, *Chatto: The Life and Times of an Indian Anti-imperialist in Europe* (Delhi, 2004), 23.

[127] DCI Report, 9 April 1910, HPB, May 1910, 18.

became a diaspora, some moving to Paris, Berlin and Geneva, a few to the United States, and only those who had broken their links with revolutionaries daring to return to India itself.

Savarkar's vision of a self-reliant and Indo-centric anti-imperialism had posed a conundrum to another Indian visitor arriving in London a few days after the assassination of Curzon Wyllie. This was M. K. Gandhi. Although he had started to use the methods of passive resistance that he would eventually bring to India, Gandhi in 1909 was still essentially a mendicant politician. He had come to London to make the case for educated Indians to enjoy equal right of immigration in the Transvaal, and—though he was feeling more and more unhappy with the technique—was working with sympathetic British officials to persuade ministers of the justice of the Indians' case and the value to the empire of meeting their demands.[128] At first, Gandhi had condemned Dhingra as a dishonourable coward, and his actions as motivated by 'ill digested reading of worthless writings' and the cowardly promptings of Krishnavarma.[129] This was because he assumed, as many did, that Dhingra was motivated by Krishnavarma's 'scientific' justification of assassination, which had been the dominant opinion at India House at the time of a visit Gandhi had made there in 1906. However, in a series of meetings over the summer of 1909, Gandhi fought out his opinions with the new strand of thinking represented by Savarkar. It was a losing battle, for as Savarkar later wrote, 'we revolutionaries used to sit on one side of the table and Gandhi and his followers on the other side. Day by day Gandhi's followers deserted him and joined our side, until a day came when Gandhi sat alone.'[130]

These encounters were of the greatest importance for Gandhi. First, practically none of the young Indians he spoke to believed that India could be free without the use of violence, a stance which his whole life and ethical stance conditioned him to oppose.[131] Secondly, they also believed—as Gandhi himself had also begun to suspect—that

---

[128] James D. Hunt, *Gandhi in London* (New Delhi, 1978), 136–9.

[129] 'Curzon Wyllie's Assassination', after 16 July 1909, *CWMG* E9/245; 'Dhingra Case', 23 July 1909, *CWMG* E9/252; Gandhi to Kallenbach, 7 Aug 1909, *CWMG* P96/15.

[130] Savarkar, *Samagra Savarkara*, iv, 407–8.

[131] Gandhi to Ampthill, 30 Oct 1909, *CWMG* E10/133; Gandhi to Gokhale, 11 Nov 1909, *CWMG* E10/151.

mendicancy was inherently demeaning and could not be made the basis of the national struggle. Gandhi was forced to accept that on this point, Savarkar was ahead of him: 'the evil, in its hideous form, of the present system of government, he saw much earlier than I did', he wrote later.[132] Savarkar and his associates' determination was not easily dismissed, and Gandhi acknowledged that he had found among them 'a high degree of morality, great intellectual ability and lofty self-sacrifice'.[133] Thirdly, their arguments did not rest on the 'worthless writings' admired by Krishnavarma but on readings of Indian history and literature. This was perhaps most clearly seen when Savarkar had invited Gandhi to preside at a dinner of London Indians to celebrate *Dassera*, the festival to commemorate the killing of the demon Ravana by Rama and the rescue of Sita.[134] Gandhi had argued that the demon was not an external enemy, but represented the battle between truth and falsehood *inside* Rama, which was won by truth through suffering. Savarkar had replied that 'Rama did not invade . . . the island of the tyrant for the sake of peace, and did not carry war abroad to kill the two-headed monster within himself. He fought for Sita the chaste, for Sita the freedom of India'. This was much better received.[135] Gandhi 'said that he considered Savarkar's teaching injurious to the well-being of the country', but his speech 'caused considerable dissatisfaction and he was cheered with much less enthusiasm at the end than he was when he rose to speak'.[136]

Although Gandhi had not succeeded in persuading the India House revolutionaries, he did not give up the idea of working out a version of Indian nationalism which was non-violent without being passive, self-reliant without rejecting the English, and based on what he understood to be the lessons of Indian myth and history. How he did this, in his great statement *Hind Swaraj* (1909), begun shortly after the *Dassera* dinner and continued on his return to South Africa, is well known.[137]

---

[132] *Young India*, 18 May 1921, *CWMG*, E23/170.

[133] 'Ethics of Passive Resistance', after 8 Oct 1909, *CWMG* E10/106; Gandhi to Ampthill, 30 Oct 1909, *CWMG* E10/133.

[134] DCI Report, 13 Nov 1909, HPB, Dec 1909, no 47.

[135] Savarkar, *Samagra Savakara*, iv, 144–6; 'Vijaya Dashami', after 24 Oct 1909, *CWMG* E10/124; Gandhi to Polak, 29 Oct 1909, *CWMG* E10/130; DCI Report, 20 Nov 1909, HPB, Jan 1910, 49; Circular 7 of 1909.

[136] Circular 7 of 1909; Raghavan, *M. Asaf Ali's Memoirs*, 70; Savarkar newsletter, 26 Nov 1909. *Samagra Savakara*, iv, 116–19.

[137] Anthony J. Parel (ed.) *M. K. Gandhi: Hind Swaraj and other Writings* (Cambridge, 1997).

Yet it was a harder task than is sometimes appreciated. Gandhi was not merely writing against mendicant and imitative nationalism but also the specific Indo-centric version of nationalism set out by Savarkar. He tried to show that Indian writings such as the *Gita* demanded self-abnegation and withdrawal rather than, as Savarkar suggested, political violence in a just cause.[138] Indian traditions of passive resistance, reworked into *satyagraha*, were not ineffective, as Savarkar suggested, but demanded greater courage, and were no less forceful for being based on soul-force rather than violence. Indeed, armed resistance of the kind favoured by Savarkar, far from reflecting Indian traditions, would, Gandhi argued, europeanise India.[139]

The implications of this conception of Indian nationalism for agitation in Britain were, in time, to be profound. Gandhi did not agree with Savarkar and Aurobindo that British sympathisers would generally prove unreliable allies. 'If we shun every Englishman as an enemy', he wrote, 'Home Rule will be delayed.'[140] But the points made about the English in *Hind Swaraj* suggest a new ambivalence towards the allies who had formed the mainstay of Gandhi's mendicant strategy up until this point. Gandhi criticised India House for insulting the British Committee, but his own endorsement of its work was hardly enthusiastic: 'Sir William [Wedderburn] does not wish ill to India—that should be enough for us.'[141] There were hints of a new basis for collaboration with the British in which the Indians would assume the lead.[142] The British, Gandhi wrote, must realise that they were not essential and had to learn from the Indians, but '[i]f the English become Indianized, we can accommodate them . . . It lies with us to bring about such a state of things.'[143] In time, Gandhi was to try and work out such a form of cooperation with British activists, in ways that Savarkar, who remained quite literally unintelligible to them, neither wished nor was able to do. These three approaches—the appeal to shared liberal values made by the British Committee, the rejectionist stance of Savarkar, and the developing Gandhian notion of self-reliant engagement—were to define the dilemma of metropolitan anti-imperialist agitation in the years to come.

---

[138] *Hind Swaraj*, 77–8; 'Discourses on the Gita', 24 Feb 1926, *CWMG* E37/81.
[139] Gandhi, 'Ethics of Passive Resistance'.   [140] *Hind Swaraj*, 17.
[141] Ibid.
[142] 'Speech at meeting of Indians', 2 Nov 1909, *CWMG* E10/135; Gandhi to Polak, 5 Nov 1909, *CWMG* E10/138; 'Deputation's Last Letter', after 6 Nov 1909, *CWMG*, E10/142; 'Last Note on Deputation', 25 Nov 1909, *CWMG* E10/163.
[143] *Hind Swaraj*, 73.

3

Edwardian Progressive Visitors to India, 1905–14

Winning the support of a political party promised to help solve one of the principal problems of organising metropolitan agitation. Parties could draw on existing affiliations and loyalties, rather than having to create them from scratch, and could deliver metropolitan expertise, pre-committed activists, and publicity opportunities, as well as the support of those who might exert a direct influence on government. The small cog of metropolitan anti-imperialism might, interlocked in this way with larger cogs, turn bigger political structures around. However, though alluring, such relationships were also fraught with hazard. For British political parties, the key question was the compatibility of Indian demands with their ideological leanings, electoral concerns and the economic interests of their supporters. For Indian nationalists the chief danger of reliance on a party was that they might be required to defer to that party's views and interests on Indian questions, or engage in irrelevant factional battles with other parties, diverting their energies and alienating existing supporters.

Despite the evident hostility of the Unionists to their aspirations, the early Congress leaders wished to win support in both major political parties, but were advised by the British Committee to give their money to support only Liberals.[1] The attempt to formalise an alliance with the Liberals had, however, proved disappointing: only around a quarter of the Liberal associations had agreed to support Congress demands, and this was insufficient to persuade the ruling bodies of the National Liberal Federation to endorse Indian demands itself.[2] Hyndman's Social Democratic Federation had given more sustained support for Congress but had proved an uncomfortable ally, likely to upset the

---

[1] *India*, 5 Dec 1890; Morrow, 'Origin and Early Years', 93; Thompson, 'Thinking Imperially?', 200–1.
[2] *India*, 23 Oct 1891.

careful strategy of seeking the support in governing circles on which the Congress leadership was set. Hyndman, who had been a student of Indian affairs since the early 1870s, had in numerous articles, some favourably reviewed by Marx, developed independently his own version of Naoroji's theory that Indian poverty was getting worse, not better, under British rule and that it was largely attributable to the 'drain' of resources to the imperial metropole.[3] But Hyndman's socialism did not always connect easily with Congress, as Naoroji was forced to admit.[4] By the late 1890s, he had moved from arguing that revolution was a likely consequence of British policies in India to encouraging it as the only route by which India could progress. '[I]t is a mistake to ask for charity instead of demanding justice', Hyndman had told Naoroji.

Men in high positions have said to me, 'Where is the evidence of discontent, Mr Hyndman? Where is the cry for justice from the people of India themselves? If the people are so poor and oppressed, as you say they are, surely we should hear a little more of it than we do hear!' What answer can I make to such a challenge? There is no answer . . . It is time to be up and stirring . . . I will help, and so will our organization, and *Justice*, as much as possible; *but* 'Providence helps those who help themselves.'[5]

Congress was irritated by Hyndman's irresponsibility, believing that he failed to appreciate how much harder agitation was in India than in Britain. Association with militancy would simply invite repression and discredit Congress in the political circles in which it aspired to move. Wacha and Congress refused in 1904 to give him any money for his election campaign on exactly these grounds.[6] 'The mass of the people yet do not understand the position', Naoroji told him. 'John Bull does not understand the bark. He only understands the bite, and we cannot do this.'[7] But Hyndman was scathing in his attacks on the servility of Congress:

'What do you judicious people gain by your moderation? What does your journal *India* gain by its dullness . . . ? To the naked eye, and even to the

[3] H. M. Hyndman, *The Bankruptcy of India* (London, 1886); *England for All* (London, 1881), 101. See also Chushichi Tsuzuki, *H. M. Hyndman and British Socialism* (Oxford, 1961); Eric Hobsbawm, *Labouring Men: Studies in the History of Labour* (London, 1964), 231–5; Norman Etherington, 'Hyndman, the Social Democratic Federation and Imperialism', *Historical Studies* 16 (1974), 89–103.

[4] Masani, *Naoroji*, 398.

[5] Hyndman to Naoroji, undated, quoted in Masani, *Naoroji*, 398–9.

[6] Wacha to Naoroji, 13 and 20 Feb 1904, 17 Sep and 28 Oct 1904, *DNC*, ii, 855–7, 870–2, 876–7.

[7] Naoroji to Hyndman, 22 Feb 1898, quoted in Masani, *Naoroji*, 401; Wacha to Naoroji, 20 Feb 1904, *DNC*, ii, 856–7.

microscope, nothing! [The British authorities] just kick you and pass seditious acts over you, and lie about you, even more than they do with us. We, at least, have the satisfaction of chasing them, deriding them, making them look ridiculous and driving them into furious anger.[8]

Chiding of this kind was not especially pleasing to the Congress leadership. Despite more sustained agitation than any other British Socialist, Hyndman became a rather semi-detached figure, neither invited to attend Congress in India, nor to participate in the activities of the British Committee at home.[9]

While British socialists and agitators could be dangerous allies, however, the support of Labour candidates and parliamentarians was more welcome. When, in the months before the 1906 election, the Congress delegates Lajpat Rai and Gokhale visited Britain, they were encouraged to seek out Labour candidates.[10] However, they differed in their estimates of the value of Labour to India. Gokhale stayed at the National Liberal Club and spent his time negotiating with Government Liberals. On his return he made cutting remarks about social democrats in the Subjects Committee.[11] Lajpat Rai spent more time touring the urban areas of Scotland, northern England and the Midlands, addressing meetings of workers. He was much more taken by the possibilities of an alliance. Gokhale's 'friends of India' spoke critically of the Government, but 'could not forget that they were Englishmen'.[12] They were a hopeless minority incapable of swinging their party behind Congress. On the other hand, the 'Socialists, the democrats and the Labour people are coming to the front every day', he wrote, 'and I am of opinion that your only chance is with them'.[13] They were poor, though, of course, this made it possible to contemplate financial support for pledged

---

[8] Hyndman to Naoroji, 19 Feb 1898, quoted in Masani, *Naoroji*, 400–1; Wilfrid Scawen Blunt, *My Diaries: Being a Personal Narrative of Events, 1888–1914* (2v., London, 1919–21), ii, 226–9.

[9] *India*, 13 June 1913; see also Tsuzuki, *Hyndman*, 195; Wedderburn to Gokhale, 3 Aug 1906, GM 11708; Hyndman to Naoroji, 9 Oct 1905, GM 11704.

[10] 'Memorandum on Indian Issues at the Forthcoming Election', undated but prob. May 1905, GM 11707; Wedderburn to Gokhale, 11 July 1905, GM 11708; Wedderburn to Wacha and Gokhale, May 1905; Wedderburn to Gokhale, 11 July and 8 Sept 1905, GM 11708; Naoroji to Gokhale, 10 Nov 1905, GM 11704.

[11] Lajpat Rai to Gokhale, 3 March 1906, GM 11703.

[12] *The Panjabee*, 17 July 1905.

[13] 'India and English Party Politics', in V. C. Joshi (ed.), *Lala Lajpat Rai: Writings and Speeches* (2v., Delhi, 1966), i, 87–9; *Hindustan Review*, Oct–Nov 1905, 349–56.

candidates.[14] Unlike the Liberals, they seemed open to suggestions about India from Indians. With them, Congress might undertake 'the work of Sappers and Miners' undermining the *raj* at its British base.[15]

In the 1906 election, 30 Labour MPs were returned, and Keir Hardie promised their 'strenuous backing' for the Indian cause.[16] The Labour parliamentary group was, of course, very small, but the proportion prepared to support Congress was much larger and voted cohesively in Parliament.[17] This worried Morley, but for quite precise reasons.[18] The new Labour MPs themselves were authorities on industrial matters, but their minds were untrained either by 'systematic and directed thought' or by the 'habits and traditions of public affairs and great duties'.[19] 'I represented workmen in Newcastle for a dozen years', he reminded Minto, 'and always felt that [they] are essentially *bourgeois*, without a bit of the French red about them' and 'only Socialist in the sense—and a grand sense—of being stirred by sympathy and pity for their comrades.'[20] But exactly this sense of fellow-feeling might be stirred by Indian agitators using the techniques that had served them so well in India. Hardie, indeed, feeling his ignorance of Indian matters, had sought advice from Gokhale for his speeches, a practice that was also followed by MacDonald and James O'Grady, the other principal Labour speakers on Indian questions.[21] The British Committee captured the majority of the Labour force for the IPC, and praise was lavished in the columns of *India* on their early forays on Indian questions.[22]

However, the prospect of an alliance between Congress and British sympathisers had its own difficulties. The Labour MPs were hardly less

---

[14] Lajpat Rai to Gokhale, 8 Aug 1905, GM 11703; Lajpat Rai to Verma 3 Aug 1905, *CWLR*, ii, 142–4.

[15] Lajpat Rai to Duni Chand, c. Sep 1905, *Panjabee*, 2 Oct 1905.

[16] *India*, 2 March 1906.

[17] Morrow, 'Origin and Early Years', 283, Table V and 331 show that in 1906 two-thirds of the Labour Party MPs were on the Indian Parliamentary Committee, compared to 43% of the Liberals, and that all of them had signed Mackarness's letter to Asquith in 1909.

[18] Morley to Minto, 8 Oct 1907, MC MSS/Eur/D573/2.

[19] Morley to Minto, 24 Jan 1908, MC MSS/Eur/D573/3.

[20] Morley to Minto, 16 and 25 Jan 1906, MC MSS/Eur/D573/1.

[21] O'Grady to Gokhale, 28 May 1906, GM 11704; Hardie to Gokhale, 13 July 1906, GM 11701; MacDonald to Gokhale, 3 Feb and 17 July 1911, GM 11700.

[22] The British Committee was, however, slower to recruit Labour MPs to its own membership. Only one Labour MP, James O'Grady, was recruited before the First World War. See Minute Book v.7, 4 Jan 1910, 13 June 1911, 27 June 1911; Cotton, *Indian and Home Memories*, 307–8.

enthusiastic about free trade than were the Liberals, which made them only weak supporters for Indian nationalist demands for protection. Matters were made worse by the impact of Congress boycotts and the *swadeshi* campaign on working-class interests, particularly in Lancashire. Neither Gokhale nor Lajpat Rai had shied away from this difficulty while speaking in Britain. Gokhale had told a Manchester audience that the intention of the boycott was not to hurt British producers but to put pressure on the Government of India.[23] At Stockport, Lajpat Rai had sought to assure cotton workers that Indian nationalists did not seek to replace imports of finished goods with local manufactures, but only to develop its production of 'cheap and coarse goods' which did not compete directly with those of Lancashire.[24] Nevertheless, as moderate nationalists came under increasing pressure from Tilak and the Extremists, the likelihood grew that Congress would be obliged to step up its boycott of all British goods and institutions, even at the expense of British workers. Labour's parliamentary attacks, like those of Radicals, thus steered clear of these thorny questions. Rather they confined themselves to deploring Britain's economic exploitation of India, resisting frontier expansionism and militarism, condemning deportations and detentions, and calling for more rapid Indianisation of the administration.[25]

The Labour MPs also had to judge the compatibility of Congress' aspirations with their own ideals. A key question for the Labour Party was whether the kinds of social reforms it wished to see in India, such as the redress of poverty, widening educational opportunity and the growth of meaningful trade unionism were more likely under Congress rule than they were under British rule. The unreformed *raj* seemed to lack the capacity or authority to undertake such a programme. Its finances were permanently squeezed by imperial military demands and those of an expensive European-dominated administration and its pension funds. It pursued agricultural policies which merely created peasant indebtedness and famine, and industrial strategies which were haphazard and compromised. Lacking sufficient authority of its own, it was forced into compromise with the existing elites and the most socially regressive elements of Indian society, the landlords and the princes. On the other hand, Congress, despite its hostility to the *raj*, seemed detached

---

[23] Nanda, *Gokhale*, 197–8.
[24] 'Lancashire and India', 27 July 1905, in Joshi (ed.), *Lajpat Rai*, i, 67–78.
[25] Moulton, 'The Early Congress', 22–53; *Hansard*, 20 July 1906, 4th ser., v.161, cols.570–637.

from the masses and their concerns. Though highly articulate, its core support came—albeit unevenly—from a predominantly Hindu urban high caste western-educated intelligentsia and had little autonomous support among workers and peasants.[26] Its primary aim was to secure its own place in the administrative and legislative work of the *raj*, but social reforms, as well as religious matters, had been sedulously avoided as divisive. Land tenure and rents were rarely discussed, and the problems of Indian rural poverty were considered mainly as evidence of the 'drain' of resources to Britain, and rarely as a problem of internal inequity.

The new style of mobilisation represented by anti-partition Extremist politics after 1904 seemed more promising, especially to those such as Hyndman who had deplored the gentlemanliness of Congress. But the methods by which this broadening was achieved itself raised questions for British sympathisers. With their own distinct traditions, the Indian peasantry and urban poor could not be mobilised by appeals couched in the language of western progressives or, for that matter, by using the techniques favoured by European working-class movements. Instead, the Extremists sought to harness their pre-existing energies, expressed in an enormous variety of causes and campaigns, in opposition to rent rises, in defence of customary rights and religious observances, and so forth. In Bengal, the methods employed were a mix of western-style petition, demonstration and boycott, combined and reinforced by the use of what Guha terms 'dharmic protest', that is, the attempt to enforce collective action through the use of religious sanctions.[27] For example, failure to comply with the demands of the boycott was treated as a religious fault, and wearing foreign cloth as polluting. Caste sanctions, such as the refusal to perform rituals of purification for offenders, were employed to coerce non-participants to join campaigns. The charismatic skills of religious leaders were deployed to win support and religious festivals and pilgrimage sites were the occasions for rallies. As well as using religious authority, Congress leaders also employed traditional techniques of social

[26] For the social, religious and regional composition of the early Congress, see the tables in P. C. Ghosh, *The Development of the Indian National Congress, 1892–1909* (Calcutta, 1960), 23–6. See also Seal, *Emergence;* S. R. Mehrotra, *The Emergence of the Indian National Congress* (Delhi, 1971), J. R. McLane, *Indian Nationalism and the Early Congress* (Princeton, 1977).

[27] Ranajit Guha, *Dominance without Hegemony: History and Power in Colonial India* (Cambridge, Mass., 1997); Gordon Johnson, 'Partition, Agitation and Congress: Bengal 1904 to 1908', *Modern Asian Studies*, 7/3 (1973), 533–88.

dominance—money-power and force—to rally support. Sympathetic *zemindars* (large landowners) and their agents enforced the boycott on their tenants and on other economic dependants. This too raised the question of the relationship between the educated, urban classes and the wider India.

This created a puzzle for Labour sympathisers with Congress nationalism. Accustomed to western notions of political progress, they had great difficult in identifying the markers of authenticity in the Indian setting. Judged by the criteria of home, the emergence of a rich urban associational life, characterised by 'moderate' politicians speaking the familiar language of western liberalism, seemed at first sight an authentic, if infant, development. Yet on closer inspection, seen in its own setting, it appeared a somewhat artificial, imitative phenomenon, lacking deep roots in Indian society. The alternative forms of mobilisation visible in 'anti-partition' politics initially offered different signs of authenticity: popular support and clear indigenous roots, and most encouragingly, self-reliance. But they were quite unlike the forms with which British politicians were familiar, relying as they did on pre-modern methods of mobilisation and on the authority of caste and class. Many of the politicians they met as heads of identifiably western organisations in London, such as Lajpat Rai, were, in India, leading narrower, communal organisations dominated by quite different methods of working. These were often reforming organisations of which British radicals approved, concerned with reforming religious practices such as widow remarriage, untouchability or prohibitions on foreign travel, in the light of new thinking. But they had unfamiliar concerns and modes of operation.

After 1907, four Labour figures—Keir Hardie, Ramsay MacDonald and Sidney and Beatrice Webb, as well as the Radical journalist H. W. Nevinson—visited India in quick succession, and their differing perceptions and recommendations provide a good cross-section of responses to the new Indian nationalism. The first arrival was Keir Hardie. As we have seen, India proved a controversial destination for Hardie, when his tour was denounced in the Anglo-Indian press as seditious. He sent several letters home to the Labour press giving his impressions, and after his return, these were collected in a small book titled *India: Impressions and Suggestions*. At first sight, the horrified reactions of Anglo-India seem quite understandable, for Hardie did not stop at urging Morley to reconsider the partition of Bengal. He went further to endorsing Extremist demands for a rapid extension of self-government. There could be 'no real pacification, no allaying of discontent, no breaking down of the barrier rising between European and Asiatic until the people of India have some effective form of self-government'. He dismissed the charge that Indians were not fit for self-government, since they were of 'the same Aryan stock as ourselves', and were proving their capacities 'in every direction'.[28] Given the lurid descriptions of Congress then in circulation, Hardie seems to have been rather surprised to find how tame it was. If treated correctly, he wrote, Congress was 'not only not seditious, [but] ultra-loyal'.[29] The Moderate faction, he wrote, was 'extreme in its moderation', while the Extremist group was 'moderate in its extremism'.[30] Nevertheless, Hardie cut through the justifications of the imperial mission in India with iconoclastic glee. The British had not civilised India, which in any case had 'centuries of civilised and refined life behind it' compared to the 'barbarous' peoples of Europe, but had exploited it. India's increasing poverty was a direct result of the British occupation.[31] Far from dedicated to serving the Indian people, the British in India were, in Hardie's uncompromising opinion, merely interested in 'comfortable billets'.[32]

Hardie proposed to make the village council—the *panchayat*—the basis of a system of indirect election by which popularly elected councils at district and municipal level would in turn elect provincial councils with enlarged powers. 'In this way', Hardie believed, 'the whole superstructure of Indian administration would rest on popular election, and the people would be given a real control over their own affairs'.[33] On his return, Hardie wrote to Morley to press this idea on him, assuring him that '[t]he process of sifting through the various Boards would be sufficient to ensure that the men finally selected to act on the Provincial Councils would be such as would command the confidence of all sections of the community.'[34] Hardie did not spell out what he thought the enlarged powers of the provincial councils might be, and his plans were merely the outline suggestions of a passing visitor rather

[28] J. Keir Hardie, *India: Impressions and Suggestions* (London, 1909), 117.
[29] Ibid. 103.   [30] Quoted in Howe, *Anticolonialism*, 45.
[31] ILP, *Report of Annual Conference*, 1905, 39.
[32] ILP, *Report of Annual Conference*, 1908, 67.   [33] Hardie, *India*, 122
[34] Hardie to Morley, 29 June 1908, Francis Johnson Correspondence, 1908/258.

than a fully evolved policy. Nevertheless, radical grass-roots democracy of this type was much more than Congress had asked for, and one might suspect, much more than it wanted. In Hardie's vision, Congress would become merely one of many parties competing for the votes of peasants, a prospect far from the ambitions of many of the pre-Gandhian Congress for the opening up of the administration to more of their number. Of course, Congress leaders were in no position to quarrel with an enthusiastic British visitor, but differences of view of this kind might help explain why Hardie was surprised by how limited their aims were. The findings of the Royal Commission on Decentralization which reported the year after Hardie's visit, suggested that *panchayats* as they then existed were an unreliable basis for village democracy. They did not exist in all of India, and were often factionalised along lines of caste, to the extent that in some cases, more than one existed in a given village. Where they commanded authority, it was usually the traditional authority of caste. Tellingly, Tilak, who gave evidence to the Commission, had wanted to see *panchayats* elected, but not for them to form the basis of Indian democracy as Hardie did.[35]

Hardie's view of the Moderates was initially shared by another visitor, H. W. Nevinson.[36] Nevinson visited India only a few weeks after Hardie. His speeches followed the same themes: the insensitivities of the *raj*, and the desirability of political concessions. However, he also made some 'rather sharp' criticisms of Hindu passivity and the lack of organisational skills. He was told by British officials that Indians made good critics and talkers, but never took advantage of the powers that were there to make practical social improvements, an impression he confirmed for himself on seeing filthy watertanks 'waiting for the municipality' to repair.[37] 'I c[oul]d hardly get them to see my point in insisting on the swadeshi of self-help', he wrote in his diary, after his first discussions with Indian politicians.[38] Indians had failed to build civil institutions above the level of the locality for themselves, were now confronted by a powerful, efficient but foreign state, and had, as a result, got into the 'habit of

[35] *Royal Commission on Decentralization in India*, Cd 4360 (1908).

[36] H. W. Nevinson, *The New Spirit in India* (London, 1908) and *More Changes, More Chances* (London, 1925), 226–83; Nevinson Diary, MSS Eng.misc.e.614.

[37] Nevinson Diary, 19 Dec 1907.

[38] Ibid. 2, 13, 15 and 20 Dec 1907. According to a contemporary intelligence report, Nevinson also said that 'Indians often showed themselves too polite and submissive; they should assert themselves more', DCI Report, 30 Nov 1907, enclosed in Minto to Morley, 12 Dec 1907, MC MSS/Eur/D573/13.

looking to Gov[ernmen]t for every single thing and of expecting all from it'.[39] Hindu submissiveness also hampered the organisation of political resistance to the *raj*. Hardie had instructed Indians that their problem was the lack of 'grit and backbone' and Nevinson was publicly critical of the 'weakness of Indians in over-politeness & taking things lying down'. They should 'stand up and meet a man face to face'.[40] There was, he told one audience, 'no glory in ruling over a flock of sheep and there was no glory in being one of a flock of sheep'. What was needed were greater efforts to develop 'self-reliance and manliness'.[41] After Russia, Nevinson found the scale of oppression 'rather petty'.[42] Like other muscular Radicals before him, such as Hyndman and Blunt, and still others later, such as H. N. Brailsford, Nevinson felt able, from a comfortable position of invulnerability to the *raj*, to urge defiance upon those in a much weaker position.

The Moderates told Nevinson that self-assertion would come from the growing confidence of Indians under British tutelage. Bhupendranath Basu told him that the Moderates were 'strongly in favour of keeping [the] Brit[ish] Gov[ernmen]t because there is no other nation th[e]y w[oul]d rather be under, all the more because we go slow & give time for internal development.'[43] To Nevinson's even greater surprise, Gokhale defended Curzon's notion that 'inscrutable providence' had brought Britain to govern India, since 'England was supplying what most was lacking in the race—love of freedom and self-assertion ag[ain]st authority'.[44] As to Hardie, this did not seem sufficiently robust to Nevinson, and it was not until he met Aurobindo Ghose that he found a nationalist of whom he could wholeheartedly approve. Aurobindo, in contrast to the Moderates, had given up on the idea that India should acquire its political skills through apprenticeship under the British and was indifferent to such tedious questions as the distribution of seats in the legislature. Instead he concentrated on building national institutions based on Indian traditions, a 'renewal of national character & spirit, reduced since 1830 more & more in each generation to condition of sheep or fatted calves'.[45] Within the Extremist camp,

---

[39] Nevinson Diary, 13 Dec 1907.

[40] *Bala-Bharata*, 1/2 (Dec 1907), 44 and 1/3 (Jan 1908), 71; Nevinson Diary, 2 Dec 1907.

[41] DCI Reports, 30 Nov 1907, enclosed in Minto to Morley, 12 Dec 1907, MC MSS/Eur/D573/13; 21 Dec. 1907, HPA, Jan 1908, 102.

[42] Nevinson Diary, 7 Dec 1907.   [43] Ibid. 3 Nov 1907.

[44] Ibid. 15 Nov 1907.   [45] Ibid. 19 Dec 1907.

moreover, Aurobindo had set himself up against the ineffectiveness of 'peaceful ashrams and swadeshism and self-help'. In its place, he advocated boycott of British goods and institutions, and the creation of national schools and courts and so forth, in their place. He also favoured ostracising those who refused to join the boycott, and believed armed struggle against repression could be justifiable and necessary.[46] Nevinson was more naturally drawn to Aurobindo because of the depth of his influence with Indians, rather than the reliance on connections in London employed by Gokhale. Better still, the Congress 'volunteers' employed to enforce the boycott, and to fend off Muslim attacks, were at least showing some manly virtues.[47] 'This is beyond doubt the true party', wrote Nevinson, 'the party with a future.'[48]

Yet Nevinson had reservations. At the end of his tour, he attended Congress itself, and was horrified to find that the dispute between Moderates and Extremists came to a fist-fight almost immediately, in a spectacular display of political incivility. The Moderates expressed their willingness to see the Extremists depart rather than give any further encouragement to their programme of agitation. Nevinson recorded a 'sleepless night of perplexity and sick passion', followed by a '[l]istless morning listening to apprehensions of fighting'. The 'petulant irritation' of the Indians on both sides was 'very disquieting'. They were 'like helpless children'.[49] Aurobindo and the Extremists received noticeably worse press from Nevinson thereafter. Lajpat Rai, who had sided with the Moderates at Surat, now, in Nevinson's view, '[stood] highest of the Indians I have known'.[50] Nevinson now placed great stress on the need for education in India, to assist with the proper growth of democracy. This would, of course, need to be liberal education, for the trouble with the schools under indigenous influence, even such as those of Lajpat Rai's Arya Samaj, was that they were more interested in religious rote-learning—'as though the mind were a passive vessel to be filled through the passage of the ears', as Nevinson colourfully put it—rather than encouraging free thought.[51] On his return to Britain, and in the book *The New Spirit in India* he later wrote, Nevinson expressed much greater faith in the Moderates and their programme of participation in local councils. Indians, he wrote, 'sh[ould] practise hard at their

---

[46] Haridas and Uma Mukherji, *Sri Aurobindo and the New Thought in Indian Politics* (Calcutta, 1964).

[47] Nevinson, *New Spirit*, 185–6   [48] Nevinson Diary, 19 Dec 1907.

[49] Ibid. 28 and 29 Dec 1907.   [50] Ibid. 21 Jan 1908.

[51] Ibid. 20 Dec 1907, 17 Jan 1908; *More Changes, More Chances*, 278–9.

municipalities'.[52] What was needed in India was benevolent western influence, not, or not yet, movements of self-reliance. For Nevinson, as for other British observers, western liberalism, confronting the new Extremist spirit in India, had hit the buffers of its understanding. 'I have never approached any subject with more overwhelming distaste and uncertainty', he wrote gloomily in April 1908.[53]

A year or so after the appearance of Hardie's heretical conclusions, Ramsay MacDonald published his own book on India, the result of a private visit to India in 1909. By then, the dispute between Moderates and Extremists had widened into a split. The unresolved question was whether the departure of the Extremists had strengthened Congress by returning it to the path of mendicant constitutionalism, or weakened it by depriving it of the unexpectedly powerful impulses of Indian cultural renaissance.

MacDonald has usually been regarded as a reactionary on India.[54] *The Awakening of India* (1910) would certainly provide an easy afternoon's work for a theorist of colonial discourse. Practically from the first chapter, in which the oriental 'spell' begins to work its magic on the arriving British traveller and 'the will of the West grapples with the acquiescence of the East', MacDonald contrasts India as 'the other': impossibly alien, mysterious, trapped in its religious traditions, and enervated by the torpor-inducing climate.[55] MacDonald, unlike Hardie, believed that religion and caste were still absolutely central to Indian social life, and that they created problems which could not be readily brushed aside. Hinduism was 'the pivot round which the life of India turns', for '[e]verything that India has been, everything that she dreams of being, she associates with her temples, her philosophies, her schools of religious learning, her devotion to her gods'.[56] It was this dominance of unreasoning, religious impulses that gave Indian nationalism its peculiar, unsatisfactory qualities. 'All Indian movements from bomb-throwing to personal purification begin in the sphere of

---

[52] Nevinson Diary, 14 Jan 1908.
[53] Quoted in Angela John, *War, Journalism and the Shaping of the Twentieth Century: The Life and Times of Henry W. Nevinson* (London, 2006), 119.
[54] David Marquand, *Ramsay MacDonald* (London, 1977), 117–18, 152; Carl Bridge and H. V. Brasted, 'The British Labour Party "Nabobs" and Indian Reform, 1924–1931', *Journal of Imperial and Commonwealth History*, 17/3 (1989), 396–412.
[55] J. Ramsay MacDonald, *The Awakening of India* (London, 1910), 8–14.
[56] Ibid. 182–3, 186.

religion, and this is particularly true of Nationalism.'[57] 'The extreme
Nationalist has no programme except a demand for elementary rights,
no ideas of what would follow upon a self-ruling India. He is a religious
votary, not a politician [and] [t]he things which are important to the
western politician are of no consequence to [him].'[58] But Hinduism,
with its caste divisions and hostility to Muslims, could neither unite
India nor sustain a political system attuned to western values. The
'struggle for civil freedom' had been 'transformed into the worship of
the Hindu genius'.[59]

MacDonald therefore did not believe that the indigenous 'new spirit',
such as that initially identified by Nevinson in Aurobindo Ghose and
the Extremists, offered any real hope of advance. Culturally, it was
doing essential work: 'creating India by song and worship'.[60] By contrast its political manifestations were 'its crudest and most ill-formed
embodiments'.[61] Nationalism demanded heroic action, while politics necessarily involved gradualism and compromise. Unlike Hardie,
MacDonald had little time for the notion that India's past provided
any basis for building democratic institutions. Where Hardie held
that the empire had merely impoverished India, MacDonald took a
much more positive view of the imperial contribution. Whatever nationalists might say, 'the historical fact remains that England saved
India'.[62] '[F]or many a long year', therefore, 'British sovereignty will
be necessary for India . . . [T]he warring elements in Indian life need
a unifying and controlling power', he wrote. 'Britain is the nurse of
India. Deserted by her guardian, India would be the prey of disruptive
elements within herself as well as victim of her own too enthusiastic
worshippers.'[63]

However, while the *raj* had brought peace, and must stay, it could
not without reform develop India further.[64] Indians did lack the
skills of government. They lacked 'discipline, steady perseverance and
courage'. But this was 'the result of generations of ancestors deprived
of all responsibility for the ordering of their own lives'.[65] MacDonald
therefore deplored the 'colossal mistake' of the official British response
to Congress: 'We spy upon it; we deport its advocates; we plan to

[57] MacDonald, *Awakening*, 181.
[58] Ibid. 186–7   [59] Ibid. 101, 184.   [60] Ibid. 70–74.
[61] J. Ramsay MacDonald, 'Introduction' to Radhakumud Mookerji, *The Fundamental Unity of India* (London, 1913), x.
[62] MacDonald, *Awakening*, 211.
[63] Ibid. 301–2; *India*, 17 Dec 1909.   [64] Ibid. 213.   [65] Ibid. 292.

circumvent it.'[66] He believed that this failure was partly the result of inadequate supervision of the *raj* from Westminster. MacDonald held, therefore, that '[w]e must govern India more on Parliamentary lines', ensuring, through greater accountability to Westminster, that Viceroys, Governors and officials maintained an appropriately 'imperial standard' of conduct in their dealings with Indians.[67]

The solvent of communal and caste divisions would be council work, education, and the greater employment of Indians in the imperial administration. Of course, MacDonald was adamant that the process could not be rushed. India would not awake 'all at once', and if Britain handled nationalism correctly, the day of her expulsion from India was 'so remote that we need hardly think of it at all'. Progress to Indian freedom, however, could not be held back, for 'her Destiny is above our will, and we had better recognise it and bow to the Inevitable'.[68] The role of the British in India now, MacDonald averred, was not ruler, but 'adviser, counsellor and guide'.[69]

Thus the early efforts of Congress to build an All-India movement seemed to MacDonald to offer the only prospect of advance. These efforts had now developed their own 'internal momentum' and could not be held back: indeed, 'the future belong[ed] to Nationalism'.[70] The pace of reform needed to be kept up. Ultimately, for MacDonald, '[r]esponsible government in the provinces and a federation of the provinces in an Indian government' was the way India might overcome her divisions.[71] 'Truly', he wrote, 'the ship of parliamentary government is launched. The hands at the helm are perhaps timorous; the officers are not certain that she is seaworthy. They had better let these feelings pass.' The manipulative electoral regulations introduced by British officials were 'not worthy of us'.[72] British officials needed to welcome the desire of Indians to be involved in their own government.

Coerced by her guardian, she will be an endless irritation and worry. Consulted by her guardian, and given wide liberty to govern herself in all her internal affairs, she may present many difficulties and create many fears, but that is the only way to abiding peace and to the fulfilment of our work in India.[73]

[66] Ibid. 107, 201.   [67] *India*, 17 Dec 1909.
[68] MacDonald, *Awakening*, 297–302, 311.
[69] *Leicester Daily Post*, 30 May 1910.
[70] MacDonald, *Awakening*, 268–70, 297.
[71] Ibid. 297.   [72] Ibid. 272.   [73] Ibid. 301–2.

After his return, MacDonald began to create a distinct role for himself on Indian affairs. Hardie used his Indian experiences and connections to lobby Government from the outside, and from a position of solidarity with the Indians. MacDonald, by contrast, sought the role of intermediary between the Indians and the British Government. This different stance had been adopted right from the start. MacDonald received introductions and advice from Nevinson about whom he should meet to get the Congress view.[74] But he took his advice from the officials as well, writing to Dunlop-Smith, the Private Secretary to the Viceroy, who sent him an alternative route: 'You must visit Peshawar & if possible, the Khyber . . . I should like you to visit the Canal Colonies in the Punjab . . . & also see something of the administration of a District.'[75] The officials of the India Office were quick to sense the possibilities of MacDonald as an ally. He was, wrote Morley to Minto, 'a. . . . Labour Member of very superior quality' and it was important to 'set him on the right path'.[76]

On his return to Britain, MacDonald became a leading parliamentary critic of the new wave of repression that had descended on India in the wake of the Morley–Minto reforms, of which he received details in correspondence from Lajpat Rai and leading Moderates.[77] Minto disliked this quite as much as he did all linked-up agitation and attacked MacDonald's 'ignorance and attempted co-operation with agitators of the worst type'.[78] But to the India Office, MacDonald was a useful critic, a good barometer of reasonable parliamentary opinion, sensitive to the difficulties they faced and, if suitably briefed, a steadying influence on Indians. He was, Wedderburn told Gokhale, 'rather a grata persona to Lord Morley'.[79] Indeed, Morley reportedly told Asquith that MacDonald had 'the front bench mind' and should be given a government post.[80] Morley wrote to congratulate him on his book; his deputy Edwin Montagu praised it publicly and even the India Office officials thought it useful,

[74] Nevinson to Gokhale, 9 Sep 1909, GM 11704; Nevinson to MacDonald, undated but prob. 1909, PRO 30/69/1217, NA.

[75] Dunlop-Smith to MacDonald, 27 May 1909, PRO 30/69/1217, NA.

[76] Morley to Minto, 20 Aug 1909, MC MSS/Eur/D573/4.

[77] Basu to MacDonald, 21 April 1910; Bannerjea to MacDonald, 1 June 1910; Lajpat Rai to MacDonald, 17 and 24 Nov 1910, 9 and 16 March 1911, PRO 30/69/1218, NA.

[78] Minto to Morley, 18 Aug 1910, MC MSS/Eur/D573/25.

[79] Wedderburn to Gokhale, 13 July 1910, GM 11708.

[80] Hugh Dalton, *Call Back Yesterday: Memoirs, 1887–1931* (London, 1953), 289.

sending many of his observations to India, marked up for Viceregal attention.[81]

This positioning provided MacDonald with a certain leverage. Both he and Hardie pressed the Government of India to release Tilak from prison in return for a promise not to engage in seditious political activity. But whereas Hardie corresponded directly with Tilak, assuring him of support and of Labour's support for his cause,[82], MacDonald's relationship with Tilak was cooler and indirect. Congress leaders hoped that MacDonald's authority at the India Office might help Tilak, and persuaded him to approach Lord Crewe, the new Secretary of State, to make the case for them.[83] But when MacDonald visited Crewe in July 1911, he was more circumspect. He was, Crewe noted, 'in no way surprised [by Crewe's refusal to release Tilak], and gave the impression of bringing the matter up in no way *de coeur*; but as he had been told that Tilak would make a public promise of the kind, he felt bound to do so'. MacDonald had added, rather unflatteringly, that it would be necessary for Tilak to make his promise public, as a Pune Brahman could not be trusted to keep his word if there were a chance of evading it.[84] '[M]y friends in the India Office have been very anxious to do things handsomely', MacDonald reported somewhat inaccurately to India, but Tilak had to wait until 1914 for his release.[85]

With the loss of so many of the British Committee's Radical MPs in the 1910 elections, Indian questions became more the work of the Labour MPs.[86] Labour, Wedderburn told Gokhale, were now India's 'most effective allies in the House of Commons' and 'the only people with both knowledge and independence sufficient to speak for India'.[87] The Committee, its British members and Indian Congress

[81] Arthur Murray Diary, 18 Jan 1918, Elibank Papers, MS 8804, NLS; MacDonald Diary, 27 July and 26 Oct 1910, PRO 30/69/1753/1, NA; Morley to MacDonald, 8 June, 14 Oct, 8 Nov 1910, and 5 April 1911, PRO 30/69/1218, NA; Montagu to Hardinge, 6 April 1911, Hardinge Papers, 92; S. D. Waley, *Edwin Montagu: A Memoir and an Account of his Visits to India* (London, 1964), 44–5.

[82] Tilak to Khaparde, 1 and 29 May 1909, in Vidwans, *Letters of Lokamanya Tilak*, 41–7; Hardie to Khaparde, 13 Jan 1911,Khaparde Coll., 3; Hardie to Tilak, 31 March 1911, HPB, July 1911, 17–19; Hardie to Vidwans, 14 April 1911, Khaparde Coll., 3.

[83] Khaparde to Ghose, 5 July 1911; Ghose to Khaparde, 11 July 1911, Khaparde Coll., 4.

[84] Crewe to Hardinge, 18 and 28 July 1911, Hardinge Papers 117.

[85] MacDonald to Khaparde, 13 Nov 1911, Khaparde Coll., 3.

[86] MacDonald Diary, 22 June 1910; British Committee Minute Book, v.7, 19 April and 25 July 1910.

[87] Wedderburn to Gokhale, 28 July and 18 Aug 1910, GM 11708.

leaders also made significant donations to Labour's depleted election fund and canvassed India for financial support for Labour's fledgling newspaper, the *Daily Herald*.[88] In return, the *Daily Herald* offered to publish whatever Indian nationalists wanted.[89] When MacDonald became leader of the party in 1911, the Moderates invited him to preside at the Congress.[90] The Government of India and Morley opposed this idea, on the grounds that the Congress should remain an Indian affair.[91] However, the attractions were greater. At a lunch with Basu in July, MacDonald explained at length his reasons for acceptance, though Nevinson, also there, wrote privately that 'no one cared in the least why, knowing vanity was the only motive'.[92] Although the Congress leaders wanted him to speak about the partiality of the Government of India to the Muslims, he planned to speak instead on industrial development, and the need for educational and administrative reforms, with the purpose of instructing Indians that '[India's] good government in the future depends just as much on Western experience as upon Eastern practice'.[93] But worsening industrial relations at home, and MacDonald's wife's severe illness intervened to prevent his visit.[94]

MacDonald was a natural choice when the India Office set up a Royal Commission on the Indian Civil Service in 1912.[95] Anticipating objections from India, Crewe told the Viceroy Hardinge that he wanted MacDonald in as the 'most level-headed exponent of views that must

[88] Bannerjea to MacDonald, 8 Feb, 11 March, 26 May, 21 Dec 1910; Basu to MacDonald, 21 Dec 1912, PRO 30/69/1218, NA; Wedderburn to Gokhale, 18 Aug 1910, GM 11708; Wedderburn to Gokhale, 1, 16 and 29 June and 31 Aug 1911, GM 11709; Allen to Khaparde, 26 Oct 1911, Khaparde Coll., 3.

[89] Seed to Khaparde, 28 Sept. 1911, Khaparde Coll., 3.

[90] Bannerjea to MacDonald, 5 Jan and 23 Feb 1911, Bose to MacDonald, 3 Aug 1911; Wedderburn to MacDonald, 13 and 18 Feb and 2 March 1911, Gokhale to MacDonald, 23 Feb 1911; Lajpat Rai to MacDonald, 20 April 1911; Basu to MacDonald, 21 Dec 1911, PRO 30/69/1218, NA.

[91] Morley to MacDonald, 22 Feb 1911, and Fleetwood Wilson to MacDonald, 16 March 1911, PRO 30/69/1218, NA.

[92] Nevinson Diary, 20 July 1911.

[93] Lajpat Rai to MacDonald, 24 Nov 1910 and 2 Feb 1911; MacDonald to Bannerjea, 1 Feb 1911; Gokhale to MacDonald, 23 Feb 1911, PRO 30/69/1218, NA; MacDonald to Gokhale, 3 Feb and 17 July 1911, GM 11700; Gokhale to MacDonald, 18 Aug 1911, PRO 30/69/1225, NA; Wedderburn to Gokhale, 16 March 1911, GM 11709.

[94] Wedderburn to Gokhale, 24 Aug and 7 Sep 1911, GM 11709; MacDonald to Gokhale, 6 Sep 1911, GM 11700; Gokhale to Gandhi, 3 Nov 1911, GM 11700; MacDonald to Khaparde, 3 Aug and 13 Nov 1911, Khaparde Coll., 3; Khaparde to MacDonald, 24 Oct 1911, PRO 30/69/1218, NA.

[95] Montagu to Crewe, 20 June and 11 July 1912, Crewe Papers, 18; Crewe to MacDonald, 3 July 1912, PRO 30/69/1225, NA.

be taken into account'.[96] Nevertheless, Hardinge protested on behalf of his Council that the ICS and Anglo-India regarded MacDonald 'with intense distrust' and disliked his nomination even more than that of Gokhale.[97] When MacDonald made some mild criticisms of the ICS in Parliament, the King protested from his quarterdeck at Cowes that he was now 'hardly fit' to be a member of the Royal Commission.[98] In reply, Crewe accepted that MacDonald was 'quite wrong', but argued that it was desirable to include men with these views in order to dispel them.[99]

Congress leaders were pleased by MacDonald's appointment, hoping he would use it to attack the autocratic and alien bureaucracy that ruled their lives.[100] However, as before, MacDonald positioned himself above the struggle. He found the experience of the gathering of evidence in India frustrating: 'merely *ex parte*—accusations and counter-accusations'.[101] Montagu, touring India himself, was disappointed when he met members of the Commission in Bombay. The trouble with MacDonald, he noted in his diary, was that he was 'very easily impressed with his latest surroundings'. In consequence, 'he has been as carefully muzzled and watched by Sly [one of the other Commission members] as a Rugby three-quarter is marked by his opponents'. MacDonald had become 'a child in the hands of the ICS who realise his extraordinary vanity, his intellectual dishonesty and his refusal to modify his views by evidence'.[102] The Commission soon divided over the question of whether to accept the Congress demand, pushed by Gokhale, that Indian Civil Servants should be recruited on the basis of a simultaneous examination in both Britain and India. The officials feared this would assist clever natives to posts at the expense of British candidates, Indian 'families of position' and 'men of character'. They therefore preferred promotion from within the provincial civil services,

[96] Crewe to Hardinge, 4 and 16 July 1912, Crewe Papers, 18; Crewe to Hardinge, 12 July 1912, Hardinge Papers, 118.

[97] Hardinge to Crewe, 5 and 12 July 1912, Crewe Papers 18; Hardinge to Crewe, 11 July and 2 Aug 1912, Hardinge Papers, 118; Hardinge to Chirol, 7 and 19 Aug 1912, Hardinge Papers, 92; Crewe to Islington, 19 Aug 1912, Crewe Papers 18.

[98] *Hansard,* 5th ser., 30 July and 6 Aug 1912, v.41, cols.1919–26, 2922–4; Knollys to Crewe, 3 Aug 1912, Crewe Papers, 18.

[99] Crewe to Knollys, 5 Aug 1912, Crewe Papers, 18.

[100] Basu to MacDonald, 1 Aug 1912, MacDonald Papers, PRO 30/69/1225, NA; Wedderburn to Basu, 10 March 1913, GM 11709.

[101] MacDonald to Reed, 16 Jan 1913, PRO 30/69/1218, NA.

[102] Montagu Diary, 1 and 8 March 1913, Montagu Papers (Cambridge), A52/10.

on the basis of proven reliability, and a requirement that new Indian applicants be approved by existing members of the Service or by reputable schools. The chairman, Lord Islington, proposed a compromise by which there would be quotas for British and Indian candidates, with separate curricula and examinations in India and Britain, but with a longer period of training in common thereafter, and a second stage of selection at the end.[103] However, a separate examination was disliked by Gokhale on the grounds that it would create a two-tier service, and opposed by the imperialist wing on the grounds that it would not prove a test of character.[104] MacDonald publicly backed the Indian demand for simultaneous examinations, although Montagu and his fellow Commissioners suspected that, disappointed by the quality of the Indian candidates, he privately favoured a separate examination in India.[105] This became clearer as the Commission's work proceeded: by the time of its second visit to India in 1913 MacDonald was, according to the Viceroy, 'extremely anti-Indian'.[106] He had become, the Commission secretary wrote, 'very ducal out here'.[107] MacDonald disliked the simultaneous examination because it set no floor to the number of successful British candidates and he believed such a floor was necessary until India became self-governing. Indianising the executive must wait for Indianising of the legislature, he wrote, since 'the faculty to administer well comes after that of forming opinion and expressing it.'[108] MacDonald, therefore, to the dismay of Gokhale, supported the Islington compromise.[109] It was, he wrote, 'far more important . . . that . . . [Indian] recruits should be good than that they should, for the moment, be numerous'.[110] He also failed to back up the Congress leaders' demand for equal pay for Indian and British members of the ICS. He had, as Chirol, another Commission member, reported delightedly to the Viceroy, 'vindicated the privileged position

---

[103] Islington's scheme, 19 May 1913, PRO 30/69/1225, NA; Chirol to Hardinge, 6 June 1913, Hardinge Papers, 93.

[104] Fisher Diary, 25 April 1913, Fisher Papers, 194.

[105] Chirol to Hardinge, 8 May 1913, Hardinge Papers, 93; Montagu Diary, 1 and 8 March 1913.

[106] Hardinge to Crewe, 11 Dec 1913, Hardinge Papers, 119.

[107] Montagu Butler to Ann Butler, 29 Jan 1914, Montagu Butler Coll., MSS Eur F225/2.

[108] J. Ramsay MacDonald, *The Government of India* (London, 1919), 110.

[109] Fisher to Mrs Fisher, 11 June 1913, Fisher Papers, 202; Wedderburn to Gokhale, 24 and 29 Sep 1914, GM 11709; MacDonald Diary, 16 and 21 Oct 1914.

[110] *Royal Commssion on the Public Services in India: Report of the Commissioners*, v.1 (Cd 8382) 1916, 121, 239, 391–3.

to be assigned to the I.C.S.'[111] These responses reflected MacDonald's dislike of Anglicised Indians, whom he regarded as 'neither Oriental nor Occidental. . . . neither at home in India nor in England'.[112]

A fourth and different perspective was offered by the indefatigable Webb partnership. The Webbs visited India for four months in 1911–12 as part of a wider Asian tour.[113] Like MacDonald and Hardie, they were shocked at the incompetence of British officialdom. Most of the British officials were second-raters sent to India because they could not hold down decent jobs at home.[114] Even 'men of capacity but without professional zeal' managed to 'go to seed' in India, as they gave way to the worst sins in the Fabian commandment: 'slackness' and 'lounging'.[115] Indeed, the Webbs, in common with many other intelligent, liberal-minded visitors to India, felt greater affinity with the colonised than with the colonisers. The British community, they noted in frustration, would only discuss tennis, dances and polo, while their Indian hosts were keen to debate public affairs, art, philosophy and religion, all regular topics around the Fabian dining-table.[116] Most of the British officials they met were, they believed, comically unaware of their own inferiority to those they governed.[117] This, for the Webbs, was the root of the Indian problem:

[A] stupid people find themselves governing an intellectual aristocracy—the explanation being. . . that the *Average man of the British race*, is far superior to the *Average man* of the Indian peoples. Until the average has been raised the aristocracy of India will be subject to the mediocrity of Great Britain—with the melancholy result of aloofness and disaffection on the part of the honourable Indians, and clever servile duplicity on the part of the dishonourable Indians.[118]

'Three months acquaintance', Sidney wrote on the journey home, 'has greatly increased our estimate of the Indians, and greatly lessened our

[111] Chirol to Hardinge, 31 July 1914, Hardinge Papers, 93; Fisher Diary, 26 Feb 1913, Fisher Papers, 194; Sidney Webb to Gokhale, 10 March 1912, GM 11708; Sidney Webb to Gokhale, 13 July 1913, GM 11702.

[112] *Hansard*, 30 July 1912, 5th ser., v.41, cols.1919–26.

[113] Niraja Gopal Jayal (ed.), *Sidney and Beatrice Webb: Indian Diary* (Oxford, 1987). See also J. M. Winter, 'The Webbs and the Non-white World: A Case of Socialist Racialism', *Journal of Contemporary History*, 9/1 (1974), 181–92.

[114] Beatrice Webb's Diary, 8–10 April 1912, Passfield Coll.

[115] Ibid. 11 Feb 1912.   [116] Ibid. 9–12 March 1912.

[117] Ibid. 16–25 April 1912.   [118] Ibid. 8–10 April 1912.

admiration for, and our trust in, this Government of officials.' The ICS carried out its own ideals well enough, but 'its ideals are still those of 1840'. Its members were 'intellectually "individualists", vaguely remembering the political economy textbooks that they crammed up twenty years before!' '[Their] conception of government is to put down internal war, brigandage and violent crime; decide civil suits and maintain order, and for the rest to leave people alone.'[119] But the Webbs did not consider that leaving people alone was an adequate solution to India's vast social problems. Accordingly, they proposed 'a bold policy of Government exploitation'. Besides its outmoded ideals, the main problem for the Government of India was the inelasticity of its revenue. The Hindu joint family stood in the way of death duties and income taxes, the consumption of luxuries was too low to make taxing them worthwhile, and home opinion precluded raising tariffs. This left the Government dependent on good harvests, which, as Sidney Webb told Gokhale, was a 'real stumbling block when Government would like to be progressive'.[120] However, there remained 'the resource of profitable Government enterprise'.

We cannot help thinking that it would be well for the Government of India to turn over a new leaf—to go in for tobacco and spirit Government monopolies, take over the railways and work them on a unified system for public ends, to put capital—perhaps attracting it out of native hoards by a 'patriotic national loan'—into the more complete and more rapid development of its 240,000 square miles of forest, to start Government factories for matches, for paper, for rope and string and what not . . . [121]

Grand schemes of this kind raised the question of the capacity of the state to support them. For state action on a modern scale in the vastness of India, the Webbs held, the whole community needed to broaden its concepts of social purpose and a small army of experts and bureaucrats would be required. The Webbs believed that, in principle, India might be '*more* adapted for collectivist enterprise by the Gov[ernmen]t (national, provincial or municipal) than for private capitalist enterprise on individualistic lines.'[122] The caste system, with all its faults, at least ensured that responsibilities were readily accepted by all the members of the community. However, the Hindu conception

---

[119] Beatrice Webb's Diary, 4 Feb and 16–25 April 1912.
[120] Sidney Webb to Gokhale, 10 March 1912, GM 11708.
[121] Beatrice Webb's Diary, 4 Feb 1912.
[122] Sidney Webb to Gokhale, 10 March 1912.

of the state as no more than the custodian of traditional ways of life was clearly highly unsuitable for the purposes of a secular, democratic and interventionist state.

It therefore seemed unlikely to the Webbs that political and social progress could be achieved quickly in India, partly because Hindus were untroubled by poverty and inattentive to material well-being, and partly because their fixed hierarchies of caste hampered collective action and active citizenship beyond the small scale of the village community.[123] '[T]he Hindu', wrote Beatrice, 'is an idealist, but alas! for his political efficiency, his ideals are "all over the place" and frequently he lacks the capacity to put them into practice—he can discover neither the means nor work at them with unswerving persistency'.[124] Associative life was restricted by the insolubility of traditional, religious alignments, and there was no real equivalent to the local bodies which gave expression to mutual obligations and civic identities in Britain. Without the framework of British rule, therefore, the modernising aspirations of educated Indians would be swamped by the incompetence, laziness and incorrigible religiosity of the mass of the population. India's leaders were, the Webbs wrote, too often 'dragged down by a multitude of lower castes—embedded in a population that seems strangely childish in intellect and undisciplined in conduct.'[125]

The Muslim community seemed no more promising. The Webbs thought the Muslims had a 'constitutional contempt for popular government', and merely wished to see the British remain in order to keep down the Hindus.[126] The Muslim teachers they met in the United Provinces and the North West Frontier Province were 'honest and pious men, no doubt, but obviously of the most narrow-minded and feeble type', cramming their small pupils' heads with Urdu and theology rather than social science and western medicine. 'These young citizens of the Oriental Empire', the Webbs wrote, 'were not learning anything that could be useful to them as independent members of a self governing State.'[127] As a result, even the educated Muslims were 'servile in dependence on the British Government, and horribly conscious (in spite of claiming to be a ruling race) of inability to organise or initiate or maintain anything without Government aid'.[128]

---

[123] Beatrice Webb's Diary, 10 Jan 1912.
[124] Ibid. 16–25 April 1912.   [125] Ibid. 16–25 April 1912.
[126] Beatrice Webb to Lady Betty Balfour, 28 Jan 1912, Passfield Coll., 2/4/F.
[127] Beatrice Webb's Diary, 11–16 Jan 1912, 9–12 March 1912.
[128] Ibid. 6–8 and 9–12 March 1912.

Finding a class of modernising experts was scarcely easier. The political leaders proved something of a disappointment. The Webbs attended the session of Congress that was to have been chaired by MacDonald, but found it rather a 'frost': poorly attended and listless.[129] Part of the problem was that the westernising of even the educated politicians was not deep enough. '[T]heir family, their caste, and their religion . . . are still the threefold centre of their life in spite of a perpetual striving to take their part in . . . European political life.'[130] Unlike the Japanese the Webbs had met earlier in the tour, Congress leaders were building their movement upon traditional loyalties rather than trying to educate on western lines. Determining to raise a popular movement as the means of ousting the British, they had fostered an 'extraordinary recrudescence of religious Hinduism'. 'The only thing to counteract the disintegrating effect of caste exclusiveness', wrote Beatrice, 'is the sacredness of the cow & appeals to the amazing superstitious mysticism of simple-minded Hindu cultivators.'[131] Worse still, Congress was unsympathetic to the social and economic needs of India. Government was to them a 'hostile force': they had 'almost a contempt for organisation and a dislike for administration—no real interest in the problems of government apart from the sentiment of Home Rule'. They were 'all individualists at heart, and think our craving after governmental efficiency wholly disproportionate to its value'.[132] This 'cripples them in political programme [sic], because they are always urging retrenchment'.[133] In the Webbs' eyes, the nationalists were just as behind in their reading as the officials they sought to replace: 'two generations' behind contemporary English thinking. 'You will not get on far until you can induce the Government of India to become *more rich*', Sidney advised Gokhale. Far from trying to reduce the Home Charges and cut salaried posts and taxation, '[y]ou ought to be aiming at *doubling* the Gov[ernmen]t expenditure'.[134]

It seemed inevitable, therefore, that the British would have to take the lead in creating the conditions of civil society. The Webbs were especially taken by the administrator Hope Simpson, chosen by the Government of India, presumably after careful thought, to guide them. Hope Simpson seemed 'almost ideal as an administrator over an alien

[129] Beatrice Webb to Lady Courtney, 28 Dec 1911, Passfield Coll., 2/4/E.
[130] Beatrice Webb's Diary, 4 Jan 1912.
[131] Beatrice Webb to Lady Betty Balfour, 28 Jan 1912.
[132] Beatrice Webb's Diary, 4 Jan 1912.   [133] Ibid. 16–25 April 1912.
[134] Sidney Webb to Gokhale, 10 March 1912.

race'. 'Tall and muscular, with a strong but kindly face, splendid nerve and health, a genuine love of guiding and serving other people, he is', wrote Beatrice, 'the exact opposite of the bureaucrat.'[135] To work with officials like Simpson, the Webbs therefore tried to identify groups sufficiently indigenous to appeal to a wide range of educated Indians, but sufficiently open to western influence to develop the public spirit they believed necessary for popular democracy to work in Indian conditions. They found themselves drawn to the Arya Samaj, the movement which was the dominant force in Congress politics in the Punjab.[136] The Aryas had dedicated themselves to reforming the superstitious caste prejudices of Hinduism by insistence on the authority of a single text: the Vedas. As such it seemed to Sidney a kind of 'Vedic Protestantism', which would contest the ritual of Hinduism while preserving its spiritual content.[137] This was very much a first step, for India was still a long way off the 'Higher Criticism' of rationalism. In its main exposition, Swami Dayanand Saraswati's *The Light of Truth*, Sidney found 'the same combination of intellectual subtlety, wide culture, with an almost childish lack of sense of perspective or of scientific critical faculty, that is so common among the Hindu gentlemen whom we have met.'[138] But a first step in breaking down Hindu orthodoxy might best be made by something 'equally dogmatic and exclusive—faith in the absolute inspiration of the Vedas'.[139] In the fullness of time, dependence on the infallibility of even one book would repel the intellectual Hindu, and religion would decline.[140] The Arya Samaj also appealed to the Webbs because it was at the forefront of practical social reform. '[T]he whole argument of the book', Sidney wrote, 'is against political agitation *until the Hindus have made themselves fit for it by a purification of their religion and an advance in personal character—in truthfulness, in public spirit, in energetic industry.*'[141]

The Webbs' search for 'the healthy, virile and free service of religious orders, self-dedicated to the progress of the race' also drew them to the Servants of India.[142] Gokhale had established this to train men for public service, and the Webbs were much struck by his 'political

[135] Beatrice Webb's Diary, 28 Jan 1912.
[136] On the Arya Samaj, see N. Gerald. Barrier, 'The Arya Samaj and Congress Politics in the Punjab, 1894–1908', *Journal of Asian Studies*, 26/3 (1967), 363–79; K. W. Jones, *Arya Dharm: Hindu Consciousness in 19th-Century Punjab* (Delhi, 1976).
[137] Beatrice Webb's Diary, 29 Feb–3 March 1912.   [138] Ibid.
[139] Ibid.   [140] Ibid.   [141] Ibid. Underlining in original here italicised.
[142] Beatrice Webb's Diary, 16–25 April 1912.

sagacity and calm statesmanship'. They became very sympathetic to his view that Indian nationalism had to be remade gradually through social and educational reform, self-education and self-discipline.[143] However, Gokhale resisted the Webbs' suggestions for developing forestry, railways, canals and government workshops 'on the ground that without increased popular control and a change of spirit, any such increase in Government action would only be used against the Hindoos'.[144] The problem with simply Indianising the administration was that the Indian officials were never given real power or authority, tended to become Anglicised and then opposed Indian aspirations more than the English. The Webbs were certainly contemptuous of the Indianised civil servants they met, none of whom measured up to Hope Simpson. The Hindu junior was cowardly, too close to the Indian population and wrote inaccurate 'whitewashing' reports designed to impress public opinion. '[I]t was almost inconceivable', the Webbs wrote, 'that he should step into Hope Simpson's place without a gradual deterioration of all branches of administration.'[145] The Muslim was not much better: '*very* slack' in his work, vain and unpatriotic, while the Indians on Hope Simpson's District Board showed 'no initiative or independence' and left the ideas to him.[146] These Anglicised creations were clearly inadequate for the Webbs' purposes.

Thus while Hardie wished to anchor the Congress elite in the interests of peasant cultivators, the Webbs sought to find ways to *detach* the aristocracy of intellect from the uncivilized masses. It did not matter to the Webbs that 'these five hundred highly educated, widely cultured and usually travelled gentlemen' were 'not representative of the 250,000,000 of peasant cultivators, petty retailers, jobbing craftsmen, artisans and labourers of India', for 'they do not claim to represent them, any more than an elected Legislature of rich men and bourgeoisie resembles the millions of wage earning labourers in whose name it legislates'. They were to gain their authority not, as some increasingly chose to do, by appeals to the religious communalism and caste prejudices of the Hindu villager, but through close alliance with sympathetic modernising British officials. Social and economic reforms might thereby be 'made to appear essentially "Nationalist", and might even be made to seem to have been inspired and demanded by the Nationalists themselves'.[147] If the British

---

[143] Beatrice Webb's Diary, 8–10 April 1912.   [144] Ibid.
[145] Beatrice Webb's Diary, 28 Jan 1912.   [146] Ibid.
[147] Ibid. 4 Feb 1912.

would 'recognise this new governing class—and would gradually take them into [their] confidence, with a view to making them party to the Government of India, then the British race might pride themselves on having been the finest race of school masters, as well as the most perfect builders of an Empire'.[148]

Although, in discussions of this kind, the political development of India was usually claimed to be decades, or sometimes centuries, behind that of the west, it is very evident that a great deal of what these five critics suggested projected on to an Indian canvas very contemporary and domestic concerns. 'The working men of England had come through their own experience to believe whole-heartedly in representation', MacDonald argued in 1909. 'This was the true secret of political progress [for] today in India exactly the same condition existed as had been experienced by English working men before the advent of the Labour Party.'[149] For MacDonald, participation in the councils would be for Congress what parliamentary work was for the British Labour Party, a necessary apprenticeship. He had, after all, visited and written his first book on India between his resignation from the National Administrative Council of the ILP and the publication of the 'green manifesto' denouncing the Labour Party's support of the Liberal Government. It is unsurprising, therefore, to find that he favoured much the same long slog of institution-building and compromise in India that he advocated at home. The elements each disliked in Indian politics—Hardie the pusillanimous Moderates and MacDonald the flamboyant Bengali impossiblists—were in one guise surrogates for their respective domestic opponents: Lib–Labs and syndicalists.

 This is perhaps clearest in their attitude to the provision that the Morley–Minto reforms made for the opening-up of work on local councils. In Hardie's view, it was most important that the British should be generous in the powers they conceded to the councils and that these powers should be subject to proper popular control.[150] MacDonald, in contrast, stressed that Indians could not excuse themselves from council work on the grounds that the powers conceded were insufficient.[151] There was natural momentum in the reforms, for 'authorities that have to be consulted must in time become authorities

[148] Ibid. 16–25 April 1912.   [149] *India*, 3 Dec 1909, 25 June 1915.
[150] Hardie, *India*, 104.   [151] *India*, 24 Dec 1909.

whose advice has to be followed'.[152] The Webbs were also keen that Indian politicians should begin with work in the local government arena. For Congress as for the British working class it was a necessary training-ground, before emergence on the national stage.[153] Council work would also allow the expression of India's own internal tendencies and forces, rather than the artificial unity provoked by the British, and thereby lead to the highly desirable emergence of party politics. 'There is no party politics in India at present', MacDonald wrote, 'only the opposition of the official and the non-official . . . This is all for the bad. But the reforms give hope that political conflict on new lines will arise. These will establish the conditions under which an extension of Reform in a Parliamentary direction will not only be necessary but desirable.' 'There will', he predicted, 'be as great a split in the old Liberal movement in India, represented by the Congress . . . as there has been in home politics owing to the rise of the Labour Party.'[154]

For Hardie, local councils were valued because they would bring Congress leaders face-to-face with the social problems of the village poor, and make them responsive to local needs and democratically accountable. This was why he wished to build self-government on the foundation of the *panchayat*. For the Webbs, however, the purpose of the reforms was different again. For them, working with the British would enable India's natural leaders—the 'aristocracy of intellect'—to acquire the technical expertise to run a modern state. This was not dissimilar to the tactics of permeation of the elite that the Webbs had employed at home. Where Hardie insisted on grassroots democracy, the Webbs saw little necessity for involving the peasantry. Sidney Webb told the students of the London School of Economics that 'India was not, and could not possibly be governed by the democracy of India', which was seen, as the working classes were at home, as an ignorant drag on the energies of the elite.[155] These ideals, projected on to India, inevitably guided them to certain allies and projects. What each most admired in the mirror of Indian nationalism was the reflection they saw of their own ideals. At

---

[152] MacDonald, *Awakening*, 269.
[153] Jayal, Introduction to Webbs, *Indian Diary*, pp. xxxix; Sidney Webb's introduction to John Matthai, *Village Government in British India* (London, 1915), ix–xviii.
[154] MacDonald, *Awakening*, 270–1.   [155] *India*, 6 Dec 1912, 22 Aug 1913.

the heart of the problem, however, was confusion over the marks of authenticity. Indian nationalism seemed to most western observers too narrow, too shallow and excessively derivative. Yet efforts to deepen and broaden it, or to 'Indianise' it, inevitably made it look even less familiar.

4

The Decline, Revival and Fall of the British Committee of Congress, 1915–22

The First World War promised to transform strategic opportunities for British anti-imperialists. Britain's need to mobilise India's resources for war put strain on existing political relationships in India, demanding a degree of cooperation from Indian politicians which, in the absence of responsible government, they had little reason to supply unconditionally. At the same time, the war emergency seemed to the Empire's rulers to justify the control and suppression of political activity in India, especially if it seemed likely to disrupt the war effort. As well as restrictions on civil liberties, war also meant price and tax rises, shortages and requisitioning. These were grievances traceable to government action, which an alien administration unused to consultation and unwilling to share power found it hard to explain. They provided a pool of new recruits for nationalism. The war also exposed the operations of the Government of India to closer scrutiny from London than before, with the possibility of unwelcome interference should it fail to prove its capacity to supply funds, troops and materiel for the war effort, especially in Mesopotamia, where the provision of soldiers, grain and fodder was largely its responsibility. Indeed, the demands of war made imperialists more open than they usually were to the possibility of offering constitutional concessions as the price of such support, if not in wartime itself then promised at its end.

This created strong incentives for renewed efforts to join up the Indian and British ends of the movement. In April 1916, after protracted negotiations sponsored by the leader of the Theosophist movement, Annie Besant, Tilak and his allies returned to Congress, ending the eight years' rupture between Moderates and Extremists. In their provincial bases, Tilak and Besant set up Home Rule Leagues, with the aim of rallying support for self-government in areas hitherto untouched by Congress politics and among villagers whose livelihoods were being adversely affected by the war. The Moderates, weakened by the deaths of Gokhale and Mehta, were unable to prevent this and at Lucknow in December 1916, Tilak confirmed his capture of Congress with resolutions demanding self-government and more radical methods of winning it. The Home Rule agitation was eventually repressed by the *raj*, which proceeded to use its wartime powers to ban political meetings and newspapers and to intern Annie Besant herself in June 1917.[1]

Both Tilak and Besant planned agitation in Britain, exploiting opportunities such as Besant's arrest and the Commission set up in 1917 to investigate military and supply failures in Mesopotamia.[2] Besant initially wanted Wedderburn to run the English Section of her Home Rule League alongside the British Committee.[3] But Wedderburn was now ill, and the British Committee was hardly meeting and financially almost bankrupt.[4] It had, in any case, lost its contacts with the Liberal Government on the formation of the Coalition Government in 1915—a 'paralysing blow', according to Wedderburn[5]—and, still Moderate in its own views, reluctant to publicise the new turn in Indian politics. Wedderburn therefore advised Besant's disciple Emily Lutyens to form an organisation of women, with the British Committee operating in a consultative capacity. However, when Lutyens attempted this, she concluded that 'women, having no political power could not accomplish anything very definite'.[6] Besant therefore ordered that a

---

[1] Hugh F. Owen, 'Towards Nationwide Agitation and Organisation: The Home Rule Leagues, 1915–18', in D. A. Low (ed.), *Soundings in Modern South Asian History* (London, 1968); 'Mrs. Annie Besant and the Rise of Political Activity in South India, 1914–1919' in his *The Indian Nationalist Movement, c.1912–22: Leadership, Organisation and Philosophy* (New Delhi, 1990).

[2] Tilak to Khaparde, 25 and 30 March 1917, Khaparde Coll., 2; Kelkar to Sastri, 13 Feb 1917, SC 176; Malaviya to Sastri, 26 June 1917, SC 178; Sastri to Vaze, 16 Aug 1917, SC 180.

[3] Sastri to Servants of India Society, 25 Sept 1915, SC 138.

[4] The Committee only met four times in 1915, and not at all from 5 Oct 1915 to 9 May 1916 (British Committee Minute Books). For evidence of financial weakness, see Annual Reports of British Committee, 1912–1916, copies in Besant Papers, 6; W. Douglas Hall, 'The British Committee and *India*', Feb 1918, Minute Book, v.7. Rs. 48,000 [£3,200] had been promised in the form of guaranteed subscriptions to *India*. By November 1915, Rs. 23,485 [£1566] had been received. For complaints about funding, see Wedderburn, 'Work in India and England', *New India*, 26 April 1915; Open Letter to Congress, 12 April 1916, Besant Papers, 6.

[5] Weddernburn to Sastri, 10 June and 8 July 1915, SC 122 and 127.

[6] Lutyens to Besant, 19 and 25 March 1915, Besant Papers, 13.

separate organisation, the British Auxiliary of the Indian Home Rule League, should be established under the direction of Theosophist and Labour activist John Scurr and Besant's old associate from her days in London politics, George Lansbury, later joined by the Theosophist (and Besant's solicitor in her numerous legal actions) David Graham Pole.[7]

The British Auxiliary was a much more active body than the British Committee. It drew on the techniques that Besant had herself developed in agitation on questions such as secularism and birth control in the 1870s and 1880s, as well as in the Home Rule Leagues: all-year-round organisation, mass meetings, petitions and high profile court cases. It also established useful horizontal alliances with other movements: Theosophy, which brought numerous monied and influential recruits with an interest in India, but also many of the organisations dedicated to socialism, democratic control and the protection of civil liberties which the war had thrown up and which had responded vigorously to Besant's arrest.[8] A police search of the headquarters of the London branch of the Besant League in November 1917 revealed to the authorities the extent and success of its meetings.[9] Lansbury asked Pole, now in India, to tell Besant that she would find 'a good solid Home Rule movement to welcome her when next she comes home'.[10]

Tilak, lacking Besant's connections, did not directly recruit British supporters, but in July 1917 dispatched his lawyer, Joseph Baptista, to London, also with instructions to make contact with Lansbury and other Labour Party activists. The ILP network proved a useful means of spreading the news of the new radicalism in India. Baptista gave a series of speeches and lectures in ILP strongholds in Yorkshire, Wales and the industrial towns of northern England. His speeches made connections between wartime illiberalism in Britain and in India, and sought to reassure Labour audiences that India's inferior cotton goods could not compete with Lancashire, but that free India would, by ending the drain and enhancing its purchasing power, actually buy more Lancashire cotton than before. Baptista also did his best to define the new nationalism in ways that would appeal. There was no class distinction in India, he insisted, because 'every man and every caste is perfectly equal' and 'every village is a republic' in 'a socialistic system which has lasted

[7] Besant to Lutyens, 28 May 1916, quoted in Emily Lutyens, *Candles in the Sun* (London, 1957), 80; Metropolitan Police Report, 7 Nov 1918, HPA, May 1918, 36–54.

[8] DCI Report, 22 Sept 1917, HPB, Sep 1917, 239–43.

[9] Metropolitan Police report, 7 Nov 1918.

[10] Lansbury to Pole, 24 Nov 1917, Pole Papers (Borthwick), 1.

2,200 years'.[11] The ILP members pressed him on the development of socialism and trade unionism, to be told that although there was little formal trade unionism in India, workers enjoyed 'instinctive sympathy' with one another, and—quite absurdly—that there was 'not a single prominent man in India who is not acquainted with the whole of the literature of the ILP'. Within a short time, Baptista had managed to address labour organisations representing 200,000 workers, which, he enthusiastically told Tilak, meant 200,000 converts, all 'pledged to support us'.[12]

At the end of 1917, Scurr tried to arrange at short notice for Baptista and Henry Polak (Gandhi's lieutenant in his South African campaigns) to address the forthcoming Labour Party Conference. Presiding at the Congress session at Calcutta in December, Besant successfully moved that they be empowered to attend and convey the movement's gratitude to Labour.[13] At the Conference the following month, at the suggestion of Baptista, Hull Trades and Labour Council put forward a resolution calling for Home Rule for India in twenty years.[14] However, radical Indian students from Cambridge pressed successfully for a more far-reaching amendment simply asserting India's right to self-government and to a status equal to that of the Dominions. Baptista himself failed to arrive in time to speak, so late on the final day of the Conference, Polak made a brief address as part of a long procession of fraternal delegates. The amended resolution was passed, but with no real discussion.[15] Nevertheless, Baptista reported to Congress that their reception had been 'spontaneous and enthusiastic'. Labour was 'very certain' to come to power 'in the not too distant future', perhaps even at the forthcoming election.[16] Scurr told Besant that relations should now be cemented through a reciprocal invitation for a fraternal delegate from the Labour Party to attend the next Congress.[17]

Scurr's invitation was circulated to the All-India Congress Committee. Of the 34 members who replied, all but one were in favour of

[11] Police Reports, 3 and 9 Dec 1917, HPB, May 1918, 158.
[12] *Mahratta,* 6 and 20 Jan 1918; Baptista to *Kesari,* 17 Dec 1917, intercepted, HPB, May 1918, 160.
[13] Zaidi, *Encyclopaedia,* vii, 254.
[14] Kelkar to Besant undated, and Clarke to Besant, undated, but late 1917, AICC 1/1917; 'Activities of the Home Rule for India League', undated, HPB, May 1918, 160.
[15] Labour Party, *Report of Annual Conference* 1918, 138.
[16] Baptista to INC Secretaries, 9 Feb 1918, AICC 4/1918; *Servant of India,* 11 April 1918.
[17] Scurr to Besant, 11 Feb 1918, Besant Papers, 14b.

strengthening the connection with Labour, in the belief that it was a growing force which had proved its sincerity through its conference vote. However, there were also fears of losing contacts with other, non-Labour supporters and in giving the anti-Labour authorities in India and Britain an additional excuse to hinder Congress work. Some respondents also worried that as soon as economic questions arose Labour support would ebb away unless Congress adopted a socialist programme.[18] Indeed, there was some evidence of this at the ILP conference in April 1918, where Indian expatriate and ILP member Shapurji Saklatvala and Scurr combined a resolution calling for 'a measure of self-government for the Indian people' with one which demanded legislation to improve industrial conditions in India, including the nationalisation of basic industries.[19] Moreover, despite the Party Conference vote, Labour's experts remained to be convinced. This was made clear in the General Election later the same year, when Labour's proposals, made in a pamphlet drafted for Sidney Webb's Advisory Committee on International Questions by the architect of dyarchy Lionel Curtis, fell squarely behind the Montagu–Chelmsford proposals, which had been announced in July and which Congress regarded as inadequate. Only a limited portion of provincial self-government was feasible at present. The commitment to an eventual transfer of power remained, but the pace was slowed to that favoured by the Liberal reformers. Where the 1918 Party Conference resolution had stated that 'the time [had] arrived' for dominion status, the Curtis proposals were more modest. India was still too divided and undeveloped for self-government to work: '[The] number of people who could understand the meaning of a vote is very small. To grant full responsible government outright, as in Canada and Australia, would place the government in the hands of a very few.' Nation building must come first. All that was offered for the present was the dyarchy of Montagu–Chelmsford and more vigorous scrutiny of the ICS at Westminster.[20]

Indian politicians themselves were divided were in their response to the Montagu–Chelmsford proposals along lines of ideology and provincial

[18] Sastri to Aiyar, 18 April 1918, AICC 4/1918; Sastri to Vaze, 19 April 1918, SC 214.
[19] ILP, *Report of Annual Conference*, 1918, 80–1.
[20] LPACIQ Memo. 26, Sept 1918, LPA.

self-interest. A Special Congress in August 1918 expressed its dissatisfaction with the refusal to make concessions at the centre and to reserve
certain subjects at the provincial level; and the regular session at Delhi
in December called for immediate self-government in the provinces.
However, Congress leaders in provinces where the prospects for winning
power under the reforms were good wanted to take what was offered.
In November 1918, a number of the senior Moderates left Congress
altogether to form the National Liberal Federation.

As before the war, control of London was a significant resource in
these battles. The British Committee, which wanted Congress to accept
the reforms, suggested a lobbying effort based on 'ripe experience of
constitutional practices, combined with calm judgement' to be provided
by British experts, and a sober, moderate Indian ambassador to negotiate
as Gokhale had done with Morley.[21] Its annual report for 1917 had
hardly made any mention of the important political developments
in India, instead calling on Tilak and Besant to exercise restraint, a
stance which led to 'much dissatisfaction' on the All-India Congress
Committee.[22] The British Committee's supporters tried to insist that
for the AICC even to discuss the activities of the British Committee
would be to act *ultra vires*. The Committee was, Wacha wrote, 'an
independent body, in no way elected by the Congress . . . a free body
of sympathetic Englishmen trying to do their best for India'.[23] But
when the Congress Secretaries wrote to request payment of arrears from
the Bombay Provincial Congress Committee, they were told by Tilak's
supporter Karandikar that there was deep resentment of the failure of
the British Committee to acknowledge the sacrifices of Indians or the
work of the Home Rule Leagues.[24]

Under these pressures, the Committee moved slightly in the direction
of the Tilak and Besant position, trying to find a basis for cooperation
with the British Auxiliary and the Home Rule Leagues.[25] But it was
not easy: in May and June 1918, Evan Cotton wrote frankly of his
dislike of this new turn in British Committee politics. The Committee
found it 'humiliating to persist in walking with a man who is hard

---

[21] William Wedderburn, 'The Indian Claim', 13 May 1917, Minute Book, v.7;
Wedderburn to Sastri, 15 April 1915, SC 109; Wedderburn to Sastri, 31 May 1915, SC
120.
[22] Minute Book, v.7, 12 March 1918.
[23] Wacha to Aiyar, 8 Feb 1918, AICC 5/18, and 24 June 1918, AICC 3/18.
[24] Karandikar to Aiyar, 6 May 1918, AICC 3/18.
[25] Minute Book, v.7, 26 Feb, 12 March, 9 and 16 April 1918.

at work kicking you all the time'.[26] Polak, who had replaced Cotton as editor of *India*, was hardly less troubled than Cotton by the 'silly antics of the H.R.Leagues'. 'I feel more and more', he wrote, 'that Mrs Besant is making successive blunders ... What is the use of all this abuse and hysteria? It is handicapping immensely our work here, for it is alienating from us the good-will of friends of long standing.'[27] In June 1918, the Committee wrote to Congress to ask for its verdict on the Montagu–Chelmsford scheme, to indicate its own desire to campaign for it, and for funds to carry our propaganda in its support.[28] It pleaded that the Committee did not think that the Montagu–Chelmsford proposals represented the final solution of the Indian problem and promised reorganisation and improvements in its propaganda work.[29] The Congress secretaries replied that there was widespread dissatisfaction with the reforms.[30] There were fresh demands that Congress funds should go instead to a Press agency under its own control, or to the British Auxiliary.[31] The Committee secretary, W. D. Hall, predicted that the Extreme faction, 'notoriously hostile' to the Committee's work, might withhold funds, but that if it did so, the Committee would side with the Moderates. 'I can hardly bring myself to believe', he wrote, 'that the majority of our members will assent to be dragged at the heels of the Tilakites and Besantines.'[32] Polak wrote to the Moderates:

With a divided Congress, in which the Moderates had control of the machinery, we could do something; but with the Extremists in control, we shall be out of touch altogether, and there is every chance of their cutting off supplies ... It is all the more necessary, if the Moderates think that their cause is a good one, that they should support an agency that is carrying on propaganda here ... It would be different if the Moderates represented a poor class of the community, but they don't. It ought not to be difficult for them to put their hands into their pockets to the tune of £2,000 ... You and those who are working with you must get to work in this affair at once.[33]

[26] Cotton to Ratcliffe, 8 May and 26 June 1918, HPD, Dec 1918, 10.
[27] Polak to Sastri, 4 July 1918, SC 235; *Servant of India*, 26 Sept 1918; DCI Report, 2 March 1918, HPB, March 1918, 399–402.
[28] Clark to Aiyar, 12 June 1918, AICC 2/1918; Minute Book, v.7, 8 July 1918.
[29] Hall to Aiyar, 7 June 1918, AICC 2/1918.
[30] Minute Book, v.7, 17 Sept 1918.
[31] See, for example, Iyer to Aiyar, 23 Aug 1918, AICC 2/1918; Minute Book, v.7, 29 Nov 1918; *New India*, 11 April 1919.
[32] Hall to Ratcliffe, 23 Aug 1918, HPD, Dec 1918, 10.
[33] Polak to Sastri, 30 Aug 1918, SC 247; Polak to Sastri, 4 Feb 1918, SC 199; Polak to Natesan, 1 and 15 Aug, 2 Oct 1918, Natesan Papers.

Polak wanted to insist on the old way of working, in which responsible British public men controlled the Committee:

[I]t is useless to expect that men of ability, position and responsibility will be prepared to join a body that may be rejected or treated with contumely, because it would, with its knowledge of affairs here and experience of the requirements and possibilities of public life in this country, refuse to be dragged at the heels of extravagance and inexperience.

The Committee, even as at present constituted, has been ignored or humiliated on more than one occasion during the last year, by one of the parties on your side. The British Auxiliary of the Home Rule League is, in its way, doing very useful work, but it is largely ignorant of Indian conditions, and its appeal is almost entirely confined to the Labour Party, whereas Indian affairs, during the next few years at least, will fall to be dealt with [by others].[34]

By this time, Tilak himself had followed Baptista to Britain to fight a libel action against Chirol and to lobby for extensions of the Montagu–Chelmsford proposals. Polak insisted that Tilak, though authorised by the Home Rule League, had no right to speak for the Congress, which was sending its own Delegation.[35] When the two met, Polak told Tilak that the demands of the Special Congress at Bombay had been 'impractical . . . and also opposed to . . . constitutional practice in this country'.[36] Polak, Tilak retorted, 'takes money from the Congress and yet uses the Congress organ ("India") to put forward a point of view opposed to that of the Congress which pays him'.[37] Tilak's hostility to the British Committee was longstanding, and cannot have been helped by its refusal to do anything to lobby for his release when he was imprisoned in Mandalay from 1909 to 1914 on the grounds that it might upset the India Office.[38] He sent a hostile report to Congress: the British Committee was in a 'moribund state' and 'either indifferent to, or . . . averse to the present Congress ideas'. Its *de facto* independence had been tolerable in the early days of Congress, but 'what was due to Wedderburn and Hume

---

[34] *Servant of India*, 3 Oct 1918.
[35] Polak to Villiers, 21 Dec 1918, in V. D. Divekar (ed.), *Lokmanya Tilak in England, 1918–19: Diary and Documents* (Pune, 1997), 214; *Mahratta*, 30 May 1920.
[36] *New India*, 11 April 1919.
[37] S. V. Bapat (ed.), *Reminiscences and Anecdotes about Lokamanya Tilak* (Poona, 1928), 29–32.
[38] Tilak to Khaparde, 1 and 29 May 1909 and Khaparde to Tilak, 6 May and 3 June 1909, in Tilak, *Samagra Lokmanya Tilaka* (7v., Pune 1974–6), vii, 709–17.

cannot be said to be due to Rutherford and Clark'.[39] Congress, meeting at Delhi in December 1918, therefore empowered its delegation to bring the British Committee in line, and to put an Indian in charge of *India*. This was reinforced by the power of the purse: the normal payment of delegates' fees from the Delhi Congress was suspended and the Committee advised not to make any financial commitments until the terms of the resolution were met.[40] However, the Committee remained defiant. It was, Tilak reported furiously to India, 'hopelessly indifferent, nay, doing positive harm'. Congress should take up a 'stern attitude' and refuse money unless it fell into line.[41] When Tilak met the Committee and demanded to know whether it proposed to accept the resolutions of the Delhi Congress, he was told by Clark that Congress had 'broken its own constitutional rules' and had 'acted upon inaccurate and misleading information'.[42] The Committee insisted on its own independence and decided that until the arrival of the Congress Deputation it would only carry out propaganda in Britain for demands on which Indians were united. It had even refused to make Tilak a member, while recognising several of the dissident Moderates as former Congress Presidents.[43] Moreover, all this went on with little actual propaganda. The Government's intelligence service reported in October 1918 that the British Committee was 'almost a dead organisation, and its influence on English politics . . . negligible'. The British Auxiliary, on the other hand, was 'unquestionably the most powerful of the organisations'.[44]

Even when the official Congress Delegation arrived in May 1919, the British Committee held out for compromise, resolving to work with both the Congress Delegation and the Moderates, and inviting each of the Indian delegations to send a single observer to its meetings. These included Besant, who now argued for the acceptance of the reforms.

---

[39] Tilak to Kelkar, undated, in Divekar, *Tilak,* 196; Report to the Subjects Committee of Congress, 28 Nov 1918, Besant Papers 6; *New India,* 15 Jan 1919; *Commonweal,* 7 Feb, 21 March, 25 April and 15 Aug 1919; *Modern Review,* May 1919, 528–32 and July 1919, 30–4.

[40] Aiyar to British Committee, Minute Book, v.7, 12 Feb 1919; Patel to British Committee, May–July 1919, in Zaidi, *Encyclopaedia,* vii, 553–61; Congress Resolution 20, Dec 1918, in Zaidi, *Encyclopaedia,* vii, 404–5; Sathaye to Misra, 5 July 1919 and Misra to Sathaye, 8 July 1919, AICC 3/19.

[41] 'How we are Getting On', 9 and 16 Jan 1919, in Divekar, *Tilak,* 229, 240; Tilak to Khaparde, 16 Jan 1919, in Khaparde Coll., 2.

[42] Minute Book, v.7, 26 Feb 1919. The correspondence between Tilak and the Committee can be traced in AICC 3/1919.

[43] Minute Book, v.7, 15 Jan 1919.

[44] DCI Report, 26 Oct 1918, HPD, Dec 1918, 10.

In response, the Delegation passed a resolution calling on the British Committee to give a definite and unambiguous assurance of its loyalty to Congress. It demanded the exclusion of the members of other Indian delegations and that all twelve of its own members be given voting rights. It also offered to assume financial and editorial control of *India*, with the clear threat that funds from India would not be forthcoming unless its demands were met. The Moderate faction on the Committee tried to prevent this takeover, arguing that until the promised delegates' fees were paid, the Congress was in no position to dictate terms to the Committee.[45] However, the newspaper's Board of Directors, doubtless realising the impossibility of continuing publication without the Indian subsidy, accepted the Congress line as editorial policy, although Polak protested bitterly that it had done so under a misapprehension, and refused to change his line.[46] By a narrow margin, the British Committee itself followed suit a week later, approving the new line and forcing Polak to resign.[47] A new constitution was drawn up, against Moderate opposition, concentrating powers in the hands of Congress, and placing control of the editorship of *India* in its gift.[48] Members of the expatriate Indian community in London, hitherto a marginal presence in the British Committee, now stood for election, displacing all the Liberal old guard in the succeeding months. Among them were prominent Tilakites, such as J. M. Parikh and Edward Delgado. Sympathetic Labour MPs were also nominated. Some of the resentment of this in traditional Radical circles was evident in the editorials of Polak's replacement, the Radical lawyer Helena Normanton, who disapproved of the newly significant Indian membership on the grounds that it made it harder for the Committee to win influence in British circles.[49] Most of the former members of the British Committee who remained active now departed to set up the Indian Reform Committee, committed to supporting the Montagu–Chelmsford reforms.

Tilak had also obtained what he termed a 'bilateral contract' with the Labour Party.[50] Initially a sceptic about the value of a link with

[45] Minute Book, v.7, 30 May 1919, 2 and 6 June 1919, 4 July 1919.

[46] Minute Book, v.7, 11 July 1919; Polak Papers, MSS Brit Emp. s.372, Rhodes House, Oxford.

[47] Khaparde Diary, 12, 14 and 15 July 1919; 'How We Are Getting On', 15 and 24 July 1919 in Divekar, *Tilak*, 720–1, 729–31; *Mahratta*, 10 Aug, 3 Nov 1919 and 11 Jan 1920; *Servant of India*, 17 April and 14 Aug 1919.

[48] Minute Book, v.7, 25 July 1919.

[49] Helena Normanton, *India in England* (Delhi, 1921); *India*, 12 Dec 1920.

[50] Divekar, *Tilak*, 229, 819–20, 870, 902.

Labour,[51] Tilak had been persuaded by Baptista that it stood on the verge of electoral victory. He had arranged for a donation of £2,000 from his Home Rule League to the party's election fund.[52] 'Tilak seems to be convinced that Labour Government in Britain is a certainty within a few years', Scotland Yard reported to India. 'He has made himself as pleasant as possible to the Labour Party in the hope that on reaching power it would grant his demands. He invariably accuses the British Government in India of being capitalistic and grinding down the workers'.[53] Further financial support from Tilak, it was alleged, went to Lansbury's *Daily Herald*, complementing that already provided by Besant.[54] However, the election result disappointed Tilak. Not merely had fewer Labour candidates been returned than he had hoped, but his principal allies, including Lansbury and Henderson, had failed to get elected. Nevertheless, Wedgwood and Spoor were in Parliament and set to work forming a Parliamentary Committee on India to support the Congress campaign against the Montagu–Chelmsford proposals. To Tilak's delight, Lansbury, with Robert Williams and Bob Smillie, signed a manifesto in April 1919 calling for immediate self-government on Dominion lines.[55] The Congress Delegation also received a substantial injection of support when reports of the repressive Rowlatt legislation and the Amritsar Massacre reached London. These events, unlike the complicated details of Montagu–Chelmsford legislation, raised clear-cut civil liberties issues of a type to which Labour instinctively and loudly responded.[56] During the summer recess, Tilak and his colleagues spoke at innumerable ILP and trade union meetings. 'It is needless to say', the delegates reported home of one Welsh mining audience, 'that the audience entirely agreed with the speakers and the heckling and interrogations though amusing [were] due to the ignorance of the realities in India [and were] nowhere adverse.'[57] Tilak addressed the

[51] Speech at Calcutta 2 Jan 1907, in Aurobindo Ghose (ed.), *Speeches of B. G. Tilak* (Madras, n.d.), 43–4.
[52] Tilak to Vidwans, 27 Nov. 1918, Divekar, *Tilak*, 194; Tilak to Khaparde, 28 Nov 1918, Khaparde Coll., 2; Tilak to D. V. Gokhale, 23 Jan 1919, copy in Khaparde Coll., 1.
[53] Bombay CID Report, undated, in Divekar, *Tilak*, 202.
[54] Bombay CID Report, 5 Jan 1920, in Divekar, *Tilak*, 870; Raymond Postgate, *The Life of George Lansbury* (London, 1951), 58, 142.
[55] 'How we are Getting On' 24 April 1919, in Divekar, *Tilak*, 628–9.
[56] Speech at Anti-Rowlatt Legislation Meeting, May 23 1919, reported in *India*, May 30 1919. For Labour responses to Amritsar, see Derek Sayer, 'British Reaction to the Amritsar Massacre 1919–1920', *Past and Present*, 131 (May 1991) 130–64.
[57] *Mahratta*, 19 Oct 1919.

Labour Party's Advisory Committee twice the following month and a meeting of Labour MPs in June.

However, Annie Besant was not prepared to surrender her Labour Party connections without a struggle. Having tried unsuccessfully to get herself adopted as a Labour Party candidate at the 1918 Election, she had rejoined the party the following July, and urged her Home Rule League to link up with it.[58] Tilak worried that her superior connections in Britain might enable her to capture the party.[59] Therefore both groups carried out extensive lobbying through the summer of 1919. The result of this was that some Labour audiences, as Tilak acknowledged later, became confused about which of the many Indian delegations really represented Congress.[60] When they returned to India, there were recriminations on this score.[61] Besant, Tilak complained to the AICC, despite having been rejected by the Congress, had 'taken advantage of . . . her position as ex-President of the Congress to mislead ignorant men and women in England'. This included the Labour leaders, who were 'put in a fix' by the conflicting claims of Besant and the official Congress delegation.[62] Yet Lansbury and others still wanted to keep lines open to Besant, despite her breach with Congress, in the hope of securing united demands. The divisions between the Indian delegations came to boiling point in October 1919, when under the auspices of Besant's League, Lansbury chaired a stormy meeting at the Albert Hall. Besant had wanted to pass a resolution which supported the Montagu reforms, while calling for further advances. It was only at Lansbury's insistence that the Congress Delegation was invited at all, and when Tilak saw the resolution, he told Lansbury that it was against Congress policy. At the meeting itself, radical Indian students, backed by a dissident member of the Congress Deputation, the editor B. G. Horniman, pushed for an amendment that rejected the reforms outright. Tilak attempted to keep the meeting focussed on the official Congress demands rather than the details of the Bill, but an acrimonious correspondence followed.[63]

---

[58] *New India*, 20 July 1919.

[59] Tilak to Khaparde, 5 March 1919, Khaparde Coll., 2; DCI Reports, 28 July and 4 Aug 1919, HPB, Aug 1919, 315–19, 432–5.

[60] Speech at Madras, 17 Dec 1919, in Divekar, *Tilak,* 896.

[61] *United India*, 12 and 19 May 1920.

[62] Reply to Mrs Besant, April 1920, in Divekar, *Tilak,* 917.

[63] Reply to Mrs Besant, April 1920; *Daily Herald,* 27, 28, 30 and 31 Oct 1919; *India,* 7 Nov 1919, *Mahratta,* 14 Dec 1919.

In Parliament, Labour's representatives, Spoor and Wedgwood criticised the Bill in debates and moved a sequence of unsuccessful amendments in committee. Their main criticisms were the limited range of subjects transferred in the provinces, the lack of advance at the centre, the limitations of the franchise, and the provision of communal and special interest representation, which it was thought would foster divisions.[64] These were all in line with demands made by Congress. As the Congress leaders prepared to leave London, one of them wrote in his diary, 'Mr Henderson promised to give us all we asked when [the] Labour Party came into power'.[65] That Labour's actions, though without practical effect, had pleased Congress was evident in a special resolution at the 1919 Amritsar Congress thanking them for their support. Motilal Nehru recommended to the Congress that it should follow Labour's advice in making the most of the reforms while pressing for more.[66] The authorities noted with concern the possibility of linked-up agitation between Labour at home and Congress in India.[67]

Tilak believed the connection with Labour to be an enormously valuable one. Unlike Besant and the Moderates, who moved easily in the circles of officials, lawyers and politicians, Tilak had few British friends. It is very apparent from his reports home that for visiting Indian activists without such metropolitan connections, the work of propaganda was extremely hard. Labour's support had been simply essential. Given the internal divisions of the British Committee, it had been only owing to the publicity provided by Labour newspapers and the audiences provided by union gatherings, conferences and election rallies that he had been able to get the Congress message across. On his return to India, he told audiences of his conviction, based on the numerous resolutions of support he had solicited, that Labour in government would support Congress proposals. Arthur Henderson, Tilak told Indian audiences proudly on his return, would be prime minister when Labour came to power, and had advised Indians to '[p]ocket what England is giving you today and continue your agitation

---

[64] *Hansard*, 5 June 1919, 5th ser., v.116, cols.2341–54, 2363–9, 2397–401.

[65] Khaparde Diary, 30 Oct 1919; *Mahratta*, 7 Dec 1919.

[66] Motilal Nehru to Adamson, 12 Jan 1920, and 'Message of Thanks to the Labour Party', 15 Jan 1920, *SWMN*, ii, 80, 85.

[67] DCI Reports 5 and 19 Jan 1920, HPD, Feb 1920, 50 and 52; 19 July 1920, HPD, July 1920, 104.

for what you want'. This, Tilak insisted, was advice which they should follow.[68] The promise, he announced, was 'not one-sided':

It is a bilateral contract as the lawyers call it. We have got the promise not only from the members of the Labour Party but also from their constituency. We have got a resolution from them that India must be granted as soon as possible full self-government on the principle of self-determination. . . . Depend upon the promise of the Labour Party as well as upon your own work.[69]

For this contract to work, however, Tilak realised that it was necessary for Congress to demonstrate through council entry and social reform its good intentions for Indian workers and peasants. The only significant difference between Congress resolutions in response to Montagu–Chelmsford and the amendments tabled by Labour had been in the emphasis the latter put upon the need to protect the Indian industrial workforce.[70] This was an obvious source of concern to Labour, both out of self-interest and fraternal concern. As Tilak left England, Wedgwood had advised him that Congress should aim to win places on the Provincial Councils and use them to tackle such problems.[71] Tilak was ready to comply.[72] Back in India, he advised Congress of the need, as Labour wished, of using the Councils for active social reform with special weighting towards the industrial worker.[73] At the Amritsar Congress in December 1919, Congress urged its organisations to promote trade unions, and made its first pledges 'to improve the social, economic and political conditions of the labouring classes'.[74] It also committed itself to working for these ends within the framework of the Montagu–Chelmsford reforms. Tilak set up a Congress Democratic Party, with the Fabian slogan, 'Educate, Agitate, Organize'.[75] Other Congress leaders were hardly less enthusiastic about the Labour alliance. Lajpat Rai told Wedgwood that he too was anxious to start an Indian labour movement, to bring the masses behind the nationalist demand and reduce religious strife.[76] 'India's tiny barque', he claimed, 'will rise or sink with that of the millions of Britain's workers.'[77] In

---

[68] Divekar, *Tilak*, 885–8.
[69] Speech at Madras, 17 Dec 1919, in Divekar, *Tilak*, 895–904.
[70] Gupta, *Imperialism*, 46–7.
[71] Wedgwood to Tilak, 6 Nov 1919, in Divekar, *Tilak*, 870.
[72] *Daily Herald*, 30 Oct 1919.
[73] *Mahratta*, 9 Nov 1919, 18 Jan and 4 April 1920.   [74] *India*, 23 Jan 1920.
[75] *India*, 21 May 1920.   [76] Lajpat Rai to Wedgwood, 3 Feb 1919, *SCLR*, 119–20.
[77] *United India*, 19 Nov 1919.

The New Economic Menace to India (1920), Pal argued that 'our only chance of safety in our present condition of political impotence and economic helplessness lies on an open, courageous and uncompromisng alliance with British Labour'. But British Labour, he noted, 'will not touch us with even a pair of tongs unless we are prepared to fight indigenous capitalism in India'.[78] It was exactly this, however, which troubled other Congress leaders. C. P. Ramaswami Iyer complained that Labour was only 'narrowly interested in sectarian matters' and had 'none of the breadth of imperialistic outlook which characterised the younger Unionist and Liberal statesmen'.[79] When Kelkar proposed that Congress should send a delegate to a Second International meeting in Switzerland, Malaviya told the Congress secretaries that he feared Congress association with Labour would 'lend colour to the idea that its aims and purposes are socialistic', and blocked Congress agreement.[80] Aurobindo Ghose, invited to endorse Tilak's Democratic Party, said that he preferred to work along authentically Indian lines:

> Your party, you say, is going to be a social democratic party. Now I believe in something which might be called social democracy, but not in any of the forms now current, and I am not altogether in love with the European kind, however great an improvement it may be on the past. I hold that India having a spirit of her own and a governing temperament proper to her own civilisation, should in politics as in everything else strike out on her own original path and not stumble in the wake of Europe.[81]

At Calcutta in September 1920, Congress approved a programme boycotting British schools, courts, councils and goods. At Nagpur in December, it swung round further to supporting Gandhi's campaign of non-cooperation, designed to win *swaraj* within a year. The logic behind this step has been extensively studied.[82] For Gandhi himself, Britain's apparent indifference to Muslim protests concerning the future of their spiritual leader, the defeated Turkish Khalifa, and to wider anger against

---

[78] B. C. Pal, *The New Economic Menace to India* (Madras, 1920), 226–7.
[79] *Hindu,* 8 Dec 1919; *New India,* 4 Feb 1919.
[80] Kelkar to Misra, 8 and 21 Jan 1919, AICC 6/1919; Kripalani to Misra, 17 Jan 1919, AICC 2/1919.
[81] Ghose to Baptista, 5 Jan 1920, in Vidwans, *Letters of Lokmanya Tilak,* 281–3.
[82] See especially Judith M. Brown, *Gandhi's Rise to Power: Indian Politics, 1915–1922* (Cambridge, 1972), 250–306.

the use of martial law in the Punjab were the decisive triggers. Taking up these issues brought him much wider support in Congress than he had hitherto attracted, allowing him to bring together Muslims involved in the Khilafat campaign with supporters of those factions within Congress who did not expect to do well out of the forthcoming elections, or who saw temporary advantages in distancing themselves from those who did. Many of the Congress leaders, however, were at best lukewarm, and at worst frankly hostile to Gandhi's plans. The need to drown these voices with sheer numbers led Gandhi to push into untapped regions and social classes, including those whose lack of western education had hitherto kept them out of Congress politics. For a variety of complex and often locally driven reasons, coupled with Gandhi's reputation as a religious leader and successful grass-roots campaigner, a large number of Indians responded to this call. This forced Gandhi's opponents to recalculate the costs of opposition to him, and enough felt that they might gain enough in the short run from acceding to non-cooperation to make a temporary retreat from constitutional politics seem worthwhile.

Congress secretaries hoped that it would be possible to persuade Labour to support non-cooperation.[83] However, the two fraternal delegates sent to Nagpur from the Labour Party and the British Committee, Spoor and Wedgwood, were bound by the Party's preference for working the reforms. In June 1920, in the same breath as it had condemned the Montagu–Chelmsford legislation as inadequate, the NEC had also asked the Indian people 'to take the reforms as far as they had gone, to make the fullest possible use of them, and to continue the agitation along strictly constitutional lines'.[84] Wedgwood was shocked by the Gandhian Congress, and especially when he found speakers shouted down at the Subjects Committee. The Irish were more bitterly divided than the Indians, he observed, but at least they behaved like gentlemen. Wedgwood had a romantic attachment to the idea of civil disobedience, and urged Congress to 'follow [Gandhi] in passive resistance'.[85] It was the weapon of dissent, and 'Labour [had] used it repeatedly in all lands'.[86] But in more reflective moments, he was highly critical of what he described as Gandhi's 'Tolstoian anarchy'. The 'basis for all

[83] Patel to Spoor, 20 Aug 1920, AICC 13/1920.
[84] Labour Party, *Report of Annual Conference*, 1920, 156–7.
[85] M. R. Jayakar, *The Story of My Life* (2v., Bombay, 1958), i, 416–17.
[86] C. V. Wedgwood, *The Last of the Radicals: Josiah Wedgwood* M. P. (London, 1951), 145–6; B. P. Sitaramayya, *History of the Indian National Congress Volume I (1885–1935)* (reprinted, New Delhi, 1969), 208.

advance' in India was the encouragement of mass education. While he was impressed by the calibre of India's political leaders, whose idealism and unselfishness he regarded as 'far higher' than those of British politicians, he remained worried by their inexperience. They had 'not yet been tested in the fire of responsibility'. He criticised their 'pathetic faith in the omnipotence of the State to do everything that one finds in all leaders who have never yet been "the State"'. Wedgwood was convinced that there was no substitute for power to teach these lessons. Therefore boycotting the councils was 'a stupid blunder' because it deprived Congress of governing experience. Wedgwood also suspected that the non-cooperation movement had come under conservative and religious influences, fearful of the implications of popular rule.[87] 'The two great bases of democracy', he wrote, 'are Education and Local Government by Panchayets. So much depends on these foundations being well laid, and foundations are so difficult to alter.'[88] Wedgwood felt that there was, in Congress non-cooperation, 'hardly conscious it may be of itself, a fear of representative and responsible institutions'.[89] Gandhi's movement was 'more a movement against western civilization than against western rule'.[90] The newly dominant Nehrus were irritated by Wedgwood's outspokenness and regarded him as a poor advocate of the new Congress ideals. 'Wedgwood', Motilal wrote to his son, 'is all that we suspected him to be... He has come here with settled convictions and for a set purpose. I think we shall soon have to expose him.'[91]

Many other Labour figures besides Wedgwood were distressed by the apparent readiness of Congress to abandon the constitutional path. Even firm supporters of Indian freedom, such as Hyndman, while accepting the Gandhian claim that non-cooperation was a powerful and justifiable tool against autocracies, did not agree with them that it assisted in the building of a nation. It 'solves no racial or economic problem whatever',

[87] Wedgwood, *Last of the Radicals*, 145–6; J. C. Wedgwood, *Memoirs of a Fighting Life* (London, 1940), 163–5; and *Essays and Adventures of a Labour MP* (London, 1924), 130–44; *Indian Annual Review*, 1924, i, 267–8.

[88] *India*, 24 Dec 1920.

[89] Wedgwood, *Essays and Adventures*, 141; Gandhi, 'Notes: On the Wrong Track', *Young* India, 8 Dec 1920 ; 'Notes', *Young India*, 2 Feb 1921, *CWMG* E22/43 and E22/151.

[90] *United India*, 2 Feb 1921.

[91] Motilal to Jawaharlal Nehru, 30 Oct 1920, *SWMN* ii, 185–7; Khaparde Diary, 7 and 28–9 Dec 1920, and Bannerjea to Motilal Nehru, undated, but prob. early 1921, AICC 4/1921.

he told Fenner Brockway.[92] The boycott of councils was scarcely likely to recommend itself to a party which had placed capture of the legislature at the heart of its programme. Direct action was something that Labour accepted might be used for political ends, but only sparingly and on important single issues, such as to counter the threat of war. It was wrong for it to be made a regular weapon in the Congress armoury when provision had been made for demands to be channelled through the new democratic machinery of Montagu–Chelmsford. While Gandhi's early campaigns had been against single oppressive laws or policies such as the Khilafat, non-cooperation challenged the whole basis of the state. The Councils offered a means of securing real advances, even if using them implied compromise with the British. They would supply Indians with a firm platform from which further demands could be made, with greater authority in Britain because they would come from elected, practising politicians not from irresponsible lawyer-agitators. In February 1922, as non-cooperation was called off, the National Joint Council of the TUC and Labour Party issued a resolution which condemned the political arrests of Indian leaders, but 'also deplores no less the action of the non-cooperators in boycotting these parliamentary institutions recently conferred upon India by which grievances should be ventilated and wrongs redressed.'[93] The boycott of British goods seemed to Labour's experts to undercut the hopes of cooperation between progressives in Britain and India. Some suspected *swadeshi* as little more than the demand for the protection of Indian bourgeois interests. However, appeals to the 'international solidarity of labour' from aggrieved British trade unionists made little headway in India.[94]

The Khilafat demand posed additional problems for the Labour Party. Labour leaders had met the Ali brothers when they visited Britain with the Khilafat delegation in 1920. Mohamed Ali had warned Labour that it would lose the confidence of Asia and Africa if it only opposed imperialism when it threatened Russia.[95] Like Tilak, he was conscious of the need to phrase his appeal to align it with Labour's concern for the underprivileged. Warned by his friends that Labour would distrust a religious appeal, he carefully stressed the points the

[92] Hyndman to Brockway, 18 July 1921, Brockway Papers, 4/112/11.

[93] Labour Party, *Report of Annual Conference*, 1922, 37.

[94] P. S. Gupta, 'British Labour and the Indian Left, 1919–1939', in B. R. Nanda (ed.) *Socialism in India* (New Delhi, 1972).

[95] *India*, 27 Aug and 3 Sept 1920.

movements had in common. After a swift look at the literature on religious nonconformity set out on the conference bookstall, he told Labour that 'the same class often abused the Turk as abused Labour and it was some satisfaction to him that centuries ago when the Turk first became unspeakable they, the Labourites, were villains. (Loud laughter).'

He represented a faith intolerant to narrow nationalism. (Cheers) His was a faith that was supernational. (Cheers) It had no church, no clergy. (Cheers) It refused to be a religion only for Sundays and Sabbaths, for churches, temples and synagogues. (Cheers) It was a work-a-day faith (cheers) and as much meant for the market place as for the Mosque. (Cheers) That is why it still retained its grip on the masses. (Cheers) It recognised wage-earners as a friend of God (cheers) and regarded poverty as a matter of pride. (Cheers)...That was the kind of faith that could keep its hold on labour and it was for respect and tolerance for such a faith that the Delegation had come to plead. (Cheers).[96]

However, despite giving Mohamed Ali this cheery reception, Labour was unable to support the Khilafat agitation on grounds that it was incompatible with demands for self-determination in Egypt and other parts of the non-Turkish Ottoman empire.[97]

The most worrying aspect of non-cooperation, however, was not its use of boycott, but the means by which it garnered support. Congress clearly now had a mass base, and it was no longer possible to argue that it was an unrepresentative clique of westernised politicians. However, there were still worries about how this base had been acquired, and the relationship the Congress leaders had with it. Gandhi shared the belief of most British observers that institutions could not simply be transplanted from Britain to India. However, he was more favourable towards the idea of revitalising existing traditions in India than to the notion of a western-led 'modernisation' of Indian politics. Gandhi himself linked the political project of *swaraj* to a religious movement of self-discipline and purification, and his techniques motivated and controlled supporters through reworked conception of Hindu duties and the celebration of an imagined and glorious Hindu past. The non-cooperation movement was therefore characterised by many of the same techniques that had troubled pre-war British observers, especially religious mobilisation,

[96] Afzar Iqbal (ed.), *Select Writings & Speeches of Mohamed Ali* (2v., Lahore, 1963), ii, 49–56; Mohamed Ali, *My Life: A Fragment* (Lahore, 1942), 194–5.
[97] Gupta, *Imperialism*, 48–9.

and although Gandhi sometimes protested against their use, caste sanctions.[98] Gandhian agitation thus gave expression to exactly those traditional and backward-looking forces which progressive British observers believed precluded genuine democratic advance. While this mode of politics was disliked—and to some extent resisted—by other Indian politicians, they were nevertheless forced to rely on it as the only effective means of rapidly building a mass movement in Indian conditions.

The price of Gandhian mobilisation, moreover, was a certain loss of control. Congress leaders had generally hitherto regarded the Indian peasantry as unruly and had doubted their own ability to halt rural unrest once it had begun. Subaltern protest had its own logic and easily slipped out of the control of Congress leaders.[99] This was most obvious when participants abandoned non-violence for attacks on landlords or peasant insurgency. But on a lesser scale, it was also evident in the transformation of Congress demonstrations from orderly marches of well-behaved middle-class petitioners into uncontrolled festivals characterised by the rowdy, undisciplined energies of the peasantry and urban poor. Gandhi himself repeatedly criticised the disorderliness of the crowds that gathered for nationalist rallies. Visiting Labour speakers shared Gandhi's distaste for the wilder manifestations of 'mobocracy'. Indeed, Wedgwood had used the same term in his criticisms of the Nagpur Congress. In Labour eyes, indeed, an Indian non-cooperation movement organised on such lines was more likely than a British movement to tip over into unrest and violence, largely because Indians were seen as less restrained and mature than British workers. Here MacDonald's prejudices about the volatility and indiscipline of Indians came to the fore. 'The mass mind of India', he had written in 1910, 'is perhaps the most credulous of mankind. It moves as the waters move under the moon. It swells with expectation. Every year it hails some Messiah. It does not seem to be a thing chained to the earth, but something floating in the air, swaying obedient to every

---

[98] Brown, *Gandhi's Rise*, 309–43; Christopher Baker, 'Non-cooperation in South India' in Christopher Baker and D. A. Washbrook (eds.), *South India: Political Institutions and Political Change, 1880–1940* (Delhi, 1975); W. F. Crawley, 'Kisan Sabhas and Agrarian Revolt in the United Provinces', *Modern Asian Studies*, 5/2 (1971), 95–109; David Hardiman, *Peasant Nationalists in Gujarat: Kheda District, 1917–1934* (Delhi, 1981); *Peasant Resistance in India, 1858–1914* (Delhi, 1992); Gyanendra Pandey, *The Ascendancy of the Congress in Uttar Pradesh, 1926–1934: A Study in Imperfect Mobilization* (Delhi, 1978); Stephen Henningham, *Peasant Movements in India: North Bihar, 1917–1942* (Canberra, 1982).

[99] Ranjit Guha, 'Discipline and Mobilize', *Subaltern Studies VII* (Oxford, 1992).

breath.'[100] When, in November 1921, the non co-operation movement collapsed into violence in Bombay, Calcutta and towns in northern India, MacDonald's fears seemed to have been confirmed. Insufficient leadership of the right type seemed to have been displayed by Gandhi and his associates.

Ironically, however, great thought and effort had been put by Gandhi and the Congress leadership into the question of how to impose discipline on the mass movement.[101] Their control over the movement had been tightened by the adoption of a new constitution which gave power over day-to-day decisions to a small Working Committee. Elaborate rules and orders were developed to govern the conduct of non-cooperators. By empowering a selfless, dedicated, enlightened group of non-violent leaders—the satyagrahis—whose orders must be followed, Gandhi aimed to bring the masses behind the freedom struggle without risking wider social unrest. However, the imposition of Gandhian discipline on the masses was not what Labour had envisaged when advising Congress leaders to base their movement on the demands of the worker and peasant. It reversed the proper relationship, as Labour saw it, between leaders and followers. The Congress leadership had not gone to the trouble of winning consent for their nationalist programme. The Indian peasantry became simply a resource to be mobilized by a Brahmanic elite using religious authority for their own purposes. Although Congress had, for official purposes, a democratic constitution, its procedures were not really democratic. Gandhi himself did not stand for election. His leadership was, it seemed, completely unaccountable to anything except his own divine inspiration. He was, Spoor told Montagu on his return from India, 'worshipped'.[102] Gandhi's early campaigns had generally won respect on the British left because they were seen as those of a practical social reformer winning justice for South African Indians or indigo planters who had themselves suffered specific injuries. However, now that Gandhi had begun to recruit the Indian peasantry for the wider cause of nationalism, it raised the questions of whose interests were being served. Too much leadership of the wrong type seemed to have been displayed.

Indeed, a further effect of the much deeper mobilisation that Congress achieved under Gandhi was that it involved the capture—or even the

[100] *India*, 16 Sep 1910.   [101] Guha 'Discipline and Mobilize'.
[102] Waley, *Montagu*, 252; Montagu to Willingdon, 16 Feb 1921, Montagu Coll., MSS/Eur/D523/17.

creation and capture—of other nascent organisations: just those types of associations which Hardie and others had welcomed as signs of recognizably autonomous political activity. The emergent associations of the Indian peasantry (*kisan sabhas*) were created, or commandeered in their early stages of development, to be used as a resource for anti-British purposes.[103] Among India's industrial workers too, much of the energy that created the trade union movement was also anti-imperial in origin, and strikes were used not merely, as British trade unions believed they should be, in labour disputes, but as a means of putting pressure on British firms or those who failed to support Congress. Universities and schools were politicised by nationalist agitators and seemed incapable of developing the secular education desired by the Webbs. The Gandhian Congress leadership thus seemed, in both senses of the word, irresponsible. It was both foolhardy and unaccountable: unwilling to give ground in negotiations but unreliable once settlements had been reached, reluctant to shoulder the burden of administration but happy to wield unaccountable power from the sidelines, prepared to raise popular emotions through demagoguery and agitation, but capable only of floundering blindly in the wake of those they had inspired when public order collapsed as a result.

By no means all the Labour Party regarded Gandhian non-cooperation in so hostile a fashion. The early 1920s also saw the emergence of a small grouping of British Gandhians who regarded non-violent non-cooperation as legitimate. Its most prominent supporters were to be found among those who had used similar methods themselves. Support was found especially among those who had been wartime pacifists, especially those who had themselves been imprisoned, such as Fenner Brockway, now secretary of the British Committee. There was also some support from the significant number in the party who believed that methods of direct action were permissible adjuncts to parliamentary action. In the early months of Indian non-cooperation, indeed, British trade unionists were engaged in their own attempt at direct action: the 'Triple Alliance' strike of miners, railwaymen and transport workers that collapsed in April 1921. Brockway welcomed efforts to link up trade unionists with campaigners for Congress in a 'Hands Off India!' campaign, trying to repeat the dockers' refusal to load weapons

---

[103] Partha Chatterjee, *The Nation and Its Fragments: Colonial and Postcolonial Histories* (Princeton, 1993).

for use against Bolshevik Russia.[104] Later the same year, the Labour councillors of Poplar, with Lansbury at their head, were conducting their own campaign of defiance.[105] Although there is no evidence of direct interaction between these movements, the two campaigns had much in common. Each limited acts of lawbreaking and civil disobedience to a select group of responsible leaders, who courted arrest and prison as a means of public martyrdom. Each released emotional energy and spontaneity of participation among wider groups outside, exhibited in demonstrations, marches and the deployment of symbolic gesture. It is no accident that those in the Labour Party who deplored Poplarism for its self-indulgence and irresponsibility were frequently also those who regarded Congress' non-cooperation in a similar light. Disagreements over Indian non-cooperation within the Labour Party showed, to a certain extent, the same clash between the participatory democracy of Poplar and the machine politics favoured by Herbert Morrison. But even Lansbury did not think that non-cooperation was justified in India: the Montagu–Chelmsford reforms offered scope for the satisfaction of Indian demands that did not exist for the Poplar councillors; and, more crucially still, working the reforms was meant to educate Indian politicians in ways that were redundant for their British counterparts.[106]

Thus as Congress made its way from respectability to agitation, the Labour Party was moving in the opposite direction. After April 1921, the Party set its face ever more firmly against the use of direct action, relinquishing its dependence on brief spurts of uncontrolled industrial militancy for discipline, organisation and sustained pressure. To enlarge its electoral support among working-class Liberal and Conservative voters, moreover, it was necessary for Labour to present itself not simply as a workers' party dedicated to the specific interests of organised labour, but as a national party, which took a broad view of its responsibilities. Electoral success, which made Labour the Opposition in 1922, now meant that it had to take the lead in debates, as it had not before. Detailed work of the kind required to oppose the Montagu–Chelmsford reforms had already made India increasingly a subject for specialists, as

---

[104] *India*, 24 Dec 1920.
[105] Noreen Branson, *George Lansbury and the Councillors' Revolt: Poplarism, 1919–25* (London, 1979); P. A. Ryan, ' "Poplarism", 1894–1930' in Pat Thane (ed.), *Origins of British Social Policy* (London, 1978); Jonathan Schneer, *George Lansbury* (Manchester, 1990), 48–67.
[106] *India*, 24 Dec 1920.

Wedgwood observed.[107] Fighting speeches were increasingly replaced by more sober exegesis. 'As long as the Socialist movement was only a propagandist body', Attlee was later to write in explanation, 'it was possible to take up a purely negative and critical attitude' on imperial questions. But as Labour moved towards government, the slogan of '[s]imple surrender of all ill-gotten gains' no longer sufficed.[108] Party discipline was tightened, restricting the capacity of mavericks to break ranks. This had implications for those in India who still looked to British Labour for assistance in winning freedom. It was no longer sufficient to win over itinerant Labour MPs, as in the days of Keir Hardie. Policy development now became more a matter of fighting longer battles through the committees. Research advisers, among them the Party's Advisory Committee on Imperial Questions, led on Indian questions by ex-ICS officials, needed to be persuaded, as well as individual leaders. These developments were, of course, neither smooth nor uniform ones. But they had the general effect of weakening the ability of Labour to propagandise for Indians in the old fashion. Those who stood outside them and challenged them, moreover, were often among the most enthusiastic supporters of Congress.

The most hurtful element of the new Gandhian strategy, however, was that it sharply downgraded the role of the British supporters of Congress. The message was given to them in a particularly brutal form in the suppression of the reformed British Committee. Tilak and Lajpat Rai favoured propaganda in Britain, along the lines they had worked out with the Labour Party. But other senior figures, including Gandhi, Malaviya and the Nehrus, were hostile.[109] In March 1920, the Congress Committee had decided to dispatch a single delegate, the Congress Secretary Vithalbhai Patel, to present its views of the latest Government proposals. Motilal saw even this as 'an absolute waste of money, time and energy'.[110]

---

[107] Wedgwood, *Essays and Adventures*, 156.
[108] C. R. Attlee, *The Labour Party in Perspective* (London, 1937), 228–9.
[109] Tilak to Khaparde, 21 Feb 1920 and 10 March 1920, Khaparde Coll., 2; Motilal Nehru to Misra, 25 Feb 1920, AICC 9/1920; Lajpat Rai, 'Need for Publicity Abroad', in Joshi, *Writings and Speeches*, i, 317–23; Lajpat Rai to Indian leaders, 25 July 1919, Lajpat Rai to Gandhi, Sept 1919, and Lajpat Rai to Hardikar, 11 Nov 1920, *SCLR*, 135–42, 150–1, 185–6.
[110] Motilal Nehru to Misra, 9, 10, 12 and 24 March 1920, AICC 9/1920; Motilal Nehru to Girdharilal, 11 and 12 March 1920, *SWMN*, ii, 108–9.

I do not believe in 'counteracting' [propaganda]. The Government acts on one plane and we on a different plane altogether. The Government man will go straight to the High Priest of Bureaucracy (Mr Montagu) and exchange confidences with him while we have the almost impossible task of serving the many-headed monster called the British public opinion. That this monster can devour all Bureaucracy and their agents admits of no doubt, but he is as impossible to awake as the Kumbhkaran of the Ramayana . . . [I] therefore have no faith in deputations'[111]

Motilal preferred the strategy of lobbying the London press, via a large grant to his own solicitor Reginald Neville.[112] When the British Committee learned of this alternative route for funds, they acted quickly to stop it, appealing successfully via Patel for the money to be sent to them instead.[113] But when Patel requested money to publicise the Congress report on the Amritsar Massacre, which he saw, rightly, as a good lever to move British public opinion, Gandhi and Malaviya were able to prevent it.[114] 'They are the men on the Punjab Committee who should have taken up the work in right earnest', wrote Tilak. '[B]ut they do not much value foreign agitation . . . [s]o the best opportunity to impress the British public . . . with the abominable despotism of the bureaucracy is being, or . . . has been, lost.'[115] Patel was left to manage on his own.[116]

In response to these worrying signals, the British Committee had loyally talked up the Congress and its decision to opt for non-cooperation, professionalising its activities to an unprecedented degree, and drawing closer to the Labour Party. The new Secretary, George Blizard, had been a labour organiser and Spoor, who became Chairman in July 1920, and other Labour MPs now provided the Committee with audiences and attention which their Liberal predecessors had been unable to

111 Motilal Nehru to Misra, 12 March 1920, AICC 9/1920.

112 Motilal Nehru to Jawaharlal Nehru, 16 Sep 1919, in *SWMN* ii, 56–7; Motilal Nehru to Misra, 12, 17 and 24 March 1920, AICC 9/1920; Motilal Nehru to Malaviya, 12 March 1920, *SWMN*, ii, 110–12.

113 Kelkar to Malaviya, 14 May 1920, Asst. Sec. AICC to Kelkar, 17 May 1920, British Committee to AICC, 29 April 1920, AICC 2/1920; Minute Book, v.8, Executive Committee meeting, 11 May 1920 and Special Committee in Connexion with the Punjab Reports, 18 May 1920; Blizard to Congress secretaries, 13 and 21 May and 14 July 1920, AICC 10/1920.

114 Patel to Misra, 3 June 1920, AICC 7/1920; Patel to Misra, 24 June 1920, AICC 13/1920.

115 Tilak to Patel, 26 June 1920, AICC 8/1920.

116 Patel to Misra, 3 June 1920, AICC 7/1920; Tilak to Patel, 26 June 1920, AICC 8/1920.

command.[117] The old style of campaigning through private conclave at the India Office or the House of Commons was jettisoned in favour of agitation and public meetings. The Committee produced an extended range of publications and a programme of national meetings and demonstrations. Efforts were made to reach audiences of British workers and to link up Indian activism with other left-wing causes. *India* offered more vigorous support for non-cooperation and boycott than before.[118]

However, precisely this desire to maximise its impact in British circles led to trouble. Some members of the Committee believed more Indians should be involved in its work. However, Helena Normanton, the editor of *India*, argued that Indians were neither trusted in Fleet Street or Westminster to write about India in Britain, nor sufficiently sensitive to 'British modes of platform procedure and [the need for] . . . brevity' to speak about it.[119] When she stepped down, Patel, Parikh and the other Tilakites on the Committee favoured the appointment of Brockway, with his experience of agitation and links to labour politics. However Horniman and some of the new Indian members put forward their own candidate Syed Hossain, on the grounds that the post should go to an Indian. When the choice between Brockway and Hossain split the Committee evenly, Spoor suggested that they appoint them both as joint-editors.[120] Motilal was told about the intrigues of the Horniman clique on the Committee. It 'discloses a disgraceful state of things', he wrote, on forwarding the letter to Gandhi and Patel.[121] The Nehrus had their own reasons for disliking Syed Hossain's candidature as editor. As Horniman's protégé and the shortlived editor of Motilal Nehru's newly founded Allahabad newspaper *The Independent*, he had all but wrecked the paper through considerable legal bills.[122] Worse still, himself a Muslim, Hossain had fallen in love with Motilal's daughter Vijayalakshmi, a development which the Brahmin Nehrus (and even Gandhi, who was summoned to help break the relationship up) viewed with deep unhappiness.[123] Thus at Motilal's instigation, Congress immediately

[117] Minute Book, v.7, 29 Aug 1919; v.8, 6 and 13 July 1920.
[118] *India*, 26 Nov and 3 Dec 1920.
[119] Normanton, *England in India*, 1–31; *India*, 13 Aug 1920.
[120] Minute Book, v.8, Executive Committee meeting, 17 Aug 1920; Parikh to Patel, 19 and 26 Aug 1920, AICC 3/1920.
[121] Bannerjea to Patel, 21 Oct 1920, AICC 10/1920; Motilal Nehru to Gandhi and Patel, 17 Sep 1920, *SWMN*, ii, 178–9.
[122] Motilal to Jawaharlal Nehru, 5 June 1919, SWMN, ii, 17–18.
[123] Viyajayalakshmi Pandit, *The Scope of Happiness* (London, 1979), 65; Stanley Wolpert, *Nehru: A Tryst with Destiny* (New York, 1996), 48.

cabled its disapproval of the appointment of Hossain without its approval, and cut off funds.[124] This seemed, even to those who wanted Brockway, an intolerable intrusion and the Committee confirmed its unanimous support for the shared arrangement.[125] Holford Knight, one of the new members of the British Committee, wrote bitterly to Lajpat Rai:

> We have reconstructed the office, obtained the best editorial assistance in Fenner Brockway and Syed Hossain, got rid of incompetent blunderers, and are about to begin splendid work on a large scale. . . . The Committee here is absolutely responsible for its work and this attempted dictation will not be tolerated by responsible public men.[126]

It would be impossible to carry on the business of the Committee, another member wrote to Patel, 'unless the Committee as a whole is treated as an autonomous body'.[127] But Patel warned Spoor that the dispute had played into the hands of the British Committee's opponents, who simply wished to see it disbanded.[128] Congress insisted on exercising control over appointments, and on Syed Hossain's removal.[129]

The propaganda work of the Congress Deputation of 1919 was supposed to have been funded by a special campaign fund from each Province. However, by October 1920, not a single Province had paid anything at all, with the result that the Deputation's costs had to be met out of the remittances normally paid to the British Committee. Motilal warned Patel that most of the Provincial Committees were unaware of the extent of their liabilities and there was little prospect of their paying them. 'People here,' his son Jawaharlal wrote from the United Provinces, 'are not over desirous of contributing for the upkeep of the British Congress Committee and most of the donors will ear-mark their donations for non-cooperation work'.[130] By the

---

[124] AICC to British Committee, 7 Oct 1920, AICC 10/1920.

[125] Minute Book, v.8, Executive Committee meetings, 26 Oct and 10 Nov 1920.

[126] Holford Knight to Lajpat Rai, 21 Oct 1920, AICC 7/1920.

[127] Minute Book, v.8, Executive Committee meetings, 12 and 26 Oct 1920; Parikh et al. to Patel, 26 Aug, 14 and 28 Oct 1920; 'Observations on the Present Constitution of the British Committee', 13 Nov 1920, AICC 10/1920.

[128] Patel to Spoor, 17 Nov 1920, AICC 10/1920.

[129] Patel to Spoor, 20 Sept 1920, AICC 13/1920; AICC to British Committee, 14 Oct 1920; Spoor to Patel, 3 Nov 1920; Parikh to Patel, 11 Nov 1920; Blizard to Patel, 14 Nov 1920; Patel to Spoor, 17 Nov 1920; AICC 10/1920; AICC to British Committee, undated, AICC 15/1920; Minute Book, v.8, 10 Nov 1920.

[130] Motilal Nehru to Patel, 23 Oct 1920; Jawaharlal Nehru to Patel, 16 Oct 1920, AICC 7/1920.

end of 1920, therefore, the British Committee was desperately short
of funds and was dispatching frantic cables to Congress warning of
closure. But the death of Tilak in August had deprived them of their
main sponsor. The Congress secretaries sent a small sum, but reported
that the performance of the British Committee had been unsatisfactory.
Gandhi, who had received worrying criticism from Sarojini Naidu in
London, attacked Brockway's salary and the extravagance of spending
so much on such worthless work.[131] For Congress to support the work
of a British propagandist body was, in Gandhi's view, incompatible with
the new emphasis upon self-reliance and non-cooperation. Propaganda
was simply unnecessary if good work was being done at home, and in
fostering a beggarly spirit among nationalists might even be harmful
to the indigenous struggle. It was better, he told Congress workers,
to concentrate attention and scarce resources on activities within India
itself. Spoor brought to Nagpur a plan for either a Congress Agency
or for Congress to appoint the Indian members of the Committee.[132]
However, at the meeting chaired by Motilal to decide the fate of the
British Committee, it was decided that the British Committee was
to be abolished and *India* discontinued. 'We have no friends outside
India', one of those present had insisted, 'and are going into the
wilderness.'[133]

   This, like the adoption of other Gandhian methods, was evidently
a controversial decision within Congress, some of whose leaders, such
as Patel, felt that the British Committee had been doing valuable
work, especially under its new Labour team. The Nagpur Congress had
therefore voted funds for continued propaganda in Britain, handing
control of it to the Working Committee. Brockway and Spoor were
asked in January 1921 to make recommendations about the best means
of spending this sum. They replied, favouring an Information Bureau,
but Brockway's precipitancy in setting one up without waiting for
authorisation evidently irritated the Working Committee, which at first
refused to reimburse the money he had spent. Gandhi therefore felt
obliged to defend the decision to abolish the Committee the following

---

[131] Naidu to Gandhi, 15 July 1920, in Makarand Paranjape (ed.), *Sarojini Naidu:
Selected Letters, 1890s to 1940s* (Delhi, 1996), 147–8.
[132] 'Observations on the Present Constitution of the British Committee.'
[133] Spoor to Nehru, 21 Dec 1920, AICC 10/1920; Minutes of a meeting of the
foreign propaganda sub-committee, 28 Dec. 1920, AICC 9/1922; Khaparde Diary, 29
Dec 1920; Zaidi, *Encyclopaedia*, viii, 372.

month.[134] Tilak's supporters remained in favour of foreign propaganda, duly regulated.[135] But the Tilak memorial fund, which they had wanted to be used for foreign propaganda, was redirected by Gandhi in the direction of 'spinning, weaving and other educational activity'.[136] When former members of the British Committee tried to revive the notion of a newspaper in Britain, they were roundly rebuked by Nehru:

[I]t is becoming clearer and clearer every day that outside propaganda is not only of no assistance to us, but not infrequently proves a drag upon our efforts within the country. It is impossible for us to take propaganda in Britain seriously at . . . present . . . and no appreciable good can result from a few articles in the English papers . . . in support of our cause. We want every penny that we can spare for the Swarajya Fund.[137]

All the factions on the British Committee, however, even the most radical, were opposed to its abolition by Gandhi.[138] In vain, they tried to speak the new Gandhian language, claiming that while they shared the Congress lack of faith in appeals to Britain, 'we do need political *sanyasis* [i.e. ascetic pilgrims] — political *Vivekanandas* [i.e. monks] . . . who will spread broadcast truths and facts and strive to convince. Appealing to others may be inconsistent with one's self-respect. Not so, *converting* others by the inner strength of a superior political evangel.'[139] However, Motilal replied that 'we attach no importance to foreign propaganda'.[140] The British Committee, therefore, was broken up, and its papers, reports and library repatriated to India.[141]

The destruction of the British Committee, therefore, did not come about through a slow process of decline at the metropole, but as the result of independent decisions at the periphery, arguably the first that had been made since the Committee's inception. Formal control had

[134] Gandhi, 'The British Congress Committee and "India"', 20 Oct 1920, *CWMG* E21/217; 'Speech on Foreign Propaganda, Nagpur', 29 Dec 1920, *CWMG* E 22/87.

[135] Kelkar to Patel, 10 Oct 1920, AICC 11/1920.

[136] Gandhi, 'All India Tilak Swaraj Fund', *Young India*, 16 March 1921, *CWMG* E22/222; Gandhi to Lajpat Rai, 8 Jan 1921, in Ravindra Kumar (ed.), *Selected Documents of Lala Lajpat Rai, 1906–1928* (5v., New Delhi, 1993), iii, 33; Mahadev Desai, 'Foundations of Swaraj', in Mahadev Desai, *Day to Day with Gandhi* (9v., Varanasi, 1968–72), iii, 202–9; Brown, *Gandhi's Rise*, 320–2.

[137] Motilal Nehru to Howsin, 3 May 1921, AICC 4/1921

[138] *India*, 3 Dec 1920.

[139] Howsin to Nehru, 26 May 1921, AICC 4/1921.

[140] Motilal Nehru to Howsin, 16 July 1921, AICC 4/1921.

[141] Report of General Secretary to Congress, 11 Dec 1925, reprinted in A. M. Zaidi (ed.), *The Story of Congress Pilgrimage*, (7v., New Delhi, 1990), vii, 114.

been achieved by Tilak in 1919 and the Committee's activity, measured by expenditure, had, in the months before its abolition, been increasing. The Committee was, judged by historic standards of activity, a healthy institution.[142] Yet Gandhi sensed that these were no longer the relevant standards. The Committee still remained reliant on British public men, who expected deference for their expertise, whose priorities were set by British left-wing politics, and whose advice might prove dangerously tempting in a crisis. 'The Congress has deliberately burnt its boats', he wrote. 'It has decided to become self-reliant. The question of the efficiency of the Committee . . . becomes irrelevant.'[143]

[142] See Figure 1, page 42 above, for evidence of a revival of funding and spending.
[143] Gandhi, 'The British Congress Committee and "India" '.

5

India and the Labour Party, 1922–8

This chapter and the next examine Labour's evolving Indian policy in the 1920s and early 1930s. There were two principal, interrelated developments. The first was Labour's closer engagement with the machinery of imperial governance, especially during its two periods of minority government. When Labour took office in 1924, officials worried that it might use its new privileges to encourage Congress intransigence in the 'linked-up' manner they had long feared. They managed to hold Labour and Congress apart in 1924, and the wedge between them was driven deeper through Labour's co-option on to the all-white Simon Commission in 1927–8. However, in 1929, a different set of circumstances provided greater scope for Labour ministers to work around official obstructions, and even build some tentative, independent connections with Indian nationalists, culminating in the first and second Round Table Conferences. Thus, with certain important qualifications, the period saw a closer and more successful engagement between metropolitan anti-imperialism and the state.

The second development, however, which tended to work against the first, was Labour's troubled relationship with the increasingly alien Gandhian Congress. Through the 1920s, it became slowly clearer that Gandhi was not simply an agitator whose short ascendancy had ended in 1922, but the defining figure of Indian nationalism. This revived the question briefly smothered by Tilak: was Congress really a modernising, progressive, even socialist, force, or not? As Congress demands were enlarged from *swaraj* (self-government) to *purna swaraj* (self-determination), moreover, this question became more urgent, for if India were to write its own constitution, the Indian poor would have to look to indigenous nationalists like Gandhi, and not British constitution-makers, for protection.

Following the collapse of the non-cooperation movement in February 1922, Congress had split between the 'no changers' who favoured continuing the Gandhian boycott of the new councils, the Independents and Liberals who favoured working the reforms while pressing for more, and the Swarajists, whose participation in provincial government was intended to be obstructive.[1] The Swarajists triumphed in the central and provincial elections of December 1923, becoming the largest party at the centre and also in Bengal. Once elected, they attempted to paralyse the councils by refusing to accept office, passing resolutions in favour of *swaraj*, and voting down government finance measures, thereby forcing governors to use their powers of certification. However, since they did not have majorities in the councils, the Swarajists needed to build coalitions with the cooperating parties to inflict these defeats, while not alienating the Gandhians who remained outside the councils and, especially in Bengal, more militant supporters who stood ready to denounce any abandonment of the principles of *swaraj*. Despite the somewhat contradictory speeches they made to these varied audiences, the Swarajists were mindful of the failure of non-cooperation and open to a quick deal with a Labour Government which would bring forward the ten year review of Montagu–Chelmsford, provided it was one which would satisfy the Gandhians and not a trap which would condemn them to working the existing councils in perpetuity.

MacDonald's primary aim in January 1924 was to convince the electorate of Labour's fitness to govern, in the hope of winning a majority at the next election. Labour's opponents had made the good government of the empire a test of Labour's capacities. Hence MacDonald began his premiership with a clear warning that there would be no surrender to non-constitutional methods and that if any attempt were made to use them it would make a liberal policy impossible.[2] Rather than appointing Labour's India expert Josiah Wedgwood, whom he considered too close to Congress, he chose—after a roster of similarly cautious alternatives—Sydney Olivier, Fabian and ex-Governor of Jamaica, a sympathiser with the Indian nationalists, but at the same time a natural bureaucrat.[3] Moreover, MacDonald's Cabinet included eight recent converts from the Liberal and Conservative Parties, including

[1] B. R. Nanda, 'The Swarajist Interlude', in Indian National Congress, *A Centenary History of the Indian National Congress* (5v., 1985), ii, 113–60.

[2] 'The Premier's Message', *Indian Annual Review*, 1924, i, 266.

[3] Francis Lee, *Fabianism and Colonialism: The Life and Political Thought of Lord Sydney Olivier* (London, 1988), 135–69.

Chelmsford, whose interest in preserving the substance of the reforms
he had introduced as Viceroy, and in supporting his successor, was an
authoritative force in the Cabinet India Committee.[4] As the outgoing
Secretary of State told the Viceroy, Labour was therefore 'unlikely to
provoke a conflict unless they are very sure of their ground, both here
and in India'.[5]

However, MacDonald and his colleagues sensed that the Swarajists
were only tactically committed to non-cooperation and that a deal with
them which got the councils working again would be a distinct political
coup, marginalising the Gandhians and setting India back on the path to
dominionhood. Wedgwood, in the Cabinet and on its India Committee,
was to be the principal advocate of this possibility.[6] 'I quite recognise
the limitations of your party, in office and not in power', Satyamurti,
the Swarajist leader in Madras wrote to Olivier. '[B]ut I want to assure
you that we are not political ogres and that we are only waiting for
a right gesture on your part. Summon a round-table conference and
you will find our leaders reasonable, practical and willing to recognise
real Imperial obligations.'[7] There was, therefore, sufficient common
ground for a deal to be done. But each party's commitment to it was
necessarily conditional: Congress needed guarantees that cooperation,
on the basis of equality of status, would deliver rapid constitutional
advance, sufficient to appease the Gandhians and radicals; and the
Government needed an end, even if temporary, to unrest and agitation
in India sufficient to enhance its reputation as an effective and safe
manager of imperial interests.

The Labour Government proved unable to deliver the guarantees that
Congress sought. But this was less because of its own reservations than
because it was forced to work through inherited state structures and
procedures which inhibited its capacity to make significant departures
in policy. There were several problems. The first was that the pathway
towards reform and the timing of steps that might be taken along it
were already defined by the 1919 Government of India Act, section 41

---

[4] Hailey to Private Secretary to Viceroy, undated but in reply to letter of 20 April
1924, Hailey Papers, MSS/Eur/E220/5D.

[5] Peel to Reading, 21 Jan 1924, RP, MSS/Eur/E238/7.

[6] Wedgwood, 'India: Constitutional Questions', 22 Feb 1924, CP 132 (24) CAB
24/165; *Daily Herald*, 21 Jan 1924.

[7] Satyamurti to Olivier, 3 April 1924, read out in House of Lords Debate, *Hansard*,
3 June 1924, 5th ser., v.57, cols.805–40; Motilal Nehru to Spoor and Wedgwood, 22
Feb 1924, *SWMN* iv, 39; Andrews to MacDonald, 22 Feb 1924, copy in JC 402 (II).

of which established a review to be held not before 1929. This provision could, of course, be amended, but only by legislation, which meant, given the parliamentary position in 1924, with the support of Liberal MPs. This was not inconceivable, for although few Liberal MPs were keen on an early review of the Montagu–Chelmsford reforms, they were also anxious not to break with the Labour Government on the wrong question. Wedgwood therefore believed the parliamentary position was secure, certainly so if the Viceroy (the Liberal former Chief Justice Lord Reading) and the Cabinet were united.[8] But this in turn effectively provided the Viceroy with a veto on Labour Government policy. This was the second problem. Reading was open to the possibility of hinting at an early advance in order to break the alliance between the Swarajists and the cooperating politicians whose support they needed to defeat his Government's budget in the Legislative Assembly. But he was adamant that such an offer needed to be made by him, and opposed any attempt to introduce it over his head from London. Within the framework of the Act, moreover, much of provincial government had been devolved or delegated to Governors and their councils. They were in most cases engaged in their own coalition-building, which sometimes required concessions along the lines of those contemplated by Reading at the centre. But like Reading they wanted to retain control of these delicate manoeuvres for themselves and resisted any suggestion that their own offers might be trumped by a better offer in London. The views of the man on the spot, if unmatched by any rival evidence ministers had gathered for themselves, was incontestably authoritative. Thus any revision of existing plans had initially to be negotiated with irremovable Governors and Viceroys appointed by previous administrations, drawn from a class which had little traditional sympathy with Labour's wider aims, which was in large measure worried about Labour's inexperience and plans for the empire, and which enjoyed considerable autonomy to block or retard measures of which they disapproved. In this way the 1919 Act had created a much less wieldy machine for direction from Whitehall. Although the Secretary of State retained formal powers to direct the Indian Governments, conventions designed to develop responsible government now made their use harder. Moreover, Labour ministers had themselves supported the Act in the belief that a period

---

[8] Olivier to MacDonald, 16 Feb 1924, PRO 30/69/199, NA; Wedgwood, 'India—Constitutional Questions'; Cabinet, 28 Feb 1924, CM17 (24)13, CAB 23/47, NA.

of uninterrupted council work would enable ICS officials to win the confidence of Indian legislators and Indian politicians to learn the political skills of compromise and responsibility. This made them reluctant to intervene. MacDonald thus advised his new Secretary of State that he should not issue directions to the Viceroy, but should make him feel his responsibility for building a working majority in the Assembly.[9]

The India Office too remained bound into procedures and strategies which made it hard for an incoming Secretary of State to alter its direction. When Reading suggested to London that a statement of the policy the new Government proposed to pursue might help to damp down speculation in the nationalist press, Hirtzel, now the Permanent Under-Secretary, argued that it would be a mistake for the Government of India even to imply that a change of Government in London might mean a change of course in India.[10] Hirtzel and his colleagues rejected Reading's request to be allowed to hint at an early review of Montagu–Chelmsford as a means of bargaining in the legislature.[11] The Council of India also remained an obstacle. Although it had lost some of its powers to approve official correspondence under the 1919 Act, its advice was still needed and carried some weight on changes of policy. In 1924, it departed from the precedent of not issuing memoranda of dissent from the Secretary of State's proposals, and its views were communicated directly to the Cabinet.[12] The Council and the India Office officials were also well connected to the India public—the constellation of learned societies, institutes and the associations of retired officials and Indian businessmen—which monopolised discussion of Indian questions in the press and with which Labour had hardly any acquaintance at all.

For these reasons, Labour ministers' task changed early and sharply, as they were forced back from the advocacy and implementation of a fresh policy regarding India to the creation of institutions and procedures to enable such a policy to be advocated and implemented. The Cabinet's

[9] MacDonald to Olivier, 14 Feb and 24 April 1924, PRO 30/69/199, NA.

[10] Minute by Hirtzel, 30 Jan 1924, L/PJ/6/1871, OIOC.

[11] Minutes by Dawson, Hirtzel and others, 29 and 30 Jan 1924, L/PJ/6/1871, OIOC; 'India: Constitutional Questions: Viceroy's Intentions', CP34(24), CAB 24/164; Olivier to Reading, 2 Feb 1924, circulated as CP55(24), 4 Feb 1924, CAB24/164; Olivier to Reading, 28 Feb 1924, RP, MSS/Eur/E238/7.

[12] Syed Anwar Husain, 'The Organisation and Administration of the India Office, 1910–1924' (London, Ph.D., 1978).

first attempt to do so was initiated by Wedgwood, who proposed to break the stranglehold of the officials on policy by making direct and official contact with the Swarajists. He persuaded the Cabinet's India Committee to agree to hold a conference in London in which ministers and MPs from all parties, with Olivier in the chair, would review the Swarajist case and the Government of India case side by side. Olivier was prepared to go along with this idea on the grounds that it would 'most uncomfortably knock the stuffing out of a great deal of . . . [the Congress] case'.[13] But it horrified his officials and the Council of India, for whom it threatened the kind of linking up they had always resisted, now backed with the authority of government. They argued that it would amount to a humiliation of the Government of India for it to be placed in the dock while its critics were given a metropolitan platform from which to attack it.[14] The Viceroy too, who had complained privately to the King about Wedgwood's backstairs diplomacy, told Olivier that he and his Council were unanimously opposed.[15] Though the India Committee and the Cabinet did not wish to abandon the plan, they felt they could only ask the Viceroy to suggest other ways of reaching the Swarajists.[16]

With the official route seemingly blocked, Labour ministers tried to use unofficial diplomacy to broker a deal with the Swarajists. In parallel with the official communications running through the India Office and the Viceroy, informal exchanges took place: between Wedgwood and Motilal Nehru; between Sidney Webb and Lajpat Rai; between MacDonald and the brother of the Swarajist President and Bengali leader, C. R. Das, as well as indirectly with Motilal; and between David Graham Pole and the Swarajist leader in Bombay, M. R. Jayakar and the Liberal leader in Madras, V. S. S. Sastri.[17] In London, the Bombay nationalist S. R. Bomanji and Baptista acted as intermediaries with the

[13] 'Indian Affairs', 3 March 1924, CP(151)24, CAB24/165, NA; Cabinet, 12 March 1924, CM20(24)3, CAB 23/47, NA.
[14] Indian Affairs Committee meetings IA(24)1 6 March 1924, IA(24)2, 7 March 1924, IA(24)3, 10 March 1924 CAB 27/229, NA; 'Opinion of Policy Towards India: Note by Members of Council' 11 March 1924, CP164(24) and amended telegram, 11 March 1924, CP164A(24), CAB 24/165, NA.
[15] Secret appreciation, 27 March 1924, Royal Archives, RA/PS/GV/N2555/63; Viceroy to Secretary of State, 21 March and 2 April 1924, CP(208)24, CAB 24/166, NA.
[16] IA(24)4 26 March 1924, CAB 27/229; Cabinet, 27 March 1924, CM 23 (24) 11, CAB 23/47; 'Indian Political Aims: Proposed Conference', March 1924, CP 208 (24), CAB 24/166; Olivier to Reading, 27 March 1924, RP, MSS/Eur/E238/7.
[17] Cabinet, 5 March 1924, CM18(24)3, CAB 23/47.

Prime Minister, Cabinet ministers and the Labour Party. The Labour ministers and their allies tried to persuade the Swarajists to abandon their disruptive tactics and be patient. 'If the Councils are worked', Pole told Jayakar, 'there is *no doubt* that when we come into [majority] power things will go on very quickly. The P.M. stands by all he has said & promised & *Lord Olivier is entirely with him.* Please convey this (privately) to Mr. C. R. Das. I have conveyed his messages to the P.M. & Secy of State'. Since the London conference had been rejected by the Viceroy, Pole tried to persuade Das to visit unofficially. 'I am very closely in touch with Cabinet ministers here & often see three or four Cabinet ministers in a day', he told Jayakar. 'I *know* things are progressing much more quickly than appears outwardly, but I am precluded from writing freely. Do try to persuade Mr Das to come over here. I can get him in touch directly with the right people, and a round table conference here will help on things in India more than I can say'.[18] Similar messages went via Bomanji to Motilal Nehru. 'Lansbury, Scurr, Wedgwood and other Labourites were firm & the Prime Minister himself is firm' and 'eager to help us', Bomanji assured Motilal. He should not judge their intentions by their speeches which had to be made to disarm Labour's critics. 'Things are moving on more quickly here than appears on the surface', Pole insisted.[19] Party channels were also employed. The Labour Party Advisory Committee on Imperial Questions, in contact through Baptista with nationalist opinion, argued that the Swarajists might settle privately on moderate terms with a Labour government if given some concessions on the workings of diarchy for the present and an accelerated Royal Commission. The concessions included the transfer of some central subjects to provinces, and, in the provinces, some reserved matters to the elected councils; conventions that Bills which could not attract 30 per cent support would be withdrawn, and the appointment of Indians to posts in the India Office and the ICS.[20] However, the India Office officials to whom these proposals were shown dismissed them as unworkable without legislation and the agreement of the Governors and Viceroy.[21]

---

[18] Pole to Jayakar, 13 March 1924, JC 402(II).
[19] Bomanji to Motilal, 20, 23, 27 and 28 March, 14 and 17 April 1924, MNC; Pole to Jayakar, 20 March, 30 April, and 5 May 1924, JC 403.
[20] LPACImpQ Memos. 6 and 6A, June 1924, LPA.
[21] Hemming to Brown, 26 June 1924; Gillies to Olivier, 7 July 1924; Minutes by Brown, Dawson, Kershaw, Hirtzel, 22–4 Jul 1924, L/PO/1/14, OIOC; TUC & Labour Party Deputation to the India Office, 31 July 1924, L/PO/1/16, OIOC.

Such unofficial intermediaries were only able to offer hints rather than guarantees and these were insufficient to tempt the Swarajists to the conference table in London. The Viceroy and the India Office continued to resist attempts to harden the invitations that ministers wanted to make into official ones, or to raise the status of the proposed conference. 'India has patiently waited for the Labour Party to extend the hand of friendship and goodwill', Jayakar told Pole, 'but it seems you have your difficulties in England, to which you have surrendered your higher ideal in your desire to retain power.'[22] Motilal managed to suspend the Swarajists' actions in the Assembly temporarily, but in the absence of guarantees, he could not stop the rejection of the Finance Bill on 17 March.[23] This action seemed to MacDonald to make it much harder to make progress behind the scenes. He told Annie Besant later in the year:

You know, it did give us an awfully difficult job when you turned down the Budget . . . We were just in, we had not got off our feet, we were floundering infants in water . . . When I came here on the 3rd January I had a Cabinet of men . . . who had never pulled their full responsibility . . . [B]efore we had five minutes to turn around and consider our Indian policy, you threw out our Budget and filled the newspapers with the riot spirit of modern India. The effect was to paralyse us. . [.] You did us a great difficulty . . . by rousing all that gang.[24]

Olivier too was angered by the impatience of the Swarajists, who seemed unprepared to give the Montagu–Chelmsford reforms a fair trial.[25] Their tactics suggested that they did 'not have enough civic intelligence to be capable of running a parish council'.[26] Olivier believed that the Swarajist movement could only count on the support of a 'comparatively small educated class' and had 'no real backing'. He distrusted its pretensions of democracy, since priests and lawyers could only be expected to govern as 'adjutants of military or plutocratic power'.[27]

[22] Jayakar to Pole, 12 March 1924, JC 402 II.

[23] Motilal Nehru to Wedgwood, 12 and 19 March 1924, *SWMN*, iv, 39–40.

[24] 'Deputation to Prime Minister re: Dominion status for India', 18 July 1924, PREM 1/40, NA. See also MacDonald to Das, 28 Feb 1924, PRO 30/69/2, NA; MacDonald to Natesan, 8 July 1929, PRO 30/69/672, NA; MacDonald to Wald, 27 May 1930, PRO 30/69/1440, NA.

[25] Olivier to Reading, 2 Feb 1924, CP55(24), 4 Feb 1924, CAB24/164; Olivier to Reading, 27 March 1924, RP, MSS/Eur/E238/7; Olivier's notes on 'Telegram from Viceroy 14 April 1924', PRO 30/69/35, NA.

[26] Bridge and Brasted, 'British Labour and Indian Nationalism', 81.

[27] Olivier to Wells, 25 April 1924, quoted in Margaret Olivier (ed.), *Sydney Olivier: Letters and Selected Writings* (London, 1948), 157.

It would take many more years of cooperation in local government before India developed 'real schools of political thought as distinct from communal, religious or caste interests'. Until then, complete self-government was 'not within the range of practical politics'.[28] Indians needed the experience of 'getting to work together for political purposes which only parliamentary experience can give'. Outlining a speech to this effect, he had promised MacDonald that he would 'lay emphasis upon the history of the progress of our own Party, now arrived at Parliamentary power'.[29]

But the Swarajists were prisoners of the Gandhians: in April they faced a trial of strength with the Gandhians at the AICC which, as Jayakar warned Pole, required them to step back from appeals to Britain.[30] Gandhi continued to advocate the no-change position and scorned efforts to link up with Labour.[31] 'People do not leave off the hope of getting hope from outside. Who can give *swaraj*? We have to take it', he insisted.[32] Although Gandhi failed to win sufficient support at the AICC to pull the Swarajists off the councils, he remained an obstacle to a private deal with the Government in London.

The India Office and its allies disliked the use of such unofficial channels. When it was revealed that Olivier had exchanged letters unofficially with Satyamurti, there was a motion of censure in the Lords, and substantial press criticism from India.[33] 'Poor Olivier!', Sastri wrote. 'Montagu was never so slanged by the Tory press. The correspondents of the *Post* and the *Telegraph* are cabling undiluted poison from India.'[34] The Government of India sent its Home Member, Sir Malcolm Hailey, to London to represent its objections to Labour's proposals. Hailey persuaded MacDonald that the Swarajists were unrepresentative of Indian opinion at large and that their pressure must be resisted. He also lobbied the Liberals to withdraw their parliamentary support

---

[28] *Daily Herald*, 14 July 1927.

[29] Olivier to MacDonald, 22 Jan 1924, PRO 30/69/199, NA.

[30] Jayakar to Pole, 29 March and 4 April 1924, JC 402(II); Jayakar to Pole, 2 April 1924, JC 403; Motilal Nehru to Bomanji, 24 March 1924 and undated, MNC; Speech at Bombay, 18 April 1924, *SWMN*, iv, 211–17.

[31] Interview, 20 March 1924, *CWMG* E27/95; Interview, 21 March 1924, *CWMG* E27/102; Interview, 27 March 1924, *CWMG* E27/126; *Young India*, 3 July 1924, *CWMG* E28/134.

[32] Interview, before 5 Feb 1924, *CWMG* E27/6.

[33] *Hansard*, Lords, 3 June 1924, 5th series, v.57, cols.805–40; Bomanji to Nehru, 3 and 9 April 1924, MNC.

[34] Sastri to Zacharias, 24 July 1924, SC 407.

from Labour, a strategy which succeeded when Sir Edward Grigg and his fellow Liberals withdrew from Pole's Indian Parliamentary Committee.[35]

The result was a progressive scaling-down of Labour's plans: from a round table conference to official talks, and then to private invitations.[36] 'It is a misfortune that your Government cannot be persuaded to invite the Swarajist leaders in the regular way as they certainly would have done, if they were dealing with a country with a white population', wrote Jayakar.[37] Since Indian leaders turned private invitations down, a move which some despairing Labour allies now recommended, the outcome announced in May was even more diluted: a restricted Government of India enquiry (the Muddiman Committee) with strict instructions to work within the bounds of the 1919 Act. It was, as Arthur Henderson admitted, a 'gesture'.[38]

This led to more or less complete disillusionment with Labour.[39] When Sastri visited London he found the Labour ministers had given up their plans for a conference. Olivier, he reported to India, was 'a simple man' but 'very weak', carrying little weight in Cabinet, who would 'dance to the Viceroy's tune'.

Lansbury says he is a log of wood. Graham Pole agreed and is even more caustic. Both he and Richards [Olivier's Under-Secretary] are bad bargains for India. [. . .] The Prime Minister is the only man that counts. He doesn't wish to do anything *now*. Lord Chelmsford counts . . . [H]e is dead against any advance. Haldane . . . is a ten-year wallah . . . [who] swear[s] by 1929.[40]

Trevelyan and Wedgwood, however, were still favourably disposed. They told Sastri and Besant that they accepted the right of the Swarajists to continue their non-cooperation from within the Councils.[41] Richards hoped for progress once the Muddiman Committee reported, a further

[35] Gupta, *Imperialism*, 105–6; Bomanji to Nehru, 17 April 1924, MNC; Pole to Jayakar, 17 and 24 April 1924, JC 403; Hailey to Private Secretary to Viceroy, undated but before 20 April, Hailey Papers, E220/5D.

[36] MacDonald to Reading, 8 April 1924 and Reading to MacDonald, 11 April 1924, PRO 30/69/35, NA; 'Viceroy's Suggestions for creating contact with leaders of Indian opinion', 4 April 1924, CP236(24), CAB 24/166.

[37] Jayakar to Pole, 13 and 20 May 1924, JC 403.

[38] Henderson to Reading, 16 April 1924, RP, MSS/Eur/E238/21.

[39] Lajpat Rai to Huebsch, 2 June 1924, *SCLR*, 246–7.

[40] T. N. Jagadisan (ed.) *Letters of the Rt. Hon V.S.Srinivasa Sastri* (Bombay, 1963), 132–8.

[41] Minutes of Deputation to Olivier at India Office, 17 June 1924, Besant Papers, 17; Sastri to Patwardhan, 19 June 1924, SC 403.

sign of how the authority of Indian officials was needed to validate Labour's policies.[42]

By the autumn, even the commitment to civil rights had gone. In June, the Governor of Bengal, Lord Lytton, had demanded Ordinance powers to detain suspected revolutionaries without trial.[43] The Cabinet had feared that this might lead to 'an entire destruction of any hope of ordered constitutional progress in India'.[44] But as over constitutional reform, they found themselves unable to resist demands from their officials, especially when questions of imperial security and intelligence were concerned. Without guarantees from Congress that its methods would remain constitutional, Labour could not afford to risk the charge that it had given way to direct action and terrorism. There had been such accusations from the Conservative benches when Olivier spoke warmly of the idealism of the Swarajist leaders.[45] Wedgwood tried to persuade MacDonald to insist that Lytton be ordered to offer to take Das into the Government as a condition of these Ordinance powers, and that the informal channel of Das's brother be used to communicate the offer privately to Das himself. 'The latest telegrams leave the Sub-Committee no option unless you take a hand', he wrote.[46] Privately, Wedgwood was sanguine about the dangers of the revolutionaries, writing to Trevelyan:

[I]f a Labour govt (the last hope) go the way of Morley & once start coercion, we shall never get over it. What does it matter if a few Englishmen are murdered? A million were killed in the war—all as it were for the good name of England. . . If we could keep it off for two months all might yet be well.[47]

At the India Committee, Wedgwood and Trevelyan favoured postponing the Ordinance; and Chelmsford and Olivier granting it, Webb remaining neutral.[48] At Cabinet, however, Olivier argued that since the

[42] Sastri to Zacharias, 24 July 1924, SC 407; Pole to Jayakar, 17 July 1924, JC 403.
[43] 'The activities of Revolutionists in Bengal subsequent to August 1923', June 1924; and 'Activities of Revolutionists in Bengal subsequent to June 1924', Aug 1924; Lytton to Reading, 26 June 1924; Reading to Olivier, 9 July 1924, L/PJ/6/1886, OIOC.
[44] Cabinet, 30 July 1924, CAB 45(24)2, CAB 23/47; 'Revolutionary Movement in Bengal', 30 July 1924, CP423(24), CAB 24/168; Olivier to Reading, 31 July 1924, RP, MSS/Eur/E238/7.
[45] *Hansard* (Lords), 26 Feb and 21 July 1924, v.56, col.320, v.58, col.766.
[46] Wedgwood to MacDonald, 12 Sept 1924, PRO 30/69/36, NA.
[47] Wedgwood to Trevelyan, 11 Sept 1924, quoted in Gupta, *Imperialism*, 107; Wedgwood to MacDonald, 12 Sept 1924, and Olivier to MacDonald, 15 Sept 1924, PRO 30/69/36, NA.
[48] MacDonald to Wedgwood, 13 Sept 1924, PRO 30/69/36, NA; Indian Affairs Committee, 15 Sept 1924, IA(24) 13, CAB 27/229, NA.

Viceroy and Lytton had advised him that Das had links with terroris[
conspirators, he could not force them to invite Das to take office.[49] The
Cabinet, Chelmsford told his successor as Viceroy, was

anxious . . . to add a rider that you should devise, without delay, some . . . policy
which would save India from the political movement drifting into the revolutionary movement . . . I pointed out that this must be in large measure
academic; that you had this constantly in mind; and that if we wanted to help
you we should indicate with greater precision the direction of our policy[50]

Indeed, Chelmsford had insisted on the authority of the Viceroy
throughout. 'It has not been an easy task combating the ignorant and
futile fanaticism of Wedgwood & Trevelyan & the Indians . . . I have
sometimes assented to foolish requests to you because I was confident
what your reply would be. This was the case when they asked for
a declaration of policy before your Committee had reported.'[51] The
Ordinance powers were duly granted, with the proviso that they were
to be used only against the 'assassination and physical revolutionary
movements', not political movements.[52]

The experience of the first Labour Government suggests how wrong it
is to regard the British imperial state simply as a neutral machine under
the direction of elected governments. Labour ministers had reservations
about Congress and did not seriously regard self-government as an
immediate objective. But even their narrower aims proved unachievable,
despite being just sufficient to form the basis of a settlement with
Congress. This was because they had to operate through institutions
and procedures devised by others with different aims, and by securing
the cooperation of political actors already committed to existing policies.
This did not make progress within the inherited structures impossible,
because such actors were themselves subject to the pressure for change:
most clearly the need to win sufficient collaboration with the reformed
councils. But it significantly raised the costs of deviating from existing
policy. This was why Labour was drawn quickly into the effort to build
alternative, parallel structures through direct contact with the Swarajists
which, being private and unofficial, might form the basis of a deal
which could then be fed back into the official policy process. Such

---

[49] Cabinet CM50(24)1, 22 Sept 1924, CAB23/48.
[50] Chelmsford to Reading, 24 Sept 1924, RP, MSS/Eur/E238/21.
[51] Chelmsford to Reading, 25 Nov 1924, Reading Private Coll., MSS/Eur/F118/104.
[52] Cabinet CM50(24)1, 22 Sept 1924, CAB23/48; Olivier to Reading, 18 Sept 1924,
RP, MSS/Eur/E238/7.

alternative structures might also have provided them with intelligence to counter the lurid accusations made by their officials. This alternative structure failed, but it did so not merely because of official opposition to it, serious though this was, but because the currencies of its dealings were understandings and promises, based on trust, rather than public guarantees, in turn the result of the estrangement of Labour and Congress since the death of Tilak. Although Indian intermediaries struggled valiantly to bring about agreement, they could speak with no authority in London. The encounter proved, as Bomanji told Motilal, 'how necessary it is for us to have some organization here'.[53] Yet, as before, the organizational fracture and the political one weakened each other: Labour still thought of Britons as the appropriate judges of Indian fitness for self-government. Congress, however, required the round table conference as the guarantor of an equality of status.

After 1924, the unity of the Swarajist grouping was broken by provincial disagreements over the terms on which office might or might not be accepted, calculations which varied according to local opportunity. As a result, a variety of Liberals, Independents, and non-Brahmans became semi-detached members of Congress, working within the legislatures. Gandhi had removed himself to the ashram, having failed in his attempts to turn Congress away from working the reforms and towards his pet schemes for non-cooperation and rural uplift.[54] Many Muslims also moved further away from Congress, some to join the Muslim League which met apart from Congress in 1924 for the first time in six years. The abolition of the Khilafat the same year had put paid to the issue that had brought them into alliance with Gandhi, and the same pressures of provincial legislative politics were forcing divisive strategic choices. Muslims in provinces where the franchise arrangements had favoured them now saw little reason to abandon separate electorates as Congress wished, while those who faced Hindu majorities began to find their exclusion from power more costly, which led in turn to an intensification of communal identities. Gandhi's efforts through fasting and conference to rebuild the earlier unity he had achieved at the time of Khilafat proved unsuccessful. The communal organizations on the fringes of Congress, such as the Hindu Mahasabha, took support both from those who felt that Congress was insufficiently attentive to Hindu

---

53 Bomanji to Nehru, 14 April 1924, MNC.
54 Brown, *Gandhi and Civil Disobedience*, 14–28.

interests, and those who feared that they would lose votes unless they campaigned under its flag.[55] By 1926, there was thus great regional variation in the texture of Indian politics. Attempts to coordinate the activities of the Swarajists by Das and Motilal Nehru failed and the commandments of AICC and even Provincial Committees too were frequently ignored. British officials welcomed these opportunities to strengthen their provincial alliances, and did their best to ignore All-India politicians except when they might be used to exert a moderating influence.

At first sight, this might seem to be precisely the kind of fragmentation that Labour leaders like MacDonald had hoped would follow the creation of opportunities for Congress to enter government. However, although there was undoubtedly now a deeper and wider politics in India, stable, responsible *party* politics, in the sense that Labour wanted to see them, did not seem to have emerged. There were parties, but they were loose coalitions based around the ambitions of individuals or communal factions, and divisions along lines of class had not formed. When Lajpat Rai set up a Hindu Party, Wedgwood hoped that the new party would exclude the 'priests and fanatics and superstition-mongers' and make the abolition of communal electorates and reserved jobs part of its programme.[56] An Indian Labour Party failed within months of its foundation, since hardly anyone except the British Labour Party wanted it: the Swarajists believed that it would act independently of their own urban movements and, in dividing industry along class lines, detract from national unity; the Gandhians had their own distinctive view of the best means of securing harmony between labour and capital, in which there was little place for a union-dominated labour party of the British type; and the Communists did not want a further rival for the support of India's industrial workers.[57] There were voters and supporters, but they had not been organised in a western sense: they continued to be recruited and rewarded largely in the old fashion. There were politicians, but they had not entirely settled to constitutional politics and remained too open to the possibility of reunifying the movement with non-cooperation when the opportunity arose. Moreover, at times like this, when politics became provincialised, it became even harder for British

[55] R. A. Gordon, 'The Hindu Mahasabha and the Indian National Congress, 1915–1926', *Modern Asian Studies*, 9/2 (1975), 145–203.

[56] Wedgwood to Lajpat Rai, 8 Oct 1925, *SCLR*, 368–70.

[57] Joshi to Pole, 22 Oct 1926, Joshi Papers; Gupta, 'British Labour and the Indian Left', 93.

sympathisers to trace the course nationalism was taking and thereby to judge its authenticity. Provincial leaders, with whom they were in any case less acquainted, could present at best a partial picture of nationalist politics, weighted in favour of their own interests. All-India figures, whom they knew better, were peculiarly vulnerable when the resources and sanctions they could deploy competed so unfavourably with the incentives available at the provincial level. Their behaviour, therefore, seemed no less wayward and capricious. These divisions were confirmed by another Labour tourist, Oswald Mosley, who circulated a report to leading politicians on his return arguing that 'bloodshed on a great scale' would follow a British departure. Mosley witnessed an attempt by Gandhi to reunite Congress with the Ali brothers, but it collapsed in disagreement. Hindus and Muslims were hopelessly divided, he concluded: 'we could stay in India as long as we wished . . . [N]ever had *divide et impera* been so easy'.[58]

Labour Party responses to these developments were correspondingly complex. The party leadership, especially Lansbury, were closest to Annie Besant, who had gathered together representatives of all the cooperating Indian groupings into a National Convention to write an Indian constitution. This had produced in 1925 the Commonwealth of India Bill, which provided for responsible self-government for an Indian Federation, with defence and foreign affairs reserved for Britain. At the 1925 Labour Party Conference it was agreed to demand that the Government call a convention of Indian politicians to discuss it. However, Congress had opposed the Bill, and the ILP wanted the conference to be on an 'all parties' basis—that is, to include non cooperating politicians too—and for it to discuss other proposals, such as the Congress demand for self-determination on the Dominion model.[59] To Besant's irritation, the Conference accepted the ILP's amendments, affirming India's right to 'full self-government and self-determination'. The Commonwealth of India Bill itself was not endorsed by the party and only introduced in Parliament, unsuccessfully, as a Private Member's Bill.[60]

[58] Oswald Mosley, *My Life* (London, 1968), 120–7.

[59] ILP, NAC minutes, 1–2 Dec 1924; ILP, Report of Annual Conference, 1925, 16, 159–1.

[60] Besant to Pole, 6 Aug 1925, Pole Papers (OIOC), MSS/Eur/F264/9; Pole to Lansbury, 12 Feb 1926, Pole Papers (Borthwick), 1; *Parliamentary Papers* (Commons), 1924–5, i, 499–556.

The ILP was therefore moving slowly towards endorsing the Congress demand for self-determination. Brockway managed to pack the ILP's Indian Advisory Committee to outnumber Besant's supporters, Scurr and Pole.[61] In 1926, the Committee produced a report which dismissed the Commonwealth of India Bill as containing undemocratic flaws 'which British Socialists must deplore', such as provision for second chambers and a franchise which would confine the vote largely to those with higher education. Instead, the Government should, as the Swarajists demanded, summon a constitution-making convention, which would contain representatives of Indian workers and peasants.[62] Besant's allies wrote a dissenting minute dismissing the need for further discussions.[63] But the ILP Conference endorsed the majority report, and its committees set to work drawing up new plans to bring round to the idea the Labour party and the trade unions.[64]

Despite this commitment, the ILP's support for self-determination was qualified. Some members of the Indian Advisory Committee were troubled by what they saw as the incapacity of Indians at devising constitutions. One member, Norman Leys, wrote directly to Gandhi to put the dilemma to him. Nationalist movements had only succeeded historically, he wrote, when they had won majority support, but this was unimaginable in India for many years. India's constitution-making would need outside help. The ILP had 'an unprecedented experience, not only of the operation of democratic institutions but of the framing of constitutions for other countries'. It might therefore devise a constitution for India in the hope that its imprimatur would win wider support in India than Congress had managed to achieve itself.[65] While Leys supported the ILP's commitment to self-determination he still found it hard to trust Indians to make the right use of it. He told Gandhi of his worry that 'the inexperience of Indians will lead them to choose to represent them bad men . . . . who will deceive the people with flattery [or] . . . fill their own pockets.' 'If I were a member of a committee with the task of giving India self-government', he wrote, 'I should feel in my bones that the whole scheme might break down.' The right men clearly existed in sufficient numbers, but could Indian voters be

[61] Gupta, *Imperialism*, 111   [62] ILP, *Report of Annual Conference*, 1926, 53–5.
[63] ILP, *The Condition of India*, Report of ILP Indian Advisory Committee, May 1926.
[64] ILP, Joint Meeting of the Indian Advisory Committee and the Empire Policy Committee, 9 July 1926.
[65] Leys to Gandhi, 29 June 1926, Gandhi Papers, SN 30/12168; Gandhi to Leys, 23 July 1926, *CWMG* E36/90

trusted to choose them?[66] Gandhi, by now used to explaining to British sympathisers that Congress was not asking for India to be given self-government, but asserting its right to it, told Leys his fears were not groundless, but that they should not deter a reformer. 'You cannot', he observed, 'wrap yourself in cotton wool and fight freedom's battle.'[67] Gandhi had also been unhelpfully honest about Leys' worry, shared by other Labour leaders, that the splitting of Congress suggested that a free India would be wracked by communal strife. While he opposed communalism himself, Gandhi replied, a fight would probably happen anyway. British officials fostered divisions, of course, but 'the fault is ours. If we were not disposed to quarrel, no outside power on earth could make us.' 'You practically admit that Muslims would resist by fighting if a democratic government were set up in India', wrote a worried Leys. 'A clash of arms will not move me', Gandhi replied. 'Any real movement for freedom is like new birth and all its attendant travail.'[68]

A second qualification concerned Congress' relationship with social-ism. Indian labour leaders and Swarajists Chaman Lall and N. M. Joshi had tried to use the Commonwealth Labour Conference in 1925 as a platform for demands for self-government, and while this was treated sympathetically, there was concern that the Swarajists were keener on winning power than troubled by the condition of Indian labour.[69] The ILP's own programme for India therefore contained a lengthy prescription of improvements that would need to be made if the masses were not to suffer under Swarajist rule, including franchise extensions, universal and compulsory education, land redistribution and labour legislation.[70] How these were to be reconciled with the commitment to self-determination was not altogether clear.

It was also soon clear that the trade unions would not easily be persuaded to support the ILP's commitment to the Swarajists. The British trade union movement had moved slowly to develop its own Indian policy, reflecting its interest in protecting British workers from sweated competition as well as the desirability of spreading trade unionism within the empire.[71] It had in essence followed a dual strategy, directed both at Congress and the *raj*. In a long series of

---

[66] Leys to Gandhi, 9 Aug 1926, Gandhi Papers, SN 30/12170.
[67] Gandhi to Leys, 3 Sept 1926, *CWMG* E36/289.   [68] Ibid.
[69] 'The Essex Hall Meeting', *Indian Quarterly Review*, 1925, v.2, 152.
[70] ILP, *Report of Annual Conference*, 1925, 16, 159–61; *Report of Annual Conference*, 1926, 53–5.
[71] See Marjorie Nicholson, *The TUC Overseas: the Roots of Policy* (1986).

debates over Indian tariffs, British trade unionists had joined their employers to lobby the British Government, and through it the raj, to take account of the interests of British exporters. The textile unions had, for example, opposed the raising of Indian cotton duties in 1917 and 1921.[72] Besides making self-interested arguments, they also suggested that while Indian workers and consumers lacked the vote, they needed protection from Indian capitalists which it was British workers' duty to provide. For this reason, they also resisted attempts to transfer powers over industrial matters to Indian hands before the franchise was widened and trade unions had grown up to defend Indian workers against their employers.[73] However, the unions did accept that India's tariff autonomy could not be curtailed. They also resisted India Office efforts to co-opt them into the work of disciplining the Indian labour force. Instead they had sought, like the Labour Party more widely, the role of intermediary: advising and helping to organise a strong and independent Indian trade union movement, speaking for it in London, and leading it towards non-Communist international organisations.

At the 1922 Trades Union Congress, it was decided to appoint a joint commission with the Labour Party to investigate labour conditions east of Suez.[74] However, very little was done to set this work going, and in March 1925, the TUC decided to act alone through a specially convened Far Eastern sub-committee of its own International Committee. Its 1925 report drew a dispiriting picture of the poor organisation of the Indian unions and proposed delegations of British trade unionists to investigate the organisation of the Indian workers.[75] Formal investigations were opposed by the Government but informal visits were made in 1925–6 by the Dundee MP and prominent ILP-er Tom Johnston, in 1926–7 by Tom Shaw for the Textile International and in 1927–8 by A. A. Purcell and Joseph Hallsworth.[76] The 1925 report, by H. W. Lee, had argued

---

[72] Deputation of UTWA, 10 March 1921, L/E/7/1062/1536 and details of proposed trade delegation, L/E/7/1066/1744, OIOC; Gupta, 'India and British Labour', 75; Montagu to Reading, 15 Aug 1921, Montagu Coll., MSS/Eur/D523/12; Labour Party, *Report of Annual Conference*, 1924, 58–9; 'Note on the Points to be Raised by the TUC and Labour Party Delegation', 23 July 1924, L/PO/1/16, OIOC.

[73] D. G. Pole and B. S. Rao, 'Industrial Conditions in India', 1926, MSS 292/954/1, TUC Archive.

[74] TUC, *Report of Annual Conference*, 1922, 457–9.

[75] Far Eastern Labour Committee, 'Interim Report', 1925, MSS 292/950/6, TUC; TUC, *Report of Annual Conference*, 1925, 71–2, 553.

[76] Deputation to India Office, 3 Dec 1925, MSS 292/954/16, TUC; Nicholson, *TUC Overseas*, 96–7; Thomas Johnston and J. F. Sime, *Exploitation in India* (Dundee,

that India posed no real threat to European industry because 'Indian workers in the mass do not seem capable of the sustained intensive effort which modern industry demands', failings it put down to the Indian workers' low standards of living, illiteracy, migratory habits and the hot climate.[77] But the visitors' conclusions were more alarmist: there would be an enormous expansion in industrial employment in the years to come. In the short term, certain sectors of British industry such as engineering, railways and shipbuilding might expect to benefit from the export opportunities afforded by Indian industrialisation. But it was only a matter of time before India developed her own industries in these areas too, with the prospect for the British working class of 'the severe shock of a very great change', as Indian workers in most industries were paid at rates from about 1/8 to 1/6 of their British counterparts.[78]

Indian trade unionism, moreover, faced very serious obstacles and was in danger of getting off on the wrong foot. For Shaw, Indian workers were trapped in a 'spider's web of criss-cross problems of religion, tradition, of method and work'. There was little sign that they even wanted improvements, let alone that they were prepared or able to insist upon having them. They seemed passive and indifferent to their poor conditions, even their faces 'seem[ing] to express an infinite patience and resignation, quite different from the expressions seen on the faces of a European audience'. The only cooperative institutions that Indian workers had evolved for themselves, Shaw reported despairingly, were moneylending ones. Even the task of local organisation was 'so complex as to appear at times perfectly hopeless'.[79] The hostility of employers and officials, poverty, illiteracy, and the rapid labour turnover associated with migration made the day-to-day work of trade unionism very hard. Worse still, unions were unable to find officers from among rank and file workers, but had to rely on 'leisured and professional people'.[80] There was also extensive doubling-up. Lee reported that in one union the President and Secretary were the same person, and that two industrious

1926); Gerald Douds, 'Tom Johnston in India', *Journal of Scottish Labour History*, 19 (1984), 6–21; Graham Walker, *Tom Johnston* (Manchester, 1988); Thomas Shaw, 'Report on India to the TUC General Council', April 1927, MSS 292/950/5, TUC; A. A. Purcell and Joseph Hallsworth, 'Visit to India', MSS 292/954/34, TUC; A. A. Purcell and J. Hallsworth, *Report on Labour Conditions in India* (1928).

[77] Far Eastern Labour Committee, 'Interim Report'.
[78] Purcell and Hallsworth, 'Visit to India'.　　[79] Shaw, 'Report on India'.
[80] Far Eastern Labour Committee, 'Interim Report'; TUC Memorandum for the Whitley Commission, 13 Sept 1929, MSS 292/954/9, TUC; Tom Johnston, *Memories* (London, 1952), 71.

Bombay solicitors occupied official positions in eight and nine trade unions respectively.[81] Given the illiteracy of nearly all the workforce, Shaw thought there was no alternative to the management of unions by benevolent outsiders.[82] It corresponded to the era in which British trade unionists had themselves been led by lawyers and humanitarians such as Robert Owen. With mass education of the workforce, this phase would pass as it had in Britain. However, Purcell and Hallsworth argued, by the time this happened, the trade union movement might have been irretrievably damaged, largely because the lawyers were primarily Congress nationalists and were using unions simply as a means of boosting their urban demonstrations and pressuring employers to join Congress.[83] The economic desperation of the workers, Purcell and Hallsworth wrote, was thus attracting them to certain unions 'only to be exploited for the purpose of helping on a strictly political and spurious nationalism'.[84] At the British Trades Union Congress in 1924, Purcell had therefore told delegates not to confuse the political and industrial movements in India:

Every year numbers of educated Indians come to this country to complain about administrative and political conditions, and to demand reforms. In nearly every case these well-intentioned gentlemen are either employers, merchants, officials or ex-officials, who are in the main very little concerned with the emancipation of the Indian worker... There is a danger that we will hand over India to mere politicians. This must be avoided. Change at the top which does not alter economic conditions and leaves the workers at the mercy of the same set of exploiters who oppress them today is no change at all. In my view, we should insist that political change should be conditional upon certain necessary and overdue industrial changes... [85]

The Swarajist demand for home rule was, Johnston commented, simply 'the pretence of the... *zemindars* and vociferous money-lenders in India that the starvation and robbery of the poor *ryot*—in which they themselves so shamefully engage—would cease instanter were only they

---

[81] Far Eastern Labour Committee, 'Interim Report'; TUC Memorandum for the Whitley Commission.

[82] Shaw, 'Report on India'.

[83] TUC Memorandum for the Whitley Commission.

[84] Purcell and Hallsworth, *Report on Labour Conditions in India*; Irwin to Birkenhead, 16 Feb 1928; Birkenhead to Irwin, 8 March 1927, HC, MSS/Eur/C152/8; TUC, *Report of Annual Conference*, 1928, 257–8, 472; Gupta, *Imperialism*, 110; *Hansard*, 2 Aug 1928, 5th ser., v.220, cols.2539–44.

[85] TUC, *Report of Annual Conference*, 1924, 71–2.

and their friends permitted to rule India'.[86] The record of the Swarajists and others in government had done little to convince British trade unionists that nationalists had any real interest in improving labour conditions. Purcell told MacDonald on his return how they had forced the Bombay millowners to lock out their own workers and, in Calcutta, had dealt harshly with strikers.[87] 'I am afraid', wrote Shaw, 'that the workers are often led to think that all India needs is political freedom in order that the worker may benefit. As a matter of fact, bad as the conditions now are, they would probably be infinitely worse if the political power were in the hands of the Indian employers.'[88] Thus although the TUC sent money to support Indian workers in their industrial disputes and lobbied the India Office with the demands of the AITUC, its support for the *political* aspirations of the trade unionists was more conditional. It accepted that, under colonialism, the national struggle necessarily preoccupied the Indian unions and that they were right to attack the legal and practical restrictions on labour organisation imposed by the *raj*. At the same time, they had to maintain their independence and build their internal strength for a larger struggle, against the landlords and capitalists who, increasingly, were taking control of Congress.[89]

Union thinking was thus and inevitably guided by its own experiences. In Britain, trade union organisation had preceded the winning of the franchise. Political objectives, important as they were, had followed on the building of an autonomous trade union movement. Indian trade unionism seemed to the TUC visitors to be emerging in a distorted form. The impulses from below that had led to the formation of the British union movement—the only valid model for British observers—were absent or being stifled. Ever alert to the dangers of allowing a working-class movement to fall into the hands of middle-class politicians, the trade unionists were adamant that Indians should concentrate on building a healthy labour movement, and only then think of political action. To get matters back on the right track, Purcell and Hallsworth proposed four organisers be appointed to work in specific industrial

[86] Douds, 'Tom Johnston', 9, 14; *Forward*, 2 Jan 1926, cited in Walker, *Tom Johnston*, 77; Reading to Birkenhead, 28 Jan 1926, RP, MSS/Eur/E238/8; Rennie Smith Diary, 8 Feb 1926, MS Eng.hist.d.287.

[87] J. Ramsay MacDonald, 'Labour Representation in the India Commission', *Forward*, 19 May 1928, quoted in Gupta, *Imperialism*, 116.

[88] Shaw, 'Report on India'.

[89] Meeting at the House of Commons, 8 July 1925, MSS 292/954/1, TUC.

sectors, with the specific provision that they should be independent of any political party. However, both plans were rejected by the General Council on the grounds of cost and the priority of domestic needs in the wake of the General Strike.[90]

What potential for fruitful links was there? Until recently, it has been very hard to answer this question because we have very little idea what the attitudes of Indian industrial workers were. However, the pioneering work of 'subaltern studies' writers in reinterpreting fragments of evidence and the gaps between them, has done a good deal to rescue the attitudes, self-images and survival strategies of the Indian workforce from the 'condescension of posterity'. The reconstructed world of Indian labour is not depicted using the models of western political sociology or history. Western scholars, it is argued, and those they influenced in India, have tended to judge the Indian labour force against the trajectories set by the European working classes. This path to modernity traces the movement of workers from the countryside, their adjustment to the disciplines of factory production and urban life, as old rural values and ties are discarded, and ultimately their acquisition of a proletarian class consciousness, expressed through labour organisation and political mobilisation. But rather than seeing the life of the Indian industrial workforce as a deviant case of western patterns, subaltern writers prefer to examine it in its own terms. Dipesh Chakrabarty's studies of the Calcutta jute-workers, for example, demonstrate how religious, communal and familial ties survived even amid modern factory conditions, and were deployed as means of cultural resistance. What western observers such as Shaw and Johnston saw as the failings of the Indian industrial movement were thus, to a greater degree than they realised, strengths. Indian workers' unwillingness to join trade unions or socialist political parties was not simply a result of their ignorance or the machinations of middle-class nationalists, but a rational response to the fight for day-to-day survival and the protection of their culture from encroachment. Ironically, as William Walker and Gordon Stewart have shown in their accounts of the Dundee jute-workers, conditions and cultural life bore a remarkable similarity there too. The jute-workers comprised in the main a poorly-paid, largely illiterate, exploited workforce of migrant female labourers from the Scottish Highlands and Ireland, which retained its rural ties, and which was engaged, like its Calcutta counterparts, in the struggle for dignified survival.

---

[90] TUC General Council, 23 May, 25 July 1928, MSS 292/20/12–13, TUC.

Indeed, its trade union activity was correspondingly attentuated. From the mid-1880s to 1906, the main workers' organisation was run by a middle-class religious leader, the Unitarian minister Henry Williamson. The jute-workers' protests, like those described by Chakravarty, were as much concerned with cultural expression as with labour or class politics. Yet despite this closeness, there was very little interaction or understanding between Indian and British workers. Even if conditions in the Calcutta *bustees* and the Dundee slums bore some similarities, cultural misunderstandings formed too high a barrier to permit any real interaction.[91]

After 1924, Labour's opponents moved to reinforce control of the structures and procedures by which political advances might be made. The promised Royal Commission was now brought forward, so that Conservative politicians would dominate it before the return of a future Labour Government. 'We could not', the new Secretary of State Lord Birkenhead told Reading, 'afford to run the slightest risk that the nomination of the 1929 Commission should be in the hands of our successors. You can readily imagine what kind of a Commission . . . would be appointed by Colonel Wedgwood and his friends.'[92] Nonetheless, Labour MPs would have to be represented on the Commission, and Birkenhead feared they might ally with the Indian members to push for a radical acceleration of the pace of self-government. Birkenhead's reasoning appealed to Reading's successor, Lord Irwin, and, once it had been decided that the Commission should be appointed early, he argued for the exclusion of Indian representatives, partly on the grounds that they might make common cause with the Labour members.[93] Birkenhead, who had at first favoured the inclusion of Indians on the grounds that it would

---

[91] Dipesh Chakrabarty, 'Conditions for Knowledge of Working-Class Conditions: Employers, Government and the Jute Workers of Calcutta, 1890–1940', in Ranajit Guha (ed.), *Subaltern Studies II* (Oxford, 1983); 'Trade Unions in a Hierarchical Culture: The Jute Workers of Calcutta, 1920–50' in Ranajit Guha (ed.), *Subaltern Studies III* (Oxford, 1984); *Rethinking Working-Class History: Bengal 1890–1940* (Princeton, 1989); Rajnarayan Chandavarkar, *The Origins of Industrial Capitalism in India: Business Strategies and the Working Classes in Bombay, 1900–1940* (Cambridge, 1994) and *Imperial Power and Popular Politics: Class, Resistance and the State in India, 1850–1950* (Cambridge, 1998); William Walker, *Juteopolis: Dundee and its Textile Workers, 1885–1923* (Edinburgh, 1979); Gordon T. Stewart, *Jute and Empire: The Calcutta Jute Wallahs and the Landscapes of Empire* (Manchester, 1998).

[92] Birkenhead to Reading, 10 Dec 1925, L/PO/6/22, OIOC.

[93] Irwin to Birkenhead, 3 and 10 July 1927, L/PO/6/27, OIOC.

expose their divisions and thereby render the Government's task easier, was persuaded.[94] Irwin had provided a liberal case for an all-white Commission: that the Commission report was really a preparatory exercise in reporting progress which could best be judged by British experts and the force of which could only be diminished by Indian quarrelling.[95] It was this which Birkenhead proceeded to press on MacDonald, who agreed that Indian opinion was so sharply divided that if Indians were to be fairly represented on the Commission it would have to be of an unwieldy size and would never reach a unanimous report. This would leave it vulnerable to diehard attack.[96] MacDonald also supplied moderate nominees to assist Birkenhead. The Conservative Chief Whip had expected Labour to nominate the party's India experts, Lansbury and Spoor, to the Commission, but the Under-Secretary at the India Office, Lord Winterton, noted that Birkenhead would 'absolutely refuse to have them'.[97] Birkenhead himself wanted J. H. Thomas and Willie Graham, but MacDonald told him that the former was needed in the event of a election, and the latter was unable to abandon his union work for so long. In their place, he suggested the 'exceedingly capable' C. R. Attlee and the miners' MP Stephen Walsh. Both had served reliably at the War Office in the 1924 administration. MacDonald reported at first that the NEC was opposed to the exclusion of Indians, but later that he had persuaded it that an all-white Commission might be appointed if it merely proposed to meet members of the Indian provincial and central legislatures and not to take evidence and examine other witnesses in India.[98] Birkenhead argued that these questions should be left to the Commission itself to resolve, and MacDonald did not press the point further.[99]

However, the party was divided. In May 1927, the Party Advisory Committee had debated whether the Party should campaign for an early Commission, even with the risk that it would be

[94] Birkenhead, 'Statutory Commission on Indian Constitutional Reforms', 12 July 1927, CP187(27), CAB 24/187, NA.

[95] Birkenhead to MacDonald, undated, July 1927, L/PO/6/22, OIOC.

[96] MacDonald to Birkenhead, 6 and 14 July, 10 Aug, 22 and 26 Sept, 10 Oct 1927; Birkenhead to MacDonald, 13 July and 28 Sept 1927, L/PO/6/33, OIOC.

[97] Notes by Lord Winterton, Statutory Commission, 4 and 14 July 1927, L/PO/6/33, OIOC.

[98] MacDonald to Birkenhead, 14 and 20 July 1927, L/PO/6/33, OIOC; Birkenhead to Irwin, 14 July 1927, HC, MSS/Eur/C152/3.

[99] Birkenhead to MacDonald, 29 July 1927; MacDonald to Birkenhead, 10 Aug 1927, L/PO/6/33, OIOC.

Conservative-dominated, which had been the position favoured by
Brockway and the ILP, or wait until Labour returned to office, as Pole
and his Indian Liberal allies wished.[100] Warned by Pole of the likely
Indian reaction to an all-white Commission, Lansbury, speaking for the
NEC, had promised the 1927 Party Conference that the Commission
'should be so constituted and its method of doing work so arranged
that it will enjoy the confidence of the Indian people'.[101] Accordingly,
when the Simon Commission's terms of reference were announced in
November, there was an outcry from Labour MPs. For the ILP, the
acceptance of an all-white Commission was a betrayal of India's right to
self-determination. At its National Council in November 1927, it accordingly called for Labour's appointees to be withdrawn unless Indian
representatives were placed on a footing of full equality with the British
ones. The PLP was not prepared to go as far as a boycott. It called on
Indian nationalists to think hard before boycotting the Commission,
and to 'cooperate heartily in making the inquiry a great contribution
to the welfare and democratic advance of the Indian people'.[102] But it
would only agree to nominate members for the British Commission on
condition that the parallel Indian Joint Select Committee appointed by
the Indian Legislative Assembly should be regarded as its equal, with
the right to examine witnesses, and submit its own report to Parliament alongside that of Simon. MacDonald, Snowden and Lansbury
therefore met Birkenhead to discuss the PLP's conditions.[103] Irwin,
facing a similar storm of protest in India, was anxious for the Labour
Party to support the Commission.[104] Birkenhead therefore agreed to
enlarge the role of the Indian Committee to allow it to take part in
the examination of witnesses. However, he told Irwin, he would 'give
[MacDonald] . . . nothing in writing':

You will observe that the formula is very guarded. It reserves to the Chairman
absolute right of determining when [the Indian] Joint Select Committee shall
take part in proceedings and what part it shall take. It also limits [the] power

[100] Pole to Woolf, 18 May 1927, LPACImpQ Memos. 36, May 1927; 39 and 39A,
June 1927, LPA.
[101] Pole to Lansbury, 3 Oct 1927, Pole Papers (Borthwick) 1; Labour Party, *Report of
Annual Conference,* 1927, 255–7.
[102] PLP, 9 Nov 1927, LPA.
[103] MacDonald to Birkenhead, 10 Nov 1927 and 23 Nov 1927, PRO 30/69/1172,
NA; Birkenhead to MacDonald, 11 Nov 1927, L/PO/6/32, OIOC.
[104] Irwin to Birkenhead, 27 Oct 1927, L/PO/6/35, OIOC; Irwin to Birkenhead, 14
Nov 1927, L/PO/6/36B, OIOC.

of [the] Committee to asking supplementary questions, and does not prevent [the] Commission from examining some witnesses separately if it thinks [it] desirable . . . [105]

The NEC, meeting without MacDonald present, was not persuaded and insisted on passing a resolution calling for a genuine equality of status between the Indian and British bodies and in threatening the withdrawal of the Labour representatives unless this were done.[106] This sent panic through the India Office and an emergency Cabinet meeting was summoned to postpone the announcement of the Commission if Labour withdrew its cooperation.[107] The PLP also met in emergency session, and was told by MacDonald that Birkenhead had agreed to make the necessary concessions, and that if this agreement were breached, Labour's nominees should report to the NEC which would consider withdrawal. Given these assurances, the PLP withdrew its threatened boycott. A motion to withdraw the two Labour representatives therefore found only nine supporters. Instead, the PLP passed a second resolution in which it accepted that Labour should serve on the Commission, but insisted that there should be at least some joint meetings, that the Commission should consult, from time to time, with the Indian Commission and that Parliament should consider both reports.[108] With less than an hour before the Lords Debate began, therefore, MacDonald provided Birkenhead with an assurance of Labour support. Government ministers were, however, careful to concede nothing beyond what had been wrung out of them by the PLP, and privately held that the Commission was entirely free to accept or reject Labour's 'pious aspirations' and decide for itself the nature and terms of its cooperation with its Indian counterpart.[109] All in all, MacDonald had, as Birkenhead wrote after the Debate, been 'most helpful'.[110]

[105] Birkenhead to Irwin, 17 Nov 1927, L/PO/6/27, OIOC; Birkenhead to Irwin, 25 Nov 1927, L/PO/6/35, OIOC.

[106] PLP, 22 Nov 1927; MacDonald to Birkenhead, 23 Nov 1927, PRO 30/69/1172, NA; *New Leader*, 9 Dec 1927.

[107] Birkenhead to Irwin, 25 Nov 1927, L/PO/6/35, OIOC; Cabinet, 24 Nov 1927, CM58(27)4 , CAB 23/55; Keith Middlemas (ed.), *Thomas Jones: Whitehall Diary*, (3v., London, 1969–71), ii, 115, 117.

[108] PLP, Special Party Meeting on India, 24 Nov 1927; Labour Party, *Report of Annual Conference*, 1928, 171–5, 303–12.

[109] Birkenhead to Irwin, 8 Dec 1927, L/PO/6/27, OIOC; *Hansard*, 25 Nov 1927, 5th ser., v.210, cols.2226–35.

[110] Birkenhead to Irwin, 25 Nov 1927 and 1 Dec 1927, L/PO/6/35, OIOC.

In giving his support to Birkenhead, it is hard not to conclude that MacDonald had missed an opportunity for Labour to influence the work of the Commission. He thought that Labour could speak perfectly well for India once evidence was given. '[W]e know your views', he told Congress, 'and you can give evidence before the Commission.'[111] This created immense and, to MacDonald, inexplicable hostility towards Labour on the part of even Indian moderates. Lajpat Rai had hitherto defended Labour to increasingly sceptical Indian audiences. In 1926, following Wedgwood's suggestion, he had withdrawn from the Swarajists and become a cooperating member of the Legislative Assembly. But the Simon Commission marked the point at which he broke with Labour. It had 'definitely adopted a fully imperialist attitude wholly in consonance with the Tory Government's attitude towards India'. None of its current leaders could match the 'pure gold' of Keir Hardie. Even Lansbury—who backed the Commission—was 'so weak and slippery', Lajpat Rai had lost faith in him. While he continued to advocate Assembly work, he called for a boycott of the Commission.[112] MacDonald and Lansbury had sent messages with Pole, in the hope of winning support for the Commission's work. MacDonald's message told Indian nationalists that '[w]hatever you may say, not only is the Labour Party in its present action sincerely wishing to help you, but it is upon the best road for doing that'.[113] Jawaharlal Nehru, having read the message, wrote that he preferred 'a frank opponent like Lord Birkenhead to gentlemen who talk and do nothing like Messrs MacDonald and Lansbury'.[114] Congress, meeting at Madras in December 1927, condemned the appointments as 'utter disregard of India's right of self-determination', and resolved to boycott the Commission's proceedings. For MacDonald, this was further confirmation of the wilful obstructiveness of Congress. The Congress declaration of its intention to boycott the work of the Commission was 'sheer rubbish'. It revealed 'a negative and destructive attitude' and was 'not the way to get things done'.[115]

---

[111] Pole to Lansbury, 3 Oct 1927, Pole Papers (Borthwick), 1.

[112] Note by Lansbury, 9 Nov 1927, Lansbury to Pole, 8 Dec 1927, Pole Papers (Borthwick), 1; Lansbury, 'Labour and India', *Daily Herald*, 25 Nov 1927; Joshi, *Writings and Speeches*, ii, 366–8.

[113] *Daily Herald*, 7 Dec 1927.

[114] Statement to the Press, 22 Dec 1927, *SWJN* ii, 2–3; Gupta, 'British Labour and the Indian Left', 98.

[115] *Daily Herald*, 19 and 31 Dec 1927.

Pole, having won no support at all for the Commission, reported to Labour leaders that he had 'never, in all my experience of India, found so much suspicion and distrust of the Labour Party and its intentions'. Only a reinforcement of the guarantees MacDonald had given, to make it clear that the two Commissions were to be of equal status, would satisfy India's politicians.[116] Lansbury wrote to Pole in confusion:

I cannot imagine this Government, or in fact any Government, giving way to the sort of clamour that has been set going. . . And if there is going to be a hartel [sic] when the Commission arrives and a general boycott, the whole situation is hopeless.

You see, people like me have understood the Indian demand to be that Indians should . . . draft their own constitution, and put this before a representative Round Table Conference, and I have always said that I cannot for the life of me see why representative Indians with such a draft constitution should not meet the Commission and have a Round Table Conference. To my mind, the only objection to this is purely one of procedure, and if there is any good will anywhere in India towards the British it should be possible for it to be overcome.[117]

Lansbury's reference to a Round Table Conference, which of course had *not* been offered, and his dismissal of the problem as simply procedural, reveals the extent to which senior Labour figures were baffled by the efforts of Birkenhead and his officials to trap them into their own mode of engagement with Congress, through their control of the Commission's remit and composition, and the India Office's co-option of MacDonald, a strategy which, as we have seen, went back to before 1914. MacDonald had chosen appropriately cautious Commissioners, who were carefully briefed on the nature of the problem as it appeared to the India Office, and whose investigations took place in an atmosphere of cross-party consensus and in the absence of Congress. At the same time, Labour's difficult but necessary links with Congress, out of which alternative solidarities might have been forged, had been effectively severed. Swarajist boycott of the Commission's work ensured that Attlee and Labour MP Vernon Hartshorn, who had replaced Walsh, met few of the non-cooperators, although they seem to have made little

---

[116] Pole, 'India', June 1927, MacDonald Papers, PRO 30/60/1283, NA; Lansbury to Hartshorn, 11 Jan 1928, copy in Simon Papers (OIOC), MSS/EurF/77/7; Note by Pole, 25 Oct 1927, Lansbury to Hartshorn, 11 Jan 1928, MacDonald to Lansbury, 12 Jan 1928, Pole Papers (Borthwick) 1; LPACImpQ, Memo 64A, June 1928, LPA.

[117] Lansbury to Pole, 19 Jan 1928, Pole Papers (Borthwick) 1.

effort to meet them themselves. 'Naturally I thought it would be an embarrassment to them', Attlee wrote a trifle defensively later on.[118] In the draft of his autobiography, he recorded their early impressions:

[Before departure] we met [Motilal Nehru] and found him completely intransigent with no constructive ideas at all, only a violent hatred for the British Raj, the result... of some social snub which had been administered to him. This is not at all [an] unusual reason for violent Indian nationalism... Hartshorn and I were brought to see [Srinivasa Iyengar] secretly, but he was quite impossible and non co-operative.[119]

The two Labour members could have drafted a minority report, or even withdrawn from the Commission on the grounds that it had failed, as it did, to honour MacDonald's agreement with Birkenhead. But both in practice worked entirely consensually. It was Simon and Irwin, rather than Attlee and MacDonald, who took the lead in expanding the role of the parallel Indian Committees.[120] Hartshorn settled into the role of specialist on Indian labour conditions, although this was weakened when he was forced to make a public apology to the Tata company for criticisms he made of its labour relations record.[121] Attlee fought more vigorously for his own ideas within the Commission, repeatedly pressing the Commission to go further in concessions of responsibility to Indians. But he did so within the framework of assumptions and codes of behaviour characteristic of a Royal Commission.

The importance of the Royal Commission setting can be seen by contrasting Attlee's recommendations with the Nehru Report of 1928. Goaded by critics who argued that the Indians could not come up with a constitution of their own, the parties boycotting Simon met in February and March 1928 in an All Parties Conference, and produced the following August the Nehru Report: a plan for an Indian Dominion, which provided for a government responsible to a central legislature, directly elected on a universal adult franchise, and no reserved portfolios, not even defence. The plan offered little to Muslims who were to lose separate electorates and the protection afforded by strong provinces in return for reserved seats, a declaration of religious rights and freedoms,

---

[118] Attlee, 'Draft of Chapter VIII of Autobiography', Attlee Papers (Churchill) ATLE 1/13.

[119] Ibid.

[120] Attlee and Hartshorn to MacDonald, 20 Feb 1928, L/PO/6/27, OIOC; Irwin to Birkenhead, 13 June 1928; Birkenhead to Irwin, 20 June 1928, L/PO/6/35, OIOC; Note by Birkenhead, 18 June 1928, L/PO/6/34, OIOC.

[121] *The Times*, 14 July 1928; details in L/PO/6/28, OIOC.

and some provincial boundary adjustments.[122] Attlee, however, regarded the Nehru Report as 'impossible'.[123] The Commission's composition and its procedure of hearing representative witnesses each speaking for their localities and communities reinforced his sense that constitutional design was primarily a matter for Britons and that India was impossibly disunited. Where, for example, the writers of the Nehru Report saw the need for a strong central legislature, with a majority party wielding the Cabinet power they believed necessary to build a modern nation, Attlee was struck by the inapplicability of the Westminster model for such a divided, complex and traditional society. 'The truth is that over here they have been trying to put an Anglo-Saxon façade on to a Mogul building', Attlee wrote, 'and the two pieces are not structurally connected.'[124] 'I fear it will be difficult to make people at home understand that we are not dealing with a *tabula rasa*, but a paper that has been much scribbled over', he continued. 'Our people, like many out here, British and Indian, are apt to make a ready-made government for India, often on some model used elsewhere, without trying to see how far it will fit [and] how far it will be suitable to work in.'[125] 'I was impressed in India with the way in which comparatively small tamperings with British institutions really destroyed their essence and left them dead and dull', he told Simon. 'Take away the electoral system, the Party system, the unity of the Cabinet, the control over the Ministry by the vote of the House, or any one of them, and the thing does not work.'[126]

Attlee had substantial reservations about the form nationalism had taken in India. All nationalisms 'thrive[d] on negatives and [bred] irresponsibility', for their nature was 'to move ever towards extremes', and while 'the fever' lasted, the nation could not apply itself to social reforms. The social exclusiveness of the British in India had made matters worse. Indian nationalism was, he thought, 'the illegitimate

---

[122] All Parties Conference, *Report of the Committee appointed by the Conference to Determine the Principles of the Constitution for India* (Allahabad, 1928) and *Supplementary Report of the Committee* (Allahabad, 1928).

[123] Attlee, 'The Central Government', 16 Sept 1929, Simon Papers (OIOC), MSS/Eur/F77/33. The following discussion is drawn from Attlee's contributions to the Simon Report, especially the memorandums of 4 Feb, 10 April, 12 July and 16 Sept. 1929, Simon Papers (OIOC), MSS/Eur/F77/32–34; various anonymous and semi-anonymous versions of a paper written by Attlee for MacDonald defending the Commission, PRO 30/69/344/4, NA; 'Draft of Chapter VIII of Autobiography'.

[124] Attlee to Tom Attlee, 14 Nov 1928, Attlee Papers (Bodleian), MSS Eng c.4792/29.

[125] Attlee to Tom Attlee, 20 March 1929, Attlee Papers (Bodleian), MSS Eng c.4792/34.

[126] Attlee, 'The Central Government'.

offspring of patriotism out of inferiority complex'.[127] While in India, he also noted 'a good deal of evidence as to the existence of jobbery and corruption and the probability that this would increase with the progress of self government'.[128] In Attlee's view, there had 'never been a field so wide as India' for the play of nationalism, nor 'one more adapted for bringing out its seamier side'.[129]

However, Attlee did believe that India's problems could only be dealt with by Indians, not an alien power. 'I think that the only line is *l'audace, toujours l'audace*', he wrote to his brother in November 1928. 'I don't think one can devise effective safeguards.'[130] He was certain that Congress '[d]espite all its follies and irresponsibility' seemed to be 'the challenging force' and 'the one movement that counts'.[131] But to work democratic institutions successfully required a level of political maturity which Attlee believed Congress lacked. It seemed to relish its oppositional role, and to eschew the discipline of governing responsibly. Like many other British left-wingers, Attlee thought that the irruption of rural and industrial unrest that he witnessed in India was only partly caused by genuine resentment of the Simon Commission. It was also a sign of 'the possibility of ignorant masses being swayed by astute politicians for purely destructive ends'.[132] Therefore, what was 'supremely important', in Attlee's view, was that 'the forces of Indian nationalism should be utilised for constructive purposes'. He told Simon that '[w]e have got to get some force at work which will give the Indians the chance of cleansing their own Augean stable.'[133] The trouble with the Montagu–Chelmsford reforms had not been that they had conceded too little, but that they had been 'almost a perfect training in irresponsibility', for the 'pleasanter departments—social service, education and the rest—were handed to Indians' while 'the unpleasant part of government'—law and order, finance, defence and foreign affairs—remained with the British.[134] Worse still had been the failure to concede any real power at the centre, which had allowed India's leading politicians the excuse of refusing to take up provincial office and blaming all India's problems on the British. Thus Attlee proposed to Simon to burden Congress with limited but genuine responsibility

---

[127] Attlee to Tom Attlee, 26 Feb 1933, Attlee Papers (Bodleian), MSS Eng c.4792/57.
[128] Attlee, 'Draft of Chapter VIII of Autobiography'.
[129] Memo for Simon, 4 Feb 1929, Simon Papers (OIOC), MSS/Eur/F77/32.
[130] Attlee to Tom Attlee, 25 Nov 1928, Attlee Papers (Bodleian), MSS Eng c.4792/30.
[131] Memo for Simon, 4 Feb 1929.   [132] Ibid.   [133] Ibid.
[134] C. R. Attlee, *Empire Into Commonwealth* (Oxford, 1961), 31.

at the centre, to an indirectly-elected Assembly in which the support of both major communities would be essential for the formation of a government.[135]

At the centre, Simon favoured weakening the hold of the Swarajists over the legislative assembly through indirect election, by empowering the provincial legislatures, on a federal rather than a unitary basis, and strengthening the central government through reserve powers. However, Attlee thought that the parties elected in this fashion would lack deep roots in the electorate. 'There has been much talk of a strong central government but not much examination of what is meant by strength', he wrote. Even 'an executive . . . composed of strong men holding similar opinions and endowed with joint responsibility would actually be very weak' unless it rested on active, popular support.[136] But Attlee was also sceptical about the Swarajists' proposed solution. In the Nehru Report, they had insisted on the Westminster system, but Attlee thought this unworkable. The Indian electorate would, with franchise extensions, become too large for direct election to be meaningful, and the central legislature therefore needed to be indirectly elected by the provincial legislatures. Given the immense variety of Indian interests, parties in a central legislature could only take the form of coalitions built around powerful individuals, single communities, or hostility to government. In the absence of clear parties and mandates, responsible government on the Westminster model, while just possible in the provinces, was simply impractical. Therefore Attlee proposed that powerful committees of the legislature should be the main engine of policy-making, electing chairmen who would be ministers in the Viceroy's Executive. This, he hoped, would destroy the artificial parties that had been built on 'barren opposition' to the Government of India and communal mistrust, and ensure that 'constructive work and responsibility' replaced 'the mere power of criticism'.[137]

In two other ways, Attlee departed from the demands of the Nehru Report. The Swarajists had argued that the powers of the *raj* with respect to the princely states would simply pass to the Government at the centre. But Attlee refused to allow that All-India matters could be handed over to Indian ministers who were responsible to persons elected from British India alone, and not also from the princely states. He therefore favoured a federal solution, or at least one to which the Indian states

---

[135] Memo for Simon, 4 Feb 1929.   [136] Attlee, 'The Central Government'.
[137] Ibid.

could readily adhere, yet in which their failure to do so did not hold up responsible government.[138] Secondly, Attlee disputed the Nehru Report's conviction that Muslim and other minority interests did not need special electoral protection. He believed that communally-defined electorates would have to remain at the provincial level, although he floated the idea of combining communal primaries with joint electorates in the hope that this would encourage the emergence of candidates who could win support outside their own communities.[139] Indirect election of the central legislature by the provincial councils, by single transferable vote, would ensure that Muslims and Hindus were represented at the centre in their correct proportions. If the support of both communities was needed to make or break government, the government could be expected to conduct itself in provincial matters on non-communal lines. This in turn would lead to non-communal Cabinets at the provincial level and eventually to the abolition of communal electorates.[140]

When Attlee put these proposals to the Commission, they were rejected. Simon and the other members thought that the analysis 'carried great weight' but that the proposals were 'too unlike anything which might have been expected to result from the course of development in India up to the present'.[141] Instead, the Commission followed Simon towards a plan for provincial self-government, but no concessions of power at the centre. Attlee warned his fellow Commissioners that a blank refusal of any advance at the centre, and no prospect of achieving it without further constitutional change, would 'drive all the politically-minded into the Independence camp'. Moreover, an irresponsible Executive at the centre would still face an irresponsible legislature, even if, through indirect election, that legislature were comprised of provincial legislators rather than politicians elected directly to it. Powers of veto and ordinance would have to be employed as often as before.[142] He and Hartshorn also opposed Simon's provision of second chambers,

---

[138] Attlee, 'The Central Government and the Problem of Federation', 10 April 1929, Simon Papers (OIOC) MSS/Eur/F77/32; Matters for Report, 28 June 1929 Simon Papers (OIOC) MSS/Eur/F77/39.
[139] Attlee, 'The Central Government'; Matters for Report, 7 Oct 1929, Simon Papers (OIOC), MSS/Eur/F77/39.
[140] Memo for Simon, 4 Feb 1929.
[141] Matters for Report, 4 Oct 1929, Simon Papers (OIOC), MSS/Eur/F77/39.
[142] 'Further memorandum by Major Attlee: The Central Government', 13 Feb 1930, Simon Papers (OIOC), MSS/Eur/F77/33; Matters for Report, 18 Feb 1930, MSS/Eur/F77/39.

and called for timetabled franchise extensions, and the full provision for electoral opportunities for labourers and the depressed classes.[143]

When the Report was published, Attlee accepted its deficiencies but argued that 'the difficulty is to support any alteration that will fit all the facts. The real difficulty . . . is that there is no feasible transitional stage between a government responsible to Great Britain and a government responsible to the Indian people.'[144] That the problem had been so configured as to ensure this does not seem to have occurred to him. The facts he continued to identify through the 1930s as obstacles to Indian self-determination—communal divisions, the size and composition of Indian electorates, the position of the Indian Army—were those to which the Simon Commission had introduced him. They increasingly put him at odds with his party. He invoked the facts in defending the Simon Report against its Labour Party critics in 1930.[145] Yet in the MacDonald Cabinet's preparations for the Round Table Conference, as we shall shortly see, hardly anyone except Attlee and MacDonald regarded these problems as insuperable.[146]

[143] Matters for Report, 24 July, 15, 17 and 29 Oct 1929, Simon Papers (OIOC), MSS/Eur/F77/39; 'Comment on the Chairman's Memorandum SC/JS/61 by Mr V Hartshorn', 10 Sept 1929, Simon Papers (OIOC), F77/33.

[144] Attlee to Tom Attlee, 27 June 1930, Attlee Papers (Bodleian), MSS Eng c.4792/36.

[145] Party criticism of the Simon Report can be found in LPACImpQ Memos. 71, Jan 1930; 80, July 1930; 81, July 1930, LPA. Attlee's responses are in LPACImpQ Memo. 80A.

[146] See Hailey to Irwin, 9 and 13 Dec 1930, HC MSS/Eur/C152, OIOC.

6

India and the Labour Party, 1929–31

When Labour took office again in June 1929, there was little reason to believe that it was any better placed than it had been in 1924 to alter the direction of Indian policy. 'The rank and file of the Labour Party is certainly friendly', Motilal Nehru's ally Iswar Saran wrote from London. 'The members in the front rank also wish to do something, if they can, but the bother is that they are committed to the Simon Commission and now they don't know how to get out of it.'[1] MacDonald told one of his Indian correspondents that '[f]or a government to say what it is going to do while a Commission is enquiring into the subject is, as you know, absolutely impossible'.[2] Pole thought that the best that could be hoped for was that the Indian Committee under Sankaran Nair would come up with recommendations better than those of Simon which Labour could then consider side by side.[3] Moreover, since Labour lacked a parliamentary majority, as before, existing legislation remained a tight constraint. When MacDonald had asked Pole what might be achieved in India without having to bring proposals to Parliament, he had been told that nothing could be done with any permanent effect. In Pole's view, the Secretary of State could not, without legislation, abolish dyarchy. He could only transfer more subjects to Indians by making recommendations to the Viceroy and Governors.[4] This was clearly insufficient to make an impression on Indian nationalists and, worse still, left it open to a successor government to undo everything Labour had done.

The India Office officials remained suspicious of contacts between the Indian nationalists and Labour ministers. When Jinnah wrote to

---

[1] Iswar Saran to Motilal Nehru, 20 June 1929, MNC.

[2] MacDonald to Natesan, 8 July 1929, PRO 30/69/672, NA; Pole to Sapru, 6 June 1929, SM, I, G112; Iswar Saran to Motilal Nehru, 4 July 1929, MNC.

[3] Polak to Sapru, 6 June, 10 July and 1 Aug 1929, SM, I, P68, P69, P71.

[4] Pole to MacDonald, 25 Oct 1927, PRO 30/69/1172, NA; LPACImpQ Memo. 50, Oct 1927, LPA.

MacDonald in June 1929 to ask him to commit the new government to dominion status, the officials condemned communication by private channels and tried to ensure that a bland reply was sent.[5] Hirtzel, as in 1924 and indeed 1907, continued to argue for the status quo. The Government should, he argued, work with the new class of cooperating politicians at the provincial level, who had now learned something of the difficulties of administration, 'not on the crumbling sand of Jinnahs & Saprus & the rest of the all-India politicians, who are politicians pure and simple'. Declarations of purpose, he wrote, 'will be hailed by the extremists at one end & the supporters of Govt at the other as another concession to clamour & violence: the former will be encouraged in their violence and the latter more half-hearted than ever'.

The moderates (for whose benefit it is intended) will, I suspect, accept it grudgingly, & in a few months time make it the basis for still further demands. . . It will thus have finally made matters worse because the present situation will be reproduced, but we shall already have shot our only bolt. . . . We have to face a trial of strength with extremism, & go through with it to the end—or else abdicate. It is impossible to buy off opposition by paying black-mail to the Congress; & as for 'rallying the moderates', we have been trying to do it for the last 20 years, with complete insuccess, because you cannot rally rabbits, least of all rabbits every one of which has one foot firmly planted in the enemy's trap!

I am afraid I am no great believer in political manoeuvres in India. You can only successfully manoeuvre people with whose mentality you have real points of contact, &—though the fact is disguised by a common language & by the use of common political *clichés*—we have no real points of contact with Indian mentality. Moreover, if it comes to a battle of wits, they will beat us every time. . . The only way to play the political game in India is to make up your mind what, on the merits, is the right thing to do, put all your cards on the table & not allow yourself to be rattled or diverted. . . .

The only manoeuvre I have ever known succeed in India is that of doing nothing. When Govt does nothing, but just carries on, the politicians fall to quarrelling among themselves, as they are doing at present. When Govt does anything, no matter what, they combine against it. For the moment there is no necessity to do anything.'[6]

[5] Minutes by Hirtzel, Dawson and Seton, 3–5 July 1929, L/PO/6/30, OIOC; MacDonald to Jinnah, 14 Aug 1929, MacDonald Papers (Manchester) RMD 1/11/5.
[6] Minutes by Hirtzel, 17 and 31 Aug 1929; Hirtzel to Benn, 16 Sept 1929, L/PO/6/47, OIOC.

However, once crucial difference transformed the situation: the Viceroy was now in favour of moving ahead of the Simon Commission. By the end of 1928, Irwin was troubled by the unity of the opposition to Simon and hoped to break it up by means of a declaration that once the Report was complete there should be a Round Table Conference to discuss it. After consulting moderates in India, he was persuaded that a declaration that Britain intended that India should achieve dominion status might be sufficient to head off the threat of Congress to resort once again to civil disobedience at the end of 1929. He had tried to persuade Simon that unless such a move were made there might be an influx of Indian delegates at the coming British election 'trying to nobble individuals' and commit Labour to a fresh move over the Viceroy's head. Simon, though he disliked the plan for a declaration, nonetheless thought this Irwin's most persuasive argument in favour of it; and that to avoid India becoming a party question at home 'might outweigh all other objections'.[7]

When Labour came into office, plans were worked out for an exchange of letters between Simon and MacDonald, setting out the Government's plans for a Round Table Conference, and commitment to dominion status. However, MacDonald was concerned that the plan might not be sufficiently radical to detach the moderates, and in response to his concerns, shared by some of the Indian Governors, the letters were redrafted so as to make the conference less restricted in scope and the promise of dominion status seem less grudging. His Commission split, Simon thereupon retreated sharply, dissociating the Commission from the declaration, although it was not apparently clear to Benn, Labour's new Secretary of State, that he was opposed to it entirely rather than merely opposed to its being endorsed by the Commission.[8] Attlee and Hartshorn were the only two members prepared to accept the idea that MacDonald should make a commitment to dominion status in his reply to Simon, but tellingly they had come to share the Commission's sense of injured pride: Hartshorn said that he was only in favour because Irwin had asked for it, and that '[i]t would certainly be regarded as surrender to the boycotters' while Attlee was strongly in favour of the Commission staying clear.[9] Nevertheless, MacDonald and

---

[7] Irwin to Simon, 27 Feb and 5 March 1929; Aide-memoire by Simon, 14 March 1929, Simon Papers (OIOC), MSS/Eur/F77/41.

[8] Moore, *Crisis of Indian Unity*, 61–7.

[9] Resumé of rough notes of 24 Sept [1929] meeting of the Commission, Simon Papers (OIOC) MSS/Eur/F77/41; Note, 24 Sept 1929, Simon Papers (OIOC), MSS/Eur/F77/42.

Benn pressed on, obtaining the personal support of Baldwin, who was led to believe that Simon had given his concurrence to the declaration. Faced with Simon's unwillingness to exchange letters, Irwin and the Cabinet agreed that Simon and MacDonald's letters should just deal with the Conference, and the statement of dominion status be made by Irwin on his return to India. However, when the Conservative Shadow Cabinet was briefed by Baldwin, it refused to be associated with the declaration on the grounds that, as had now become clear, the Simon Commission had not agreed to it. Simon too, informed that Baldwin had only given conditional assent to the declaration, made it clear the Commission also opposed its being made. However, their efforts to block the declaration failed, principally because Irwin, who had tried out the ideas on the Indian moderates with success, was now committed to making it.[10] Benn had told him: 'If you refuse to budge I will support you absolutely and we can succeed.'[11] Irwin had spoken, the declaration was certain to survive an admittedly stormy party debate in which Simon, wishing to hold his Commission together, and to get whatever advantage remained from a good response in India, made a pacifying speech.[12]

In contrast to 1924, therefore, the Labour Cabinet were able to use the machinery of imperial governance to their own advantage. Irwin's initiative had met with very broad opposition at home: the principled opposition of diehards like Churchill and Austen Chamberlain, the wary concern of Reading, the pique of Simon and the ambitions of Lloyd George and a number of disaffected Tories to unseat Baldwin from the Conservative leadership, and restore the Conservative–Liberal coalition of 1918–22.[13] The Irwin–MacDonald policy was thus supported only by a shaky and narrow coalition that extended from Fenner Brockway, through some, though not all, the Liberals (Reading was an important exception) to Baldwin and a handful of other Conservatives, and highly vulnerable to the twists and turns of parliamentary intrigue. But in dealing with this opposition, MacDonald and Benn were prepared to

---

[10] Moore, *Crisis of Indian Unity*, 79.   [11] Quoted in Ibid. 76.
[12] MacDonald Diary, 5 and 6 Nov 1929.
[13] Moore, *Crisis of Indian Unity*, 80; G. R. Peele, 'A Note on the Irwin Declaration', *Journal of Imperial and Commonwealth History*, 1/3 (1973), 331–8; Carl Bridge, *Holding India to the Empire: The British Conservative Party and the 1935 Constitution* (Delhi, 1986) 29–38; Stuart Ball, *Baldwin and the Conservative Party: The Crisis of 1929–1931* (New Haven, 1988), 109–12; Philip Williamson, *National Crisis and National Government: British Politics, the Economy and Empire, 1926–1932* (Cambridge, 1992), 125.

take greater risks than Labour had in 1924. They had told neither Baldwin of the Simon Commission's decision to disassociate itself from the declaration, nor Simon about the conditional nature of Baldwin's support of it, nor Irwin about the extent of Conservative and indeed Liberal opposition. This prevented opponents of the declaration from forming a bloc until it was too late. Another significant difference was that the decision of Congress to delay civil disobedience until the end of 1929 meant that Labour did not yet have to contend with boycotting and non-cooperation. But the crucial difference was that on this occasion they had the Viceroy's support. Once assured of this, Benn and MacDonald were evidently determined to make the declaration no matter what Simon said. Simon's opposition had been on the grounds of the declaration's inexpediency, wrote MacDonald in the middle of the crisis, '& upon that the Viceroy was the one man in the world to advise'.[14] This blunted much of the criticism directed at the plan from its opponents. The King even told the diehard Burnham that he 'would not be allowed to resign' from the Simon Commission over Irwin's declaration.[15] Hirtzel had tried to tempt Benn himself to clarify the position regarding dominion status in a speech. This, he argued, was 'less capable of being twisted into a pledge' and, of course, though he did not say this, easier for Conservatives to oppose and non-binding on future governments.[16] Rather than a Round Table Conference, Hirtzel had argued for a small delegation of Congress Indians to be asked to offer their views to a Cabinet committee, leading later, once legislation was drawn up, to invitations to Congress and other Indian parties to give evidence to a Joint Parliamentary Committee.[17] But he too could not, on this occasion, appeal to the need to defer to the Viceroy.

The Irwin declaration thus represented a secure platform from which further advance could then be made, and from which future governments could not easily resile. Where Labour in 1924 had been trapped in the procedures created by the commitments of 1919 and the institutions they inherited from their predecessors, Labour and Irwin in 1929 broke free to define their own policy pathway, defined by the commitment to dominion status, and novel institutional and procedural forms—principally the Round Table Conference. Equality

---

[14] MacDonald Diary, 3 Nov 1929.   [15] Ibid. 5 Nov 1929.
[16] Minute by Hirtzel, 31 Aug 1929, L/PO/6/47, OIOC.
[17] Hirtzel to Benn, 16 Sept 1929, L/PO/6/47, OIOC.

of status at the Conference gave the opportunity for the linking-up of Indian agitators and their British supporters in ways that earlier, asymmetric institutional structures such as Royal Commissions and parliamentary select committees had hindered. Its location in London made it much easier for linking-up to occur, and also harder for Indian officials to interfere. These and the Government's powers to define the Conference's procedures all combined to allow Labour to extricate itself from its false association with Conservatives and estrangement from the Indian moderates. 'We have the right cause and, what is equally important, the *right enemies*', Benn told Beatrice Webb.[18] Indeed, the effects of this realignment of forces were rapidly obvious to their opponents as the rules governing the form and structure of the Conference were drawn up. On two occasions, Benn and his colleagues defied the attempts of the Opposition to determine their strategy at the Conference, first over the status of the Simon Report and its principal author, and subsequently over the composition of the British delegations and agenda.[19] The inwardness of these negotiations over machinery and procedure, as Benn told Irwin, was that such questions would largely determine whether the Conference was merely an occasion for discussing the Simon Report or, as he and MacDonald wished, one in which progress towards a dominion constitution for India might be made. 'Everything is being done so to shape the machinery we propose to use', Benn wrote, 'that it can only produce a certain result.'[20] Hirtzel called in vain for a conference which excluded discussion of independence and which made the Government's proposals the agenda, rather than affording open discussion. '[M]ore important than letting people have their say', he complained, 'is getting them to say the right thing, i.e. what we want them to say.'[21]

However, this time Hirtzel did not win. Labour ministers disarmed their opponents by referring their objections to Irwin, in the knowledge that he would reject them and in so doing would reinforce the Government's policy. Benn reminded him, 'You must decide in the light of the needs of India, and you will be supported unflinchingly

[18] Beatrice Webb Diary, 4 Nov 1929.

[19] Memorandum by Benn for Cabinet Committee on British Delegation for Round Table Conference BDG(30)4, 29 Oct 1930, CAB27/470 NA; Williamson, *National Crisis*, 90; Bridge, *Holding India* 44–5, 50.

[20] Benn to Irwin, 20 June 1930, HC, MSS/Eur/C152/6.

[21] Minutes by Hirtzel, 4 and 28 May 1930, L/PO/6/48, OIOC.

by the Government.'[22] The Labour ministers decided that they would not construct a common line with the other British parties, before or during the Conference. They agreed to note the Government of India's own proposals rather than adopt them as their own, to allow other, potentially more far-reaching schemes to come forward at the Conference itself.[23] Nor were they prepared to be diverted by any notion of dividing and ruling. The communal question and the issue of federation were 'questions Indians must settle'.[24] But if they were not settled in a period of time, the Government must make an award to allow the reforms to continue. Arthur Henderson told Hugh Dalton that if 'all the Indians unite in asking for Dominion status, it can't be refused, so far as the Government are concerned'.[25] Labour ministers believed that Irwin had given them the chance to take advantage of their incumbency to create their own precedents. Meeting Benn, Sapru recorded: '[He said that] if we could come to a mutual understanding among ourselves we should win all along the line, and that even though Labour might come out of office, the Government that succeeded it would not and could not go behind that agreement.'[26]

The institutions and procedures put in place by the Round Table Conference were insufficient on their own to guarantee political advance without the leverage of a working alliance between British left-wingers and Congress. This remained as hard as ever to achieve. The professional Liberal mediators, especially Sapru, moved between the Government and the Congress, reassuring each other, and the semi-official status they acquired under Irwin made it easier for each to know the other's mind.[27] But relations had been harmed by Labour participation in the Simon Commission and by the refusal of Congress to give anyone in London any authority. 'If you and a few others were here', Motilal Nehru's London ally pleaded, 'and could meet privately and informally with some members of the Government it would be splendid. Those who talk

[22] Benn to Irwin, 4 July 1930, PRO 30/69/344/1, NA.
[23] British Delegation Meeting, 20 Oct 1930, BDG (30) 1 CAB27/470 NA.
[24] Benn, Memorandum for British Delegation on Strategy at the Round Table Conference, 19 Nov. 1930, BDG(30)8, CAB27/470, NA.
[25] Ben Pimlott (ed.), *The Political Diary of Hugh Dalton* (London, 1986), 129.
[26] Quoted in Moore, *Crisis of Indian Unity*, 125.
[27] Sapru to V. J. Patel, 5 Dec 1929, SM, I, P18; Pole to Sapru, 17 Jan 1930, SM, II, Reel 7.

must be in a position to deliver the goods.'[28] Gandhi, however, remained central but mysterious. In the autumn of 1929, his position shifted from one of cautious welcome of the Irwin Declaration, to rejection of it and threats of civil disobedience. Over the coming eighteen months, he would move from this to an unexpected truce and parleying with Irwin, to an agreement to join further discussions in London, to withdrawing this agreement, and finally agreeing again. There was a complex logic to each of these steps, little of which was apparent to the British supporters of Congress who urged rapprochement.[29] This was partly because, for familiar reasons, they lacked many of the necessary contacts. Polak wrote in irritation from London to the Mahatma to point this out.

'Gokhale was far wiser in the work that he undertook along these lines, and the absence of co-ordinated effort here on the part of your people has been a real disaster . . . [Y]ou really have no concept of the extent to which the psychology here has been changed for the better . . . We . . . are much more sensitive to this change than you can possibly be, and I feel very strongly that you ought to allow us to be better judges of the extent to which this has altered matters'.[30]

However, feeling in Congress was divided: the Liberals favoured acceptance, but Bose, Jawaharlal and the radicals believed that Irwin's declaration was vague, and argued for its rejection. They feared that participation in a conference without a solid guarantee of advance would expose Indian differences and make it impossible to reconstruct the united platform agreed at Calcutta in 1928.[31] Gandhi was instinctively attracted to the idea of responding positively to Irwin, but his priority was the unity of Congress in whatever response was made. Hence he

---

[28] Iswar Saran to Motilal Nehru, 20 June 1929, MNC.

[29] Congress decision-making can be traced in Brown, *Gandhi and Civil Disobedience*. For Labour urgings, see Brockway to Benn, 21 Nov 1929, Home-Pol 1929/299, NAI; Benn to Irwin, 24 Oct 1929, HC, MSS/Eur/C152/5; Brockway to Sastri, 27 Nov 1929, SC 534; *Servant of India*, 21 Nov 1929; Brockway to Gandhi, 31 Oct 1929, Gandhi Papers, SN 15730; Brockway to Nehru, 1 Nov 1929, AICC G113/1929; Polak to Gandhi, 2 and 12 Nov and 13 Dec 1929, Gandhi Papers, SN 15735, 16211 and 16278; Polak to Sapru, 8 and 28 Nov 1929, Polak to Naidu and Iyengar, 22 Nov 1929, Sapru to Polak, 5 Dec 1929, SM, I, P18, P73, P74 and P76; Pole to Sapru, 6 June, 11 and 31 July, 1, 8 and 26 Nov. 1929, SM, I, G112, G113, G114, G116, G117 and G118; Kunzru to Rao, 29 Nov 1929, SC 530.

[30] Polak to Gandhi, 5 Dec 1929, Gandhi Papers, SN 16286; Polak to Sapru, 1 Aug 1929, SM, I, P71.

[31] Low, *Britain and Indian Nationalism*, 41–71.

told Brockway and Polak that he could not 'take things quite on trust'. 'I would', he wrote, 'far rather wait and watch and pray than run into what may after all be a dangerous trap...'[32] Gandhi therefore demanded that the British Government state that the purpose of the Conference was not merely exploratory, but to draft a dominion constitution; that Congress should have the largest delegation and that there should be an amnesty for political prisoners. Brockway did his best to persuade Benn of the need for the last of these conditions, but the first two were much trickier, and Irwin was unable to agree to them.[33] Polak told Gandhi he was 'indulging in suspicions' and making impossible demands. 'I cannot understand why you should fear a trap, unless you believe that your colleagues are weak, divided, untrustworthy and unpatriotic... [T]he Government have even more to risk in extending the invitation, than you have in accepting.'[34] But at Lahore in December 1929 Congress leaders formally declared for *purna swaraj* and began making preparations for civil disobedience. The Congress leaders had failed to react with the gratitude that the Labour leaders felt their bravery deserved. Critical comments from Britain therefore persisted, but Gandhi was adamant about his conditions:

It is open to those English friends who are sincerely anxious for India's welfare to assist India in her fight for freedom and on her terms. She knows best what she needs. Complete independence does not mean arrogant isolation or a superior disdain for all help. But it does mean complete severance of the British bondage, be it ever so slight or well-concealed.[35]

Few of Congress' supporters in Britain really understood the decision to embrace *purna swaraj* when dominion status was, in their eyes, indistinguishable except for its greater acceptability among the British electorate. They understood even less resort to civil disobedience when a Conference beckoned. Their responses split and ran along familiar channels: disappointment, frustration, withdrawal and anger.[36] The

---

[32] Gandhi to Brockway, 14 Nov 1929, *CWMG*, E47/495; 'My Position', 14 Nov 1929, *CWMG*, E47/486; 'Some Significant Questions', 8 Dec 1929, *CWMG*, E48/59; Sastri to Aiyar, 2 Dec 1929, Sastri to Rao, 7 Nov 1929, in Jagadisan, *Letters of Sastri*, 183–5.

[33] Benn to Irwin, 14 and 21 Nov, 24 Dec 1929, HC, MSS/Eur/C152/5; Pole to Sapru, 26 Nov 1929, SM, I, G118.

[34] Polak to Gandhi, 5 Dec 1929, Gandhi Papers SN 16286; Gandhi, 'The Issue', *Young India*, 6 Feb 1930, *CWMG*, E48/304.

[35] 'To English Friends', 23 Jan 1930, *CWMG*, E48/257. See also 'An English Friend's Difficulty', 10 April 1930, *CWMG*, E49/54; 'Notes', 1 May 1930, *CWMG*, E49/236.

[36] For example, Beatrice Webb, *Diary*, 4 May 1930.

Labour Government set its face firmly against the campaign, and found little difficulty in persuading its backbenchers to fall into line. As in 1924, MacDonald thought Gandhi had made a liberal policy impossible.[37] A friend who had criticised his Indian policy in a letter to the press was told:

[I]magine yourself not the producer of a paper but the leader of a progressive movement, which was not merely a propaganda one, but an affair of practical action. . . It is the easiest thing in the world for one with no responsibility to talk of 'the cruelties of the authorities in dealing with the followers of Ghandi' [sic] . . . Is your idea of democratic government that whoever is responsible for it is to allow social fabrics of order and civic relationships to go to wreck and ruin, because somebody comes along claiming to be inspired by God? . . . Why do you not face the facts and refrain from taking the easy-oozy way of facing life in a half dreamy and. . . rather cowardly way? . . . I am just as anxious to help India to liberty as you are, but unfortunately for me, I am not free to withdraw myself and sit on a hill-side . . . What you do not seem to understand is that public opinion has to be brought into line.[38]

When in mid-1930, attempts were made by Sapru and Jayakar to get Gandhi released from prison to attend the forthcoming Round Table Conference, Polak and other Labour figures pressed him to make the necessary concessions. But Gandhi was obdurate, though no more forthcoming with his reasons.[39] 'As a prisoner, I may not write to you as fully as I would like', he told them. ' [I]f you knew the circumstances as much as I do, you would not press me to go to the R.T.C. I should be perfectly useless there.'[40] As both Congress and Irwin started to put out feelers to negotiate an end to civil disobedience, MacDonald warned Benn to beware of laying himself open to accusations of 'surrender or bargaining'.[41] MacDonald's stance on India often looked more negative than it in fact was, because of the need to protect himself and his minority administration against opposition attacks.[42] Nevertheless, so low was the stock of Congress that his policy of resisting its pressure

[37] MacDonald to Andrews, 5 May 1930, PRO 30/69/1440, NA.
[38] MacDonald to Villard, 27 Oct 1930, PRO 30/69/1440, NA.
[39] These were his desire to retain the support of Jawaharlal and his supporters. See Brown, *Gandhi and Civil Disobedience*, 157–67.
[40] Gandhi to Wellock, 11 July 1930, *CWMG*, E49/378; Gandhi to Polak, 16 July 1930, *CWMG*, E49/397.
[41] Marginal notes by MacDonald on Irwin to Benn, 5 July 1930, Irwin to Benn, 14 July 1930, PRO 30/69/344/3, NA.
[42] See his annotations to Irwin to Benn, 14 July 1930, and MacDonald to Benn, 3 Sept 1930, PRO 30/69/344/3, NA.

met little Labour opposition. At a PLP meeting in May 1930, Benn's defence of the *raj* was received with 'loud cheers'.[43] At the 1930 Party Conference, Brockway protested in vain. The only alternative to the conference method, announced one speaker, was to quit India immediately:

Was that the kind of policy that men with a sense of the fitness of things would say ought to have been adopted? . . . There was no united India. The Hindus and the Mohammedans had not sunk their differences of creed. Caste had not been wiped out . . . Did they want India to go through all the . . . bitterness and civil war that had characterised China in the last ten years? That was what was likely to happen if there was a hasty ill-considered departure from India.[44]

At a meeting of the PLP in November, it was agreed that further discussion of Indian unrest would be 'inopportune'.[45]

At the Conference itself, the willingness of leading Princes to consider All-India federation was seized upon by Sapru and the Labour Government delegation as a vehicle by which rapid dominion status with safeguards might be realised. For Labour, it offered the prospect of a speedy and consensual solution of the Indian problem. The counterweight of the Princes would allay Opposition fears of untrammelled Congress rule, and a federal centre would have built-in safeguards for the protection of minorities. There would be no need to add extra safeguards to the constitution, and it would thus be possible to transfer powers much more freely and swiftly than had been expected. Moreover, there was, Benn considered, a better chance of experienced statesmen rather than 'lawyer demagogues' emerging as the central players within a federal framework.[46] For a moment, even the Muslims at the Conference were prepared to accept the federal ideal, and establish specific communal safeguards later. Much to Labour's delight, Congress agreed to attend a further session, after the release of some political prisoners. When the Conservatives demanded that communal agreement should precede a new constitution, MacDonald again made it clear that Labour believed that adjustments of the Lucknow Pact would suffice.[47] Sankey,

---

[43] Benn to Irwin, 8 May; 29 May 1930, HC, MSS/Eur/C152/6; PLP Exec. Cttee, 20 May 1930, PLP Meeting, 21 May 1930, PLP Special Party Meeting, 27 May 1930, LPA.

[44] Labour Party, *Report of Annual Conference* 1930, 217–18.

[45] PLP Party Meeting, 25 Nov 1930, LPA.

[46] British Delegation Meeting, BDG(30)8, 19 Nov 1930, CAB27/740, NA.

[47] 'Indian Situation and the 2nd Conference', 24 May 1931, Note of Meeting on 21 May 1931, PRO 30/69/698, NA.

meanwhile, had begun work on a draft constitution. The safeguards were contained in a single, general clause, and all portfolios including finance were to be transferred to Indian ministers.[48] The display of communal antagonism by some of the Indian delegates and the prospect put before them by Malcolm Hailey of 'Europeans being murdered in communal riots' was enough to frighten the Cabinet Committee into abandoning the plan of Henderson and the Party Advisory Committee for provincial governors to become figureheads, and restoring their powers to intervene.[49] But, on the whole, the Labour Party was very pleased with the results of the conference method. On 19 January 1931, MacDonald closed the Conference with a pledge of central responsibility with safeguards. The Labour ministers planned a mission to India to finalise the communal and federal aspects of the plan, in the hope of pushing to a final settlement at a second Conference in London.[50] In 1929, Labour had found India, in Benn's words, 'sullen, resentful and unwilling to co-operate'.[51] Before the Round Table Conference, even Harold Laski privately believed that India was 'really not fit to govern itself'.[52] Now the 'great change' in Labour thinking, Benn recorded, was 'the growing belief that the Indian problem, if well handled, could be an asset to the Party'.[53]

Every significant advance in Indian policy made by the Labour Government since taking office had been either a result of the Viceroy's initiative or subject to his approval. This made the Viceregal succession a question of great importance. MacDonald and Benn first asked Irwin to undertake an extended term of office, and, when this was refused, proposed Irwin's nominee, the Marquess of Zetland.[54] Baldwin also favoured Zetland, whom he had asked to assist with drafting the Conservative response to the Simon Report, and subsequently appointed a

[48] Sankey, 'Constitution of India', May 1931, Sankey Papers, C538.

[49] Gupta, *Imperialism*, 213.

[50] British Delegation Meeting, 9 Feb. 1931, BDG (31)1, CAB 27/470, NA; Gupta, *Imperialism*, 215, 223.

[51] Labour Party, *Report of Annual Conference*, 1932, 180.

[52] M. Wolfe de Howe (ed.), *The Holmes–Laski Letters* (2v., London, 1953), ii, 1261.

[53] Benn to Irwin, 18 Feb 1931, HC, MSS/Eur/C152/6.

[54] Philip Williamson, '"Party first and India second": The appointment of the Viceroy of India in 1930', *Bulletin of the Institute of Historical Research*, 55 (1983), 86–101.

Conservative delegate to the Round Table Conference. The appointment of Zetland would therefore have had several advantages for the Labour Government, most obviously so in tying the Conservative Party more closely to Irwin's policy, and in strengthening Baldwin's hand against his diehard opponents. However, it came into conflict with a more radical strategy: that of appointing a Labour Viceroy. This would signal to Indian nationalists that Irwin's policies would be continued, and also allow the Labour Party to show that it was capable of filling even the most prestigious offices of state from within its own ranks. This last argument was particularly strongly felt by Henderson, who told Beatrice Webb that he found it 'intolerable that when these great appointments were to be made, they should always be given to members of the other parties'.[55]

After refusals from Jowitt, J. H. Thomas and Charles Trevelyan, the Cabinet agreed on Lord Gorell, author, publisher and Labour peer.[56] However, the King's Private Secretary, Lord Stamfordham, was horrified by the prospect of a candidate with no experience of governing Indians and set about trying to wreck the Cabinet's nomination. He seems to have realised that the Palace could not expect to get its way in a direct clash with the Government, but that a period of delay and selective leaking might provide time sufficient for a public, or semi-public, discussion of Gorell's deficiencies. He seized on a minor breach of protocol to delay the public announcement of Gorell's appointment, but allowed Geoffrey Dawson, editor of *The Times*, to learn of it.[57] Dawson's opinion of Gorell, who had once worked for the newspaper, was very low, and his own preference, like that of his friend Irwin, was for

[55] Webb Diary, 23 Nov 1930; Gorell Diary, 16–17 Oct 1930, and his 'Unpublished Chapter of autobiography re offer of Viceroyalty, 1930', Gorell Papers; Schuster to Irwin, 13 Nov 1930, HC, MSS/Eur/C152/19.

[56] Gorell Diary, 17 Oct 1930, 14 May 1931; 'Unpublished Chapter'; Cabinet, 9 and 17 Oct 1930, CC 59(30) and 61(30), CAB 23/65, NA; Trevelyan to Lady Trevelyan, 15 Oct 1930, Trevelyan Papers, CPT EX124; Gregory Blaxland, *J. H. Thomas: A Life for Unity* (London, 1964), 243; MacDonald Diary, 12–16 Oct 1930.

[57] Dawson Diary, 29 Oct 1930. Dawson saw Stamfordham the following day when they discussed the Viceroyalty, and again on 14 and 25 November (Dawson Diary, 30 Oct and 14 and 25 Nov 1930). MacDonald to Stamfordham, 29 Oct 1930, PRO 30/69/577, NA; MacDonald to the King, 29 Oct 1930, PRO 30/69/676, NA; MacDonald to Stamfordham, 30 Oct 1930 (2 letters), PRO 30/69/577, NA; Stamfordham to Irwin, 26 Nov 1930, and Irwin to Stamfordham, 16 Dec 1930, HC, MSS/Eur/C152/1. See also Stamfordham to Dawson, 2 and 4 Dec 1930, Dawson Papers, 75; Hailey to Irwin, 9 Dec 1930, and Irwin to Dawson, 16 Dec 1930, HC MSS/Eur/C152/19.

Zetland.[58] *The Times* carried an editorial arguing that neither Gorell's 'temperament nor his interests' suited him for the task.[59] This opinion mattered to MacDonald, since Dawson's support for Irwin had been important.[60] He invited Dawson to Chequers, possibly with the hope of persuading him to support Gorell. 'I came away thoroughly dejected', Dawson wrote. '[MacDonald] was apparently "powerless" to appoint a good Viceroy.'[61] After the opening of the Round Table Conference, Dawson published a second editorial on the qualities needed by the new Viceroy, in which Gorell continued to score poorly.[62]

After a lengthy period of limbo, in which he briefly considered taking the post himself, MacDonald withdrew his support for Gorell.[63] '[T]he Gorilla is absolutely dead', Stamfordham wrote to Dawson in triumph.[64] MacDonald told Gorell that 'Baldwin . . . and Lloyd George. . . had both been to him and told him that they would not even give a negative consent to a Labour Prime Minister, in a minority, making the appointment of a Viceroy without first obtaining their approval: they had told him that if they did they would either combine to turn the Government out there and then or at all events would reverse the appointment at the first opportunity.'[65] Baldwin had certainly told MacDonald that the Conservatives would 'never accept G[orell]', [66] but there is no evidence of quite so direct a threat from either of the Opposition leaders. Had Gorell been appointed, their interest in upholding the dignity of the office and of bipartisan consensus at home would have made his recall very difficult. What seems to have troubled MacDonald was the lack of support for Gorell among the broad yet fragile coalition of support that was needed to underpin his Indian policy at home. Without the support of men like Dawson, Gorell could

[58] Dawson to Irwin, 6 and 25 Nov 1930, HC, MSS/Eur/C152/19.

[59] *The Times*, 30 Oct 1930.

[60] See J. E. L. Wrench, *Geoffrey Dawson and Our Times* (London, 1955), 281–9.

[61] Dawson Diary, 2 Nov 1930; Dawson to Irwin, 25 Nov 1930, HC, MSS/Eur/C152/19; MacDonald Diary, 2 Nov 1930.

[62] *The Times*, 19 Nov 1930; Gorell Diary, 19 Nov 1930.

[63] MacDonald Diary, 26 Nov–14 Dec 1930; Gorell Diary, 14 Dec 1930; MacDonald to Gorell, 22 Dec 1930, and Gorell to MacDonald, 24 June 1937, in 'Viceroy File', Gorell Papers; Margot Asquith to MacDonald, 11 Dec 1930, PRO 30/69/1440, NA; Inchcape to MacDonald, 11 Dec 1930, and reply, MacDonald Papers (Manchester) RMD 1/11/9; Note by Reading, 8 Dec 1930, RP, MSS/Eur/E238/106; Dalton Diary, 5 Dec 1930.

[64] Stamfordham to Dawson, 10 Dec 1930, Dawson Papers, 75.

[65] Gorell, 'Unpublished Chapter'; Gorell Diary, 24 Nov 1930.

[66] MacDonald Diary, 3 Dec 1930.

not be used, as Irwin had been, to trump Conservative opposition to the reforms. The episode also confirmed the horror felt by men like Stamfordham when contemplating Labour not merely criticising the Empire's natural rulers but exercising its own unnatural stewardship. It also showed that Labour's engagement with the imperial state had to take the form neither of simple occupation of the system they had inherited, nor of straightforward opposition to it, but the securing of political alliances with fractions of the non-Labour governing elite. The failure to build them on this occasion was costly: Willingdon, as MacDonald privately feared, turned out to be a poor tactician, and uninterested in a rapprochement with Congress.[67]

The second Round Table Conference provided the first time that large numbers of British left-wingers had seen Gandhi in the flesh and tried to debate with him. In a public exchange of letters with the Communist MP Shapurji Saklatvala in 1927, Gandhi had stated his distrust of socialism and its schemes for the amelioration of the lot of the poor. Indian labour should be organised by 'efforts from within':

It is not so much discontent with capital that I want to inculcate as discontent with themselves. I want real co-operation between labour and capital. I shall convince the labourers that in many things they are to blame themselves instead of blaming the capitalists. As in the political so in the labour movement, I rely upon internal reform, i.e., self-purification.

Labourers in India needed leadership by others, and to be kept away from the international labour movement while they purified themselves.[68]

   In some ways, of course, this reflected what British trade unionists themselves had said about the Indian labour movement, and Gandhi's view that labour and capital could be brought into harmony through the mutual observance of responsibilities and duties was not in itself incompatible with the British trade unions' own strategy of industrial cooperation after 1926. His concern that Indian labour should not become a pawn in the political struggle, but should develop its own internal strength, was also close to the verdict of Labour visitors in the 1920s. Yet his idiosyncratic ideas of how this internal strength should

   [67] Ibid. 1 Jan 1932.
   [68] Gandhi, 'No and Yes', 17 March 1927, *CWMG*, E38/194; 'Interview', 24 March 1927, *CWMG*, E38/219; Gandhi to Saklatvala, 10 May 1927, *CWMG*, E38/366.

be developed convinced them much less. Gandhi dismissed western methods of organisation as a model. 'Let us not be obsessed with catchwords and seductive slogans imported from the West', he would later tell students. 'Have we not our own distinctive Eastern traditions? Are we not capable of finding our own solutions to the question of capital and labour? . . . Let us study our Eastern institutions in that spirit of scientific enquiry and we shall evolve a truer socialism and a truer communism than the world has yet dreamed of.'[69] His own union of Ahmedabad millworkers was, as Tom Shaw and other Labour visitors to India had found, distinctively Gandhian. It was run by Anusayaben Sarabhai, sister of the leading millowner. It enjoined its employees to work hard to obtain the maximum production at minimum costs. Indeed, Shaw wrote, 'the workmen are admonished quite as much as the employers'. [70] The year before Shaw's visit, Gandhi had told its workers that when times were hard for their employers, workers should not press their grievances and some should work without pay.[71] The union relied absolutely on the good faith of the employers and had no provision whatsoever for the creation of a strike fund or even the holding of a strike. In Indian conditions, Shaw found, this did not detract from its effectiveness. It was the strongest and most effective of the textile unions and had a good track record of resolving disputes and of constructive educational and social services. Nevertheless, it was bound to make some British left-wingers think it a humanitarian gesture but not a trade union.

Visiting Britain in 1931, Gandhi had also needed to convince British trade unionists of the purity of his motives for endorsing the boycott of British goods. In the previous two years, annual sales of British cloth to India had fallen from 1,248 million yards to 376 million yards.[72] This was partly the result of the world depression and uncompetitive pricing, but this was of little comfort to its producers.[73] Gandhi's own response to the plight of the Lancashire unemployed had been less than convincing. Saklatvala had tried without success to persuade him that the boycott was not non-violent because of the injury it did to Lancashire

---

[69] Gandhi, 'Discussion with Students', 21 July 1934, *CWMG*, E64/254.
[70] Shaw 'Indian Report'. See also H. N. Brailsford, *Rebel India* (1931),116; Purcell and Hallsworth, *Report on Indian Labour Conditions*.
[71] Gandhi, 'Speech at Meeting of Labour Union', 6 Sept 1925, *CWMG*, E32/242.
[72] B. R. Tomlinson, *The Political Economy of the Raj, 1914–1947: The Economics of Decolonization in India* (London, 1979), 122–3.
[73] Gupta, *Imperialism*, 216–23.

textile-workers.[74] C. F. Andrews had made the same argument after a visit to Lancashire.[75] It was hardly the time, the Labour MP Philip Noel-Baker commented privately to a British Gandhian in March 1930, for Gandhi to complain about the British exploitation of India, 'when Lancashire is absolutely starving'.[76] Margaret Bondfield, the Minister of Labour, told MacDonald that Lancashire was sceptical of the Congress claim that Indian freedom would really 'improve the standard of life and purchasing power of the population generally'.[77]

Andrews therefore arranged for an economist to assemble some statistical evidence and pressed Gandhi to visit Lancashire to see the distress for himself.[78] However, Gandhi was not convinced by this data. He told Andrews that although he sympathised with the unemployed, the solution was not for India to lift the cotton boycott. 'If it was wrong any time for Lancashire to impose its cloth upon India by hook or by crook it is wrong also today and more so because India has become conscious of the wrong.' The boycott was 'undoing the wrong done by Lancashire. That the labourers were not conscious of the wrong . . . is no justification for the wrong itself being sustained.' Gandhi's solution for the Lancashire unemployed, as expressed to Andrews, was to 'find some other employment'. '[B]etter still', he continued, 'why should not the machinery be scrapped and the unemployed take to handicrafts?' England, like India, needed to 'return to simplicity'.[79] A further idea was that the millworkers should refuse the dole and starve in public, thereby shaming the Government into action.[80] It was small wonder that Ernest Bevin, requested to chair a meeting for Gandhi in Bristol, told its organiser that he was anxious to ask him some 'difficult questions from the working-class point of view'.[81]

During the second Round Table Conference, the opportunity to make these suggestions to Lancashire millworkers in person arose. But Gandhi did not do so. Instead, he argued that the boycott was only

---

[74] CPGB, *Is India Different? The Class Struggle in India: Correspondence on the Indian Labour Movement and Modern conditions by S. Saklatvala, M.P., and M.K. Gandhi* (London, 1927).

[75] Hugh Tinker, *The Ordeal of Love: C. F. Andrews and India* (Delhi, 1979), 248.

[76] Noel-Baker to Alexander, 11 March 1930, Noel-Baker Papers, 4/368.

[77] Bondfield to MacDonald, 30 April 1931, quoted in Gupta, *Imperialism*, 220.

[78] Andrews to MacDonald, 24 June 1931, Andrews to Gandhi, 26 June 1931, Alexander Papers (NMML); Gandhi to Polak, 15 June 1931, *CWMG*, E52/466.

[79] Gandhi to Andrews, 19 and 24 June 1931, *CWMG*, E52/498, E52/547.

[80] Hunt, *Gandhi in London*, 194.

[81] Menon to Merrie, 11 Aug 1931, KMP 9/3/41.

a minor cause of the unemployment, which owed more to the world slump and Japanese competition. He also held out the possibility that after independence, Lancashire would be given a preference in, or even sole access to, the Indian market to provide those goods which the home spinner could not yet produce, but which would be demanded on a large scale by an 'awakened India on her road to prosperity'.[82] These promises were much more satisfactory to the workers and their representatives than Gandhi's earlier reported comments. While there was some disappointment that Gandhi did not promise an end to the boycott, there was also a good deal of realism. Gandhi convinced most of those he met of the sincerity of his campaign and of the prospects for trade to increase after independence.[83] Thereafter, the deleterious results of the cotton boycott were rarely laid at the nationalists' door. At the 1932 Party Conference, a speaker from Lancashire blamed not Congress, but 'the wooden-headed Generals and the soulless civil servants' for its effects.[84] Indeed, Gandhi's visit did much to endear him to Labour's natural supporters, especially his decision to stay in the East End with the workers, convinced, as he told Brailsford, that to win them would win the political class as a whole.[85]

However, the enthusiasm of the workers of Bow and Clitheroe was not matched among Labour's party managers in London. Gandhi was, in many ways, an anti-politician, who did not take naturally to the work of practical negotiation and compromise. Those who corresponded with him had often found his letters infuriatingly ambiguous. 'I beg you to think of one thing only', Leys had written in 1926, after receiving a particularly delphic utterance on religion and communalism: 'how you

---

[82] Gandhi, 'Lancashire v. Japan', *CWMG*, E53/164; 'Interview to "Textile Mercury"', 17 Sept 1931, *CWMG* E53/422; Statements to the Press and meetings with representatives and workers in the cotton industry, 25–7 Sept 1931, *CWMG*,E53/448–54; Gandhi to Andrews, 19 June 1931, *CWMG*, E52/498. See also C. Rajagopalachar and J. C. Kumarappa (eds.), *The Nation's Voice: Being a Collection of Gandhiji's Speeches in England and Sjt. Mahadev Desai's Account of the Sojourn (September to December 1931)* (Ahmedabad, 1932), 279–88.

[83] Account of Meeting with Representatives of Cotton Trade, 26 Sept 1931, *CWMG*, E53/451.

[84] Labour Party, *Report of Annual Conference*, 1932, 179; Resolution of United Textile Factory Workers' Association, 15 May 1933, William Gillies Correspondence, WG/IND/83ii, LPA.

[85] Gandhi, however, was saddened that the workers of Bow had 'no conception of what India is suffering'. 'They sincerely believe that India is the brightest jewel in the British crown. They are honestly proud of the record of British rule. It never enters their mind that there can be anything amiss.' Interview to H. N. Brailsford, undated, but probably Oct 1931, *CWMG*, E53/516.

would act if your name were not Gandhi but Leys, and God had given you some responsibility for coming to decisions which may conceivably become the decisions upon which some day a British Government may act.'[86] Gandhi met Labour MPs on several occasions during breaks in the Conference proceedings.[87] He clearly impressed many of them with his honesty, but they felt the limitations of his approach. While they could admire Gandhi's *satyagraha* as a fine example of personal spiritual growth, they found it much harder to see it as an adequate solution to the deep national, class and communal problems of India. Moreover, Labour's sensitivity to questions of class interest was particularly raw as Gandhi came to address them. Only a few days before, Parliament had reassembled for the formalities of the end of the second Labour Government. Its first business thereafter had been for Snowden and MacDonald to introduce an emergency budget and cuts in unemployment benefit even more drastic than those that had been dividing the party for months. At his first meeting with Labour MPs, therefore, Gandhi was subjected to some fairly rough questioning. There was incredulity about his attitude to machinery, the Middlesbrough MP Ellen Wilkinson demanding to know 'if it was not a reactionary policy to refuse to use the inventions of science . . . [and] the human mind', the effect of which was simply to keep India poor.[88] But most of the points the Labour MPs raised concerned the Lancashire boycott and Congress' attitude to questions of industrial relations. The County Durham MP Manny Shinwell told Gandhi that the Indian coalowners were 'much more reactionary and brutal to their employees than British coal-owners' and that he wanted to know how Gandhi reconciled that with his claim that Britain exploited India. Gandhi replied that when he spoke about exploitation, he 'was not thinking about these few thousand labourers in the coal-mines, or in the factories of Bombay or Calcutta' but of India's immensely larger rural population. The Indian coalminers were 'oppressed but . . . not starving' like the villagers. Gandhi also insisted that the cotton boycott was designed only to serve the interests of

---

[86] Leys to Gandhi, 29 June 1926, Gandhi Papers, SN 12168; Gandhi to Leys, 28 May 1926, *CWMG* E35/360.

[87] There were meetings with Labour MPs alone on 16 Sept 1931, and among others on 23 Sept, 2, 12 and 30 Oct, 12 Nov, and 3 Dec 1931. Edited extracts of these meetings are given in *CWMG*, E53/421, 442, 498, 519; E54/59–60, 94, 138. A full report of the first is in *Manchester Guardian*, 17 Sept 1931.

[88] Speech at Meeting of Labour MPs, 16 Sept 1931, *CWMG* E53/421 See also 'Account of Meeting with Representatives of Cotton Trade', 26 Sept 1931.

these villagers in year-round employment. However, the anti-imperialist Norman Angell, now MP for Bradford North, pointed out that its likely effect was that Lancashire goods would be replaced by the products of the industrial mills of Bombay and Calcutta rather than homespun cloth. The Sowerby MP and weavers' leader, W. J. Tout asked Gandhi to deny the rumour that the boycott was paid for by the Bombay mill-owners for precisely this reason. Gandhi was unable to deny the financial involvement of the mill-owners, but claimed that the hand-spinners would be able to take them on and win when independence came.[89] Another Labour MP asked Gandhi what the Indian villagers would answer if asked why they were led by Gandhi. Gandhi replied that he led them 'because they could not express themselves [and] that he was expressing their aspirations for them'.[90] 'Bloody hopeless' had been the verdict of Tout afterwards.[91]

A second meeting, held at the National Labour Club, was little better. Here the questioning touched on the issue of communal tension in India. Gandhi had not been given to offering assurances to British socialists about this, as Leys had learned in 1926. In a letter to Leonard Woolf, Leys wrote of the 'the obvious fact that scarcely any Asiatics and Africans do govern themselves and also when alone, as in China, they relapse into anarchy'. Democracy would not work in Africa, Leys wrote, because 'tribal ideas and habits are incongruous with democracy', nor in Asia because of 'the prevalence of ideas of authority in religion, politics—everything'. These made it 'a wicked thing to think for oneself and . . . without personal liberty and independence, democracy withers'.[92] Asked now whether he was not risking a communal war after a British withdrawal, Gandhi told the Labour MPs:

It is likely that we the Hindus and Muslims may fight one another if the British Army is withdrawn. Well, if such is to be our lot, I do not mind it. It is quite likely. Only if we don't go through the ordeal now, it will simply be postponement of the agony and therefore, I personally do not mind it a bit and the whole of the Congress . . . has decided to run the risk of it . . . Did

[89] For details of support for the cotton boycott by Indian business interests, see Brown, *Gandhi and Civil Disobedience*, 127–30, 147–8, 309–11. 'Account of Meeting with Representatives of Cotton Trade', 26 Sept 1931.

[90] Gandhi, 'Speech at Meeting of Labour MPs', 16 Sept 1931, *Manchester Guardian*, 17 Sept 1931.

[91] Dalton, *Political Diary*, 16 Sept 1931, 155; M. A. Hamilton, *Remembering My Good Friends* (1944), 248.

[92] Leys to Woolf, 8 Nov 1931, Leonard Woolf Papers, General Correspondence.

the British people themselves not run the maddest risks imaginable in order to retain their liberty? Did they not have the terrible Wars of the Roses?[93]

There was little more reassurance for questioners eager to know Gandhi's plans for Indian defence. This was important because Congress had made control of defence a sticking point in their demands at the Conference. Foreign rule, Gandhi announced at the National Labour Club, had fostered a 'rot of emasculation' which was worse than fighting. Invasion would therefore simply be met by non-cooperation with the invader.[94] Gandhi, Dalton had already concluded after an earlier meeting, had 'a terrible physical inferiority complex' on this question.[95] Asked whether the constitutional 'safeguards in India's interest' he had agreed to accept included trade, he was less reassuring than he had been when talking to the cotton operatives in Lancashire. He would not have adjustments that did 'moral harm' to Britain, though some of them 'might mean material loss'.[96]

Attlee, although he is not recorded as having spoken at these meetings, also had substantial reservations. He had told the Fabian Society earlier in the summer that there were three difficulties that a socialist must encounter with the proposal to leave India. The first was the likely effect on the Indian economy, for the British, far from impoverishing the country, had created an artificial prosperity which would collapse into confusion and famine on their departure. Conditions in native-owned industry were worse than those in British-owned factories, and Indian trade unionism was 'largely racketeering run by the lawyers'. The second difficulty was the question of defence, which Attlee continued to believe could not be transferred to Indian ministers without removing British officers, and thereby stripping it of all its senior ranks. Finally, there was the problem of religious minorities. The Muslims formed a kind of 'diffused Ulster'. On the Hindu side, few inroads had been made into caste prejudice, and the Brahmins would certainly oppose democratic growth. Attlee thought that the only solution was what he had pressed on Simon: the concession of limited central responsibility to Indians, to attract the 'best nationalists' who, in Attlee's view, were those who were

[93] Gandhi, 'Speech at Meeting of Labour MPs', 16 Sept 1931; 'To English Friends', *Young India*, 23 Jan 1930, *CWMG*, E48/257; Rajagopalachar and Kumarappa (eds.), *The Nation's Voice*, 203–4.

[94] Speech at National Labour Club Reception, 12 Oct 1931, *CWMG*, E53/519.

[95] Dalton, *Political Diary*, 16 Sept 1931, 155.

[96] Speech at National Labour Club Reception, 12 Oct 1931; 'Speech at Meeting of MPs', 23 Sept 1931, 'Interview to H. N. Brailsford', undated but probably Oct 1931.

currently occupied in provincial government. With franchise extensions, 'unscrupulous lawyers' would give way as 'parties in the proletariat' rose against them. But there could be no immediate clearing out of India: the result would be 'the loss of the North-West Frontier and of the bulk of our Indian trade'.[97]

At the Conference itself, the Conservatives attempted a reversion to the Simon Commission plan. They proposed a plan to introduce provincial autonomy first, with progress at the centre delayed until agreement was reached on the structure of a federation. Gandhi was briefly won to this idea, seeing it as a means by which the provinces could pull powers from the centre. But Sapru persuaded him and other Indian delegates that strengthening the provinces would make it harder to achieve federation and central responsibility, an opinion shared by MacDonald and Sankey, now in the National Government. In his closing statement, MacDonald announced that the Government would therefore work towards the production of a single India Bill. To this end it would make its own settlement of the communal impasse, and set up expert committees and an Indian consultative committee to deal with the outstanding difficulties and continue the work of the Conference.[98]

This seemed to Labour's India experts a significant victory and a sign that even the Party's loss of office did not mean the end of political progress. However, Gandhi dismissed it as of little consequence. On the eve of his departure, therefore, leftist sympathisers pleaded with him to go some way to meeting it.[99] At the very least, the proposals were, as Horrabin put it, 'dangerously plausible'. British sympathisers would have 'real difficulty in getting public opinion to grasp the objections to them'. Gandhi was pressed by Laski, Brailsford and Kingsley Martin to recognise that MacDonald had outsmarted Hoare, giving Congress more than it had got from the minority Labour Government. On that ground, Martin insisted, Gandhi should restrain himself and neither dismiss the Conference so readily, nor resort to civil disobedience. 'We may be too stupid to know when we are beaten', Brailsford commented, 'but you may be too clever to see when you have won.' Harold Laski too urged Gandhi to look at the situation from a British point of view. '[F]rom our angle', he pointed out, 'the Prime Minister made a brilliant strategic move' which made it impossible for Gandhi or his

[97] Meeting at Easton Lodge, 13 June 1931, Fabian Society Papers J2/3/80–2.
[98] Moore, *Crisis of Indian Unity*, 232–9; Brown, *Gandhi and Civil Disobedience*, 254.
[99] Discussion with J. F. Horrabin and Others, 3 Dec 1931, *CWMG* E54/138.

British supporters to respond in an immediate or impetuous way. He advised Gandhi to declare his support for the future programme of Conference work MacDonald had announced. He might legitimately insist on conditions: an end to the Bengal Ordinance, proper places for Congress on the proposed committees, and more Indians on the Viceroy's Executive. But beyond these demands, he should go slow in order to strengthen MacDonald's hand against the Conservatives and win British opinion, and thereby provide the left with a task 'upon which we can embark with a good heart'.[100]

Gandhi was no help at all. There was, he insisted, no real room for manoeuvre in what had been wrung from the Conservatives, and the Labour experts' suggestions that he should welcome the prospect of future conference work merely revealed 'the paralysis of the British mind'. 'You throw logic to the winds', Gandhi declared. 'I should have certainly patience, but not the patience of a stone . . . Do you want me to sit still in the hope that things are coming right?' Gandhi was unhelpful because he now knew that civil disobedience was inevitable on his return. But Gandhi's British supporters concluded that he thereby played into the hands of the right. He had insisted on speaking for the whole of India and he had refused to trust the Labour Government which was both well intentioned and hamstrung by its political opponents. But this was not the only problem. Gandhi genuinely found the insincere politics of coalition, as the Labour experts explained them to him, simply incomprehensible. He could not see how MacDonald could make an equivocal declaration at the behest of the Conservatives and expect to please Congress at the same time. When Laski told Gandhi that some members of the coalition Cabinet did not support the use of repression in India, Gandhi snapped back 'No? Then the members should resign. It is a sickening thing. It is positively horrid . . . If you remain silent in a matter of this kind you are guilty.'[101]

This was no less than an irreducible clash of moralities. One of those present, the writer George Catlin, later wrote of the occasion:

Everyone was, I think, a little stiff and a little embarrassed. The politicians and worldly men did not know what might be said next. They might be asked whether they had been saved, as by a Salvationist . . .

I was impressed—impressed by the signs and wonders, by Gandhi as an unusual kind of politician; but I had, as yet, no insight. . . . Even some of those at the

---

[100] Discussion with Horrabin and Others.   [101] Ibid.

party . . . dismissed him as 'too much of a Jesuit for them'. His religiosity offended their Fabian common sense, their Marxist prejudices, and indeed their Bloomsbury good taste . . . [A] god in a drawing room . . . [is] always liable to say things in bad taste . . . There is a collision of two worlds. [102]

British interest in Gandhism in 1931, which was considerable, reflected neither sympathy nor hostility, but a desire to find a place for the seemingly anomalous Gandhi in the belief-systems and political world-views of the progressive left. Gandhi was not so alien that this task was impossible. Some aspects of his thinking were undoubtedly attractive, notably those which had been derived from familiar sources. Ruskin, for example, who had provided Gandhi with his belief in the dignity of labour and the necessity of service to the poor and marginalised, had also been one of the dominant influences on the thinking of the British left. Gandhi's disparagement of western materialism, technology and uncritical scientific progress aroused distant echoes of similarly-inclined critiques by Edward Carpenter and other 'new age' critics, which had been influential in *fin-de-siècle* socialist circles.[103] The popularising of Gandhi by Romain Rolland and others in the 1920s had also helped to assimilate Gandhi to dissident Christian traditions, especially the Franciscan one of poverty and service, which resonated among Christian Socialists and others influenced by Christianity.[104] The Gandhian ashram seemed to offer an ideal of equality, simplicity and austerity and Gandhi himself the incorruptibility of a man of the people, an exemplar which had a special place in Labour mythology. His concern for the *harijan* was a useful counterweight to their suspicions of the entrenched caste system.

However, in the Labour Party of the interwar years, alternative visions of modernity and radical approaches to realising socialism and democracy, which had been quite prominent before 1914, had been marginalised, if not squeezed out altogether, in a drive for electoral growth and state power.[105] While Gandhi's personal integrity and commitment to social experiment could be admired, therefore, most

---

[102] George Catlin, *In the Path of Mahatma Gandhi* (London, 1948), 201, 223.

[103] Fox, *Gandhian Utopia;* Leela Gandhi, *Affective Communities.*

[104] Claude Markovits, *The UnGandhian Gandhi: The Life and Afterlife of the Mahatma* (London, 2004); Mark Juergensmeyer, 'Saint Gandhi' in J. S. Hawley (ed.), *Saints and Virtues* (Berkeley and Los Angeles, 1987).

[105] Logie Barrow and Ian Bullock, *Democratic Ideas and the British Labour Movement, 1880–1914* (Cambridge, 1996).

thought his ideas too retrograde, anarchic or utopian for nation-building. For example, Keir Hardie, as we saw in Chapter 3, wanted the Indian nation-state to rest on a structure of provincial and local councils, and ultimately on the village *panchayat*. This would ensure that it was properly accountable but also that it acquired authority sufficient to eradicate poverty and under-development. Gandhi, by contrast, wanted a structure which was not pyramidal, but made up of 'ever-widening, never ascending circles' in which the village would resist control from the centre.[106] Gandhi's hostility to machines which displaced manual labour, for example, suggested an admirable concern for rural employment, and appealed to the dwindling numbers of ruralist or handicraft socialists in the William Morris tradition. But to the majority of British socialists, Gandhi's 'absurd economic dreams', as Beatrice Webb termed them, offered no solution to the material impoverishment of the Indian peasant.[107] Industrial modernisation, with its accompanying clash of class interests, was seen as quite inevitable if India was to be free. 'Rejection of the machine is always founded on acceptance of the machine', wrote Orwell, 'a fact symbolised by Gandhi as he plays with his spinning wheel in the mansion of some cotton millionaire.'[108] Such examples could be proliferated, and are evident in the tough questioning Gandhi received from Labour MPs in 1931.

Of course, many of Gandhi's *Indian* critics agreed with much of this critique, and certainly with its underlying assumptions. As we shall see in the next chapter, this made them, especially Jawaharlal Nehru and the Congress Socialists, closer allies of the British left than Gandhi ever managed to be. But in making such alliances, they were neither willing nor able to disown Gandhi. While they disagreed with many of his beliefs, they were dependent on him to reach supporters and voters to whom their own ideals remained unintelligible. They were also in awe of him as a strategist. Congress leaders who hardly agreed with a word of Gandhian thinking on the questions that mattered most to Gandhi—spinning, self-purification, *harijan* uplift, and so on—nonetheless deferred to his leadership of political campaigns, even when he was not formally placed in charge of them. Thus Gandhian

[106] 'Independence', 21 July 1946, *CWMG*, E91/378
[107] Beatrice Webb, Diary, 11 Aug 1942.
[108] Orwell, Review of Lionel Fielden's *Beggar My Neighbour* in Sonia Orwell and Ian Angus (eds.), *The Collected Essays, Journalism and Letters of George Orwell* (4v., Harmondsworth, 1968), ii, 306–15.

ideas, for all their novelty and complexity, remained the force field within which Congress policy was made even when Gandhi was not directing the campaign.

This was problematic because Gandhian political strategy also seemed alien and unfamiliar. This was not exactly its use of non-cooperation, which had a legitimate, if limited, place in the British left's armoury. Rather it was its use by Gandhi as a technique for building and cementing a movement, rather than as a tactic of last resort. This was one reason why George Lansbury, a Poplar rebel, opposed its use in India. In British debates over the efficacy of passive resistance or the defiance of unjust law, the Labour Party had generally been on the side of caution. This was one of the principal commitments which defined it as a party. Its preference was for the capture and use of legislative power and, above all, the exploitation of the opportunities that office-holding permitted for a party to strengthen its position. This was why, from the Montagu–Chelmsford reforms to Stafford Cripps' Offer in 1942, Labour had invariably advised Congress to stand for election or take office as a stepping stone to further advance. From Congress' point of view, however, such offers looked more like traps than stepping stones. To step forward risked splitting the movement and diverting its energies, as occurred in the mid-1920s. Hence those who did enter the councils always kept one foot outside, and one eye on those who had not entered, above all on the irresponsible Congress Working Committee, and, of course, Gandhi.

Gandhi thus remained the key. Labour had been able to create a useful working alliance with Tilak in 1919, despite differences of view about India, because they shared with him a sense of how politics worked. Tilak had been mildly misleading about his commitment to socialism, and doubtless this, had he lived, would have become evident sooner or later. But this would not have wholly surprised his Labour friends, because they understood the business Tilak was engaged in. In their hearts, they suspected that, whatever he said, Tilak was probably only entering the councils in order to use the leverage they provided to push for more. While Labour's leaders did not altogether like this, they did understand it. Gandhi's more principled refusals were harder to construe. 'Politics is a game of worldly people and not of *sadhus*', Tilak told Gandhi reproachfully in 1920.[109] But Gandhi was engaged

---

[109] Tilak to Gandhi, 18 Jan 1920, quoted in *Young India*, 28 Jan 1920, *CWMG*, E19/182.

in building a largely new form of *sadhu* politics much better adapted to the position of weakness in which Congress found itself. The capacity of these techniques to put the *raj* on its back foot are well known.[110] Labour, especially when in Government, shared this sense of impotence they created. 'If I were to start a bonfire in Whitehall', MacDonald raged, 'they would certainly arrest me.'[111] Benn too preferred 'a straight fight with the revolver people' rather than this indirect moral struggle with Gandhi.[112] But Gandhi's strategy was not simply designed to wrong-foot the officials of the *raj*. Had it been so, it would have formed a more secure base for an alliance with British Labour, which had its own reasons to bait the Blimp for his hostility to popular demands. Gandhi, as Nandy observes, 'wanted to liberate the British as much as he wanted to liberate the Indians', awakening dormant or undeveloped elements in their civilisation and making them aware of the wrongs they had committed.[113] This was an unsettling and largely unwelcome reversal of the awakening of India by western modernity that MacDonald had described. It was not Blimp-baiting either, because it ranged the British left-winger with the officials of the *raj*, not as enemies, of course, but as penitents who needed to examine their consciences over their treatment of India and engage in dialogue with those they had wronged. To Indians who asked for their advice and leadership, therefore, Labour offered support and apprenticeship. Those who simply refused to address them at all, like Savarkar, they ignored. But the Gandhian proposal bewildered and at times infuriated them because it did neither. It spoke to them, but as equals.

[110] See Dalton, *Mahatma Gandhi*, 91–138.
[111] MacDonald to Pickthall, 6 March 1929, PRO 30/69/1174, NA; MacDonald to Walsh, 20 Oct 1930, PRO 30/69/676, NA; MacDonald to Andrews, 5 May 1930, PRO 30/69/1440, NA.
[112] Benn to Irwin, 30 Jan 1930 and 22 April 1930, HC, MSS/Eur/C152/6.
[113] Nandy, *Intimate Enemy*, 51. See also 'From Outside the Imperium: Gandhi's Cultural Critique of the West' in his *Traditions, Tyranny and Utopias: Essays in the Politics of Awareness* (New Delhi, 1987).

7

An Anti-Imperialist Junction Box?
Metropolitan Anti-Imperialism
in the early 1930s

This chapter returns to Congress' dilemma of metropolitan organisation. It examines the constellation of anti-imperialist groups in Britain in the early 1930s, identifying their relationships with, and dependence on, British associations and parties. In doing so, it also tests the theory that London acted as an anti-imperialist 'junction-box', providing connections between anti-colonial nationalists from India and metropolitan radicals, as well as those from other colonised countries. This theory, long present in historical accounts of nationally-specific anti-imperialisms, has been much favoured by postcolonial theorists, for two principal reasons: first, because they tend to see diasporic encounters as distinctively productive, suffering few of the drawbacks associated with nationally-grounded movements; and secondly, because the possibility that the imperial capital could be, against its own inclinations and without its knowledge, a site of resistance, its concentration of power and nodal centrality turned against it by actors from the periphery, is so pleasingly subversive. It is, Homi Bhabha argues, 'by living on the borderline of history and language, on the limits of race and gender, that we are in a position to translate the differences between them into a kind of solidarity'.[1] In such a view, the metropole is a fertile place at which hybridity occurs, offending and disrupting the coloniser's insistence on purity and boundaries.[2]

---

[1] Bhabha, *The Location of Culture*, 170.

[2] See, for example, Elleke Boehmer, *Empire, the National, and the Postcolonial, 1890–1920: Resistance in Interaction* (Oxford, 2002), 20, 172. See also Jonathan Schneer, *London 1900: The Imperial Metropolis* (New Haven, 1999); John McLeod, *Postcolonial London: Rewriting the Metropolis* (London, 2004).

Since the abolition of the British Committee at Nagpur in 1920, no one had spoken authoritatively for Congress in London. Efforts by some Congress leaders to reinstate British work were invariably blocked by the Gandhians. In December 1921, Congress had voted to draw up a definite scheme of foreign propaganda. To forestall Gandhian objections it was agreed that it be run by Indian expatriates, not British sympathisers, and that it be directly supervised by Congress.[3] Gandhi, however, had reiterated his objections, invoking the 'automatic capacity of Truth to spread itself' without the need for propaganda.[4] 'My own impression', he wrote, 'is that sufferings constitute the best and most eloquent propaganda.'[5] '[N]atural and organic' interest in India would grow anyway in countries intrigued by the Gandhian movement, and could not be artificially stimulated by the press.[6] This did not satisfy everyone: at the Gaya Congress in 1922, C. R. Das called for a revival of foreign propaganda and the Swarajists made it part of their programme in 1923.[7] In 1925, with Gandhi having removed himself to the background of its affairs, Congress managed to set up a foreign department to protect the interests of overseas Indians, with a small Rs. 5000 (£375) grant for educative propaganda overseas. But less than half this small sum was actually spent, none of it in London.[8] Even the Swarajists' official London representative, P. B. Seal, had found it difficult to extract funds from India, thanks to the opposition of Motilal Nehru.[9] The growth of political opportunities in India at the provincial level meant that Congress leaders preferred more than ever to devote their money and activists to the capture of local office than to the distant and uncontrollable efforts of 'All India' lobbyists in Britain. Throughout the 1920s, Gandhi continued to insist on the undesirability of foreign

[3] 'Interview to the Daily Herald', 16 March 1921, *CWMG*, E22/228; 'Interview to the Bombay Chronicle', 24 Dec 1921, *CWMG*, E25/160; AICC 3/1921 generally; Ansari to Patel, 5 Jan 1922, and Hardikar to Patel, 7 Jan 1922, AICC 9/1922.
[4] Gandhi, 'Letter to Chairman, AICC', 22 Feb 1922, *CWMG*, E26/93; Minutes of Working Committee, 26 Feb 1922, in Zaidi, *Encyclopaedia*, viii, 494.
[5] 'Interview to "The Bombay Chronicle"', 5 Feb 1922, *CWMG*, E26/45.
[6] 'Letter to Chairman, AICC', 22 Feb 1922, *CWMG*, E26/93; 'Foreign Propaganda', *Young India*, 9 March 1922, *CWMG*, E26/131.
[7] *Hind*, 13 and 20 Dec 1922; Nanda, 'The Swarajist Interlude', 117; Swaraj Party meeting, Allahabad, 28 Feb 1923, *SWMN*, iv, 517–20.
[8] AICC accounts for this are in files F25/1926, G21/1926–7 and F43/1928–9. Rs. 1,897 [£142] was spent from March 1926 to Sept 1927 and Rs. 20 [£1/6s] in 1928–9.
[9] Sarat Bose to Seal, 2 Dec 1924, 22 Jan, 4 March, 21 Oct, 19 Nov, 3 and 10 Dec 1925, 7 Jan 1926, P. B. Seal Coll., MSS/Eur/Photo Eur/446/2.

propaganda, and his acolytes stamped on any suggestion that it was needed.[10]

The intangible incentives enjoyed by British activists before the war were no longer available either. Like many other idealistic and altruistic causes, India had attracted many supporters who were activated by a sense of specifically British responsibilities. This is one reason why anti-imperial campaigns, like those of pacifists, were more effective at the national than the international level. Satisfaction of these duties required British activists to take the moral lead in demolishing or transforming empire, as in the tradition of 'Members for India' in Parliament. But in the Gandhian strategy, the part of the British sympathiser in the drama of Indian independence was to be reduced from that of principal to that of chorus. British supporters had lost nearly all the authority they once commanded in the nationalist movement. Indeed, their role was a very uncertain one: they were clearly no longer leaders, but could they even be advisers, representatives or delegates? Gandhi had reversed the relationship as it had evolved under the British Committee: it was no longer the duty of Britons to instruct Indians in governance, but the mission of India to save Britain, through its use of *satyagraha*. He told Polak in 1925, 'It is contrary to my nature to distrust a single human being or to believe that any nation on earth is incapable of redemption. I have hope of England because I have hope of India.'[11] Many felt rebuked by this reorientation.

In the absence of direction or encouragement from India, campaigners for Indian freedom in Britain were left to find their own resources and the quality of campaigning slumped accordingly. The authoritative, if often tedious and patronising, columns of *India* were replaced by an unpredictable succession of cyclostyled news-sheets with small print-runs, and groups of activists became more dependent on the hospitality offered by other progressive causes. Indeed, in effect the story of metropolitan anti-imperialism in the 1920s and 1930s is that of a search for such homes. Since campaigners for India lacked the authority and resources to win sufficient supporters on their own, they needed to tie themselves to campaigns or parties that could. Hitching the Indian issue in this fashion thus promised the instant

---

[10] Gandhi, 'Interview to "The Hindu"', 17 May 1924, *CWMG*, E27/350; Gandhi to Nehru, 14 May 1927, *CWMG*, E38/383; 'Foreign Propaganda', *Young India*, 2 Aug 1928, *CWMG* E42/349; C. Rajagopalachari, ibid. 1 March 1928, *CWMG*, E41/273; E41/App III.

[11] *Young India*, 29 Jan 1925, *CWMG*, E30/82.

adhesion of large numbers of new recruits and opportunities for publicity and influence, provided campaigners could identify a well-supported movement with aims which neither clashed with that of Indian freedom nor alienated too many existing supporters. Increasingly, therefore, the tendency of metropolitan anti-imperialism was to become more parasitic, working not through direct connections between British anti-imperialists and Indian nationalists, but through the delicate and intermittent connections between the nationalists, on one hand, and a variety of British progressive causes, loosely defined, on the other. Of course, to describe such relationships as parasitic need not imply that they could not also be mutually advantageous. However, it was not always easy to identify causes which reliably delivered the kind of metropolitan support that anti-imperialists needed. Theosophists, socialists, communists, feminists, Christians and pacifists each served this purpose at times. Each cause had, for its own reasons, certain affinities with the Indian freedom struggle, but each had other priorities too, and often rivals anxious to contest its claim to speak for India.

The first such host was the Theosophical Society, which provided considerable support for Congress in the First World War and afterwards. The great utility of Theosophy for anti-imperialists lay in its 'affirmative orientalism'.[12] Unlike western liberalism and socialism it did not need to squeeze India into an existing ideology, for in Theosophical belief, Hindu India was the starting point. It was in the ancient texts of the Vedas that Theosophists believed that they had found the potential for global spiritual rediscovery and growth; in traditional Indian social arrangements a more satisfactory means of reconciling private interests and mutual responsibilities than that offered by mass democracy; and in Indian values an ethic with which to counter a godless and acquisitive west. Unlike some of the other neo-Hindu revivalist movements of the time, moreover, the Theosophists did not merely celebrate ancient India, but used it to stimulate modern questions about social development. These included questions troubling sections of the British Victorian professional middle classes, such as the reconciliation of scientific discovery with Anglican Christianity, or the place for spirituality in the modern

---

[12] Richard G. Fox, *Gandhian Utopia: Experiments with Culture* (Boston, 1989), 105–11.

age. Theosophy, though not the most popular form of spiritualism among the autodidact poor, nonetheless appealed to some British socialists, especially those hostile to traditional Anglican authority or keen to respond to accusations that socialism was merely materialistic.[13] But Theosophy did not confine its attentions to finding Indian solutions to the spiritual crises of the west, for it also addressed questions which worried Indian westernised elites, such as how to reform the social practices of Hinduism without conceding leadership to missionaries or British officials.[14] The critique of modern India made by Theosophists focussed not just on the adequacy of Hindu culture in its response to modernity, but on the damage wrought by the incursion of the west on an admittedly idealised vision of pre-colonial India.

In complex ways, therefore, Theosophy partially reversed imperialist conceptions of Indian inferiority while also providing a specific and powerful anti-imperial charge. Its Indo-centric approach was reflected in its institutional configuration: the headquarters of the Theosophical Society were in Adyar, near Madras, though London was also an important centre for the English-speaking world; its annual conventions brought British and Indian supporters together on Indian ground; and Indians rose to positions of seniority in the movement.[15] In India, the Theosophical Society supplied organisation which could not readily be repressed even when its activities embraced the political: this was one of the reasons why Annie Besant's internment in 1917 had been so controversial. In Britain, Theosophy was very well resourced: membership in England and Wales grew strongly in the spiritual crisis of the First World War and after, peaking at about 5,000 in 1922.[16] Many of these members were also affluent and well-connected, which, as funding from India dried up, put large sums of money into the organisation's coffers for Indian work and gave it a certain

---

[13] Logie Barrow, *Independent Spirits: Spiritualism and English Plebeians, 1850–1910* (London, 1986).

[14] Peter Van der Veer, *Imperial Encounters: Religions and Modernity in India and Britain* (Princeton, 2001).

[15] Mark Bevir, 'In Opposition to the Raj: Annie Besant and the Dialectic of Empire', *History of Political Thought*, 19/1 (1998), 61–77; Mark Bevir, 'Theosophy as a Political Movement', and Carla Risseuw, 'Thinking Culture Through Counter-Culture: The Case of Theosophists in India and Ceylon and their Ideas on Race and Hierarchy', in Antony Copley (ed.), *Gurus and Their Followers: New Religious Reform Movements in Colonial India* (Oxford, 2000), 159–79, 180–205.

[16] *General Report of the Year's Work of the Theosophical Society in England & Wales* gives the figures as 1918: 3,281; 1919: 3,802; 1920: 5,105; 1921: 5,261; 1922: 4,625 England and 209 Wales.

legitimacy among officials and MPs.[17] In India, the Theosophical convert was an awkward and destabilising figure, as Gauri Viswanathan suggests, through his or her refusal to respect the efforts of the *raj* to secularise and assimilate Indian elites.[18] In Britain too, Theosophists adopted transgressive positions, and redrew the lines of solidarity which usually divided Britons from Indians. Virginia Woolf paid an inverted compliment to this in a comment on a lecture by Annie Besant in 1919. Besant, she wrote, 'a massive and sulky featured old lady . . . pitched into us for our maltreatment of India, she apparently being "them" and not "us" '.[19]

Theosophy might therefore have validated an effective anti-imperialist politics in Britain. That it did not do so very effectively after the mid-1920s was the result of a number of causes. Politically, as had been painfully apparent in the clashes between the Besantines and the ILP in the mid-1920s, Theosophists were cautious and elitist. Few were sure that the solution to India's problems lay in political self-determination alone. Most, with Annie Besant herself, favoured home rule within a commonwealth led by Britain, in the belief that India needed the political guidance of Britain as much as Britons needed to learn from India's spiritual strengths. This, as noted earlier, had led Besant in 1919 to oppose Gandhian non-cooperation, which she thought was impatient and risked social disorder. It was to lead to a more marked divergence after 1928. Other Theosophists exhibited a less affirmative 'middle-brow orientalism'[20] in their dealings with India. They imbued India with unworldly virtues which proved hard to reconcile with the immediate needs of the nationalist movement, which in turn they came to see as a grubby struggle for worldly political gains, incapable either of developing India spiritually, or enabling it to act as a beacon for the rest of the world. Furthermore, while Theosophists were generally committed to international brotherhood and racial equality, their political activities usually had to be carried on semi-independently through 'Action Lodges', partly because of the distrust of action in the

[17] DCI Report, 3 Nov 1917, HPB, Nov 1917, 471–4; Veer, *Imperial Encounters*, 58.

[18] Gauri Viswanathan, *Outside the Fold: Conversion, Modernity and Belief* (Princeton, 1998); 'The Ordinary Business of Occultism', *Critical Inquiry*, 27/1 (Autumn 2000), 1–20.

[19] Leonard Woolf (ed.), *A Writer's Diary: Being Extracts from The Diary of Virginia Woolf* (New York, 1954), 17.

[20] Joy Dixon, *Divine Feminine: Theosophy and Feminism in England* (Baltimore, 2001), 11.

'outer world' by some Theosophists, and partly due to a desire to avoid laying down a common political line in an organisation dedicated to the pursuit of personal spiritual pathways.[21] The more narrowly political drive came mostly from Annie Besant herself. Since the Society was a strongly hierarchical organisation, with status conferred by degrees of spiritual insight, Annie Besant's political priorities enjoyed, at least while she lived, an authority they might not otherwise have had. Nevertheless, there were splits and secessions in the movement in the late 1920s over the direction in which she had taken the Society, and under G. S. Arundale, her successor in 1933, there was a noticeable retreat from 'causes' in favour of the occultist and esoteric side of its work. By this time, in any case, the organisation had been badly shaken by Jiddu Krishnamurti's renunciation of the role of World Teacher assigned to him by Annie Besant, for which the Theosophists had been working for over a decade. Its membership slumped accordingly.[22]

In the late 1920s, the political expression of Theosophy on Indian questions in Britain was the Commonwealth of India League (CIL), the organisation that Annie Besant had set up to publicise her demand for the Commonwealth of India Bill in 1925. Its day-to-day leader was Pole, from 1929 Labour MP for South Derbyshire but also the Theosophical Society's treasurer. Its increasingly influential secretary was a student and Theosophist recruited in south India for teacher training in Britain, V. K. Krishna Menon. Menon, who rapidly gave up teaching in favour of graduate work at the London School of Economics, gathered around him younger allies from the Indian student population. He was initially very much Annie Besant's creature, and took some time to build up the confidence and support to launch a challenge to seize control of the CIL.[23] But it is clear that from early on his ambition was to disconnect the movement from Theosophical patronage and build a more independent organisation more directly under Indian control.

This, however, was neither easily nor quickly achieved. After Congress formally adopted *purna swaraj* as its goal in 1929, the CIL entered a period of schism. The previous year, when Congress had passed its resolution for *purna swaraj* within the year, Besant had been in the

[21] See *Theosophy*, Jan and May 1924 for debate over the political work of Theosophists.
[22] Dixon, *Divine Feminine*, 228.
[23] See Janaki Ram, *V. K. Krishna Menon: A Personal Memoir* (Delhi, 1997), 19–20, 32–4; Suhash Chakravarty, *V. K. Krishna Menon and the India League, 1925–47* (2v., Delhi, 1997); *Crusader Extraordinary : Krishna Menon and the India League 1932–36* (Delhi, 2005).

minority which opposed it. She had refused to allow the CIL to campaign for *purna swaraj* until the year was up.[24] This had left the CIL vulnerable to attacks from British Congress supporters, including ILP-ers, who denounced it for holding a 'pro-government, anti-Congress and anti-Gandhi stance'.[25] From further left still, the CIL was attacked by Communists such as Saklatvala as an ally of bourgeois reformists.[26] The CIL's response to the Irwin declaration had nonetheless been a Besantine one: Congress should attend without conditions, but should make a unified demand on arrival for dominion status.[27] When Congress refused to come, Besant argued that the non-Congress groups should attend the Conference to put the Congress case in its absence. Menon tried to argue that *purna swaraj* meant little more than dominion status, which itself logically entailed the right of secession, and to which the League was already committed. But even this alienated Pole and most of the CIL's financial backers among British Theosophists, who believed it placed too much emphasis on secession and too little on unity and commonwealth. They were only prepared to endorse home rule within the empire. However, a radical element within the CIL insisted that the Congress demand should be supported in full.[28] Menon was well aware that to fail to support Congress was to risk marginalisation. Other groups were springing up to endorse and explain Gandhi's position *in toto*. In August 1930, Quakers and ILP-ers committed to self-determination and support for non-violent civil disobedience, including Gandhi's associate Reginald Reynolds, formed the Friends of India.[29] Horace Alexander and Wilfred Wellock's Council for Indian Freedom brought together Quakers, pacifists and ILP-ers in support of Gandhi.[30] G. S. Dara's Indian National Congress League (INCL) was founded at around the same time, and received the support of Brockway's ILP.[31] These groups were also starting to win over the Indian student body, many of

---

[24] Chakravarty, *Menon*, i, 119; *Indian News*, 14 Nov 1929, 23 Jan 1930.

[25] Chakravarty, *Menon*, i, 201; *United India*, 11 Nov 1929.

[26] *United India*, 11 Nov 1929; Scotland Yard Reports, 23 June 1929, L/PJ/12/362; 10 Dec 1930, L/PJ/12/356; *Indian News*, 21 Oct and 4 Dec 1930; Chakravarty, *Menon*, i, 315; Housman to Reynolds, 3 Dec 1930, Housman Corr., v.1.

[27] *Indian News*, 14 Nov 1929.

[28] Chakravarty, *Menon*, i, 133, 137–9, 229–30, 327, 337–8, 345, 352–4.

[29] Reginald Reynolds, *India, Gandhi and World Peace* (London, 1931); Friends of India, *India Bulletin* (1931–3).

[30] Chakravarty, *Menon*, ii, 59–63.

[31] Scotland Yard Reports, 28 June 1929, 28 May 1930, L/PJ/12/225; Chakravarty, *Menon*, i, 361–4; *United India*, Nov 1930.

whom regarded Menon's CIL as a 'another snare'.[32] Yet to ditch the Theosophists would risk losing the bulk of funding and support hitherto accumulated. After Congress confirmed its choice of independence, Pole stepped down as chairman of the CIL and Besant put her efforts into the Liberal Federation. However, despite these departures, the CIL itself remained an unconvincing advocate of Congress policy. It was still formally committed to dominion status and its platforms therefore contained both supporters and opponents of the Congress stance.

The most promising alternative to Theosophy as a metropolitan host was the ILP, which offered the kind of access to left-wing audiences that had proved so useful during the First World War, and which had generally backed the Congress line since 1925. With a reputation for pushing at the Labour Government from within the left, a healthy membership of some 17,000, a branch structure of around 650, and a press outlet in the form of the *New Leader*, the ILP was clearly the brightest star in the constellation of cause groups interested in India. Its organiser, Fenner Brockway, had begun to see the CIL, with its hardworking secretary, as worth capturing. Menon saw the ILP as a useful ally, but feared the loss of the remaining Theosophists with their financial support and commitment to dominion status. He was wary of being used by the ILP against the Labour Government, whose intentions towards India the CIL still trusted. However, ILP branches persisted in regarding the CIL's commitment to dominion status as at best simply too ambiguous in meaning, and at worst 'a kind of capitalist scheme designed to keep the masses in subjection'. The ILP, Menon was told, would only assist the CIL insofar as it insisted that the Indian people should decide their future for themselves. Yet these clarifications were unacceptable to many of the League's remaining supporters, and Menon was understandably reluctant to make them.[33] Brockway offered him the support of the ILP to compensate for the exodus of Theosophists that would follow a clearer endorsement of *purna swaraj*.[34] In October 1930, he told Menon bluntly that there were now too many groups and that their

[32] Scotland Yard Reports, 29 Oct, 12 Nov and 5 Dec 1930, L/PJ/12/356

[33] Chakravarty, *Menon,* i, 369–74, 376–7, 379–81, 384; ii, 120; Besant to Pole, Sept–Oct 1931, Pole Papers, MSS/Eur/F264.

[34] Chakravarty, *Menon,* ii, 17–18, 64–9, 94–5, 114–15, 127–8; Scotland Yard Reports, 12 Nov and 10 Dec 1930, L/PJ/12/356.

disunity hampered effective work for India. He proposed coordination and agreement on some minimum demands.[35] However, Menon wished to resist the League's work being swallowed up entirely in that of the ILP.[36] This was not merely for reasons of organisational pride. Menon told C. F. Andrews that he feared the ILP's socialism did not make enough room for the legitimate demands of nationalism.[37] In his reply to Brockway, he therefore dismissed many of the rival organisations as mere paper bodies and refused to attend Brockway's meeting or to cooperate with his plan to establish a united council.[38] Brockway managed to bring together representatives of a number of the smaller Indian groups, but clearly concluded that they were insufficient without the CIL too. He told CIL members that he wanted to see them agitate about India without the traditional nervousness of Besant's supporters and to extricate the organisation from the 'mental mess' of Theosophy.[39] Rival groups such as that of Dara as well as the Communists attacked the CIL as a 'government gramophone' for its refusal to condemn the suppression of the civil disobedience movement.[40] With the prospect of a visit from Gandhi looming, it was clear to Menon and others that with the departure of so many existing members, and the growth of rival Gandhian groups speaking for Congress, a deal with Brockway was unavoidable. In March 1931, the CIL newspaper, *Indian News*, brought ILP members on to the editorial board, and in June, at the CIL AGM, a commitment to self-determination was made.[41] A further, but final wave of resignations from the older members followed.[42] Brockway now joined the Executive and the profile of the CIL—renamed the India League (IL)—was raised by the agreement of Bertrand Russell to become its Chairman. In November 1931, the Executive Committee decided formally to reword the League's object to support India's claim to *purna swaraj*.[43]

The same day, the Committee met Gandhi.[44] Gandhi was as suspicious of the India League as he was of all such organisations. He had been advised by Andrews, Polak and Horace Alexander to be wary of

[35] Brockway to Menon, 14 Oct 1930, Brockway to Redfern, 5 Feb 1931, KMP 7/1/a.
[36] Chakravarty, *Menon*, i, 321, 362–3, 380.   [37] Ibid. ii, 115–6.
[38] Ibid. ii, 17–18.   [39] Ibid. ii, 67, 94–5, 114.
[40] For example, *United India*, March, June-July and Oct–Nov 1931.
[41] Chakravarty, *Menon*, ii, 113–14; *Indian News*, 19 March 1931; Scotland Yard Report, 24 June 1931, L/PJ/12/356.
[42] Chakravarty, *Menon*, ii, 127–8.   [43] Ibid. ii, 159.
[44] Speech at Commonwealth of India League Meeting, 12 Nov 1931, *CWMG*, E54/94.

it, partly because its commitment to the Congress goal was so recent, but also because, they believed, it was too associated with Brockway and the political left to reach the wider opinion they believed he should be trying to convince.[45] When Brockway had attempted to get Gandhi to endorse his leftist campaigns, Gandhi had refused, saying that to do so might 'damage the cause which you and I want to espouse'.[46] When Gandhi met the IL, he insisted that it make its new orientation absolutely clear. In line with his distaste for foreign outposts, he also advised the League to remain organisationally independent of Congress and that it should, contrary to Menon's feelings, link its work with that of other British groups, including Alexander's Quaker organisations and Reynolds' Friends of India.[47] After Gandhi's departure, therefore, Alexander proposed an equivalent of the National Peace Council to link up the various groups working for Indian freedom, to be run not by Menon but by Agatha Harrison. Brockway, seeing his chance to bring together all those supporting the Congress platform, supported the proposal, but Menon was understandably opposed and offered his resignation, winning the crucial vote to keep the IL independent.[48]

Menon's alignment with the ILP was initially fairly successful in providing him with leverage within the British party system. Although the new commitment to the Congress programme made some branches and party leaders suspicious, the electoral defeat of October 1931 and the emergence of Lansbury as party leader had an independent radicalising effect on Labour's programme. This allowed Menon to challenge the monopoly Pole enjoyed on providing advice.[49] As the Conservatives tried to arrest the Round Table Conference method that Labour had put in place, Lansbury told Gillies that the Party should 'accept no responsibility for [the] present policy but stand four square for our own'.[50] Menon was able to provide Lansbury with information directly from India, and later in the year staged a great coup in organising a high profile delegation of three Labour Parliamentary candidates to

[45] Alexander to Andrews, 26 Nov 1931, Alexander Papers (NMML).

[46] Brockway to Gandhi, 24 Sept 1931, Gandhi Papers, SN 17840; Gandhi to Brockway, 29 Sept 1931, *CWMG*, E53/469.

[47] *Indian News*, 3 and 26 Nov 1931.   [48] Chakravarty, *Menon*, ii, 167–72.

[49] Ibid. ii, 159, 165, 241–2; *India Review*, 12 March and 27 Feb 1932; Scotland Yard Report, 16 March 1932, L/PJ/12/448.

[50] Lansbury to Gillies, 12 Aug 1932, William Gillies Correspondence, WG/IND/192 LPA.

India to investigate the repression of Congress.[51] The activities of the Delegates caused much concern in the India Office. Ellen Wilkinson, who seemed to the officials an unbiased and dangerously articulate critic, was a particular worry. Officials therefore went to great lengths to ensure that the Delegation got the right impressions, and to discredit their conclusions when they emerged. Nevertheless, the Delegation provided Labour with some useful ammunition against the abuses of civil rights sanctioned under the suppression of civil disobedience. Its report, *The Condition of India*, was used by Morgan Jones in moving the Adjournment on 22 December 1932, and at the Party Conference the following year, where two speakers compared British action in India with Nazi Germany.[52]

As the ILP split over whether to remain affiliated to the Labour Party, Menon was to be found among the affiliationists, and when, in July 1932, this cause was lost, he moved with them into support for the Socialist League. Although Brockway felt betrayed, this decision turned out to be wise. Over the coming three years, ILP support underwent a haemorrhage: its membership fell from 16,800 in 1932 to 4,400 in 1935, and it lost on average more than two branches a week. It was quite unable to provide the funding and speakers that Menon had expected, leaving his meetings dependent on the same groups as before.[53] In December 1932, Brockway resigned from the IL and took the ILP's shrinking assets across to support Dara's INCL, commenting that the 'association with the [India] League of so many Labour Members of Parliament who were completely silent when the Labour Government was repressing the Indian Nationalist Movement convinces me that they are not reliable friends of India'.[54] Though Brockway denied it, it was clear that this was principally the result of the disaffiliation of the ILP from the Labour Party earlier in the year. He had known of the IL's reluctance to criticise the second Labour Government at the time he had sought its cooperation.

[51] India League, *The Condition of India: Being the Report of the Delegation Sent to India by the India League in 1932* (London, 1933); official correspondence in Home (Political) 40/XII/1932, NAI, and Home-Political 35/3/34-Poll(I) NAI; Indian Political Intelligence file L/PJ/12/448 and Information Department file, L/I/1/50, OIOC.

[52] *Hansard*, 5th ser., v.273, cols.1249–58, 22 Dec 1932; Labour Party, *Report of Annual Conference*, 1933, 228–30; [Indecipherable] of India Office to MacGregor, 26 Nov 1932, L/I/1/50, OIOC.

[53] See Report of India League Conference, 26 Nov 1932, L/I/1/50, OIOC.

[54] Brockway to Horrabin, Dec 1932, printed in *United India*, Dec 1932; also *United India*, Jan 1933.

With the loss of the ILP's backing, the IL came close to closure. Menon was reduced to writing begging letters to India, almost all of which went unanswered.[55] Closeness to Sir Stafford Cripps' Socialist League initially looked like a means of recovery, since the SL's anti-fascism led it easily to an anti-imperialist position, with British actions in India interpreted as the first signs of an indigenous strain of fascism.[56] Its early success in pressing its programme on the Party, first seen at the 1932 Labour Party Conference, had given Menon hope that it would do what he had wanted the ILP to do: remain in the Labour Party and try and push it from the left towards the Congress position. But although the SL's membership and general strength never matched that of the ILP, its rebelliousness increasingly did, condemning its suggestions unheard. Worse till, the strengthening of party discipline in the Labour Party restricted the room for dissident factions within it, while efforts to get the Labour Party itself committed to the new Congress goal of a constituent assembly failed, with the bulk of the party throwing itself behind Attlee's cautious amendments to the 1935 Act and the recommendation that Congress work it. 'We have done our best to defeat this Bill', George Lansbury announced. 'I say [to my friends in India] "We hate the Bill, but take it. Use it and do the best you can with it." '[57]

A third, rival home for metropolitan anti-imperialism was offered by the British Communist Party.[58] In theory, British Communists had

---

[55] IL Executive Committee meeting, 2 March 1933, cited in Chakravarty, *Crusader*, 167–71, 202–6. 260–1; Janaki Ram, *Menon*, 40.

[56] David Blazaar, *The Popular Front and the Progressive Tradition: Socialists, Liberals, and the Quest for Unity, 1884–1939* (Cambridge, 1992), 156; Michael Bor, *The Socialist League in the 1930s* (2005), 281–90.

[57] *Hansard*, 5 June 1935, 5th ser., v.302, col.2003; *Servant of India*, 10 Jan 1935; George Lansbury, *Labour's Way with the Commonwealth* (London, 1935), 47–8; Hugh Dalton, *Practical Socialism for Britain* (London, 1935), 366.

[58] Stuart MacIntyre, *Imperialism and the British Labour Movement in the 1920s: An Examination of Marxist Theory* (London, 1975), 17; Howe, *Anticolonialism*, 53–66; John Callaghan, 'The Communists and the Colonies: Anti-imperialism between the Wars', in Geoff Andrews et al., (eds.), *Opening the Books: Essays on the Social and Cultural History of the British Communist Party* (London, 1995); Marika Sherwood, 'The Comintern, the CPGB, the Colonies and Black Britons', *Science and Society*, 60/2 (1996), 137–63; and reply by John Callaghan, *Science and Society*, 61/4 (1998), 513–25; Matthew Worley (ed.), *In Search of Revolution: International Communist Parties in the Third Period* (London, 2004); Sobhanlal Datta Gupta, *Comintern and the Destiny of Communism in India, 1919–1943* (Calcutta, 2006).

certain strengths as allies of Indian anti-imperialism. Believing that imperialism formed the basis of capitalism in its current stage, they were usually unpersuaded by notions of empire socialism. They were also generally better internationalists, or at least resisted claims about British civilisation designed to justify liberal imperialism.[59] Communists saw the British state as not accidentally committed to imperialism but as constitutively and deeply entangled in it. With some exceptions, they were also generally optimists about the possibility, or even inevitability, of its being transformed. Moreover, they brought metropolitan anti-imperialism a level of commitment, intellectual consideration and organisation that it had usually lacked, even if this fell considerably short of the task and their own ambition. These were a product of Communists' distinct sense of vocation, seriousness of purpose, and loyalty to leaders. The CPGB was in design not a loose, horizontal affiliation of mutually affable individuals, like other anti-imperialist groups, but a vertically-integrated and hierarchical structure. This deterred, if not altogether removing, the individual defaulting which generally characterised other metropolitan anti-imperialist campaigns.

The other principal distinction of Communist anti-imperialism was its political subordination to an international organisation: the Comintern. This was meant to neutralise national sentiment about empires, and also provide a common framework of analysis and action within which specific struggles could be situated, with supporting propaganda, training and funds. Comintern's prodding of the CPGB on colonial questions, as well as its funding, were very apparent: without them it seems certain that less would have been done. However, Comintern activities were directed above all to the protection of the Soviet state. The heavy financial dependence of the CPGB on Comintern funding limited further such autonomy as these arrangements permitted. Control was not total: the somewhat erratic nature of Comintern advice on Indian questions permitted a certain looseness of application. Had the CPGB obeyed Comintern instructions to bring M. N. Roy to Britain to stand in the 1924 General Election, for example, he would have been arrested and deported to India, where he had been convicted in his absence earlier in the year. Questions of immediate tactics usually

---

[59] See Eric Hobsbawm, *Interesting Times: A Twentieth-Century Life* (London, 2002), 364–6; Raphael Samuel, *The Lost World of British Communism* (London, 2006).

remained the responsibility of the national sections, one CPGB member cheerfully observing that the Party did not defer to the Soviet Union on colonial or Indian matters, because 'we knew far more than they did'.[60] Certainly, too, there were recognised CPGB authorities on Indian questions, such as C. P. and R. P. Dutt, Saklatvala and Robin Page Arnot, who provided, as well as received, advice. But it is clear that even tactical questions were reviewed by Comintern, and wider strategy was a matter of direct instruction. The international structure of Communist anti-imperialism also multiplied the difficulties of co-ordination in anti-imperial work. There were four principal parties to synchronize: the Comintern, the Indian Communists in exile under M. N. Roy and others in continental Europe, a growing Party in India itself, and the CPGB. Much of Comintern's time was spent demanding reports, dispatching and seconding inspectors, and inventing bureaus and committees in the hope of achieving coordination between them.

As a substitute for the leadership and influence that Gandhi had removed from the metropole, the Communists supplied the status of vanguard in the global struggle against capitalism. However, this risked the re-appropriation of leadership from the Indian movement. From about 1925 to about 1934, for example, the progress of Indian Communism was formally the responsibility of the British Communists, with their greater experience of organising proletarian action. On the face of it, this seems an extraordinary arrangement, replicating the colonial model in its privileging of British expertise, and it did lead to resentment among Indians. In theory, the Communists' notion of vanguard leadership, by which the Party acted not directly *for* the working class, but so as to raise its consciousness and action to the level demanded by its world-historical role, provided a model of leadership without detachment which, suitably adapted, could also be used to govern the relationship between the CPGB and the colonised Indians. In practice, leadership on such terms often entailed the subordinating of the needs of the Indian movement to international demands. But, unlike most other metropolitan anti-imperialists, vanguard leaders led from *within*, in solidarity with those they led, sharing the risk of persecution, arrest and imprisonment. Hitherto, British allies of Congress had dealt with it from *above*, activated by a sense of social conscience. They prescribed courses of action from a position of riskless dominance of the Indian movement. They related to the Indians as victims of an

---

[60] Malcolm MacEwen, *The Greening of a Red* (London, 1991), 114.

imperialism which they, as radicals, disavowed, but which they also, as Britons, sought to engage in the role of constructive, internal critics. Their Britishness thereby remained undissolved. Communists were not wholly immune to such thinking, and some of their propaganda in the 1920s has a distinctly paternalist character. But at least the 'help the poor Indian' attitude, as Arnot described it, was recognised as a weakness: '[a] reflection of imperialist ideology within the ranks of the working class'.[61]

This orientation was most visible in the Communists' commitment to direct engagement with the subcontinent. A succession of CPGB emissaries arrived initially undetected in India, and helped to build up Workers' and Peasants' Parties (WPPs) and trade unions independently of Congress. Accusations of 'bossing' were made frequently by Roy and other émigrés, who were cut out of such arrangements, but rather less by the Communist trade unionists in India among whom the emissaries worked. The CPGB emissaries generally worked in solidarity with their Indian counterparts, running the same risks. However, the WPPs were never fully under Communist control, and the Comintern's growing distaste after 1928 for cooperation with bourgeois nationalists forced their liquidation. In March 1929, the arrest and subsequent trial of the emissaries at Meerut alongside their fellow-communists and trade unionists did much in India to reinforce admiration for the solidaristic aspects of Communist anti-imperialism.

The CPGB's metropolitan agitations, however, were less successful. The Party insisted on primary, even exclusive loyalties, although it was not alone in this: the social democratic parties by the end of the 1920s were also refusing to tolerate multiple allegiances. The Communists were, at times, energetic constructors of common fronts with non-Communist anti-imperialists, but in all such organisations, Communist leadership had to be maintained. The Communists were suspicious of non-party elements, and were rightly suspected of entering front organisations in order to disrupt them or build them to a point at which their supporters could be harvested for a purely Communist organisation. Fissiparous tendencies of this kind were fatal to numerous small Indian organisations in Britain. At the international level, they had carried off the League Against Imperialism (LAI), an international Communist front set up in 1927 to unite anti-colonial nationalists and

---

[61] CPGB Central Committee, 1 June 1930.

Communists.[62] Jawaharlal Nehru had succeeded in getting Congress to associate itself with the LAI, though he refused to seek affiliation, which would have committed Congress to endorsing the LAI's position.[63] However, under the sectarian pressures of the Third Period, there was a sharp lurch towards exposure and confrontation. At the July 1929 LAI Congress at Frankfurt-am-Main, Congress was denounced as a bourgeois-dominated ally of imperialism.[64] When Nehru wrote to the LAI to point out that it was not permitted to instruct the Congress, the Berlin secretariat responded by expelling him.[65]

On specifically Indian matters, the same pattern was repeated in the Indian National Congress (London Branch). This had been established in June 1928 by the ILP with the blessing of Congress left-wingers Iyengar and Nehru. Brockway provided initial advice, but after a long battle the work of the London Branch came to be dominated by the CPGB. The Branch was warned by a visiting nationalist that it could not expect recognition, let alone any financial support, from the parent body in India unless it acquired a large membership and substantial funds, and that it would be expected to do as it was told by Congress.[66] But the CPGB wished to instruct the parent body: Saklatvala, indeed, hoped that the London Branch would become 'the tail that wags the whole dog'.[67] Under his influence, the Branch passed resolutions endorsing the demands of the Congress left-wingers for *purna swaraj* and socialism.[68] This pleased Nehru, who persuaded Congress to affiliate the London Branch, although it was barred from making any official statements.[69]

---

[62] Mustafa Haikal, 'Willi Munzenberg und die "Liga gegen Imperialismus und fur nationale Unabhangigkeit"', in Tania Schlie et al., (eds.), *Willi Munzenberg (1889–1940): Ein Deutscher Kommunist in Spannungsfeld Zwischen Stalinismus und Antifachismus* (Frankfurt-am-Main, 1995). On the British work of the League Against Imperialism, see John Saville, 'Reginald O. Bridgeman' and The League Against Imperialism', in Joyce M. Bellamy and John Saville (eds.), *Dictionary of Labour Biography*, vii (London, 1984), 26–40, 40–50; Howe, *Anticolonialism*, 71–7; Jean Jones, *The League Against Imperialism* (London, 1996).

[63] Nehru, 'Report on the Brussels Congress', 19 Feb 1927, *SWJN*, ii, 278–97; Nehru to Iyengar, 7 March 1927, *SWJN*, ii, 298–303; 'Note for the Working Committee', 4 April 1927, *SWJN*, ii, 316–18.

[64] Manifesto of the Second World Congress of LAI, 1929, LAI Archive, IISH, File 78.

[65] Munzenberg to Comintern, 12 Aug 1929, CI, RGASPI 542/1/30; Nehru to Secretariat of LAI, 30 Jan 1930, CI, RGASPI 542/1/44.

[66] Scotland Yard Report, 28 July 1928, L/PJ/12/361, OIOC.

[67] Ibid. 9 Dec 1931, L/PJ/12/441, OIOC,

[68] Ibid. 1 Sept and 3 Oct 1928, L/PJ/12/361, OIOC.

[69] Ibid. Nov 1928, L/PJ/12/361; 28 March 1929, L/PJ/12/362, OIOC; Minutes of All India Congress Committee meeting, 3–4 Nov 1928, and Minutes of Working

However, from the middle of 1928, the Third Period ruling on keeping a distance from bourgeois nationalists split the London Branch between those who endorsed Gandhi's methods and the CPGB fraction which wished the Congress campaign to be transformed into an unfettered social revolution. The CPGB members published attacks on Gandhi for tactical errors, culminating in a denunciation of Congress' response to the Irwin declaration. When the Branch revolted against this, the CPGB leader Harry Pollitt himself went to meet it, but reported to the Politburo that the Branch had demanded that the CPGB cease to attack the Congress leaders, which he regarded as an impossible condition to meet.[70] Gandhi's pact with Irwin and its endorsement at Karachi in March 1931 encouraged the Communists to make renewed attacks, driving much of the moderate element out in disgust.[71] Learning that Gandhi was to visit London, the Branch debated whether he should be met with a black flag demonstration or merely not welcomed at all. It was clear that without the support of the non-Communists they would be at a disadvantage during Gandhi's visit. The Communists therefore concocted a plan to resign temporarily from the Branch so as to put it in a position to welcome him, and to return to it in force when, as expected, his strategy failed to win independence. However, this rather elaborate scheme threatened to leave the non-Communists in a position to capitalise on Gandhi's visit, so the Communists soon decided that it would be preferable to break up the London Branch altogether.[72] The breach came at the second Indian Political Conference in June 1931. Saklatvala launched a vituperative attack on the Congress-supporting Indians as 'London Indian sycophants who were too ready to attend . . . feasts in honour of State Secretaries, and ex-Viceroys' and 'young Indians who profess to love Communism but hate or fear to join the Communist Party'.[73] When the visiting Congress veteran Vithalbhai Patel told the Branch that it must support Congress unequivocally, the meeting collapsed into fighting, driving him from the hall. Nehru

Committee meeting, 3–4 Feb and 16–19 Nov 1929; Congress Secretaries' report to the Congress, 23 Dec 1929, in Zaidi, *Encyclopaedia*, ix, 498, 524, 529–30, 638, 680–1, 685.

[70] CPGB Politburo, 23 Oct 1930; Central Committee, 22 Nov 1930; see also Scotland Yard Report, 2 April 1930, L/PJ/12/382, OIOC.

[71] ALEXANDER to Pollitt, 22 April 1931 (CA 246), HW17/69, NA.

[72] Scotland Yard Reports, 18 Aug 1930, Oct 1930 and Jan 1931, L/PJ/12/363; Jan to June 1931, L/PJ/12/364, OIOC.

[73] *Daily Worker*, 26 June 1931.

wrote to the London Branch to insist on its remaining loyal to the Congress, but any reply that was sent to him was lost in the upheaval of the civil disobedience campaign.[74] The remaining non-Communists left to join Dara's INCL, which promised to back the Congress civil disobedience campaign unquestioningly. These departures reduced the active membership of the London Branch to fewer than twenty members, with Saklatvala in control. The remaining moderates moved to expel the Communists in time for Gandhi's visit, but it was too late. On Nehru's recommendation, the London Branch was disaffiliated in August 1931.[75]

The CPGB proved much better at destroying existing organisations than at building up its own independent campaigns. This was despite the unexpected gift, for campaigning purposes, of the trial of the CPGB emissaries and the WPP and Indian Communist leadership at Meerut.[76] The CPGB did little to win the wider opinion that the trial had aroused, and a good deal to alienate it. It initially set up a Meerut Defence Committee on the 'united front from above' lines; that is, including ILP leaders, left-wing Labour MPs and non-Communist trade unionists. However, after criticism from Comintern, this was disbanded and replaced with a sectarian campaign from below based in the factories.[77] This was a disaster, as is very clear from the CPGB's own records. The new Meerut Committees were merely 'the Party meeting itself under another name', the Party's leaders were told.[78] There was almost no spontaneous enthusiasm or interest in colonial matters. When the CPGB asked what the local parties wanted included in its Charter (1930) not a single mention was made of the empire or India.[79] When it wrote to the districts offering to pay for leaflets on Meerut, it only received a single

---

[74] Nehru's Note for the Working Committee on Foreign Branches of the Congress, 8 Aug 1931, *SWJN*, v, 250–3.

[75] Congress Working Committee meetings, 4–7, 9 and 11–14 Aug 1931, in Zaidi, *Encyclopaedia*, x, 196–204; Scotland Yard Reports, June–Aug 1931, L/PJ/12/364, OIOC.

[76] John Saville, 'The Meerut Trial, 1929–33', in Joyce M.Bellamy and John Saville (eds.), *Dictionary of Labour Biography*, vii (1984).

[77] Central Committee, 12 Jan 1930; CPGB Secretariat to DPCs, LPCs and comrades in charge of colonial work, 20 Jan 1930; and Scotland Yard Report, 22 Jan 1930, L/PJ/12/382, OIOC.

[78] Central Committee, 1 June 1930; 'Plan for Reorganising and Enlivening the British Section of the League Against Imperialism', 11 Aug 1930, with Politburo 1930 papers; Politburo, 1 Oct 1931.

[79] Politburo, 4 Sept 1930.

reply.[80] The districts merely waited for instructions from the centre, and when they got them, demanded literature, speakers and organisers, rather than developing any local capacity. They did not even have much knowledge of the Asian communities in their own districts.[81] The British Section of the LAI was also an elite organisation *par excellence*: it had no factory-level presence at all, only one trade union affiliate (the Furnishing Trades Association), no functioning Indian section, and very little support outside London.[82] The districts were sternly told of the need to 'root out the opportunist attitude to colonial work as something extra'. They 'must re-act energetically and on their own initiative to all important news from India'.[83] But despite these orders, the Meerut campaign was a top-down affair, only catching fire when sparked from the centre or where it could win the support of the non-Communists. The Party itself, the Politburo was told at the end of 1931, had done 'practically nothing' over Meerut: it was 'dead in relation to the trial', relying wholly on the efforts of the remaining non-Communists in the LAI.[84] When repression of Congress began again at the start of 1932, 'not. . . a single resolution. . . from any group of workers' was received.[85] Around £1,000 had been collected under the auspices of the Meerut Defence Committee, most of it in its early non-sectarian phase. A second *Daily Worker* appeal in early 1932, on more sectarian lines, received not a single factory contribution, and raised just £3.[86] By the time the CPGB lifted its sectarian approach, there was little trust left. In late 1932, with the Meerut prisoners due to be sentenced, it set up a Prisoners Release Committee on a broader basis. But of 130 letters sent out to potential non-Communist supporters, only a few even received a reply, and these were conditional or non-committal. At its initial meeting, only four people turned up.[87]

---

[80] Central Committee, 12 Jan 1930; see also CPGB circular to local parties, 12 April 1929, copy in L/PJ/12/381, OIOC.

[81] Politburo, 21 Aug 1930.

[82] Politburo, 17–18 July 1930; 'Plan for Reorganising and Enlivening the British Section'; Politburo, 21 Aug 1930, 13 Feb 1931.

[83] Scotland Yard Reports, 11 June and 23 July 1930, L/PJ/12/382, OIOC; ECCI to CPGB, 26 May 1931 (CBP3), 30 June 1931 (CBP6), 20 July 1931 (CBP9), HW17/77, NA.

[84] Politburo, 1 Oct 1931.   [85] Politburo, 9 Jan 1932.

[86] Politburo, 1 Oct 1931, 4 Feb 1933; Report of 3rd LAI Annual Conference, 1933, copy in L/PJ/12/273, OIOC; Estimates of Meerut Fund, 17 Sept 1932, L/PJ/12/345, OIOC; Scotland Yard Report, 22 Nov 1933, L/PJ/12/273, OIOC.

[87] Politburo, 4 Feb and 9 March 1933.

There are dangers in taking this dismal record at face value: some of what was said in Politburo meetings reflected the Communist practice of self-criticism and the admission of errors, even when these might be thought trivial or excusable. Factional rivalries sometimes expressed themselves as critiques of theory and practice even where the theories and practices concerned were held with small variation by the critics. The intense scrutiny of performance undertaken by the Comintern was sometimes unfair and often a reflection of larger battles. Nevertheless, the party's commitment was qualified by a deep pessimism about making India, rather than unemployment, wages and conditions, a means of persuading workers to abandon their existing loyalties to reformist unions and parties. Efforts to create a satisfactory relationship with Indians in Britain were also slow work. In the dock towns, the job insecurity and discrimination suffered by the Indian workforce made them potential recruits for Communist anti-imperial work, but most were reluctant to embrace anti-imperial politics which risked their livelihoods or status.[88] In the universities, the political cautiousness of students, and their commitment to Gandhism or moderate nationalism also held back many, to the disgust of the CPGB leadership.[89] An Indian Bureau of expatriate Indians, mostly students, was grudgingly established, though the CPGB never liked it because it was secretly influenced by Roy and because it sent its criticisms of the CPGB direct to Moscow, in the hope of independent recognition.[90]

---

[88] On the Indian seamen in Britain, see especially Laura Tabili, '*We Ask for British Justice': Workers and Racial Difference in Late Imperial Britain* (Ithaca, NY, 1994) and Gopalan Balachandran, 'Circulation Through Seafaring: Indian Seamen, 1890–1945', in Claude Markovits et al. (eds.) *Society and Circulation: Mobile People and Itinerant Cultures in South Asia, 1750–1950* (New Delhi, 2003).

[89] CPGB Young Communist League Report and Resolution on Colonial Work, July 1925, *Communist Papers: Documents selected from those obtained on the arrest of the communist leaders on the 14th and 21st October, 1925* (1926), Cmd 2682, doc.43; Tom Bell, Report to Colonial Commission, 26 March 1925, CI, RGAPSI 495/100/260; Scotland Yard Report, 28 May 1930, L/PJ/12/382, OIOC; Summary of draft of resolution prepared . . . for the Central Committee of the British Young Communist League, undated but probably 1931, and Scotland Yard Report, 4 May 1932, L/PJ/12/272, OIOC; Scotland Yard Report, 25–6 Jan 1936, LPJ/12/275, OIOC; *Daily Worker*, 27 Jan 1936.

[90] 'Colonial Conference held at Amsterdam, July 11th and 12th, 1925', *Communist Papers*, doc 42; 'Suggestions of Indian comrades in London', [?1925], Dutt and others to CPI European Bureau, 6 July 1925, and reply, 15 Sept 1925, in Purabi Roy et al. (eds.), *Indo-Russian Relations, 1917–1947: Select Documents from the Archives of the Russian Federation* (2v., Calcutta, 2000), i, 202–5; Submission to Comintern by Communist

In his long opposition to foreign propaganda as conventionally understood, Gandhi made several arguments concerning its cost and
inefficiency.[91] But his most powerfully-felt argument concerned its
weakness as strategy. He believed that set against the official line,
Congress claims would always be discounted, as long as audiences
believed that Indian voices were not to be trusted. The propaganda
techniques that sympathisers like Brockway wanted would be, Gandhi
argued in a telling image, 'like a bullock-cart competing with a train'.[92]
In a separate article, I have traced the reporting of the civil disobedience
movement in Britain to test this belief, which indeed had a lot to it.[93]
Here, however, it is sufficient to note that Gandhi's conception of propaganda and of foreign agitation followed directly from his notions of
truth, self-reliance, non-violence and from the need to counter the sense
of inferiority created in India by western domination. 'I do not discount
the value of propaganda . . .', he argued. 'But my propaganda is unlike
the ordinary. It is that of truth which is self-propagating.'[94] Too much
attention to world opinion was a symptom of Indian under-confidence,
and detracted from the main task: the building of internal strength to
take independence. In 1929, therefore, as he contemplated a return to
civil disobedience, Gandhi had resisted efforts to publicise his movement
in ways he saw as inappropriate.[95] Indeed, although Gandhi is often
credited with mastery of the means of mass communication beyond India's borders, he was ambivalent about many of them. When Tilak had
proposed using the new medium of the cinematograph to instruct the
British people on the iniquities of General Dyer, for example, Gandhi
had dismissed the suggestion as ludicrous.[96] He himself regularly refused requests to go on foreign visits, despite frequent invitations.[97] He
also refused to cooperate with the demands of the film companies for

Group of Indians in Great Britain, 4 Sept 1934, CI, RGASPI 495/68/487; Saklatvala, *A Few Thoughts on Party Work*, 1934, CI, RGASPI 495/100/938; *Daily Worker*, 20 July 1934; Statement of the Indian Members of the CPGB, undated, but prob. Sept 1936, CI, RGASPI 495/16/34.

[91] 'Interview to the Daily Herald', 16 Mar 1921, *CWMG*, E22/228; 'Interview to the Bombay Chronicle', 24 Dec 1921, *CWMG*, E25/160.

[92] Gandhi to Premabehn Kantak, 28 Sept 1935, *CWMG*, E68/26.

[93] Nicholas Owen, 'Reporting the Indian Civil Disobedience Movement in Britain, 1930–32', unpublished paper (2006).

[94] 'Interview to Fox Movietone News', 30 April 1931, *CWMG*, E52/18.

[95] Gandhi to Rolland, 2 May 1929, *CWMG*, E45/415.

[96] Gandhi, 'Lokmanya', *Young India*, 4 Aug 1920, *CWMG*, E21/78.

[97] 'To American Friends', *Young India*, 17 Sept 1925, *CWMG*, E32/261.

interviews and his answers to press questions were often gnomic, almost unhelpful. It is often forgotten that he sent the press away from his Salt March.[98]

Gandhi left the recruitment of foreign supporters to the working of conscience, stimulated and shamed by the sight of the suffering *satyagrahi*. '[Y]ou must feel call[ed] to study the question because you represent the wrong doers and we the wronged', he told sympathisers in 1931.[99] This was why he generally opposed the dispatch of Indians to foreign countries for agitational work. At various times, he allowed solo associates and disciples to return, or report to, the west: Reynolds was Gandhi's messenger to the Viceroy in 1931, C. F. Andrews visited Britain regularly, especially after 1928, as did Madeleine Slade (Mira Ben) in 1934, while another priest, Verrier Elwin, was asked to report the atrocities of the North-West Frontier Province in 1931–2. But there were important qualifications for this kind of work. None of these disciples had been in any meaningful sense recruited by Gandhi: they had come to him voluntarily, and each had undergone a kind of rite of passage through work among the rural poor and in prison (Mira Ben),[100] ashram work (Reynolds),[101] work among tribals (Elwin),[102] or the abandonment of his missionary career (Andrews)[103] which served to reorient them to the task of service to ordinary Indians and away from any sense of doing good for them.[104] Moreover, Gandhi did not make them his emissaries: he frequently expressed reservations about their going and made no transfer of authority to them. They did not speak for him, let alone negotiate, while abroad or in print.[105]

Gandhi neither created an organisation for his supporters in Britain, nor endorsed those that grew up independently, despite the fact that many of them wished he would. This was not, of course, because

[98] Thomas Weber, *Gandhi as Disciple and Mentor* (Cambridge, 2004), 141, 157, 274.

[99] 'Rough Notes of a Talk with Gandhi', Dec 1931, Indian Conciliation Group Archive, TEMP MSS 41/1.

[100] Madeleine Slade, *The Spirit's Pilgrimage* (London, 1960), 66–90, 100–3, 155–77.

[101] Gandhi to Chintamani, 4 Feb 1930, *CWMG*, E48/300; 'We are all One', 16 March 1930, *CWMG*, E48/462.

[102] Ramachandra Guha, *Savaging the Civilized: Verrier Elwin, His Tribals and India* (Chicago, 1999).

[103] Hugh Tinker, *The Ordeal of Love: C. F. Andrews and India* (Delhi, 1979), 73–97.

[104] This was evidently also a necessary qualification in the case of the ICG secretary Agatha Harrison. See Gandhi to Patel, 29 March and 18 April 1934, *CWMG*, E63/359 and E63/452.

[105] See Gandhi to Andrews, 15 June 1933, *CWMG*, E61/211; Gandhi to Harrison, 4 April and 1 May 1935, *CWMG*, E66/568 and E67/39.

he shared Savarkar's sense of hostility to the British. On the contrary, Gandhi repeatedly stated his admiration for aspects of British society and culture, incorporated many British writers' ideas into his own thinking, and maintained an extensive and generally amicable correspondence with friends in Britain. He demanded, however that organisation should grow out of British reflection on the wrongs of imperialism rather than by direct instruction or funding from India. Gandhian organisations were not discouraged, but had to find their own lines of work, and, of course, their own funds.[106] The British Gandhians regularly asked for advice and leadership which Gandhi deliberately refused to provide. They were told that Gandhi wanted them neither to try to explain his actions, nor—most particularly—to offer excuses for them.[107] Instead, British supporters were given Gandhi's own thoughts, which often seemed contradictory and obscure, and were told to try and find their own 'inner voice' to guide them to their own conclusions. To Mira Ben, who wrote from Britain in 1934 suggesting a more intensive Gandhian campaign there, Gandhi recommended his own practice, phrased in the misremembered words of Shakespeare's Polonius, 'Give thy ear to everyone, thy voice to none.'[108]

The closest institutional expression of this approach to metropolitan agitation was the India Conciliation Group, set up after Gandhi's departure from Britain in 1931.[109] The ICG was dominated by Quakers, pacifists and others committed to non-violence and Gandhism. It did not contemplate offering *satyagraha* itself, but tried instead to persuade policymakers of the justice of Indian demands, through private lobbying of the India Office, Parliament and Fleet Street. Its intentions were not propagandist, since this would harm its capacity to broker, but simply the establishment of trust and the opportunity for conciliation between British and Indians. Its membership was small, metropolitan and chosen for its influence, and its budget was tiny.[110] It was well connected, with

---

[106] Weber, *Gandhi as Disciple and Mentor,* 175–6.

[107] Gandhi to Harrison, 20 Sept 1932, 29 Sept and 16 Nov 1933, *CWMG,* E57/133, E61/533 and E62/193; Harrison to Sastri, 4 June 1932, quoted in Tinker, *Ordeal of Love,* 256.

[108] Gandhi to Mirabehn, 21 Aug 1934 and 12 Oct 1934, *CWMG,* E64/371 and E65/218. The line is, 'Give every man thy ear, but few thy voice' (*Hamlet,* Act I, Sc. 3).

[109] See Hugh Tinker, 'The India Conciliation Group, 1931–1950: Dilemmas of the Mediator', *Journal of Commonwealth and Comparative Politics,* 14 (1976), 224–41.

[110] Membership is in Tinker, 'India Conciliation Group'. Accounts for 1937–8 in Alexander Papers (Friends House) TEMP MSS 577/103 record annual spending of £155.

links which initially ran to Cabinet ministers, bishops and other church leaders, senior judges and academics; and it had a membership which included leaders of women's organisations, and church and voluntary bodies, especially those connected with peace.[111]

These connections were in principle powerful ones. British pacifists had been drawn to Indian nationalism ever since its Gandhian turn in the early 1920s.[112] They had found in *satyagraha* an attractive answer to perhaps the principal dilemma of their own movement: the apparent powerlessness of non-violence to effect change in the real world. Gandhi seemed to have developed a technique for pacifists which was more robust in directly engaging with violence, than merely bearing witness to it, or giving lectures about it.[113] His commitment to individual struggle and example and to the promptings of the 'inner light' had led many Quakers, among them Reginald Reynolds and Horace Alexander, to admit themselves, as Reynolds put it, 'completely out-quakered by a Hindu'.[114] British pacifism had, even more than Theosophy, a legitimacy in British public life that made its advocates respected figures, whose support was worth cultivation.[115] Similarly, some Christian groups were also responsive to Gandhi's moral stance against imperial domination. Gerald Studdert Kennedy has shown the importance of British Christianity as the base of a 'structure of assumptions about. . . western rationalism that gave Empire its coherence as a historical fact and a continuing obligation', or even as a justification of the imperial mission.[116] But it seems equally clear that, for nonconformists especially, Gandhi seemed to embody moral dissent and struggle, and a view of politics that placed ethics before utilitarian considerations.

At the same time, each group had reservations. Anglican theologians were divided over the meaning of Gandhi and Congress. For some, such as C. F. Andrews, they represented a manifestation of God's unfolding purpose in India, and, as such, the best means of arresting

---

[111] Tinker, 'Indian Conciliation Group', 240–1.

[112] See for example, Wilfred Wellock, *India's Awakening* (London, 1922), 66.

[113] Martin Ceadel, *Pacifism in Britain, 1914–1945: The Defining of a Faith* (Oxford, 1980), 28–9.

[114] Reynolds, *To Live in Mankind*, 47.

[115] Martin Ceadel, 'A Legitimate Peace Movement: The Case of Britain, 1918–1945', in Peter Brock et al. (eds.) *Challenge to Mars: Essays on Pacifism from 1918 to 1945* (London, 1999).

[116] Gerald Studdert-Kennedy *British Christians, Indian Nationalists and the Raj* (Delhi, 1991).

the moral atrophy of Empire.[117] For others, they constituted a threat to the fulfilment of the Christian purposes that had been entrusted to the British *raj*. Gandhian challenges to civil authority threatened the moral and social order within which Christian cooperation between Britain and India might be realised.[118] Those who thought in this way made their support for Congress heavily conditional on its openness to negotiation and its non-violence. Similarly, not all pacifists were Gandhians. For some, Gandhi's techniques, not in shaming wrongdoers but in incapacitating them through boycott or ostracism, were a veiled form of coercion, and inattentive to the need for reconciliation. For example, not all pacifists thought Gandhi's decision to fast in order to reverse the decision to award separate constituencies to the Untouchables in 1932 justifiable.[119] Gandhi denied his actions were coercive, but he did accept that they designedly hurt his opponents and were intended to leave them no choice.[120] The Quakers, by contrast, aimed through organisations like the ICG at compromise between imperialists and nationalists. 'They called themselves a Conciliation Committee [sic]', the pacifist Clifford Allen reminded the Group in 1932, 'but the name was not applicable unless they attempted to conciliate both sides . . . Indian friends should be urged to give up their systematic undermining of authority.'[121] Yet the ICG was uncomfortably aware that its location on the British side of the divide was a weak place from which to make such prescriptions. Gandhi, though open to honourable compromises, disliked the presupposition of a moral equivalence between different forms of suffering regardless of where justice lay, believing that it gave a spurious value to negotiation for its own sake. 'Argument has never convinced any man', Gandhi told the pacifists, 'but on the contrary, conviction precedes argument.'[122]

Gandhi was also, for reasons with which we are familiar, not interested in linking up organisationally with the peace movement in Britain, believing that it had its own work to do, and must not seek to be directed

---

[117] Tinker, *Ordeal of Love*.   [118] Studdert-Kennedy, *British Christians*, 143–82.
[119] Gandhi to Alexander, 20 Sept 1932, *CWMG*, E57/132 and 23 Dec 1932, E58/379; and Alexander to Gandhi, 3 May 1933, Gandhi Papers, SN 21120; Gandhi to Reynolds, 13 Oct 1932, *CWMG*, E57/393.
[120] 'Interview to Journalists', 1 Dec 1931, *CWMG*, E54/132.
[121] Allen to Heath, 27 Jan and 4 May 1933, ICG TEMP MSS 47/6; see also Alexander to Wilson, 22 May 1934, Alexander Papers 577/82a; Note on meeting of the Indian Conciliation Group, 5 April 1932, L/I/1/252.
[122] 'Interview to Journalists', 1 Dec 1931, *CWMG*, E54/132; Gandhi to Heath, 10 Dec 1934, *CWMG*, E65/542.

or funded from India.[123] When he met pacifists in London in 1931, he had criticised some of them for their quietism and their vacillations in support of the Indian cause: 'There are people who sometimes hug me and sometimes revile me . . . I want them to assimilate the truth about the movement in India so they are not easily changed . . . This study must also be followed by corporate action based on the truth they have assimilated.'[124] Thereafter, while Gandhi continued contact with the ICG and admired much of what it did, he told its members that he was neither eager to know the details of its work, nor for it to speak for or explain his actions. [125] Nor did he permit the ICG to be funded by Congress, though here as in other places, the millowner Gandhian G. D. Birla stepped in to pay for things that Gandhi disapproved of but were nonetheless valuable.[126] Gandhi was also sometimes irritated by the ground that the ICG was prepared to give in conciliation.[127] For its part, the Group accepted that it could not speak for India, but it insisted that Gandhi understand that 'whatever our deep sense of the claims of justice to India may be, we cannot look at things just as India would. We naturally are concerned for England in a special way. . .'[128] Gandhi wrote in reply that he could not understand this request, even with Andrews' help. It reinforced his sense that the struggles were, at least organisationally, separate ones in which the Group should 'do your level best according to your lights'.[129] Lacking any real authority to represent Gandhi or Indian opinion, the ICG generally failed to make much impact on the policymakers.[130] Its secretary was, in the view of the India Office, a 'sentimental, well-intentioned and harmless person'.[131]

Quaker and pacifist cautiousness also irritated Reginald Reynolds and his Friends of India group. Reynolds, who had returned from India in 1930 determined to campaign for Gandhi, had found the

---

[123] Gandhi to Alexander, 16 July 1936, *CWMG*, E69/277; Minutes of Fellowship of Reconciliation Executive Committee, 18 Nov 1931, cited in Ceadel, *Pacifism*, 88–90; *The Friend*, 18 Dec 1931.

[124] 'Interview to Journalists', 1 Dec 1931, *CWMG*, E54/132.

[125] Gandhi to Harrison, 8 March 1932, *CWMG*, E55/106; 20 Sept 1932, E57/133; 29 Sept 1933, E61/533.

[126] Gandhi to Trikumji, 8 March 1934, *CWMG*, E63/280; interview with Horace Alexander, Oral History Project Transcript, NMML.

[127] Gandhi to Harrison, 24 May 1935, *CWMG*, E67/153.

[128] Heath to Gandhi, 19 Nov 1934, ICG TEMP MSS 44/4.

[129] Gandhi to Heath, 10 Dec 1934, *CWMG*, E65/542.

[130] Tinker, 'India Conciliation Group', 238.

[131] Joyce to Stephens, 16 Feb 1934 and MacGregor to Stephens, 4 May 1934, L/I/1/1394, OIOC.

Quakers much less committed to Gandhi than were the ILP. 'While the Quaker support, which I had tried to invoke, was not available', he wrote, 'the ILP support (with regard to which I was at first very doubtful) was forced on me.'[132] He managed nonetheless, as secretary of the No More War Movement from 1932 to direct its efforts towards support and publicity for Gandhi, though principally by not telling the NMWM what he was doing, and not without the kind of controversy he enjoyed.[133] There was friction between the Friends and the pacifists, not least over the desire of the latter to insist that the Indians always stand prepared to negotiate. '[T]he proposed bridge [of conciliation] could not be built save on the basis of absolute equality', Reynolds told the ICG firmly.[134] Atma Kamlani, the Friends' secretary, told the ICG's Horace Alexander that too many Quakers had 'got into the comfortable groove of conciliation':

As regards your impression that the *[India] Bulletin* [the Friends' newspaper] shows no faith in the [British] statesmen and generally attacks them . . . you are right . . . We must be stern with the wrong doer. . . . We cannot always conciliate because it takes a long time and sometimes many lives . . . for the divine spark [in human nature] to come out . . . [A] great deal of weakness lurks behind this talk [of conciliation] . . . I see many charming Quakers doing nothing but trying to convert Sir Samuel Hoare.[135]

Rather than conciliating the wrongdoer, the Friends published reports of the atrocities directed against civil disobedients in 1932.[136] But it was no luckier in gaining Gandhian endorsement or funds from India than was the ICG and before long was running precipitously short of funds.[137]

ICG and Friends' appeals were also frequently signed by 'leading women'. British feminists were, like other progressives, conditional allies of Congress. Before 1914, 'imperial feminists' had made the case for female enfranchisement by stressing their commitment to strengthening the empire through the uplift of downtrodden colonial women.[138] In 1927, the American Katherine Mayo, in *Mother India*,

[132] Reynolds, *My Life and Crimes*, 71.   [133] Ibid. 100.

[134] Note on House of Commons meeting of the Indian Conciliation Group, 13 April 1932, L/I/1/252, OIOC.

[135] Kamlani to Alexander, 19 June 1932, Alexander Papers (Friends House) TEMP MSS 577/101.

[136] *India Bulletin,* March, April, July–Aug and Sept 1932.

[137] Scotland Yard Reports, 12 Oct 1932, 5 July 1933, 6 Dec 1933, L/PJ/12/428, OIOC.

[138] Antoinette Burton, *Burdens of History: British Feminists, Indian Women and Imperial Culture, 1865–1915* (Chapel Hill, NC, 1994).

had, through lurid depiction, made child marriage and other Hindu patriarchal practices a justification for alien rule.[139] By no means all British feminists followed this logic: many criticised the alien rulers for their failure to legislate effectively to protect Indian women, and some supported the demands of Indian women's organisations for self-government. The conflict over the Sarda Act in 1930, for example, which aimed to limit child marriage, showed that the *raj*, with its fear of creating religiously-inspired opposition, was less willing to reform than the modernising elements of Congress and the nascent Indian women's movement.[140] But British feminists' main concern was to ensure that the interests of Indian women were protected in whatever political settlement was reached, and this left them open to the proposals of a reforming imperialism. In their work, moreover, the voices of Indian women were not always audible. Eleanor Rathbone's 1929 conference to consider Mayo's claims invited British women who had not visited India, but did not trouble Indian women in London for their views or experiences.[141] Rathbone's sensitivity on such matters improved thereafter, and she supported many of the demands of Indian women's organisations over the 1935 India Act. But she never fully shared the priority they placed on national independence, or, later, their support for Congress strategies of civil disobedience.[142]

In the mid-1930s, at least half a dozen significant groupings claimed to represent Congress views in London: Pole's British Committee on Indian Affairs, which advised the Labour Party leadership; Menon's IL, tied to the left of the Labour Party and the Socialist League; Dara's INCL, attached to the ILP; the CPGB-run New Indian Political Group and Indian Independence League, which Saklatvala continued to claim, quite inaccurately, were, as successors to the London

---

[139] Mrinalini Sinha, *Specters of Mother India: The Global Restructuring of an Empire* (Durham, NC, 2006).

[140] Mrinalini Sinha, 'The Lineage of the "Indian" Modern: Rhetoric, Agency and the Sarda Act in Late Colonial India', in Antoinette Burton (ed.), *Gender, Sexuality and Colonial Modernities* (London, 1999).

[141] Barbara N. Ramusack, 'Catalysts or Helpers? British Feminists, Indian Women's Rights and Indian Independence', in Gail Minault (ed.), *The Extended Family: Women and Political Participation in India and Pakistan* (Delhi, 1981); 'Cultural Missionaries, Maternal Imperialists, Feminist Allies: British Women Activists in India, 1865–1945', *Women's Studies International Forum*, 13/4 (1990), 309–21.

[142] Susan Pedersen, *Eleanor Rathbone and the Politics of Conscience* (New Haven, 2004), 241–64.

Branch, officially accredited by Congress; and the unaffiliated, though generally pacifist and Quaker-supported, Friends of India and Indian Conciliation Group. None of these had any official, endorsed status. When the London Branch had been disaffiliated by Congress, Brockway had written to Nehru hoping that one of his preferred organisations might replace it, but the request was swiftly refused by the Working Committee of Congress. '[W]e have had bitter experiences of our branches', Nehru replied, 'and our Committee is against all foreign commitments.'[143]

This fragmentation was less the product of differences in India than of differences on the British left. Communist and non-Communist groups worked largely apart until the calling-off of civil disobedience in April 1934. The opening of the Communist-inspired Third Indian Political Conference in June 1933 was attended by only twelve people, and at least some of them were hecklers from Reynolds' Friends of India who turned up to protest at the attacks the speakers made on Gandhi.[144] The Communists' New Indian Political Group heckled Friends of India meetings in return, but won almost no support at all outside the usual circles. Contemplating the state of its accounts in November 1934, its secretary noted sadly that 'You can't fight British imperialism on £14'.[145] The India Independence League, which replaced it, remained dominated at the top by Communists, and was now, in the spirit of the United Front favoured by Communists on other issues, also designed to bring in non-Communist supporters. But this strategy was generally unsuccessful, largely because the Communist and non-Communist factions found it impossible to work together after past experiences of distrust.[146] Menon was not interested, doubtless in part because the CPGB had collapsed the Bristol branch of the IL through hostile takeover.[147] Relations among the non-Communists were scarcely better. When Lansbury suggested that his British Committee on Indian Affairs might work with the IL and the Friends of India, Pole declined on the grounds that they were too quarrelsome.[148] Pole, as a creator of the CIL, was particularly resentful of the way Menon had deserted Theosophy.

[143] Nehru to Brockway, 20 Aug 1931, *SWJN*, v, 17.
[144] Report of Third Indian Political Conference, June 1933, L/PJ/12/372, OIOC.
[145] Scotland Yard Report, 8 Nov 1934, L/PJ/12/371, OIOC; 'New Indian Political Group', Oct 1933, L/PJ/12/372, OIOC.
[146] Scotland Yard Report, 22 Nov 1934, L/PJ/12/371, OIOC.
[147] Merrie to Macnamara, 28 Aug 1932, quoted in Chakravarty, *Crusader*, 21.
[148] Pole to Lansbury, 10 Feb 1932, Pole Papers (Borthwick), 2.

He had, he told Sapru bitterly, helped to pay for Menon's London education, and had expected him to go back to India to teach rather than remain in London and involve himself in Congress politics.[149] The IL's views, he told party officials, were 'not those of the Party', and 'statements [it had] made about events in India and sent to George Lansbury turned out to be unreliable'.[150] Menon resented the ICG's guarding of its links with Gandhi and tried hard to break them.[151] The ICG with its desire for reconciliation viewed the 'neurotic demagogues' and 'theoretical babblers' of the IL with tolerant disdain, sceptical of how much cooperation there could be with an organisation with such leftist and confrontational views.[152]

Cutting across these lines of division was a further and no less familiar one: the respective roles of British and Indian activists in metropolitan anti-imperialist movements. The IL was a very British-dominated organisation, as the CPGB and others pointed out.[153] However, Menon responded by pointing out that the Communists sent to heckle his meetings were also mostly British and not Indian, a weakness the CPGB had itself spotted.[154] Hence, at a Friends of India meeting in 1933, it was Saklatvala who denounced his fellow Indians present as 'either friends of the Government or "well-meaning fools"':

SEAL [CPGB Indian] here stood up and vociferated that Gandhi had completely duped India and acted treacherously towards Indian nationalism—the Mahatma was the friend of the British. RAY CHOUDHURY, who was seated next to SEAL here shouted out that he did not wish to see Britishers at the gathering, as they were not the friends of India. English girls (Communists) accused Indian members of the Friends of India of being 'traitors'. An Indian called out, "They are not the friends of the Communists. They are our friends."[155]

But British allies were indispensable. If Menon did not realise this already, his Labour allies were ready to remind him that Indian voices

---

[149] Pole to Sapru, 2 Sept 1947, Pole Papers (OIOC), MSS/Eur/F264/14.
[150] Pole to Gillies, 12 Sept 1934, William Gillies Correspondence, WG/IND/238, LPA.
[151] Menon to Masani, 26 April 1935, cited in Chakravarty, *Crusader*, 636
[152] Harrison to Alexander, 7 March and 8 Aug 1932, Alexander Papers (NMML); Harrison to Pyarelal, 24 Aug. 1932, ICG TEMP MSS 41/1.
[153] Scotland Yard Reports, 23 Nov 1932, L/PJ/12/448, OIOC, and 18 Jan 1933, L/PJ/12/449, OIOC; *India Bulletin,* June, Oct, Dec 1932 and Jan 1933.
[154] *Daily Worker,* 14 July 1932; *Indian News,* 21 Oct 1930, 4 Dec 1930; CPGB Colonial Committee, 20 Oct 1930, CI, RGASPI 495/100/699.
[155] Scotland Yard Report, 5 July 1933, L/PJ/12/428; *India Bulletin,* July–Aug 1933.

alone would not be heard or trusted.[156] The tricky and still unresolved question was what role they should play. Mulk Raj Anand, a perceptive contemporary observer of such things, noted Menon's anxiety that Indian students must not shout slogans or walk out of meetings when influential British sympathisers such as Bertrand Russell were present, and commented wryly on the 'undercurrent of pink warmth' and shy glances shared between the British members at IL meetings.[157] Anand felt a certain ambivalence himself, admiring and deferring to the Bloomsbury intelligentsia, while at the same time resenting or despising their often considerable ignorance of Indian culture and history, and assumptions of the west's superiority in political matters.[158] But Menon too was, at least for Indian audiences, scornful of the value of the Friends of India, before taking up the post in the IL which forced him into such alliances:

[H]ow can India think differently from what her 'friends'. . . think?. . . Have they not 'loved India all their lives'?. . . India is not seeking friends. India is seeking to find herself. She might welcome friends in that search. But if the friends take upon themselves to decide on the goal and the form of the search India has no use for them and she must seek to save herself from her friends.[159]

Visitors to Britain from India were unimpressed by these displays of disunity. In 1934, Gandhi's disciple Mira Ben found plenty of enthusiasts for India, but '[t]hey do not seem prepared for India to have any advance except on *their* terms'.[160] She disliked the ICG which she thought was over-cautious, and unwilling to put her in contact with leading political figures, for fear it would compromise its own lobbying efforts.[161] She was more taken with Dara's INCL, attending the ILP Summer School where she was plied with criticisms of the IL—the 'Anglo-Indian League', as Dara termed it—and the Friends of India.[162] But Gandhi refused to endorse Dara: 'Let them all do their little bit or

[156] Owen, 'Reporting'.   [157] Mulk Raj Anand, *The Bubble* (Delhi, 1984), 441.
[158] Mulk Raj Anand, *Conversations in Bloomsbury* (New Delhi, 1981).
[159] V. K. Krishna Menon, 'Friends of India', *Indus*, VII, 8 (May 1928).
[160] *India Bulletin*, Dec 1934.
[161] MacGregor to Stephens, 30 Aug 1934, L/I/1/1517, OIOC; Slade, *Spirit's Pilgrimage*, 183–6, 189.
[162] *United India*, Jan–Feb 1932, Oct–Nov 1934.

their utmost there. It is enough for us that they are all well meaning', he told Mira.[163]

In October 1933, the Congress leader Vithalbhai Patel, who, it will be recalled, had always favoured foreign propaganda, had died in Switzerland, leaving some £7,500 to Subhas Bose for the work. The various groups in Britain sniffed the possibility of funding. The ICG, backed by C. F. Andrews, proposed a London centre to speak unequivocally for India.[164] The Friends of India wrote to Gandhi in the hope of a grant. Bose and his supporters in Calcutta demanded that the money be used for the improvement of foreign propaganda, possibly in Vienna, where Bose was now resident.[165] But exactly as he had done over the Tilak Fund in 1920, Gandhi opposed the wishes of the deceased. His supporter Vallabhbhai Patel, Vithalbhai's brother, managed to tie up the money through lengthy legal proceedings which ended with the court deciding that Vithalbhai's wishes were unclear.[166] Gandhi, though he claimed not to want the legal action, nonetheless persuaded the family that the money should be given to Congress and used for national reconstruction.[167] 'People have to work out their salvation here', Gandhi wrote to the Friends of India, '[and] what will be effective there [i.e. London] is equal mass realization . . . of the consciousness of the wrong being done to India in every way . . .. But the conviction that came to me in 1920 has grown stronger. Even in the heyday of the struggle I never felt the want of an Indian organization in foreign lands'.[168] 'On this point', he told the ICG, 'I am perhaps the only "whole-hogger" but there it is.'[169] It was clear from the refusal of normally sympathetic newspapers such as the *Manchester Guardian* to

[163] Gandhi to Mira Ben, 21 Aug 1934 and 12 Oct 1934, *CWMG*, E64/371 and E65/218; Gandhi to Patel, 25 Aug 1934, *CWMG*, E64/417

[164] ICG Group Meetings 26 Sept and 14 Nov 1934, ICG TEMP MSS 41/2/2b; Heath to Harrison, 17 March 1935, ICG TEMP MSS 44/4; Note to ICG, 17 March 1935, ICG TEMP MSS 42/1.

[165] Scotland Yard Report, 15 March 1934, L/PJ/12/214, OIOC; *Modern Review*, Aug 1935, 244–5.

[166] 'Vithalbhai Patel's Will', Aug 1934; Bose to Woods, 4 March 1936; 'India Abroad', *CWSCB*, viii, 144–5, 283–4, 357–67; Scotland Yard Report, 13 Feb 1936, L/PJ/12/216, OIOC; Gordharibhai Patel, *Vithalbhai Patel* (2v., Bombay, 1950), ii, 1256, 1270.

[167] Gandhi to V. Patel, 9 Nov 1933, *CWMG*, E62/158; Gandhi to D. Patel, 6 April 1934, *CWMG*, E63/393.

[168] Gandhi to Kamalani, 1 Feb 1934, *CWMG*, E63/79.

[169] Gandhi to Harrison, 1 Feb 1934, *CWMG*, E63/77; Gandhi to Guieyesse, 25 July 1935, *CWMG*, E67/436; Gandhi to Harrison, 4 April 1934, *CWMG*, E66/568; Gandhi to Kantak, 28 Sept 1935, *CWMG*, E68/26.

publish reports from Indians about the extent of repression, that Indian claims still required validation by sympathetic Britons.[170] It was this dependence that Gandhi could not accept. 'My own opinion has been and still persists that English audiences will not take instruction from Indians', he wrote.[171]

When Nehru came to review the question of foreign representation during his visit to Britain at the end of 1935 he too was much struck by the ineffectiveness of most of the organisations.[172] Congress work was, he wrote, badly hampered by the 'mutual rivalries and jealousies' of the Indian residents and the impossibility of controlling semi-independent bodies from so far away. To his embarrassment, he had been practically torn apart on the platform at Victoria Station by rival deputations, including one from yet another organisation, the Indian National Congress in Great Britain, set up by K. D. Kumria and Anand, which handed him leaflets condemning the official reception committee. Saklatvala denounced the INCGB at length: it was a 'bogus and mischievous organisation' activated by 'malice, spitefulness and jealousy' that had put on a 'sectarian, futile and feeble show'.[173] Nehru doubted if it was a real organisation at all and criticised the 'petty mischief' of its use of the Congress name without official accreditation. Although he felt strongly the need for Congress to develop its international connections, therefore, Nehru argued that the most that Congress could do was to encourage groups and societies to form, without funding them, affiliating them or giving them any right to speak for Congress or make commitments on its behalf. [174]

The rich diversity and pluralism of British associational life in the 1930s meant that there were many possible homes in which anti-imperialists might lodge. The various organisations and causes involved were firmly rooted organisations, avowedly political in their goals and organisation and both willing and able to criticise the state directly and more easily than could their Indian counterparts. Of course, few of their members

---

[170] Owen, 'Reporting'.

[171] Rough notes of a talk between Mr Gandhi and Mr Heath in India, 6 Dec 1936; Heath to Wilson, 7 Dec 1936, ICG TEMP MSS 44/1.

[172] Nehru to Prasad, 20 Nov. 1935, *SWJN*, vii, 38–44.

[173] Saklatvala to Kumria, 28 Dec 1935, copy in Seal Papers, MSS/Eur/Photo Eur/446/3.

[174] Nehru to Prasad, 20 Nov 1935; Nehru to Menon, 31 Dec 1935, KMP 10/1/K.

were anti-imperialists *first*. Their anti-imperialism grew out of other commitments. But since these commitments were often deeply-felt, galvanising ones, that did not necessarily impede the generation of anti-imperial energy. The difficulty was not the amount of energy, but its dissipation. If London was a junction-box, it seems a poorly-wired one, containing unfastened cabling and loose connections, in which anti-colonial energies were lost in a shower of unproductive sparks. Rather than crossing boundaries, the anti-imperialists often found them immovable, or even that in trying to cross them, their movements were split. Some found the metropolitan centre enabling, but others that its self-confidence and indifference to them paralysed them, only permitting action once they returned to the colony. Although there are signs of individual empowerment and acts of imaginative border-crossing, there is little sign that the borders could be dissolved, or that individual transgressions could be built upwards into strong or durable organisational or political forms. It was all too easy for Indians at the metropole to be sucked into other debates and organisations and while this could provide new perspectives on India, it could also prove a distraction. As for connections with other nationalist movements, there seems to be little more than distant, gestural hand-waving in their direction. The Indians focussed on their own struggle, whatever the rhetorical value they found in allusion to larger allegiances. Possibly this is the result of the removal of authority from London by the Gandhian Congress after 1920, which left it a place where only rather limited and unofficial types of interaction were possible. More generally, it seems to be true that as nationalist movements gain in influence at the periphery, the metropole becomes itself peripheral and isolated from the real work, its leaders becoming exiles unable to transmit so much of their own ideas and influence back home as had been possible at earlier, less formed, stages of the struggle.

Nevertheless, it is important to be sensitive to the many ways in which 'junction-box' connections might be made even in these later stages. Although the interactions of Congress nationalists with British pacifists, Communists and others seem often to have been characterised by acrimony rather than mutually profitable exchange, it may be possible to read them as dialectical engagement, in which an initial conflict between opposed positions ultimately produces a higher synthesis owing something to both. In such a reading, the apparent clashes are in fact productive mutual questioning, and the heat of disagreement is energy thrown off by the fusion of hitherto incompatible positions. The multiple demands to which anti-imperialists were subject neither paralyse them, nor pull them apart, but enable them to operate in many different registers, and hence to work across and dissolve borders. The synthesis they produce may be invisible for long periods, even at first to the participants who create it, or occur without much organisation or even formal interaction. Boehmer, for example, writes, of 'silent borrowing' and exchanges which operated at an 'interdiscursive level' in which no more than terms and concepts are shared, with no sign of any contemporary connection at all.[175] Even quite small exchanges could set an example, or break a mould, or set in train contagious effects which, in time, went much wider.

However, in order to distinguish such dialectical engagement from a straightforward and unproductive fight, and 'silent borrowing' from silence, it is necessary to define and adhere to concepts and evidence quite precisely. First, proximity is not sufficient for there to be a connection between anti-imperialists: engagement is required. This does not necessarily mean a physical encounter: it is quite possible that connections were made between people who never met, but corresponded, or read and responded to each other's writings. But writing in the same journal does not alone entail engagement, and nor does having mutual friends, or living in the same city. The metropole, to be a 'junction-box', must not merely provide the location for these encounters, but facilitate them, even if unknowingly. Secondly, for the connection to be a strong and productive one, the engagement must exhibit certain features: durability; a capacity for spreading itself wider through further connection; flexibility, that is, the capacity of the parties to adjust position to achieve greater closeness; reciprocity and voluntariness. The junction-box must afford a meeting on equal terms, not a forced surrender of one party to the will of the other.

What kind of signs of mutual engagement would we expect to see in the metropolitan anti-imperialist movements of the 1930s if their inter-connections were of this type? We might expect to find the parties encountering each other with a certain suspicion, but then adjusting their positions as trust grew and the gains of cooperation became visible; the identification and claiming of common ground which is in turn made the basis for a new synthesis of ideas; and perhaps, with growing confidence, the formation of strategic political campaigns. Memberships

---

[175] Boehmer, *Empire*, 24, 106.

of the organisations would begin to overlap, perhaps prompting the formation of durable single associations to prolong and apply the energy thrown off by the initial encounter; and money as well as rhetorical support might begin to flow. Borders should become permeable, and we might expect to see the alliances forged at the metropole transferred back to the colonial periphery. We might also expect to see all of this leave historical traces in the form of common, well recorded memories of mutual support.

What we actually find is more fragile than this: a series of often unsatisfactory couplings, none of which delivered the necessary hybridisation. Indian nationalists at the metropole were forced to be largely parasitic on other struggles, which sucked them in and drained their energies, or split them. They were dependent on single, driven hyperactive individuals as a substitute for broadened appeal and the refusal of many to forge connections across borders. Indeed, the secretaries of the two principal organisations suffered nervous breakdowns through overwork—Atma Kamlani of the Friends of India in 1934 and Krishna Menon in 1935.[176] The groups were usually quite far from mutually supporting: more commonly they were rivals, much of their energies spent pushing each other aside in the desire to win the small authority that Indian nationalists were prepared to make available to them, or to speak alone for India. Menon was at the heart of this. Many years later, Brailsford told Gandhi that Menon seemed 'always to create round himself an atmosphere of suspicion and intrigue'. 'He split the Indian community in London and for years it gave a painful exhibition of disunity.'[177] 'There are so many groups and parties here', Indira Nehru wrote to her father from London, 'and Krishna is not popular with any of them'.[178] But this was not simply a personality trait, but the result of the need for Menon to monopolise the League's political contacts and speak uninterruptedly for India. To other groups, the Indians were only able to offer rhetorical endorsement, rather than practical support, and their wider affiliations were largely gestural, signalling support but little more; the alliances were ad hoc and temporary rather than principled and resilient, and almost always fractious. These weaknesses were not

---

[176] Gandhi to Mira Ben, 7 Aug 1934, *CWMG*, E64/328; Janaki Ram, *Menon*, 51–7.

[177] Brailsford to Gandhi, 24 Oct 1947, quoted in Sudhir Ghosh, *Gandhi's Emissary* (Boston, 1967), 222.

[178] Indira Nehru to Jawaharlal Nehru, 2 April 1938, in Sonia Gandhi (ed.), *Freedom's Daughter: Letters Between Indira Gandhi and Jawaharlal Nehru, 1922–39* (Delhi, 1989), 388.

often created by the authorities, which monitored the metropolitan anti-imperialists' activities but hardly ever felt the need to intervene in them.

This is not to argue that there was no significant engagement at all, but that it lacked the necessities for sustained growth. The movement certainly grew at times, through its parasitic dependence on other growing movements, such as anti-fascism in the late 1930s, as the next chapter will show. But these formations were brittle: it took only minor crises, often unrelated to India, to disrupt them. Given the left sectarianism of the 1930s, a group's rivals could usually be relied upon to supply a crisis, should none independently arise. Major changes of line, such as those made by the Communists, could destroy otherwise reasonably healthy organisations. This was because the encounter was not usually reciprocal: it involved the assimilation of the Indian cause to the British one, not the other way around. This had certain campaigning advantages: it enabled those who lacked the time or inclination to master the complexities of India to speak out for it, and to gain the support of fighters on other fronts. But it often took a good deal of hammering to make the distinctive shape of the Indian independence movement fit the contours of these other struggles. At times, it had the awkward habit of springing out of the frame into which they had set it.

8

An Anti-Fascist Alliance, 1934–42

In the late 1930s, a fresh alliance based on anti-fascism was built between Congress and the British left. Its principal architect was Nehru. In 1935, after a visit to Britain, Nehru was pleased to find that there were 'individual English socialists, and they are a growing number, who have got over this imperialist complex, and who can think of India on real socialist lines'.[1] Nehru's optimism was reciprocated, not least because in his speeches in Britain and in his *Autobiography* (1936) he seemed to answer so many of the doubts that the British left had harboured over Gandhi. 'I wish you could realise how much good your visit has done among the heathen', Ellen Wilkinson told him.[2] Labour found it easier to listen to Nehru than to his colleagues because he was the most anglicised of the Congress leadership. Congress under Gandhi had become less intelligible to its British supporters. From Europe, Nehru had told the Congress President, Rajendra Prasad, that 'some of our prominent Congress leaders might be so out of tune . . . as to be hardly comprehensible here'.[3] But Nehru did speak the right language, and his writings, as C. F. Andrews told him, were much more accessible than those of Gandhi, which 'had to be condensed and explained over and over again', or the obscure and prolix texts of other Congressmen.[4] Nehru was also much more open than his colleagues to familiar, western models of how India should develop. 'In many ways', he wrote, 'I have far more in common with English and other non-Indian socialists than I have with non-socialists in India'.[5]

The first mystery to be unravelled for British sympathisers was Gandhi. Nehru explained why Gandhi was vital to the nationalist

---

[1] Nehru to Amiya Chakravarty, 29 Nov 1935, *SWJN*, vii, 12–14.
[2] Wilkinson to Nehru, 17 Feb 1936 in Jawaharlal Nehru, *A Bunch of Old Letters: Written Mostly to Jawaharlal Nehru and Some Written by Him* (Delhi, 1960), 171–2.
[3] Nehru to Prasad, 20 Nov 1935, *SWJN*, vii, 38–44.
[4] Andrews to Nehru, 6 Nov 1935, in Nehru, *Bunch of Old Letters*, 126–7.
[5] Nehru to Chakravarty, 29 Nov 1935.

struggle at the same time as denying that his views would prevail in Congress. Gandhi, he wrote in the *Autobiography*, was ' a very difficult person to understand' and 'sometimes his language was almost incomprehensible to an average modern'.[6] *Hind Swaraj*, Gandhi's great denunciation of western modernity, was an 'utterly wrong and harmful doctrine, and impossible of achievement'.[7] Gandhi thought in terms of 'personal salvation and of sin, while most of us have society's welfare uppermost in our minds'.[8] Yet, for all this, Gandhi had a unique and inexplicable ability to reach the peasantry.[9] By sharing the doubts Labour had felt about Gandhi's techniques, explaining why in the specificity of the Indian situation they were needed, but stressing that they would not carry weight in an independent India, Nehru defused them. As Congress learned of India's problems, and the peasantry learned of Congress, these struggles came to be fused as part of a seamless campaign for freedom.[10] This two-way process of discovery, by which Congress did not dictate its terms to the peasantry, but learned from it, was much closer to the ideal of mobilisation favoured by the British left, especially among middle-class socialists, for whom it mirrored their own discovery of the British working class.

In other ways too, Nehru reversed what Labour had been told by Gandhi. In 1931, there had been three principal objections. The first and most important was socialism. Nehru had long argued that Congress must adopt socialism if independence were to be meaningful.[11] In 1934, when the Working Committee passed a resolution denouncing class war and favouring the Gandhian ideals of a 'wiser and juster use of private property' and 'a healthier relationship between capital and labour', Nehru told Gandhi that he thought it showed 'such an astounding ignorance of the elements of socialism that it was painful to read . . . and to realise that it might be read outside India'.[12] Gandhi replied disarmingly that while he valued the contribution the Socialists were making to Congress, he must insist that they go at his own pace.[13] British socialists were troubled by the dominance of the right in Congress: a British Socialist government, Patrick Gordon Walker wrote, 'should proclaim its right to remain in India in the interests of the

---

[6] Nehru, *An Autobiography* (London, 1936), 72–3.   [7] Ibid. 511.
[8] Ibid. 512.   [9] Ibid. 72–3.   [10] Chatterjee, *Nationalist Thought*, 131–66.
[11] Jawaharlal Nehru, *Whither India?* (Delhi, 1933).
[12] Nehru to Gandhi, 13 Aug 1934, in Nehru, *Bunch of Old Letters*, 115–20.
[13] Gandhi to Nehru, 17 Aug 1934, in ibid. 120–1.

[Indian] working class'.[14] However, the emergence of Masani's Congress Socialist Party had already impressed some of the younger Labour MPs as a sign of progress. Advised by Krishna Menon that the CSP represented the 'younger men who are not wedded to the spinning wheel philosophy',[15] Anthony Greenwood had told the 1935 Party Conference that India now had 'a virile and determined Socialist movement' which the Party should support.[16] In his *Autobiography*, Nehru, while not endorsing the Congress Socialists, nonetheless distanced himself from Gandhi's support for handicrafts and unmechanised agrarian policy. Ellen Wilkinson, who had herself questioned Gandhi on this point in 1931, assured him that his 'socialist summing up [would] give a great impetus to the interests of the socialists in England'. There had been 'a very general assumption', she told him, 'that you were G[andhiji]'s spiritual son and heir'.[17] Nehru, she announced at an India League meeting in May 1936, 'openly embraced international socialism, in preference to the blatant nationalism of Motilal Nehru and the Mahatma'.[18]

In 1931, Gandhi had hardly reassured Labour MPs when he had predicted communal war at independence. But Nehru was much more reassuring here too. Like Gandhi, he blamed the British for fostering discord. But he also recategorized communal tension as class conflict in disguise. 'Every one of the communal demands put forward by any communal group is, in the final analysis, a demand for jobs', he wrote. 'Religious passion was hitched on to them in order to hide their barrenness.' In this way, 'political reactionaries came back to the political field in the guise of communal leaders'.[19] 'It does not affect the masses at all', Nehru told his British audiences.[20] Nehru also managed to collapse the complicated problems of caste into a problem of class. '[The] depressed classes. . .', he told the Indian Conciliation Group, 'are the proletariat in the economic sense; the others are the better-off people. All these matters can be converted into economic terms, and

[14] *United India*, July–Aug 1934. See also 'The Indian Worker and the Indian Constitution', SSIP pamphlet 3, 1934, copy in Fabian Society Papers J6/3.
[15] Menon to Greenwood, 19 Sept 1935, cited in Chakravarty, *Crusader*, 634.
[16] Labour Party, *Report of Annual Conference*, 1935, 240–1.
[17] Wilkinson to Nehru, 17 Feb 1936 and 22 March 1936 in Nehru, *Bunch of Old Letters*, 171–2, 176–8.
[18] Scotland Yard Report, 20 May 1936, L/PJ/12/293, OIOC.
[19] Nehru, *Autobiography*, 138.
[20] Nehru, 'Indian Problems', in his *India and the World* (London, 1936), 238.

then one can understand the position better.'[21] All these problems could thus be spirited away by economic development under a free national government.

The final obstacle, which had become more important since Gandhi's visit, was defence. Nehru mocked the idea that Japan would ever contemplate invading India, promising that if it did, a national movement such as Congress could resist it better than an army of mercenaries. The means of resistance, which were controversial in India, were not often discussed. Nehru did not just tell British sympathisers that the nationalist movement had moved on: he represented progress himself, as an embodiment of India's aspirations.[22] 'When I speak', he wrote, 'I do not speak as an individual but I speak with the authority of the hundreds of millions of India.'[23] All this ensured that British socialists came to regard Nehru as 'one of us' (Brailsford), and as a man who 'does not quarrel with history' (Brockway), 'worlds above Gandhi in strength of character and insight' (Laski).[24]

Unlike most of his colleagues, Nehru also valued work undertaken in Britain. Ever since the late 1920s, he had been trying to persuade Gandhi that his hostility to foreign propaganda was mistaken.[25] Gandhi had been unconvinced, and had argued that the European states were partners in imperialism and Congress could not expect to retain their sympathy in the 'final heat of the struggle'.[26] As we have seen, these objections seemed to be vindicated when Nehru's chosen vehicle, the League Against Imperialism, tried to direct Congress in the interests of Communism. Nehru therefore tried to develop a form of action abroad which did not offend Gandhian concerns for self-reliant struggle or risk appropriation by foreign allies. He did not believe that Congress should focus solely on Britain in its international work, but it was clearly an

---

[21] Nehru, talk with Indian Conciliation Group, 4 Feb 1936, ICG TEMP MSS 42/1.

[22] Nehru, 'A Visit to England', in *India and the World*, 210.

[23] Quoted in Guha, *Dominance without Hegemony*, 128.

[24] Brailsford in *New Statesman and Nation*, 9 May 1936 and in his *Subject India* (London, 1943), 31; Brockway, 'Gandhi and Nehru', in Sheila Dikshit (ed.) *Jawaharlal Nehru: Centenary Volume* (New Delhi, 1989), 678; Kramnick and Sheerman, *Laski*, 359.

[25] Nehru to Gandhi, 22 April 1927, *SWJN*, ii, 325–6; Nehru, 'A Foreign Policy for India', 13 Sept 1927, *SWJN*, ii, 348–64.

[26] Gandhi to Motilal Nehru, 14 May 1927, Gandhi to Jawaharlal and Motilal Nehru, 25 May 1927, *CWMG*, E38/383 and E38/435–6.

important centre, and Nehru decided to force unity on the warring groups there by providing one of them with informal authority to speak for Congress. His choice was Menon's India League, on the grounds of its socialist inclinations (shown by its closeness to Masani's Congress Socialists), Menon's own abilities and, of course, the fact that the IL, unlike Reynolds' Friends or the ICG, was controlled by an Indian.[27] Nehru's endorsement of the IL transformed it from an organisation facing collapse into the most significant anti-imperialist organisation in London. He and Masani withdrew support from the other groups. They told the ICG that they were not interested in discussing 'amiable trivialities' with it.[28] 'I do not think it takes us anywhere, and it may sometimes add to our difficulties', Nehru wrote of the ICG's conciliatory work.[29] He 'evidently felt [there was] little [the Indian Conciliation] Group could do save "temper" and "help" when clash comes', the ICG concluded sadly after meeting him.[30] Nehru also withheld his endorsement from the Indian Swaraj League, which had been set up by Kumria and Mulk Raj Anand when he had refused them permission to use the Congress name.[31] Similarly, Dara's INCL, to which the ILP continued to provide limited backing, also withered through lack of authority. At Brockway's instruction, Dara had formed a 'Socialist Committee for Indian Independence' in the hope of winning some support from the British left, but he was an unconvincing advocate of socialism, with much of which he disagreed.[32] By 1936, his was effectively a paper organisation only and even Brockway had abandoned it in despair.[33]

Menon's links to Nehru made him newly attractive to the CPGB. From late 1934, the CPGB edged towards cooperation with bourgeois

---

[27] Nehru to Prasad, 22 Nov 1935, *SWJN*, vii, 38–44.
[28] Harrison to Heath and Alexander, Oct 1935, 15 Jan. and 9 Feb 1936, Alexander Papers (NMML); Harrison to Wilson, 25 Sept 1936, ICG TEMP MSS 42/1.
[29] Nehru to Prasad, 22 Nov 1935.
[30] Meeting with Nehru and Masani, 1 Nov 1935, ICG TEMP MSS 41/2/2b.
[31] Scotland Yard Reports of activities of Indian Congress League and other groups, 1934–5, L/PJ/12/365, OIOC; Reports of activities of Indian Swaraj League, L/PJ/12/373, OIOC.
[32] *United India*, Feb–March 1935.
[33] Scotland Yard Reports, 24 Sept 1935, L/PJ/12/215, OIOC; 13 Feb 1936, L/PJ/12/216, OIOC; Feb 1936 and Feb 1937, KV2/1917, NA; *United India*, Oct–Nov 1937.

nationalists, a shift of strategy confirmed in the summer of 1935 at the Comintern's Seventh Congress, when Communists were instructed to participate in and seek to lead the anti-imperialist struggle.[34] R. P. Dutt moved quickly to woo Nehru and Masani, whom he had already identified as the key figures in India.[35] At meetings at the end of 1935, Nehru agreed to consider the possibility of affiliating outside bodies such as the trade unions to the Congress so as to create mass pressure on the right-wing leadership.[36] Dutt asked Nehru the crucial question: 'why, if Congress [is] based on [the Indian] masses . . . it fails to voice masses, and voices instead leadership which is dominantly right wing and bourgeois?' Nehru's reply persuaded Dutt that 'the exclusion of the masses (the vociferous attenders without votes) takes place already in the lowest organs of the Congress; the balance is inevitably magnified at each successive higher state to the final bourgeois leadership'. The solution of collective affiliation was attractive to Nehru who believed it would fortify Congress in periods of civil disobedience, when the middle-class elements, hit with confiscations and loss of privileges, had caved in. But he knew the Gandhians and the right would not easily surrender their claim to speak for the masses. He was also reluctant to lose his own position and popularity. Dutt therefore feared that Nehru would express sympathy with leftist demands, but suppress them in the name of unity if they could not be obtained.[37]

To Dutt's delight, however, Nehru called on his return for Congress 'to develop democracy in the lowest rungs of the . . . ladder' through the functional affiliation of trade unions and peasant associations and

[34] 'Problems of the Anti-Imperialist Struggle in India', *Inprecor*, 15/10, 9 March 1935.

[35] John Callaghan, *Rajani Palme Dutt: A Study in British Stalinism* (London, 1993), 107, 124, 156–62; CPGB to Pollitt in Moscow, 19 Aug 1935 (3677), HW17/19, NA; Dutt to Arnot, 12 Jan 1935, Dutt to Bradley, 19 Jan 1936, Dutt Papers, K4/1935–6; 'Notes regarding the CPGB, the Anti-War Movement and the LAI', 1 July 1936, L/PJ/12/384, OIOC; Note on Masani by Bradley, 23 Aug 1935; Masani to Pollitt, 24 Aug 1935, CI, RGASPI 495/16/25; Scotland Yard Report, 28 Aug 1935, L/PJ/12/492, OIOC.

[36] Meeting between the CPGB and Nehru, 31 Oct 1935, report in CI, RGASPI 495/16/30, also 'Don' to 'Johnson', 29 Nov 1935, same file.

[37] Pollitt to ECCI, 21 Jan 1936 (5071) and ECCI to Pollitt, 27 Jan 1931 (5241), CPGB to ECCI, 3 Feb 1936 (5101), DISRAELI to Pollitt, 10 Feb 1936 (5200); CPGB to ECCI, 17 Feb 1936 (5235), HW17/20, NA; Pollitt's report to ECCI on his meeting with the Professor (Nehru), undated, CI, RGASPI 495/16/30; Dutt's report, 19 Feb 1936, is in Dutt Papers K4/1935–6, reprinted in John Callaghan, 'Jawaharlal Nehru and the Communist Party', *Journal of Communist Studies*, 7/3 (1991), 357–66.

for an agrarian programme that struck at peasant debt and high rents.[38] But his attempt to persuade Congress to accept these proposals got nowhere. The plans for agrarian reform were shelved to allow Congress to fight the elections without a commitment to attack the landlords. Research confirmed Nehru's suspicion that Congress membership was confined to the elite, with an almost total absence of agricultural and industrial labourers.[39] However, the right feared that functional affiliation would crowd out their own efforts at recruitment and empower peasant and trade union leaders to defy them. The Congress right forced Nehru to concede the lack of any real base of socialist advance in India before freedom was won, and would only allow the poor to be recruited as non-voting associate members.[40] Nehru was regularly outvoted in the Working Committee, and when he attacked Bombay capitalists its right-wing majority threatened resignation and appealed successfully to Gandhi who publicly rebuked him.[41] In a conciliatory speech, Nehru criticised his fellow socialists for divisiveness, and acknowledged that socialism could not come until after independence and only then if it could prove itself.[42] Within a few months of his return to India, therefore, Nehru's socialism had effectively been silenced.

At home, the CPGB needed an organisation of Indians in London to support its new interest in collaborative anti-imperialism, but its track record did not inspire confidence. Saklatvala had hoped for a revival of the London Branch and approached the ILP, but this got nowhere, thanks to bitter memories of its earlier incarnation.[43] The best prospect of influencing Nehru, and also avoiding sole reliance on the CPI with its ingrained hostility to working with nationalists, was Menon's India League, so the CPGB began to identify causes on which common

---

[38] Nehru, Presidential Address at Lucknow Congress, April 1936, *SWJN*, vii, 170–95; 'The Indian National Congress at Lucknow', 17 April 1936, Dutt Papers, K4/1935–36.

[39] D. A. Low, 'Congress and 'Mass Contacts', 1936–37: Ideology, Interests and Conflict over the Basis of Party Representation', in his *Rearguard Action: Selected Essays on Late Colonial Indian History* (New Delhi, 1996); 'Which Way Ahead? Nehru and Congress Strategy 1936–1937', in his *Britain and Indian Nationalism*.

[40] See Low, 'Mass Contacts'; B. R. Tomlinson, *The Indian National Congress and the Raj, 1929–42: The Penultimate Phase* (London, 1976), 58–9, 132–5, 170.

[41] Nehru, 'Socialism the Only Way', 'The Role of Big Business', Nehru to Menon 18 June 1936, *SWJN*, vii, 250–4, 288; Gandhi to Nehru, 12 May, 8 and 15 July 1936, *Bunch of Old Letters*, 183, 198, 203.

[42] 'Address to the Congress Socialist Conference', 20 July 1936, *SWJN*, vii, 329.

[43] Scotland Yard Reports, 22 Nov 1934, L/PJ/12/371, OIOC; 3 July 1935, L/PJ/12/274, OIOC; Aug 1935, L/PJ/12/373, OIOC.

platforms could be built.[44] Menon naturally did not want the India
League to be captured. India, he had told one Communist in 1929,
would gain little from being 'a convenient stick for the Communists to
beat their enemies'.[45] The Communists' denunciation of his every move
in the early 1930s cannot have helped. But access to Nehru, which he
could use as a means of preserving independence, made a conditional
alliance more attractive. His existing Labour Party allies had refused
to endorse the Congress goal of a constituent assembly, insisting that
Congress should work the 1935 Act first. But the CPGB had come
out in favour of a constituent assembly, and its pursuit of left unity
and affiliation to the Labour Party through a Unity Campaign with
Cripps' Socialist League promised a reconfigured left which might assist
Congress' cause. Indeed, the CPGB was the keenest to include Indian
independence in such an alliance: in the negotiations for the Unity
Manifesto at the end of 1936, it had insisted on including colonial
independence, against the opposition of more domestically-oriented
socialists such as Bevan who thought '[p]eople wanted to know more
about [the] unemployed and things that concerned them'.[46] By 1936,
the CPGB also had over four times the membership of 1930 and
offered welcome publicity, speakers and finance: 'massive support in
every form'.[47] Menon could not afford to allow any of his rivals, such
as those in the Indian Swaraj League, to seize such gains for themselves.
Also personally persuaded, like Nehru, that India's struggle could not be
isolated from wider world events, he found himself drawn ineluctably
closer to the CPGB.[48]

Through 1936 and early 1937, Menon tried at IL meetings to offer
support for left unity, while marking out a position on India which was
independent of the CPGB.[49] But as the Unity Campaign collapsed over
Spain, and the Labour Party's tightening of discipline made it harder to
maintain multiple affiliations on the left, he found himself orbiting the

[44] Bridgeman to Menon, 15 Feb and 26 April 1935, Pollitt to Menon, 6 and 10
March 1935, cited in Chakravarty, *Crusader*, 439, 645–6.
[45] Houghton to Menon, 12 Oct 1929; Menon to Houghton, 16 Oct 1929, quoted
in Chakravarty, *Menon*, i 169–70; Menon to Bridgeman, 18 July 1935, cited in
Chakravarty, *Crusader*, 646.
[46] CPGB Politburo, 13 Nov 1936.
[47] N. K. Krishnan, *Testament of Faith: Memoirs of a Communist* (New Delhi), 52–3;
Jyoti Basu, *Memoirs: A Political Autobiography* (Calcutta, 1999), 10; see also comments
by Douglas Hyde, quoted in Callaghan, *Palme Dutt*, 201, 215.
[48] Menon to Mehta, 19 Sept 1936, KMP 9/4/53.
[49] Scotland Yard Report, 6 May 1936 and 10 Feb 1937, L/PJ/12/450, OIOC.

CPGB. By early 1937, the Security Services had picked up signs of an 'undeniable entente' in Menon's meetings with CPGB leaders.[50] The following month the CPGB was exhibiting 'ever-increasing intimacy' and an 'almost proprietary interest' in Menon. He attended the LAI British Section conference, despite his protestations labelled as the delegate of the Congress.[51] On May Day, Menon took the place of honour alongside Pollitt at the CPGB demonstration.[52] From this time, intelligence reports suggest, 'he took no important action of any kind without prior consultation with the higher Communist Party leaders'.[53] A police report concluded:

MENON . . . has taken great pains to ensure that the British Communist leadership should regard him as the only Indian in London whose views . . . can be taken as correct. He has pointed out that he alone has any authority to speak for NEHRU and that he is invariably advised by the Congress Socialist Party on matters of importance. He is exceedingly contemptuous of other Indian organisations in London . . . He has compelled BRADLEY to admit that owing to the conflicting cross-currents in Indian circles . . . it is difficult for them to know who are really their friends. Finally he has made it clear that if the British Communists want to get anything done in India, they must . . . forward their projects through him in order that they may be considered on their own merits by Congress, and not turned down straightaway on the score of Communist dictation.[54]

However, alliance with the CPGB inevitably ruled out other alliances, notably that with Masani and the CSP. In early 1937, Menon began pressing the CPGB's concerns on the CSP and Congress, especially over Spain and the Soviet Union.[55] Masani, however, told Menon that in India the Communists were not proving reliable allies of Congress and that he could not work in unity with them.[56] The CPGB also insisted on a firm break with Brockway's ILP, which it now regarded as the political home of Trotskyists. Menon did not agree, but he was nonetheless forced to exclude the ILP from a conference on 'Socialism

---

[50] Scotland Yard Report, 1 Feb 1937, L/PJ/12/323, OIOC.
[51] 'The United Front Activities of the Communist Party of Great Britain', 17 March 1937, L/PJ/12/384, OIOC; Scotland Yard Report, 7 April 1937, L/PJ/12/450, OIOC.
[52] Scotland Yard Report, 5 May 1937, L/PJ/12/384, OIOC.
[53] 'V. K. Krishna Menon', 10 June 1940, L/PJ/12/323, OIOC.
[54] 'V. K. Menon's Views on the Political Situation in India', 1 Feb 1937, L/PJ/12/323, OIOC.
[55] Menon to Masani, 2 Jan, 6 Feb, 14 May 1937, KMP, 9/4/70.
[56] Masani to Menon, 21 May 1937, KMP, 9/4/66.

and India' on the grounds they were 'Trotskyists and splitters'.[57] He told Masani that a 'new alignment is appearing here and we must either recognise it or be in a backwater'.[58]

The greatest thing that has happened here is the U[nited] F[ront] Movement.. . . [T]he Communists are behaving with great tact and complete honesty. And they do work hard! . . . The international situation is such that the defence of the Soviet Union against enemies is the primary concern of all Socialists. I am sick of the ILP talk of revolutionary socialism though I am for working even with them. Any way there are not a lot of them about. . . . [T]he world changes. Fascism has made such a difference. . . The Unity campaign is sound on India and with regard to the CSP. Both Stafford [Cripps] and Pollitt are well informed and Maxton never bothered about it.[59]

Masani wrote in protest: 'I am afraid that you have now transferred your old bitter antagonism to the C.P. to the Trotskyists. . . . Personally I don't share your views regarding. . . [Spain] or the Moscow Trials . . . But surely you and I and comrades in the Party can hold differing views in a matter like this without worrying about it?'[60] But they could not. The CPGB insisted that Menon cut his links with Masani as well as Brockway. 'I have not heard from you for some time', wrote Masani sadly in July 1938. 'I guess that you have given me up as hopeless because of my "heresies." '[61]

Menon also lost some support among expatriate Indians, as well as the expatriates of other colonised countries in London, many of whom believed that the CPGB had restrained its anti-imperialism in the interest of stiffening the western powers against Hitler. The 1938 CPGB statement 'Peace and the Colonial Question' offered British colonies interim democratic charter rights, but not independence.[62] The CPGB acknowledged that it was losing its hold over colonial émigrés for this reason.[63] Thus while Menon's meetings were now better attended, the ratio of Indians present had fallen. One in December 1936 had an attendance of 180 but only 12 Indians, a feature commented on by the

[57] Menon to Masani, 30 March 1937, KMP, 9/4/70; Brockway to Menon, 31 May 1937, KMP, 9/4/71.
[58] Menon to Masani, 9 June 1937, KMP, 9/4/70.
[59] Menon to Masani, 30 March 1937, KMP, 9/4/70.
[60] Masani to Menon, 7 July and 7 Aug 1937, KMP, 9/4/70.
[61] Masani to Menon, 12 July 1938, KMP, 9/4/70; Menon to Mehta, 30 Aug 1938, KMP, 9/4/71.
[62] 'Peace and the Colonial Question', 2 May 1938, Dutt Papers, K4/1937–8; CPGB Central Committee, 23 April 1938; Politburo, 1 June 1938.
[63] Central Committee, 24 June 1939.

Trinidadian socialist and Trotskyist C. L. R. James.[64] Indians attending meetings of the League Against Imperialism also demanded to know why they were so under represented in the League's upper structures, a complaint which others, such as George Padmore and Jomo Kenyatta, were to make subsequently.[65] The asymmetry of the relationship between Menon and the CPGB is revealed in the police reports of turnout at their respective marches. In February 1938, the CPGB delivered 1,200 marchers to the Indian Independence Day procession organised by the IL. However, at the CPGB's own demonstration in May, few Indians reciprocated: Menon led only 5 or 6. [66]

As the price of its support, the CPGB insisted that Menon bombard Nehru with its views concerning office-taking, the priority of the defence of the Soviet Union, and the need to resist Gandhism.[67] Nehru noted in one letter that Menon had sent him a 'formidable list' of demands for evidence of united front activity in India: 'peace movement, cultural cooperation, civil liberties, youth and students, socialists, labour and peasant'. 'We have all these in varying degrees', he told Menon, somewhat vaguely. 'You want my authority to represent India on some kind of an executive dealing with this Spanish affair', he continued wryly. 'I do not quite understand what this central committee is, but you can certainly join it and represent us there. Exactly whom you will represent, I do not know.'[68] When Menon wrote to attack Trotskyism in India, Nehru was bewildered: '[t]here is no such thing here'.[69] Nehru tried to persuade Menon to return to India to renew his acquaintance with the 'human material' of Indian politics.[70] 'Try to imagine', he wrote, '. . . how they think, how they act, what moves them, what does not affect them. It is easy enough to take up a theoretically correct attitude which has little effect on anybody.'[71] But

[64] Scotland Yard Reports, 30 Dec 1936, L/PJ/12/384, OIOC; 10 Feb 1937, L/PJ/12/450, OIOC.

[65] Compare Scotland Yard Reports of LAI Conferences, 25 May 1932, L/PJ/12/272, OIOC; 25–6 Jan and 2 Dec 1936, 27–8 Feb 1937, L/PJ/12/275, OIOC; 20 Dec 1936, L/PJ/12/384, OIOC

[66] Scotland Yard Reports, 9 Feb, 4 May, 21 Sept, 19–20 Oct, 2 and 16 Nov 1938, L/PJ/12/451, OIOC.

[67] Menon to Nehru, 19 March, 9 April, 1 May, 23 June, 11 Aug, 25 Sept, 29 Dec 1937, KMF, 2/3.

[68] Nehru to Menon, 3 Sept 1936, *SWJN*, vii, 429; 7 and 30 Aug 1937, *SWJN*, viii, 293–5, 614–16.

[69] Nehru to Menon, 11 Nov 1937, *SWJN*, viii, 197.

[70] Nehru to Menon, 29 Oct 1936, *SWJN*, vii, 438.

[71] Nehru to Menon, 28 Sept 1936, in *SWJN*, vii, 470–1.

Menon refused to return home, asking instead to be made a formal deputy to the Congress President in London, so as to be able to speak in Congress' name with greater authority. Denied a formal Congress mandate, his usual practice was, he told Nehru, to say 'that I spoke in the name of the [Congress] President and that he spoke for India'.[72] But Nehru refused this degree of licence which he must have sensed would compromise Congress.[73]

The main demand that the CPGB wanted Menon to press on Nehru was Congress support for their anti-fascist 'peace front', as a reply to those critics, such as the Trotskyists and pacifists, who argued that it bought security for the imperialist powers at the expense of the colonised. Nehru had managed to secure the passage of Congress resolutions of solidarity with Abyssinia, China and republican Spain.[74] As long as appeasement continued, he could easily denounce fascism and British imperialism in the same breath, and argue that the former was simply an extreme outgrowth of the latter. But beyond this, Congress had done almost nothing for Spain, despite Menon's entreaties. 'I pressed hard but almost all the others felt that we could not do anything effective', Nehru told him.[75] At Haripura in February 1938, Congress resolved that India could be no party to an imperialist war, but that a free India would 'gladly associate herself' with an international world order based on disarmament and collective security. This formula was designed by Nehru to commit Congress to conditional support for an anti-fascist alliance while taking account of Gandhian principles of non-violence and the view of Subhas Bose and others that a war between Britain and Germany would necessarily be an imperialist one which should be exploited to push the British out of India. Neither Nehru nor other Indian leaders expected the war to touch India's borders and expose the incompatibility of these positions. However, in Britain, where these matters were more urgent and divisive, the CPGB wanted something more precise than Nehru's formula.[76] Menon, on the Communists' behalf, attacked Bose's views as 'mistaken and muddled' and Gandhi's

[72] Menon to Nehru, 9 and 23 Jan 1936 [misdated: 1937], KMF, 2/3; Menon to Nehru, 23 Jan 1937, KMP, 10/1/D.
[73] 'Subhas Bose and Foreign Propaganda', 28 April 1936, *SWJN* vii, 205–7; Nehru to Menon, 22 Feb 1937, KMF 2/3; Scotland Yard Reports, 10 Feb 1937, L/PJ/12/450, OIOC; 30 March 1939, L/PJ/12/452, OIOC.
[74] *Indian Annual Register*, 1936, i, 248, 279; ii, 201.
[75] Menon to Nehru, 29 Nov 1936, KMF, 1/8; Nehru to Menon, 14 Dec 1936, KMF, 1/10; Nehru to Menon, 20 Jan 1939, KMF, 1/1.
[76] Menon to Nehru, 9 and 16 April 1938, KMF, 1/6.

as objectively helpful to fascism. The 'methods of the fascists are not to be ruled out by some of our members', he warned Nehru. 'It will be covered up in mystic language and no doubt we shall have philosophical explanations in the *Harijan* about the necessity for them.'[77] Nehru remained unable to oblige: 'I doubt that much could be done at this end.'[78]

In March 1938, Menon proposed approaching Labour leaders to promise Congress support for collective security. 'Obviously it is not a matter for a Working Committee decision', Menon told Nehru, 'but one which Nehru communicates in the most informal manner and they all know what it means.'[79] Nehru agreed but told Menon not to commit Congress.[80] Later in the year, Nehru himself visited Britain again, shepherded by the Left Book Club and the CPGB, with which Menon was now holding daily meetings.[81] In Britain, Nehru was more definite than he had been in India about Congress' anti-fascism. He told the *Manchester Guardian* that 'Indian opinion is entirely anti-fascist' and that a free India would unhesitatingly throw itself behind the democracies in a war with fascism.[82] In an article for the *Daily Worker*, Nehru even explored the idea of replacing the Indian Army with a people's militia and declared—not altogether accurately—that the Congress ministries were starting to investigate military training.[83] He addressed the CPGB's Central Committee, which responded in flattering terms.[84] Nehru told the Working Committee that his discussions in Britain had been dominated by the question 'of what India might do at a time of grave international crisis, such as war. . . Crudely put, India had a tremendous nuisance value.' Hence Labour was now 'prepared to go almost to the full extent of meeting India's demands for independence and a constituent assembly'.[85] An important meeting was held at Cripps' Cotswold home, Goodfellows.[86] A draft agreement by Laski proposed

[77] Menon to Nehru, 25 Sept 1937, KMP, 10/1/D; Menon to Nehru, 9 and 19 Feb 1938, KMF, 1/6.

[78] Nehru to Menon, 5 March 1938, *SWJN*, viii, 378–9.

[79] Menon to Nehru, 22 March 1938, KMP, 10/1/f.

[80] Nehru to Menon, 2 April 1938, KMP, 10/1/A.

[81] Scotland Yard Report, 20 Oct 1938, L/PJ/12/451, OIOC.

[82] *Manchester Guardian*, 8 Sept 1938.   [83] *Daily Worker*, 29 June 1938.

[84] CPGB Central Committee, 1–2 July 1938.

[85] Nehru, 'Note to the Congress Working Committee' 1 Aug 1938, *SWJN*, ix, 93–105; 'Report on his Travels', Interview to the Press, 17 Nov 1938, *SWJN*, ix, 202–6; 'India and the British Labour Party', 18 July 1938, *SWJN*, ix, 78–80.

[86] Menon to Nehru, 16 March 1938, KMP, 10/1/D.

that the Viceroy be instructed to summon a constituent assembly to be elected by universal suffrage, with the task of drawing up a new constitution for India, which the British Government would ratify subject only to the negotiation of a treaty.[87]

But Nehru's task was a difficult one. He had to (and wished to) align Congress with collective security without offending Gandhian non-violence or compromising the fight for independence. Gandhi had hitherto tolerated Nehru's anti-fascist resolutions partly because he saw them as fundamentally irrelevant and partly because Nehru had been careful only to deplore fascist actions and not to express even tentative support for physical sanctions except under circumstances of unprovoked aggression.[88] But the pace of international events was putting pressure on Nehru to make firmer commitments. After 1936, some British pacifists on the left found themselves drawn away from Gandhism, with its strict injunction against even the limited violence that socialist or revolutionary pacifists like Brockway and Reynolds were now willing to contemplate in anti-fascist self-defence. This, however, did not make them advocates of the 'peace front', which they believed sacrificed the interests of the colonised and the working class to capitalist and imperialist war.[89] Instead, they advocated war resistance, and a general strike in Britain, supported by a colonial rising.

Many of Nehru's former allies among these groups, such as Brockway and Reynolds, were thus frustrated by their hero's support for the 'peace front'. 'I want to warn you very earnestly', wrote Brockway to Nehru, 'against the clever intrigue that is going on to capture you for the Communist Party.'[90] Brockway worked hard during Nehru's visit to get him to stress that India's priority was independence and that it would be no party to an imperialist war.[91] Nehru replied warning Brockway against allowing the ILP to get into a sectarian position at a time of international crisis. Brockway, dissatisfied, threatened to take the question up with the Congress Working Committee, which he knew

[87] Laski's handwritten draft is dated 25 June 1938, the Saturday of the weekend Nehru spent at Goodfellows, and is in CAB127/60, NA. There is also a typed copy of this in KMP, 11/19/A. There is also a later typed draft dated 13 July 1938, presumably of what was actually agreed, in CAB127/60, NA.

[88] For example, 'India and Britain', 6 July 1938, *SWJN*, ix, 34–55.

[89] *No More War*, Jan 1935, quoted in Ceadel, *Pacifism*, 170; Housman to Menon, 27 Sept 1938, Housman Corr., v.2.

[90] Brockway to Nehru, 6 Aug 1938, JNC v.10.

[91] Brockway to Nehru, 20 and 30 June 1938, JNC v.10; Brockway to Menon, 30 June 1938, KMP, 9/4/39; *New Leader*, 1 July 1938.

did not back Nehru's position.[92] Reynolds also wrote to India to tell Congress Socialists of Menon's close links with the CPGB.[93] Both the official CPGB resolution and the ILP amendment for the India League's 'Peace and Empire' Conference thus welcomed Congress's position: the former for its declaration in favour of collective security and the latter for its refusal to involve India in any war on Britain's side.[94] Nehru backed the former, but his right to do so was challenged by Reynolds and the ILP delegate, who protested that the resolution gave people the false impression that Indians were prepared to fight for collective security. Nehru accepted in his concluding speech that the Conference resolution did not contain all that had been agreed at Haripura. But he insisted that it was compatible with it.[95]

At the end of the year, having assured the British left of the intensity of Congress anti-fascism, Nehru returned home. But in India, he could hardly find any allies. Sympathy with fascism was actually growing among the communal parties. There was little support for the Spanish republicans and a 'great deal of passive opposition' to taking in Jewish refugees.[96] The Congress Socialists were in the main supporters of the line taken by Brockway and the ILP: the coming war was one between imperialists which was of no interest to India.[97] Nehru was forced to admit privately to Menon that the collective security platform he had hoped to build had failed to materialise.[98] Matters were made harder by Bose's desire to use the coming struggle as an opportunity to push the British out of India through civil disobedience. Whether India would take any part in the war was, for Bose, to be decided along the lines of narrow self-interest and an unsentimental approach to the choice of allies.[99] Nehru wrote to Bose for clarification in February.[100] But Bose replied angrily that Nehru's international policy was 'nebulous'.

I was astounded when you produced a resolution before the Working Committee some time ago seeking to make India an asylum for the Jews. You were

[92] Brockway to Nehru, 6 Aug 1938, JNC v.10.
[93] Scotland Yard Report, 20 Oct 1938.   [94] Copies in Bridgeman Papers, 27/3.
[95] Speech at 'Peace and Empire' Conference, 15 July 1938, *SWJN*, ix, 61–71; 'Indian Freedom and World Politics', *Tribune*, 28 Oct 1938; Scotland Yard Report, 27 July 1938, L/PJ/12/293, OIOC; Menon to Mehta, 30 Aug 1938, KMP, 9/4/71.
[96] Nehru to Menon, 4 and 6 April 1939, KMF, 1/1.
[97] Gupta, 'British Labour and the Indian Left', 116–17.
[98] 'Boycott of Japanese Goods', 30 Sept 1937; Nehru to Menon, 30 Aug, 30 Sept and 7 Oct 1937, *SWJN*, viii, 718–19, 725–6.
[99] Speech at Haripura, *CWSCB*, ix, 27.
[100] Nehru to Bose, 4 Feb 1939, *SWJN*, ix, 480–5.

mortified when the Working Committee . . . turned it down. Foreign policy is a realistic affair to be determined largely from the point of view of a nation's self-interest . . . It is no use championing lost causes all the time and it is no use condemning countries like Germany and Italy on the one hand and on the other, giving a certificate of good conduct to British and French Imperialism.[101]

In his reply, Nehru confirmed his disapproval of Bose's lack of sympathy with anti-fascism.[102] But on foreign policy questions, Congress was speaking with three voices—Nehru, Bose and Gandhi—and had evolved no common position on defence at all. In his letters to Cripps, Nehru kept up the impression that all was well.[103] Menon was keen to press for a more vigorous anti-fascism, but Nehru was unable to oblige him since only Bose could speak for Congress and his views differed considerably from his own. Bose's Working Committee had not taken long to move against Menon's ill-defined right to speak for Congress in London. It had ordered that he should only speak in the name of Congress if given instruction to do so.[104] 'You should carry on', Nehru told Menon, 'but you will no doubt realise the difficulty of your, or for that matter of my, committing the Congress to a policy which might be objected to by Subhas [Bose] or others.'[105] Nehru's ability to rally India for collective security was therefore already starting to crumble.[106]

In 1934, the India League had been small, financially weak and characterised by a floating and irregular membership. By the middle of 1939, Menon was the leading figure in anti-imperialist politics in London. Support for the Indian independence struggle in Britain probably peaked in the summer of 1938, when Nehru addressed a packed Albert Hall on 'Peace and Empire' with Menon at his side. It was mostly indirect and self-interested support, provided in expectation of reciprocal endorsement of the 'peace front' and anti-fascist struggle, and it was contested by others who hoped that Congress might provide support for their own project of anti-imperialist war resistance. At one level, that this

---

[101] Bose to Nehru, 28 March 1939, *CWSCB*, ix, 198–9.
[102] Nehru to Bose, 3 April 1939, *SWJN*, ix, 534–49; Nehru to Menon, 4 and 6 April 1939, KMF, 1/1.
[103] Nehru to Cripps, 21 Jan 1939, CAB127/143, NA.
[104] Kripalani to Nehru, 11 Aug 1938, JNC v.41; Nehru to Kripalani, 24 Aug 1938, *SWJN*, ix, 114–15; Nehru to Menon, 24 Aug 1938, KMF, 1/6.
[105] Nehru to Menon, 31 March, 4 and 18 April 1939, KMF, 1/1.
[106] Nehru to Menon, 16 March 1939, KMF, 1/1.

enthusiasm *for* India was not much *about* India did not matter. Parasitic anti-imperialism was not necessarily weak: its strength depended on its success in identifying suitable and reliable hosts. The relationship was, to use the language of parasitology, mutualist: the 'peace front' got Nehru, which helped it to represent itself as anti-imperialist, and Menon got endorsement and support for the Indian struggle and, specifically, for the India League. But the relationship was also brittle. It relied almost wholly on a single figure: Nehru, a man who had come to Britain precisely because his own views were increasingly out of line with those of Congress, but who had while in Britain created a powerful illusion of control, both his of Congress and Congress of the nation.[107] Above all, it forced Congress into a mould that suited its new allies, but at the cost of flattening its distinctive shape. Whatever its campaigning advantages, this ran the risk of arousing expectations which could not be met.

When war broke out in September 1939, both the Labour Party and the CPGB expected that, in return for their support for Indian freedom, Congress would support the war effort. Labour therefore called on the Chamberlain Government to offer Indian politicians a genuine part in wartime government. The thrust of Labour's campaign of 'constructive opposition' was the claim that socialist measures were necessary to increase the efficiency of the war effort. The alienation of potential support in India, apparent in the Viceroy Linlithgow's failure to consult any Indian politicians before declaring India to be at war, was easily integrated into it.[108] Menon and Nehru lobbied the party leaders to seize the opportunity, assuring them that Congress was 'against fascism and wholly favouring democracy'. But 'India must have democracy to defend.'[109] Menon found Labour receptive.[110] Attlee, not normally one

---

[107] 'I have felt out of place and a misfit. This was one reason . . . why I decided to go to Europe.' Nehru to Gandhi, 28 April 1938, in Nehru, *Bunch of Old Letters*, 283–4.

[108] Zetland to Linlithgow, 11 Oct and 15 Nov 1939, Linlithgow Coll., MSS/Eur/ F125/8; Cripps to Nehru, 11 Oct 1939, JNC v.14; Menon to Nehru, 18 Oct 1939, KMP, 11/18/57; 'Statement by Mr. Attlee and Mr. Greenwood', 20 Oct 1939, ID/IND/1/72vi, LPA; Menon to Nehru, 4 Oct 1939 and undated, but probably written early Oct.1939, KMP, 10/1/B; NEC, 25 Oct 1939, LPA; Annexure to *NEC*, 20 Dec 1939, LPA.

[109] Menon to Grenfell, 15 Sept 1939, KMP, 5/18/14; Nehru to Grenfell, 18 Sept 1939, *SWJN*, xiii, 714–16; Menon to Greenwood, various dates from 2 to 14 Oct 1939, KMP, 5/18/14.

[110] Menon to Nehru, 4 Oct 1939 and undated, but probably written early Oct 1939, KMP, 10/1/B; Menon to Nehru, 18 Oct 1939, KMP, 11/18/57.

of Menon's allies, raised India as part of a general debate on the war and told Zetland, the Secretary of State, of Labour's 'dissatisfaction' and 'profound regret' at the failure to rally India.[111] Cripps urged Congress to stand 'as firm as a rock' on its demand for a say in wartime government, though his own ability to deliver the Labour Party was now weak: it had expelled him earlier in the year.[112] Menon also advised the CPGB that Congress would support the war.[113] A cable from India which seemed to hold out this prospect was received by Menon on 17 September, and the CPGB, to which he showed it privately, thought it 'magnificent'.[114] In his letters to Nehru, Menon continued to warn against the siren call of Gandhian pacifism and Bose's opportunism. To British audiences, he continued to insist on India's potential to fulfil its side of the Goodfellows bargain.[115]

However, the war had upset the delicate balance in Congress in favour of those who favoured confrontation over working constitutional reforms. Gandhi opposed war on principle, and hoped that his philosophy of non-violence might render armed defence unnecessary. In 1940, he threatened to start a fast if Congress joined a national government, and 'fostered a war-like spirit'. Others, including Rajagopalachari, were prepared to enter government in return for immediate independence. The leadership was also divided over whether to exploit Britain's difficulties by threatening civil disobedience. Bose, though now outside Congress, continued to lead a disaffected group of younger Congressmen and Congresswomen who pressed for direct action. Other Congress politicians had settled to the work of provincial government, and were loath to give up the spoils of office. Accordingly, Congress embarked on a series of unstable compromises designed primarily to allow the agitators to let off steam without giving the British an excuse to crush the movement, and to provide limited support for the war effort without alienating the Gandhian wing. The leadership first called upon the provincial ministries to resign, allowing their powers to revert to the Governors. This was a move that Gandhi privately admitted was a way

---

[111] Zetland to Linlithgow, 11 Oct 1939, Linlithgow Coll., MSS/Eur/F125/8; 'Statement by Mr. Attlee and Mr. Greenwood ', 20 Oct 1939, ID/IND/1/72vi, LPA.

[112] Cripps to Nehru, 11 Oct 1939, JNC, v.14.

[113] 'India and the War', 18 Sept 1939, L/PJ/12/323, OIOC.

[114] 'The Statement of the Indian National Congress in Regard to the War', undated but Sept 1939, L/PJ/12/323, OIOC.

[115] Menon to Nehru, 28 and 30 Sept 1939 and undated, KMF, 1/1; 'India and the War', 18 Sept 1939; *Colonial Information Bulletin*, 18 Sept 1939.

of 'cover[ing] the fact that we were crumbling to pieces'.[116] Nehru told Edward Thompson that cooperation in Britain's war effort would in reality be 'an unknown and dangerous adventure':

We shall have nothing to do with it even if the whole Viceroy's Council is offered to us, with the Viceroyalty thrown in. . . We could not do this even if we wanted it. The Congress would throw us overboard. It is a complete change in the outlook, the system, the structure, the objective that is an essential preliminary. If that does not take place we shall wait for a better day.[117]

The resignation of the ministries dismayed the allies of Congress in Britain.[118] Polak told the Mahatma that it was 'a weak and silly policy' and that Congress increasingly exhibited signs of 'intrigue, dishonesty, rancour and dangerous authoritarianism'.

The Congress Party lives in the past, in a realm of suspicion and fear. . . It cannot convince either of its sincerity or of its understanding of major problems affecting the welfare of the nation. . . I should have thought that when the Allied countries are fighting a life and death struggle to destroy all that the Hitler regime stands for. . . you, at least, would have understood that. . . with the ultimate resort once more to argument, reason and conciliation. . . the problem of India's future. . . would be automatically solved.[119]

When Laski asked that Labour should now publicise the terms agreed with Nehru at Goodfellows, Attlee refused.[120] As Congress began to make threats of wartime civil disobedience, Labour criticisms of Congress multiplied and officials noticed a dramatic falling-off of attacks on Government policy.[121] Nehru raged bitterly at the desertion of some of the Labour MPs who had feted him in 1938 but whose support was now so clearly conditional.[122] When Menon suggested that Nehru, not as a Congress leader but 'as a socialist' should appeal 'direct to the

---

[116] Nehru's notes of a lecture by Gandhi 'W[orking] C[ommittee] Wardha, Bapu, June 18 1940', Jawaharlal Nehru Papers, Misc. Draft Resolutions I, NMML.

[117] Nehru to Edward Thompson, 11 Nov 1939, *SWJN*, x, 235–9.

[118] Wedgwood to Linlithgow 5 Jan 1941, Linlithgow Coll., MSS/Eur/F125/130; Zetland to Linlithgow, 18 Jan 1940; 21 Feb 1940, Linlithgow Coll., MSS/Eur/F125/9.

[119] Polak to Gandhi, 23 Nov 1939, Polak Papers, S24, NAI; Polak to Sapru, 8 Feb 1940, SM, I, P120.

[120] Laski, 'Note on Indian Policy', Nov 1939, ID/IND/1/6, LPA; Newman, *Laski*, 222–3; NEC, 6 Feb 1940, LPA; Attlee to Middleton, 22 April 1940, Attlee Papers (Bodleian), MSS.Attlee dep.1.

[121] Zetland to Linlithgow, 24 April 1940; Linlithgow to Zetland, 26 April 1940, Linlithgow Coll., MSS/Eur/F125/9; LPACImpQ Memos. 212A, Jan 1940; 215A, Jan 1940; 218, April 1940, LPA; NEC, 22 May 1940, LPA.

[122] Nehru to Menon, 27 April 1940, *SWJN*, xi, 22–4.

British Labour Movement', he was told angrily that this was impossible and that British socialists were indulging in wishful thinking if they thought Congress would accept 'odd jobs on the Viceroy's Council'.[123]

On joining the Government in May 1940, Labour ministers were remarkably silent on India for the whole of the first year, and seemed reluctant to support even the modest measures of reform that the new Secretary of State, Leo Amery, proposed. Amery's early attempt at a settlement, which would have given India dominion status at the end of the war subject only to the agreement of her politicians and a defence and trade treaty, won Laski's enthusiasm, but bafflingly was not supported in Cabinet by Labour's ministers.[124] The result was a watered-down compromise, the 'August Offer', in which the right of India to make her own constitution and the time-limit were lost, but Britain's continuing duties and responsibilities to the minorities and the defence of India emphasised.[125] Indian leaders were unimpressed by the Offer, and plans for civil disobedience were almost immediately approved.[126] This further alienated and confused Nehru's left-wing allies, because they still believed that, as Nehru had told them, Congress was strongly anti-fascist.[127] 'I have gained a definite impression in my recent conversations with Members—especially Members of the Labour Party—that there has been a genuine stiffening of attitude about India', one MP wrote. 'They feel both bewildered and exasperated by Mr. Gandhi's new line and the anti-war speeches . . .'[128] When the Parliamentary Party met to discuss India, Attlee told Labour MPs that 'Congress played politics all the time. It w[oul]d not accept any responsibility. It w[oul]d not move until it had a date for Dominion Status, when, during the war no one c[oul]d fix a date. There was not much democracy about Gandhi. The minorities everywhere insisted on protection. The Moslem Punjab

[123] Menon to Nehru, 1 Nov 1939, KMP, 10/1/B; Nehru to Menon, 18 Sept 1939 and 13 Nov 1939; Nehru to Menon, 13 Nov 1939, KMP, 10/1/B; Nehru to Menon, 16 May 1940, JNC, v.47.

[124] Amery Diary (unpublished), 7 April 1946, in possession of late Sir Julian Amery; John Barnes and David Nicholson (eds.), *The Empire At Bay: The Leo Amery Diary Vol.2, 1929–45* (London, 1988), 12 July 1940, 632; 25 July 1940, 635–6.

[125] *Hansard*, 5th series, v.364, cols.870–924, 14 Aug 1940; Labour Party, *Report of Annual Conference*, 1941, 59; intercepted telegram from Menon to Nehru, 14 Sept 1940, in L/PJ/12/323, OIOC; Butler to Cripps, 12 Aug 1940, Butler Papers, E3/3/150–55.

[126] Nehru to Carter, 10 Aug 1940, *SWJN*, xi, 114; see also Nehru to Menon, 8 Sept 1940, ibid. 134–135; 'The Parting of the Ways', speech at Allahabad, 10 Aug 1940, ibid. 101–14; Sapru to Shiva Rao, 7 Nov 1940, SM, II, Reel 78.

[127] Wilkinson to Menon, 30 Nov 1940, KMP, 4/22/1.

[128] Schuster to Harrison, 20 Dec 1940, ICG TEMP MSS 48.

contained 70% of the fighting men of India.'[129] After the silence of Greenwood and Morrison allowed Churchill to savage his proposal to release some civil disobedients, Amery wrote bitterly, 'These Labour Members are incredibly feeble creatures.'[130] In October 1941, Laski suggested to a special committee of the PLP and NEC that a Government minister should take an updated version of the Goodfellows agreement to India.[131] But the committee refused most of Laski's recommendations, contenting itself with a reaffirmation of self-government within three years of the war's end and a representative empowered to 'emphasise the importance attached by His Majesty's Government to the full co-operation of all parties in India in the War effort'. Reconstruction of the Viceroy's Council was not even mentioned.[132]

The other principal party to the Goodfellows agreement, the CPGB, was less troubled than Labour by the failure of Congress to support the war. Although for the first month of the war, it had argued for a war on two fronts, against both Nazi Germany and British imperialism, it was soon instructed by the Comintern that the war was a struggle between two imperialisms, which the CPGB should not support. To some, this suggested that rather than 'demand[ing] democracy for the colonies, we must now . . . support colonial insurrection'.[133] Indeed, the Indian Communists, released by the shift of Comintern policy from the obligation to work with the despised bourgeois politicians of Congress, did move to a revolutionary position.[134] But the CPGB does not seem to have seriously adopted revolutionary defeatism at home, let alone a policy of encouraging colonial unrest abroad. It advised the Indian Communists, unsuccessfully, to preserve unity on the left,

---

[129] James Chuter Ede Diary, British Library Additional MSS. 59690–59701, v.1, 29–30 July 1941; Menon to Nehru, 14 Sept 1940, in L/PJ/12/323, OIOC; Draft Reply to NUR in ID/IND/1/17, LPA; NEC, International Sub-Committee, 29 April 1941; NEC, 7 May 1941, LPA.

[130] Amery, *Diary*, 17 Nov and 20 Dec 1941.

[131] NEC International Sub-Committee, 10 Oct 1941; NEC, 22 Oct 1941; Laski to Gillies, 11 Dec 1941, ID/IND/1/41, LPA. Laski's original proposals are in 'Laski's Pamphlet', undated, ID/IND/1/42i–iii, LPA; his first draft for the International Sub-Committee is in 'ISC draft', undated, ID/IND/1/50, LPA.

[132] Laski's handwritten draft of the Joint Committee's conclusions is in ID/IND/1/48, LPA. A second draft in typescript is in ID/IND/1/65, LPA. The amended report as finally submitted to the NEC is in ID/IND/1/49, LPA.

[133] Francis King and George Matthews (eds.), *About Turn : the British Communist Party and the Second World War: The Verbatim Record of the Central Committee Meetings of 25 September and 2–3 October 1939* (London, 1990), 102, 128, 249.

[134] Overstreet and Miller, *Communism in India*, 171–90.

possibly because it feared that India might be used as a base to attack
the Soviet Union which a sectarian policy of agitation might find it hard
to prevent.[135] At home, it raised India as an effective example of the
vagueness of Chamberlain's war aims, and the imperialist character of the
war.[136] Menon found the new CPGB position got him off the hook on
which Congress' war policy had threatened to impale him. His speeches
and writings such as *Why Must India Fight?* (1940) argued that Congress
was justified in refusing to participate in what was now an imperialist
war.[137] He became a prominent and popular speaker for—and member
of the Executive of—the People's Convention, a Communist-inspired
campaign of popular demands designed to position the CPGB as
the defender of working-class interests in a period of rationing and
growing labour regulation. The resolutions adopted by the Convention
included a call for Indian independence.[138] Against the background
of an otherwise unpopular set of commitments, indeed, the CPGB's
line on India was a relatively strong one, which reduced the pre-war
tensions between its position and that of Congress. It could be put
forward undiluted by the shift to a more defencist and nationalist
stance—effectively an unacknowledged shift back towards the 'war on
two fronts' line—which followed the fall of France and the threat
of invasion in May 1940. But it was fragile too: what made the war
imperialist to Congress—the absence of any commitment to freeing
India as one of its aims—was not the same as what made it imperialist
to the CPGB—the fact that the Soviet Union was not engaged in it.

This drove Menon's India League closer to the CPGB, reducing
further his independence. When he had tried to set up student branches
of the IL in university cities, the CPGB students swamped them, through
their growing control of the student Majlises.[139] The organisation of

[135] Michael Carritt, 'India Before the Storm', *Labour Monthly*, May 1940, 294–5;
R. P. Dutt, Notes of the Month, *Labour Monthly*, May 1941, 209–10.

[136] R. P. Dutt, Address to Federation of Indian Students, 18 April 1940, Dutt Papers,
K4/1939–40; Michael Carritt, 'The Crisis in India', *Labour Monthly*, Feb 1941, 75–82;
Harry Pollitt, 'India: A Call to the British People', *Labour Monthly*, June 1941, 263–5;
King and Matthews, *About Turn*, 83, 222, 247, 270; Morgan, *Against Fascism and War*,
186.

[137] V. K. Krishna Menon, *Why Must India Fight?* (India League, 1940); 'V.K.Krishna
Menon', 11 Oct 1939; Scotland Yard Report, 13 Dec 1939, L/PJ/12/323, OIOC.

[138] 'V. K. Krishna Menon's Activities', 9 Aug 1941, L/PJ/12/323, OIOC; Morgan,
Against Fascism and War, 185–9, 205; Neil Redfern, *Class or Nation, vol.1: Communism,
Imperialism and Two World Wars* (London, 2005), 146.

[139] 'The India League and other Indian Societies in London', 30 March 1939,
L/PJ/12/452, OIOC. For the CPGB's organisation of Indian students, see Scotland

students, Pollitt told Menon, was a party matter, and the IL must remain a propagandist body. It was the same story with the Indian seamen: Menon was told that he should no longer organise them himself, but must work through the CPGB's organisations.[140] When Menon feebly told the CPGB leaders that unless they stopped undermining his work, he would come out against them, they withheld their support and threatened to favour Kumria's Indian Swaraj League—now, through the CPGB's anti-war stance, a possible alternative—until he fell back into line.[141] Nevertheless, as long as he did as he was told, Menon was provided with much-needed support. IL branches with strong Labour Party membership were folding though irritation at Congress's hesitation over the war, and the division between Labour and non-Labour members on other issues.[142] In 1940, Scotland Yard commented that Menon was 'suffering on the one hand from fear that without aid from the CPGB he cannot fill the Kingsway Hall . . .[and] on the other from apprehensions that the meeting may be turned into a battleground on the question of the [Soviet] invasion of Finland, which would be definitely distasteful to orthodox Labour Party Members.'[143] More damagingly still, Menon's Labour parliamentary candidacy at Dundee was revoked. The main issue was not his advocacy of Indian independence or even of the Congress position, but his closeness to the CPGB, especially over Finland and the advocacy of peace councils.[144] The National Agent recommended that Menon be deselected on the grounds that he had a 'double loyalty'.[145] Following Menon's deselection, and his resignation from the Party, IL meetings attracted very little support from Labour.

When the Soviet Union entered the war in June 1941, however, the CPGB's expectations of Congress altered sharply again. It was now

Yard Reports, 16 Dec 1936, 23 Nov 1937, 23 March 1938, L/PJ/12/4, OIOC; 30 June 1938, L/PJ/12/293, OIOC; 16 June 1937, 12–14 April 1938 and 14–15 April 1939, L/PJ/12/475, OIOC.

[140] Scotland Yard Report, 30 March 1939, L/PJ/12/452, OIOC.

[141] 'The India League and Connected Organisations', 1 Aug 1939, L/PJ/12/452, OIOC; 'V. K. Krishna Menon', 10 June 1940, L/PJ/12/323, OIOC; Scotland Yard Reports, 30 June 1940, L/PJ/12/384, OIOC; 27 Nov 1940, L/PJ/12/4, OIOC.

[142] Scotland Yard Report, 16 Oct 1940, L/PJ/12/453, OIOC.

[143] Scotland Yard Report, 17 Jan 1940, L/PJ/12/323, OIOC.

[144] Middleton to Bell, 20 Jan 1941, KMP, 1/10/14, OIOC; 'V. K. Krishna Menon', 10 June 1940, L/PJ/12/323, OIOC; 'Indian Communist Activities in London', 29 July 1940, L/PJ/12/384, OIOC.

[145] 'National Agent's Opinion on the Parliamentary Candidature of Mr. Krishna Menon', annexed to NEC, 27 Nov 1940, ID/IND/1/13, LPA.

expected to return to government on the best terms obtainable, and to mobilise India's resources for war.[146] There was not much enthusiasm for this in India. Now outside the Labour Party, Menon needed the CPGB more than ever, and therefore oscillated uncertainly between the priorities of Comintern and Congress, pleasing neither side. Almost continually from June 1941 onwards, he frantically cabled Nehru in India to ask for a clear offer of mobilisation against fascism. Nehru was unable to help and criticised Menon's 'complete misunderstanding' of the situation.[147] When Menon took this news to the CPGB, its response was frosty.[148] The IL continued to promise that an anti-fascist India was ready to support the war, if only a national government were provided.[149] By the end of 1941, the Communists were accusing Menon of the 'dangerous fallacy' of supposing that India could not help the USSR until it was free.[150] Nevertheless, Menon and the CPGB remained unhappily yoked together. The CPGB had concluded that Menon was 'not sufficiently opportunist for Communist purposes' but found its new priorities made it hard to find an alternative. Menon, depressed by the inability of Nehru to help him, struggled for independence of the CPGB, but realised that his close identification with it since 1938 had reduced his alternatives: the CPGB could now 'make or mar his meetings'. By late 1941 the India League actually contained very few Indians, and even fewer who exercised any influence over it. Each local branch Menon tried to set up, the police reported, 'more often than not falls on sterile or already over-occupied ground and . . . either fails to germinate or turns into a sickly plant'.[151] Those branches which survived did so because of the support the CPGB gave to them, and they proved refractory as a result, taking their orders from the Party, and, 'addicted to using their Communist talents for organisation over his head and in directions contrary to

[146] Dutt to Menon, 1 Aug 1941, Dutt Papers, K4/1941–2.

[147] Menon to Nehru, 15 and 30 Dec 1941, 22 Jan and 31 May 1942, JNC v.47; Nehru to Menon, 16 and 31 Dec 1941, 2 Feb 1942, 5 June 1942 *SWJN*, xi, 32, 60; xii, 116, 339.

[148] 'Note on Krishna Menon and the India League Office, London', 27 Jan 1941; 'V. K. Krishna Menon's Activities', 5 Aug 1941; 'The Present Position of the India League', 5 Nov 1941, L/PJ/12/453, OIOC.

[149] V. K. Krishna Menon, 'Freedom's Battle', *Labour Monthly*, Aug 1941, 364–7; 'India in the War', *Labour Monthly*, Jan 1942, 26–8.

[150] 'V. K. Krishna Menon's Activities', 5 Aug 1941; 'Reactions to the release of Nehru, Azad and others', 9 Dec 1941, L/PJ/12/323, OIOC; 'The Present Position of the India League', 5 Nov 1941, L/PJ/12/453, OIOC.

[151] 'The Present Position of the India League', 5 Nov 1941.

his wishes', issuing statements which subordinated Congress demands to those of the CPGB. They also increasingly demanded that the IL be run in a more democratic fashion, a move clearly intended to facilitate greater Communist control, which Menon refused to accommodate.[152]

By the end of 1941, therefore, the anti-fascist alliance with the British left that Nehru had helped to construct in 1938 was in tatters. 'You do not seem to like Mr Gandhi, though you have a partiality for me', Nehru wrote angrily to one Labour MP. '[P]erhaps what I have written will lead you to revise your opinion of my "statesmanship".'[153] With the defections of both Labour and Communists, support in Britain for Nehru was now reduced to a handful of rebels in Parliament such as Bevan, and, outside, a loose collection of progressive activists, writers and intellectuals. Ironically, Nehru's most loyal supporters were now those whom his 1938 policy had excluded, such as Brockway and the pacifists.[154] Nevertheless, the entry of Japan into the war, combined with an unexpectedly powerful groundswell of popular distress at military losses in the east, created political pressure sufficient to justify a fresh approach by the British Government: the Cripps Mission to India of March 1942. I have explored the origins and failure of the Mission in some detail elsewhere.[155] Here it is sufficient to note that the pressure for the Mission came not from the Labour Party leaders in government, keen but now sceptical about the possibility of a wartime deal with Congress, but from lower down in the party, and a plethora of other left-inclined groups, which still had unrealistic expectations about the scope for an agreement. However, the prospect of invasion and British defeat had further polarised the already divided views within Congress, shattering the formula that had hitherto held non-violent Gandhians, socialists and nationalists in uneasy unity. The Gandhians regarded the threatened invasion as an important test of their pacifism. Others opposed participation in war not because of its violence but because it would deprive the movement of Gandhi's leadership at a crucial time. It would be 'nothing short of a calamity', Prasad, Patel and two other senior Congress leaders

---

[152] 'The India League and other Indian activities in the United Kingdom', 10 March 1942, L/PJ/12/454, OIOC.
[153] Nehru to Wedgwood, 21 Nov 1941, intercept in Hallett Coll., MSS/Eur/E251/61.
[154] *New Leader*, 27 Oct and 3 Nov 1939, 25 April 1940.
[155] Nicholas Owen, 'The Cripps Mission: A reinterpretation', *Journal of Imperial and Commonwealth History*, 30/1 (2002), 61–98.

announced, in which Congress would 'lose everything including what
we have achieved for the last twenty years'. If Congress chose it, then
they would resign.[156] Others still believed that for Congress to take
office under the British would make it much harder for it to settle
with the Japanese when they arrived.[157] Most of the Congress leaders
doubted their ability to improve India's chances of repelling invasion.
On the contrary, association with the necessary activities of resistance
was likely to make Congress less, not more popular.[158] Siding with
the British would entail asking Indians to fight those 50,000 other
Indians training in Malaya under Bose's leadership in support of the
imminent Japanese invasion of the subcontinent. For Congress to associate itself with these activities, in support of a power which few
believed could defend India effectively, was for most of the Working
Committee simply too risky.[159] There were some willing to take the
risk, but their price for doing so had sharply risen. Rajagopalachari
demanded a share in power for Congress at the centre, not merely
in the provincial governments.[160] Nehru thought even this too little,
accusing Rajagopalachari of 'lining up with British policy almost as
it is'.[161] 'Nothing could be more dangerous', he told Rajagopalachari,
than to be 'saddled with responsibility without complete power'. It was
'inconceivable' to suppose that the British would part with complete
power in wartime, and 'partial power will make our position worse'. '[I]t
is much too late for any compromise to take place', he wrote, 'for the
very minimum conditions on our part are far beyond what the British
Government might do.'[162] But the Cripps Offer fell far short of the

---

[156] Statement to the Press by Prasad, Patel, Kripalani and Ghosh, 3 Jan 1942, in
Valmiki Choudhary (ed.), *Dr. Rajendra Prasad: Correspondence and Select Documents* (20
v., New Delhi, 1984–95), v, 331–2. The extract is wrongly dated in this source. For the
correct dating, see *Indian Annual Register*, 1942, i, 31.

[157] Nehru, reported in Linlithgow to Amery, 12 Feb 1942, *TP* I 108. See also speeches
in *SWJN*, xii, 61–72, 93–9, 102–16, 133–6.; G. B. Pant, 'Responsibility for India's
Defence', in B. R. Nanda (ed.), *Selected Works of Govind Ballabh Pant* (17 v., 1993–) ix,
389–91.

[158] Note by Sir S. Cripps, 'My Interview with Jawaharlal Nehru', 30 March 1942,
TP I 449; *Harijan*, 22 March 1942.

[159] Report of a meeting between Nehru and Col. Johnson, 6 April 1942, *TP* I 540.

[160] Rajagopalachari, Speech at AICC meeting, 16 Jan 1942, cabled Linlithgow to
Amery, 18 Jan 1942, *TP* I 17; 'My interview to Sri C. Rajagopalachari', 28 March 1942,
TP I 412.

[161] Nehru to Sampurananand, 14 Dec 1941, *SWJN*, xii, 15–16.

[162] Nehru to Rajagopalachari, 26 Jan 1942, *SWJN*, xii, 91–2; Shiva Rao to Sapru, 26
Jan 1942, SM, I, R184/1; Report of the Working Committee meeting of 1 April 1942,
Home Political 221/42-Poll(I), NAI.

complete power Nehru needed.[163] It could only have succeeded had the British War Cabinet been prepared and able to expand the terms of the Offer to guarantee that the Viceroy's Executive would normally operate like a cabinet. But although they wished to see representative Indians brought on to the Executive, they had already rejected full Indianisation and the adoption of new Viceregal conventions.[164] Attlee remained very reluctant to allow the unreformed and undemocratic Congress leadership to assume control in the Executive without either a strong legislature or special powers for the Viceroy to hold it in check. Cripps too, though desperate to get Congress to enter government, believed that it should do so under existing constitutional arrangements, confident that its powers would grow with their exercise.[165] Thus hardly anyone in the British Government was prepared to see Congress given strong guarantees in advance that the Viceroy's Council would operate in wartime as a cabinet, and hardly anyone on the Congress Working Committee was prepared to enter wartime government unless they got them. Both the War Cabinet, keen to show its critics that something was being done to win Indian support for the war, and the Congress leaders, anxious to preserve their movement's unity and popularity, had good reason to negotiate, and to lay the blame on the other for the failure of the negotiations. But neither had sufficient reason to give way.

After Cripps returned, both the Labour Party and Congress still hoped for the reopening of negotiations.[166] But Congress soon began plans for renewed civil disobedience. Its policy of seeking accommodations with the British now discredited, the leadership now had to move quickly in the opposite direction to outflank the increasing numbers who favoured pushing the British out without delay. The renewed threat of civil disobedience brought all Labour's suspicions back to the surface again. Now even Laski turned against Gandhi, accusing him of tactical naivety. 'Alongside his errors', he wrote, 'even

---

[163] Amery to Hardinge, 2 March 1942, *TP* I 208; Amery to Linlithgow, 2 March 1942, *TP* I 218.

[164] This was suggested by Amery (*TP* I 165); considered by India Committee (*TP* I 191); and redrafted by Cripps (*TP* I 223 and 229).

[165] Reginald Coupland, *Diary* (Rhodes House Library, Oxford), 184, 203, 227.

[166] *World News and Views*, 25 April 1942; Dutt to CPI, 10 May 1942, Dutt Papers, K4 1941–2; Scotland Yard Reports, 12 May and 10 June 1942, L/PJ/12/454, OIOC; NEC, 5 June 1942, LPA; Report of Joint Committee (Sub-Committee), 21 July 1942, NEC, 22 July 1942, LPA; 'Indian Notes', 10 June 1942, L/PJ/12/646, OIOC.

the follies of the India Office are small.'[167] The Labour ministers in Cabinet raised no objection to Churchill's proposal to arrest Gandhi if it seemed necessary.[168] The NEC statement argued that the 'very contemplation' of civil disobedience was 'proof of political irresponsibility'.[169] The CPGB had privately regarded the Cripps offer as inadequate, but argued nonetheless that Indians should accept any reasonably progressive compromise.[170] It regarded civil disobedience as 'disastrous, harmful and weakening', even 'suicidal', and urged the CPI to seize the leadership of a united national front to prevent it.[171] Menon was paralysed by the severity of the conflicting pressures on him: the India League postponed its planned protest meeting and, the police reported, 'he personally does not know what to do or say'.[172] When the War Cabinet, chaired by Attlee, was presented with fresh evidence, Linlithgow's plans to arrest Gandhi and the Working Committee were approved.[173] Amery was impressed by the Labour members' resolution.[174]

On 8 August, by a majority of 250 to 13, the All-India Congress Committee ratified the 'Quit India' resolution, which sanctioned 'a mass struggle on non-violent lines on the widest possible scale'. Early the following morning, Gandhi and the Congress Working Committee of Congress were arrested, marking the start of spontaneous and popular outbursts across India.[175] Labour's India committee approved

---

[167] *Reynolds News*, 12 July 1942.

[168] Amery to Linlithgow, 15 July 1942, *TP* II 269.

[169] Labour Party, *Report of Annual Conference*, 1943, 39–40; *The Times*, 23 July 1942; Amery to Linlithgow, 24 July 1942, *TP* II 323.

[170] 'India', 31 March 1942, Dutt Papers, K4/1941–2; 'The India League and other Indian activities in the United Kingdom', 10 March 1942, L/PJ/12/454, OIOC; 'Indian Notes', 9 May 1942, L/PJ/12/323, OIOC; Intelligence Report, 3 June 1942, in Home-Poll 1/1/42 Poll (I), NAI.

[171] Political Letter—India', 29 July 1942, Political Statement on the Indian National Congress, 7 Aug 1942, Dutt Papers, K4 1941–2; Scotland Yard Report, 25 Aug 1942, L/PJ/12/454, OIOC; Clemens Dutt, 'India and Freedom', *Labour Monthly*, Aug 1942, 247–50; R. P. Dutt, 'India—What Must be Done', *Labour Monthly*, Sept 1942, 259–68; Pollitt to Nehru, 29 July 1942, CPGB Individual Coll (Pollitt), CP/IND/POL/3/11; Resolution of CPGB Central Committee, 20 Aug 1942, CPGB Central Committee, CP/CENT/CIRC/01/02.

[172] 'Menon's Private Views', 16 July 1942, L/PJ/12/454, OIOC; Scotland Yard Report, 19 Aug 1942, L/PJ/12/323, OIOC.

[173] Government of India Home Dept. to Secretary of State, 3 Aug 1942, *TP* II 393.

[174] Amery to Linlithgow, 8 Aug 1942, *TP* II 474; Amery, *Diary*, 7 Aug 1942, 824–5.

[175] F. G. Hutchins, *Spontaneous Revolution: Gandhi and the Quit India Movement* (Cambridge, Mass., 1973); R. K. Frykenberg, 'The Last Emergency of the Raj', in H. C.

a statement endorsing the arrests and condemning Congress.[176] For Cripps too this was the final blow. He told Cove and Sorensen that 'it was now a case of open war between India and Britain' and broadcast a justification of the arrests.[177] Nehru wrote bitterly in his prison diary that Cripps had thereby attacked 'injured Indo-British relations far more than any other Englishman could have done'.[178] A very small number of Labour backbenchers criticised the Government, but they spoke 'amid constant jeers' and the majority supported their leaders.[179] Only twelve Labour MPs defied party instructions by voting against the renewal of Governors' rule in the formerly Congress Provinces.[180]

Over the previous twenty years, Labour responses to Congress campaigns had become well oiled.[181] Each wave of non-cooperation—1917, 1930, 1940—had begun with a wave of interconnected agitations, which were then drawn together and focussed on a non-violent, small-scale Gandhian *satyagraha*. The usual Labour response in these early stages had been to express sympathy with Indian grievances and to put pressure on the British Government to respond generously to them. However, when offers were made, no matter how inadequate their terms, Labour applied stronger pressure in the opposite direction: on Congress to engage with the offer made and to enter into formal negotiations. On each occasion, acceptance had proved divisive for Congress, and the offers had been rejected, or accepted on such restricted terms as to make negotiation difficult. This had been so over discussion of the Montagu–Chelmsford legislation in 1919, over participation in the Round Table Conferences of 1930–1, and over the Cripps Mission in 1942. In each case, Labour had urged Congress to make greater concessions, especially when the Party itself had gone out on a limb

Hart (ed.), *Indira Gandhi's India* (Boulder, Color., 1976), 37–66; Stephen Henningham, 'Quit India in Bihar and the Eastern United Provinces: The Dual Revolt', in Ranajit Guha (ed.), *Subaltern Studies* II (Oxford, 1983), 130–79.

[176] Joint Committee Meeting, 4 Aug 1942, reported to NEC, 23 Sept 1942, LPA; Attlee to Churchill, 13 Aug 1942, *TP* I 530.

[177] Report of India League Executive meeting, 19 Aug 1942, L/PJ/12/454, OIOC; *Manchester Guardian*, 27 July 1942.

[178] 'Reply to Stafford Cripps: Statement to the Press', 27 July 1942, *SWJN*, x, 419; Linlithgow to Amery, 4 Aug 1942, *TP* II 404; Amery *Diary*, 7 Aug 1942, 824.

[179] Chuter Ede Diary, v.6, 9 Sept and 6–7 Oct 1942; PLP, Party Meeting, 7 Oct 1942, LPA.

[180] *Hansard*, 5th series, v.383, cols.1458–60.

[181] I owe the idea of this cyclical progression to D. A. Low, who discusses it briefly in his introduction to *Congress and the Raj*, 7–10.

at home to secure any offer at all. The breakdown in negotiations was in turn followed by a secondary wave of wider, less controlled agitation; respectively, the non-cooperation movement of 1920–2, civil disobedience in 1932–3 and the Quit India movement of 1942–5. In each case the British crushed the movement, drawing as they did so some of the Congress leaders into cooperation. It was normal at this stage for British sympathisers to regret the use of repression, and to call for the resumption of negotiations. But they generally doubted that this could achieve real results without some movement from Congress, which in no case came. This second phase of agitation, indeed, was generally characterised by a reversion to wholly *self-reliant* struggle and minimal contact between Congress and its British friends. This in turn led to despair and the condemnation of Congress irresponsibility. Long periods of minimal contact between Labour and Congress then generally followed, mirroring the deadlock in India. In the last of these three cases, Labour responses were much harsher than before, partly because of the repetitiveness of the cycle of expectations and recriminations, partly because of the urgency of wartime cooperation, and partly because Labour had invested much more in securing a settlement.

Quit India shattered what was left of the unity Nehru had briefly achieved. Although the CPGB continued to demand the release of Congress leaders, this was always explicitly for the purposes of the war, not for elections and a constituent assembly, which was the Congress demand.[182] Such a position required a revisionist account of Quit India. Menon and Dutt argued that since the arrests had been preemptive, Congress had never formally answered Gandhi's call to civil disobedience, and that the disturbances were not a national struggle, but just anger at the arrests, fanned by a handful of unrepresentative quislings.[183] This was found insulting by the Congress leaders and by

---

[182] CPGB, *Unity and Victory: Report of 16th Party Congress*, July 1943, 26, 40; R. P. Dutt, 'Mr Amery's Last Chance', 25 July 1944, Dutt Papers, K4/1943–44; Scotland Yard Report, 16 Sept 1942, L/PJ/12/454, OIOC; 'Indian Notes', 14 July 1942, 'Indian Activities', June–July 1943, L/PJ/12/646, OIOC.

[183] *World News and Views*, 15 Aug 1942; V. K. Krishna Menon, *India Faces Peril* (London, 1942); 'Activities of the India League', 8 Sept 1942, L/PJ/12/454, OIOC; Report on India for Politburo, 19 Aug 1942, Dutt Papers, K4/1941–2; Notes for India Debate, 6 Oct 1942, Dutt Papers, K4/1941–2; Preface to the American edition of 'A Guide to the problem of India', 31 March 1943, Dutt Papers, K4/1943–4.

Indians in Britain, as was the CPGB's new-found and opportunistic interest in concessions to Jinnah which it had hitherto opposed. The Indian membership of the IL slumped further as a result, leaving it more British and Communist in membership than ever before.[184] With Nehru in prison again with little prospect of a wartime release, India dropped out of the CPGB's sights. '[T]he same crowd turns up at each successive [IL] meeting', the police found, 'its numbers varying only in proportion to the amount of Communist support lent for the occasion.' The CPGB still held the IL tightly, however, as a guarantee against any reversion to Gandhism or anti-war sentiment.[185] An enquiry into Menon's finances in 1943 found that his personal accounts and those of the IL were intermingled, and dependent on the CPGB, but none of them was much in credit.[186] By 1944, the IL was 'virtually without funds' and being sued by its creditors, entirely reliant on the CPGB for its survival, with the official Labour Party and TUC indifferent or hostile.[187] When the Viceroy asked about interning Menon, the India Office decided there was no evidence that the IL had had sufficient success to warrant it.[188]

Many of those who left the IL joined the Committee of Indian Congressmen (CIC), run by Menon's longstanding rival Pulin Seal and Amiya Bose, Subhas's nephew and a Cambridge student.[189] Its purpose was to articulate the Congress case in Britain without Menon's equivocations.[190] It also worked to protect Indians in Britain from conscription, an objective that Menon and his CPGB backers could not so easily support, given their pro-war stance, but which matched the Congress view that non-resident Indians should not serve in the

---

[184] 'Indian Notes', 13 April 1943, L/PJ/12/455, OIOC; 'Indian Organizations in the United Kingdom: A Review, 1942–43', L/PJ/12/646, OIOC.

[185] 'Indian Notes', 10 June and 14 July 1942, Sept–Oct 1942, 24 Feb 1943, 'Indian Activities', June–July 1943, L/PJ/12/646, OIOC; 'Indian Notes', 13 April 1943, L/PJ/12/455, OIOC.

[186] Special Branch Report on Menon's finances, 23 April 1943, MEPO 38/107, NA.

[187] India League Executive Committee minutes, esp. 10 Aug and 2 Sept 1942, 3 Feb, 2 and 9 June, 7 July, 4 Aug 1943, KMP, 6/20; 'Indian Activities in the United Kingdom', 25 Sept 1944 and 4 March 1945, L/PJ/12/646, OIOC.

[188] Linlithgow to Amery, 23 June 1942, *TP* II 181; Amery to Linlithgow, 16 Dec 1942, *TP* III 280; Note by Patrick, 8 Aug 1942, Note by Morley, 12 Feb 1943, L/PJ/12/323, OIOC.

[189] 'Activities of the India League', 8 Sept 1942, L/PJ/12/454, OIOC.

[190] Committee of Indian Congressmen in Great Britain, *M. K. Gandhi: To Every Japanese* (1942); *Gandhi, Azad and Nehru speak to India and the World: Fateful proceeding of the A.I.C.C. Meeting on August 8 & 9 1942* (London, 1942).

British armed forces.[191] It won considerable support from the ex-patriate Indian community, including such catches as Surat Ali, the CPGB's organizer of the Indian seamen, who seeing that the war offered a chance to improve the dreadful conditions under which the Indian seamen worked, had established a new union free of their control.[192] A further, deliberate contrast with Menon's organ-isation was that the CIC adopted a dual structure: only Indians could join the Committee proper, with foreign (including British) supporters only permitted after May 1943 to join a separate body, the Council for the International Recognition of Indian Independence (CIRII), of which 'complete and absolute control [was] in the hands of Mr P. B. Seal'.[193] This won over most of Menon's former parliamentary allies, including the MPs W. G. Cove, James Glanville, Aneurin Be-van, Frederick Messer, Sydney Silverman, Lord Strabolgi, Rhys Davies and Charles Ammon, as well as the pacifists George Catlin and Vera Brittain.[194]

But there was no escape from engagement with the rivalries of the British left. Bose and Seal took up Brockway's offer to organise a wider Indian Freedom Campaign (IFC), comprising ILP-ers, pacifists, liberals such as Edward Thompson, and the British Centre Against Imperialism, the latest attempt by the ILP to establish an international anti-imperialist front. It stood for complete independence for India without reference to the war issue at all, or any promises of joint action against fascism. Brockway appointed himself its chair and used it to publicise the 'fundamental difference of principle' it had with the IL over the war.[195] Its devotees, who included Reginald Reynolds

---

[191] See Committee of Indian Congressmen, 'Indians and Military Conscription', 4 Feb 1944, Catlin Papers, 137; Brockway to IFC supporters, 18 Jan 1944, Catlin Papers, 159; Swaraj House, 'Conscription of India Residents in Great Britain', 1 Feb 1944, P.B.Seal Coll., MSS Eur/Photo Eur/446/3; Brockway to Bose, 28 Jan, 4 and 5 Feb 1944, intercepts in Home-Political 51/3/44, NAI; *New Leader*, 26 Feb 1944; *Tribune*, 28 Jan 1944.

[192] Visram, *Asians in Britain*, 239–53.

[193] 'Propaganda in Britain and other European Countries', undated, P.B.Seal Coll., MSS/Eur/Photo Eur/446/5; Report of meeting of CIC, 7 May 1943, in L/I/1/892, OIOC; Catlin, *In the Path of Mahatma Gandhi*, 139, 267–9.

[194] Scotland Yard Report, 19 Aug 1942; 'Activities of the India League', 8 Sept 1942, L/PJ/12/454, OIOC.

[195] Report of ILP Conference, 6 Dec 1942, KV 2/1920, NA; *New Leader* 22 Aug, 19 Sept 1942.

and former Indian Leaguer J. F. Horrabin, turned up at Menon's meetings to insist on amendments to this effect. However, it was almost entirely dependent on the ILP and the pacifist Peace Pledge Union for distribution, mailing lists and funds.[196] These arrangements were soon resented by the Indians, who found Brockway exercised a tight and political control over whom he would work with. The details of this are not altogether clear from some very angry correspondence. Possibly Brockway remembered Seal's days as an ally of the CPGB in the destruction of the London Branch and Dara's Indian National Congress League. Certainly the Indians recalled Brockway's preference for Dara. '[I]t is clear', Amiya Bose wrote, 'that what you require is not real Indian support, but an Indian protégé whom you can parade before the public as a representative of Indian opinion and get a hearing... You have... spoken against... everyone who has been helpful to us.'[197]

The IFC was a very mixed collection of bedfellows, defined more by those who were missing than those who were there. British pacifists had, under the pressures of war and a growing sense of the impracticability of Gandhism as an anti-fascist manoeuvre, largely rejected political Gandhism—that is, the intention of using collective non-violent resistance directly to confront the aggressor—in favour of quietist exercises in communal living and personal witness-bearing.[198] Nevertheless, they still looked to India and Gandhi in particular to set a moral example to a world at war.[199] Thus while they campaigned vigorously for the release of Indian prisoners, they were keen that this should not be for any warlike purpose.[200] On the IFC they clashed with fellow-members

[196] Manifesto for Indian Freedom Campaign, Catlin Papers, 78; 'Indian Independence: What Must be Done', Catlin Papers, 137; Minutes of Indian Freedom Campaign Working and Campaign Committees, 19 Oct, 24 Nov, 8 Dec 1942, Catlin Papers, 159; Housman to Reynolds, 1 Sept and 30 Nov 1942, Housman Corr., v.2; Brockway *et al.* to Murry, 25 Sept 1942, copy in KV2/1920, NA; *Peace News*, 9 and 30 Oct, 27 Nov 1942; *New Leader*, 17 and 24 Oct 1942, 9 Jan, 13 and 27 Feb, 6 Mar, 1 May 1943; Pittock-Buss to Pope, 12 July and 12 Sept 1944, intercepts in Home-Political 51/3/44, NAI.

[197] A. N. Bose to Brockway, 4 Feb 1944, copy in Catlin Papers, 143; Brockway to Pope, 31 Aug 1944, intercept in Home-Political, 51/3/44, NAI.

[198] See, for example, comments of Murry, *Peace News*, 23 Feb 1940.

[199] Vera Brittain, *Wartime Diary* (ed. Aleksandra Bennett and Alan Bishop) (London, 1989), 193, 209–10.

[200] *Peace News*, 11 Sept 1942.

such as Edward Thompson who wanted to enlist Congress for war.[201]
The ILP, which also supported the IFC, was internally divided between
those who wanted to support Congress demands for immediate independence, and the Trotskyists, powerful in some ILP branches, who
regarded even the Congress left as irretrievably bourgeois, and called
for a mass struggle in India under proletarian leadership, as they had
from the start.[202] Certainly, some Indians too, used to working with
the CPGB, found it hard to re-align themselves towards the Trotskyists
and pacifists of the IFC. To one of them, Seal wrote that although his
private sympathies were with the CPGB and not the ILP and PPU,
he was guided by the latter's support for Congress, no longer available
from the former.[203]

The CIC also suffered slow atrophy through its association with
Subhas Bose, now widely known to be developing a fighting force
to assist Japan in the war. Amiya Bose and Seal were regarded by
officials as potential fifth columnists and were listed for internment
in the event of a German invasion of Britain, although the CIC does
not seem to have endorsed Subhas Bose's arguments publicly.[204] Those
Congress Indians in Britain more sympathetic to Nehru and Gandhi
than Bose therefore left the CIC, not to return to the India League,
but to form a third bloc of support in yet another organisation: Swaraj
House. This stood for Congress and its demand for independence
without any recourse to British support at all, but in opposition to Bose.
Along with the Indian Workers Union, which successfully took away
from Menon those Indian workers in British provincial towns hitherto
loosely allied to the IL, it formed a Federation of Indian Associations
in the UK.[205]

---

[201] *Peace News*, 6 Feb, 10 April and 12 June 1942; Housman to Reynolds, 30 Nov
and 30 Dec 1942, Housman Corr., v.3; Brockway to Naidu, 22 Feb 1944, intercept in
Home-Political 51/3/44, NAI.

[202] Howe, *Anticolonialism*, 109–10, 116; *New Leader* 1 May 1943; Trotsky, 'An
Open Letter to the Workers of India', *New International*, 5/9 (Sept 1939), 263–6; 'India
and the War', *Workers' International* News, 2/12, Dec 1939, 10–12; Ajit Roy, 'Friends
of India', *Workers' International News*, 5/8, Jan 1943, 8–9.

[203] Seal to Sankara [?Mitter], undated but 1943, P.B.Seal Coll., MSS/Eur/Photo
Eur/446/3.

[204] 'Propaganda in Britain and other European Countries', undated, P.B.Seal Coll.,
MSS/Eur/Photo Eur/446/5; Scotland Yard Report, 10 March 1942, L/PJ/12/454,
OIOC; 'Indian Notes', 9 May 1942, LPJ 12/323, OIOC.

[205] Sasadhar Sinha, *Indian Independence and the Congress* (London, 1943); 'Indian
Notes, Sept—Oct 1942', 'Indian organizations in the United Kingdom: A Review,

Menon rightly recognised the IFC and the CIC as directed against the IL. They were, he lamented, 'doing more harm to the cause of Indian independence than all the British officials put together'.[206] The CPGB summoned a meeting of British-based Indians in the hope of bringing them back to the India League. But Dutt, chairing it, could not resist railing against the 'pathetic' advocacy of Quit India, the 'complete impotence' of pacifists, the 'absolutely hopeless' CIC and the 'very heavy liability' of Gandhi's leadership. As an effort to achieve unity, this predictably failed, perhaps because as Anand argued at the meeting itself, Dutt had not asked the Indian audience for suggestions for achieving unity.[207] When Reginald Sorensen, one of Menon's few remaining parliamentary supporters, spoke on an IFC platform, Menon threatened to resign unless he withdrew. The IFC, he insisted, was 'not a pacifist body with religious convictions but . . . a cover for ILP and other hostile elements'. Its policies could ' do nothing but harm to India and the cause of freedom'.[208] Sorensen resented such exclusiveness, and angrily pointed out that he had spoken on platforms with CPGB speakers without protest.[209] Menon wrote back no less bitterly that it was a mistake to 'regard everyone interested in India as one wholesome lot of friends'.[210] The results of this fragmentation were predictable and damaging, as the India League and its rivals organised their meetings competitively, briefed against each other to their respective British audiences, and fought each other for support, even establishing separate relief committees to raise funds for the victims of the Bengal famine, which they interpreted according to predictable and distinct political positions.[211] All this went on with almost no interaction with India itself. From 1942 to 1944, the CIC and Swaraj House wrote regularly to Congress to persuade the Gandhians that

1942–43', L/PJ/12/646, OIOC; 'Indian Notes', 13 April 1943, L/PJ/12/455, OIOC; Federation of Indian Associations in the United Kingdom, 'Our Search for Unity' (1943), copy in AICC G55/1942.

[206] Scotland Yard Report, 17 Feb 1943, L/PJ/12/455, OIOC.

[207] Invitation Meeting, 11 Feb 1943, Dutt Papers, K4/1943–4; 'India League', 6 Jan 1943, L/PJ/12/455, OIOC

[208] Menon to Sorensen, 10 and 15 May 1943, KMF, 2/2.

[209] Sorensen to Menon, 10 May 1943, KMF, 2/2.

[210] Menon to Sorensen, 20 July 1943, KMF, 2/2.

[211] 'Indian organizations in the United Kingdom: A Review, 1942–43'; Indian Freedom Campaign, *Indian Famine: The Facts* (London, 1944); V. K. Krishna Menon, 'Famine in India', *Labour Monthly*, Oct 1943.

the IL's failures over Quit India and its CPGB connections damned it as only a 'fairweather friend' of the Congress.[212] But like every other attempt to gain authority to speak for Congress in Britain, these failed.[213] 'They are all, of course, a great nuisance,' wrote one official of the metropolitan anti-imperialists, 'but to some extent cancel each other out.'[214]

[212] Kumria to Nehru, 19 July 1942 and undated, Kumria to Kripalani, 1 June 1946, Iqbal Singh to Nehru, 14 July 1946, AICC G55/1942; A. N. Bose to Catlin, 9 Dec 1944, 13 and 31 Jan, 11 March 1945, Catlin Papers, 143; Brockway to Naidu, 22 Feb 1944, Surat Ali to Gandhi, 2 Oct 1944, Pope to Shah, 8 Nov 1944, intercepts in Home-Political 51/3/44, NAI.

[213] 'Indian Activities in the United Kingdom', 4 March 1945, L/PJ/12/646, OIOC.

[214] Morley to Dudley, 12 May 1943, L/I/1/892, OIOC.

9

Labour and India, 1942–7

The history of the constitutional negotiations leading to Indian independence is already well known, and it will not be profitable to repeat it here.[1] Assessments have usually been made using managerial and technical criteria: the Government's sensitivity to the details of the multiply-constituted 'Indian problem', its capacity to build and impose a consensus, to honour pledges and protect the national interest: in sum, its *grip*. The assessors have usually awarded it high marks. For R. J. Moore, this was an 'escape from empire'. For Kenneth Morgan, Attlee emerged as 'a liberator, the leader of his government and the architect of the new Commonwealth'.[2] Attlee's official biographer is equally fulsome: 'From start to finish, he moved steadily and unshakeably, coolly and adroitly according to his plan, stepping up the pace towards the end with fine judgement.'[3] I have suggested elsewhere that this picture of calm, logical grip is slightly at odds with the pessimistic and sometimes panicky process revealed in the Cabinet and private papers.[4] Nonetheless, it is clear that the Attlee Government did not find it as hard as the MacDonald Goverments had to control policymaking, so it is worth considering what had altered by 1945, and how Labour's engagement with the machinery of imperial governance took place on changed terms. We shall also examine the endgame of Indian decolonisation in the light of the other themes of the book: the Labour Party's long debate over the compatibility of socialism,

---

[1] See Moore, *Escape from Empire*.

[2] Kenneth O. Morgan, *Labour People* (Oxford, 1987), 142.

[3] Kenneth Harris, *Attlee* (London, 1982), 386. See also Carl Bridge and H. V. Brasted, 'Labour and the Transfer of Power in India: A Case for Reappraisal?' *Indo-British Review*, 14/2 (1987), 70–90 and '15 August 1947: Labour's Parting Gift to India' in Jim Masselos (ed.), *India: Creating a Modern Nation* (New Delhi, 1990).

[4] Nicholas Owen, 'Responsibility Without Power: The Attlee Government and the End of British Rule in India', in Nick Tiratsoo (ed.), *The Attlee Years* (London, 1991).

democracy and colonial freedom, and the Indian nationalists' search for a form of engagement with Britain which satisfied its desire and need for self-reliant struggle.

In 1945, the Labour Government discovered swiftly that its room for manoeuvre was restricted by hostility between Congress, keen for immediate independence, but fearful that the British were set on encouraging separatist demands, and Jinnah's Muslim League, no longer satisfied with the paper guarantees promised in the Cripps Offer and determined to maintain the strong national claims it had popularised in wartime. Labour's desire was to engineer a reconciliation of these divergent interests which also satisfied its desire to preserve a united India, within the Commonwealth, capable of making a useful contribution to imperial defence, and providing dollar-earning raw materials and a market for industrial exports and capital goods. However, its capacity to achieve such a settlement was set by several interlocking constraints: overstretched global military commitments, financial weakness created by wartime debt and a crippled export trade, a moribund and unpopular civil administration and an increasingly Indianised Indian Army. The tightness of these constraints essentially forced policymaking down a single, narrowing road towards independence and partition. Other, perhaps for Labour more attractive, routes to Indian freedom proved impassable and were soon forgotten. Since this was so, they are almost wholly unknown, though they tell us something important about Labour's attitudes and priorities. It will therefore be worthwhile to start a little earlier than 1945 and examine three initiatives taken in the years between the suppression of Quit India and the 1945 election: first, Labour interest in sponsoring a new political party in India, M. N. Roy's Radical Democratic Party; secondly, the plans drawn up by Cripps and Bevin to use social and economic development schemes in India to salve anti-British grievances and break the unnatural hold enjoyed by Congress over the Indian poor; and thirdly, Attlee's keenness to make an appeal over the heads of the imprisoned Congress leaders to a new generation of more representative local politicians.

After Quit India, the charge that Congress was controlled by the interests of Indian landlords and capitalists found fresh support in the Labour Party. Hugh Dalton, who believed that Indian capitalists were behind Gandhi's 'appeasement [of] the Axis', argued that since Congress did not represent Indian society, the British ought to 'organise, indirectly and discreetly, some alternative political party to Congress . . . to prevent the latter from winning so many elections'.[5] In 1942 just such a fresh opportunity seemed to Labour to present itself. The Party was sent a document entitled 'A People's Plan' by the Radical Democratic Party (RDP). It informed Labour that it had broken away from Congress in order to support the war against fascism. The Congress had become 'a party of industrialists and financiers', but the RDP was 'a party of the . . . people', and its purpose 'the accomplishment of the long-delayed democratic revolution as a necessary precondition for the eventual growth of a socialist society'.[6] The RDP had been founded by M. N. Roy in December 1940 out of the League of Radical Congressmen he had formed to support the war. Roy proposed that Britain should offer non-Congress Indians the chance to form autonomous provincial ministries, and a share of the responsibility for national defence. In return for this, they would guarantee Britain wholehearted support in the war effort.[7] At the head of an anti-fascist front, with British support, Roy hoped the end of the war would find him entrenched in power in Delhi, with a mass movement behind him, confronting a war-weary and discredited British administration.

Roy also sought to win British Labour support by taking control of the AITUC from Congress on the issue of wartime co-operation.[8] In November 1941, he founded the Indian Federation of Labour (IFL), a rival to the AITUC. Ernest Bevin welcomed this development, as he already had the secession of Aftab Ali's Indian seamen's union from the AITUC in 1941.[9] Roy had provided one of the Indian Bevin Boys with RDP propaganda and orders to contact Bevin and other labour leaders on his arrival in England.[10] For Labour, the RDP had impeccable credentials. It was the nationalist party they secretly believed Congress ought to be. Roy had often been regarded by British Labour as an unreliable politician, but his diagnosis of the faults of Congress rang true. RDP attacks on Congress for its 'nationalistic bellicosity [and]

---

[5] Dalton, *War Diary*, 25 Aug 1942 and 16 Dec 1942, 481–3, 537–8.
[6] V. B. Karnik, 'A Short Statement About the Radical Democratic Party', undated copy in ID/IND/2/9, LPA.
[7] M. N. Roy, *India and War* (RDP, Lucknow, Dec 1942).
[8] Karnik, *M. N. Roy*, 460–1; Roy to Karnik, 3 and 5 Sept 1940, M. N. Roy Corr., IC/VBK/Supp-2, NMML.
[9] Aftab Ali to Bevin, 6 Dec 1940; Amery to Bevin, 3 Jan 1941, 1 and 4 Feb 1941, Bevin Papers BEVN(I) 3/1; Amery to Linlithgow, 4 Jan, 6 Feb 1941; 12 June 1941, Linlithgow Coll., MSS/Eur/F125/10.
[10] Roy to Karnik, 21 April 1941, M. N. Roy Corr., IC/VBK/Supp-4 NMML.

reactionary social outlook'—a combination which formed 'the essence of Fascism'—were well calculated to appeal to Labour in the aftermath of Quit India.[11] The RDP's 1942 Party Manifesto provided a critique of Congress which matched that of Labour critics point by point. Congress had refused to resist fascism, the RDP argued, because 'they were never inspired by the modern ideas of democracy and progress. They are an association of conservatives, with a decidedly reactionary outlook' dominated by Gandhi, whose 'idiosyncrasies' they accepted as 'divinely inspired wisdom': '[The RDP] rises on the ruins of the Congress to blaze a new trail .[.]. Its programme is the same as should have been adopted by the Congress, if the latter could be transformed into the political party of the people.'[12] Better still was the RDP's vision of a postwar alliance with 'British Democracy', with the aim of building a post-war socialist 'commonwealth of free nations'.[13] It offered economic cooperation, while darkly hinting that the business-dominated Congress would favour autarchy, and suggested that '[t]he prospects for British exports would be much improved' if an independent India were controlled by 'democratic forces with an internationalist outlook'.[14] Imperialism, Roy assured British Labour, 'could be transformed into a relation of cooperation and mutual inter-dependence'.[15]

In the summer of 1941, a letter from M. N. Roy sent to delegates at the Labour Party Conference had already caused a minor stir.[16] After the failure of the Cripps Mission, interest in an alternative to Congress grew appreciably. The TUC resolved to work with the IFL as well as the AITUC.[17] With the defeat of Quit India, and Congress proscribed, the RDP set up house in London and began making connections with British Labour.[18] Until the outbreak of 'the sabotage movement in India', one of its officials observed, 'the phrase "Indian question" [in Britain] was interchangeable with the "Congress question". Now...

---

[11] *This Way To Freedom: Report of the All India Conference of the Radical Democratic Party* (Dec 1942), 4.

[12] *An Address to British Democracy* (RDP, Dec 1940); Linlithgow to Amery, 1 April 1942, *TP* I 491; *The New Path: Manifesto and Constitution of the Radical Democratic Party* (Delhi, 1943); M. N. Roy, *PostWar Perspective: A Peep into the Future* (London, 1945).

[13] *This Way To Freedom*, 53–7.   [14] Ibid. 97–100.   [15] Ibid. 35–45.

[16] *Manchester Guardian*, 10 Sept 1941; Karnik, *Roy*, 479.

[17] TUC Report to National Council of Labour, 25 July 1942, copy in ID/IND/1/66, LPA.

[18] Karnik, *Roy*, 529; Karnik to Mukherji, 19 Aug 1945, intercept in Home Political 20/20/45-Poll(I), NAI.

the Congress is losing caste with many of its erstwhile admirers.'[19] The RDP's London office was responsible for the production of a steady stream of pamphlets, including *The New India*, which might have been written to reinforce every doubt of Congress legitimacy that Labour had ever entertained. The nationalist movement had started with good intentions, it argued, but as years passed it had become 'more and more narrowly nationalistic in outlook', and less and less representative of the Indian workers and peasants. The war had revealed it in its true colours as the ally of fascism and reaction, and in doing so was creating the conditions for the growth of authentic nationalism rooted in the aspirations of the 'toiling millions'.[20]

Some of this propaganda went home. In January 1944, the RDP was invited to address Labour's Imperial Advisory Committee.[21] In a debate on Indian reconstruction, Labour MP Fred Montague used RDP materials in offering as the 'unexpressed views of large numbers of Members of the Labour Party' a condemnation of the 'great financiers' of Congress.[22] The International Sub-Committee of the NEC agreed that the RDP should be given all the assistance in its power, and its manifesto circulated to senior Party members.[23] It was probably through Montague's influence that the RDP's London head was also invited in March 1945 to a meeting with members of the PLP.[24] At the 1944 Party conference, the NEC spokesman told delegates of a new party which was 'gaining strength all over India', with 'a programme akin to the programme of the Labour Party . . . a working class Party and not a capitalist Party which some of our friends seem to think so much about in the Congress Party'.[25] The RDP's influence was also visible at the TUC.[26] Those closest to Congress did hesitate. Learning from

[19] *This Way to Freedom*, 1–14, 46–8 (the pagination of this pamphlet is rather confused); Pillai to Maxwell, 30 Nov 1943, Home-Political File 7/15/44-Poll(I), NAI.

[20] V. B. Karnik, *The New India: A Short Account of the Radical Democratic Party, Its Programme and Policy* (London, 1944).

[21] LPACImpQ, 24 Jan 1945.

[22] Hansard, 5th ser., v.402, cols.1087–91, 28 July 1944; Amery to Wavell, 1 Aug 1944, *TP* IV 618; Pillai to K. S. Shetty, 4 Oct 1944, intercept, Home-Political 7/15/44-Poll(I), NAI.

[23] NEC, International Sub-Committee. 24 Oct 1944, LPA; LPACImpQ Memo 280, Dec 1944, LPA.

[24] PLP, Admin. Cttee, 15 and 27 March and 19 April 1945, LPA.

[25] Labour Party, *Report of Annual Conference*, 1944, 188–9.

[26] Enclosure in Joshi to Citrine, 5 Oct 1942, AITUC, 23; 'Some Notes on the Present Indian Political Situation' and Gillies to Ridley, 8 Nov 1943, ID/IND/1/83, and ID/IND/1/95, LPA; TUC, *Report of Annual Conference*, 1943, 333–6; *Report of Annual*

Menon that the Labour Party and TUC were contemplating recognition of the RDP, Laski argued that while there might be something to be said for a fight against the capitalist interests in Congress after independence, the multiplication of parties could only delay Indian freedom.[27] But the work of the RDP had, Amery told Wavell, 'thrown a very big brick into the somewhat muddy pool of Labour thought on India'.[28]

After Quit India, Cripps too contemplated a 'flanking attack on the problem now that the direct attack has failed'.[29] In alliance with Bevin, he advocated an appeal over the heads of the party leaderships to the masses rather than Congress. Talking to Patrick Gordon Walker, Cripps stated frankly that his 'only practical aim [was] to split Congress'. There was '[n]o other way of getting any Indian settlement'.[30] The lever was to be socio-economic development. This was not entirely a new idea. In March 1941, the Socialist Clarity Group—a loyalist successor to the Socialist League—had published 'A Policy For India', which argued that '[o]nly a sentimentalist can press for an immediate declaration of Indian independence... leaving an unprepared India to make her way amid the tremendous economic and military-political forces of the twentieth century', and that nation-building under British auspices must precede it. Time for development would allow genuine working-class parties to emerge, 'limit the power of the [Indian] bourgeoisie, and give India a chance to progress towards socialism'.[31] In India in 1939–40, Cripps too had filled his Indian diary with the details of the stirrings of industrial modernisation: rural cooperatives, housing projects, scientific farming and technical institutes. It bears strong similarities to the diary kept thirty years before by his aunt Beatrice Webb on her own visit.[32]

Conference, 1944, 304–5; Pillai to Holland, 24 Oct 1944, intercept, Home Political File 7/15/44-Poll(I), NAI; Nehru to Menon, 31 July 1945, *SWJN*, xiv, 383–7.

[27] Laski to Middleton, 27 Aug 1944, Middleton Papers MID73/92; Middleton to Laski, 30 Aug 1944, Middleton Papers MID73/93; *New Leader* 1 and 15 July 1944.

[28] Amery to Wavell, 19 Oct 1944, *TP* V 58.

[29] Cripps to Harrison, 4 Sept 1942, CAB127/132, NA.

[30] Robert Pearce (ed.), *Patrick Gordon Walker: Political Diaries, 1932–71* (London, 1991), 1 Oct 1942, 113.

[31] Socialist Clarity Group, 'Policy for India', *Labour Discussion Notes*, 21, March 1941; Pearce, *Gordon Walker Diaries*, 5 Aug 1938, 77.

[32] Stafford Cripps and Geoffrey Wilson, Indian Diary, 1939, Cripps Papers (Bodleian), uncat.

Cripps was prompted by Bevin, who suggested to the War Cabinet in August 1942 that the repression of Congress might be accompanied by a more progressive policy to improve social and industrial conditions.[33] With his habitual enthusiasm, Cripps rapidly produced proposals which sought to appeal to Indians, not on the basis of community but class. '[T]he struggle in India would no longer be between Indian and British on the nationalist basis', he wrote, 'but between the classes in India upon an economic basis. There would thus be a good opportunity to rally the mass of Indian opinion to our side.'[34] Officials opposed Cripps' plans, ostensibly on the grounds that to impose a fresh social policy on the Indian provinces was incompatible with existing commitments to self-government, but in practice because they knew that the *raj* did not possess the administative capacity or authority to deal with the conflict that reconstruction would create or the costs of providing it.[35] But the scheme proved impossible to strangle at birth, mainly because, perversely, Churchill was much taken by the idea. For Churchill, Quit India confirmed that Congress only represented 'lawyers, money-lenders and the Hindu priesthood'. Therefore 'it would really pay us to take up the cause of the poor peasant and confiscate the rich Congressman's lands and divide them up'.[36]

Nevertheless, once detailed work was done, and the Viceroy consulted, it was clear that little could be done under British auspices. The war effort precluded any large-scale diversion of resources to social reform, which would in any case only be regarded by Indian opinion as 'death-bed repentance'.[37] '[I]t began gradually to dawn on Cripps and Bevin that we were trying to do something that . . . should have been done

[33] War Cabinet WM(42)117, 24 Aug 1942, WM(42)119, 31 Aug 1942, *TP* II 621, 664; Alan Bullock, *Ernest Bevin: Minister of Labour 1940–1945* (London, 1967), 206; Ernest Bevin, *The Job to Be Done* (London, 1942); Bevin, 'Co-Ordination in the Empire', *The Spectator*, 3 Feb 1939.

[34] 'Note by Sir S. Cripps', 2 Sept 1942, *TP* II 678; Amery to Linlithgow, 30 Oct 1942, *TP* III 128.

[35] Harrison to Cripps, 4 Sept 1942, CAB127/132, NA; Schuster to Cripps, 24 Sept 1942, CAB127/81, NA; Amery to Linlithgow, 1 Sept 1942, *TP* I 673; Amery to Cripps, 2 Oct 1942, *TP* III 54; official discussion of proposals in L/E/8/2527 OIOC.

[36] Amery to Linlithgow, 1 Sept 1942, *TP* II 673; Churchill to Amery, 20 Sept 1942, *TP* II 775. 'I am by no means sure', Amery wrote in his diary after hearing this, 'whether on this subject of India he is really quite sane.' Churchill, he observed in a note pushed across the Cabinet table to Wavell, knew 'as much of the Indian problem as George III did of the American colonies'. Amery, *Diary*, 4 Aug 1944; Amery to Wavell, 10 Aug 1944, *TP* IV 635; Wavell, *Journal*, 27 July 1943, 12.

[37] Linlithgow to Mudaliar, 25 Dec 1942, *TP* III 217; Linlithgow to Amery, 21 Aug 1943, *TP* IV 87.

about 30 years ago at the latest', wrote Amery. The Government of India also advised that 'it was not worth doing anything unless we were prepared to give four to five hundred million pounds free without any controlling conditions'.[38] These were amounts far in excess of the modest £5 million voted for tied schemes in the whole of the colonial empire under the 1940 Colonial Development and Welfare Act. Cripps too was 'considerably shaken'[39] and Amery was able to report to Linlithgow that the scheme was 'very much deflated'.[40]

But Cripps was rarely shaken for long, and kept pushing his ideas on Amery. He and Bevin hoped to use Wavell's appointment as the new Viceroy as a fresh opportunity.[41] Bevin proposed that India's sterling credits be used to pay for industrialisation and the modernisation of agriculture, so as to 'raise the whole standard of living in the East'. '[P]olitically-minded Indians', Bevin asserted, could be 'sidetracked . . . by just paying no attention to them', for with rising Indian living standards, 'the Indian peoples as a whole . . . [would] not trouble their heads about political development.'[42] Cripps' team produced a 'Social and Economic Policy for India' which called for 'a growth of scientific rationalism in the village and the emancipation of the peasant from his ignorance and superstition', to be achieved through an increase in the number of village schools, the introduction of adult education and modern teaching methods. '[A] programme of this kind could be started tomorrow', he claimed, 'if the necessary impulse were given from the centre.' Agricultural productivity was to be improved by technical education, model villages, cooperative methods of production and the provision of credit, rent control and western farming methods. To reduce the isolation of the Indian village, 'nothing would do more than a great road-building campaign'. For town workers, the proposals offered factory legislation, 'estates' of cheap housing, and poverty relief schemes. Industrialisation could not be expected in wartime, but 'there was no reason why India should not make use, straight away, of modern techniques of economic planning

[38] Amery, _Diary_, 29 Sept 1942, 838.
[39] Mudaliar to Linlithgow, 2 Oct 1942, _TP_ III 53.
[40] Amery to Linlithgow, 4 Dec 1942, _TP_ III 251.
[41] Cripps to Amery, 15 Dec 1942, enclosing 'Social and Economic Policy for India', dated 10 Dec 1942, _TP_ III 276; War Cabinet WM(43)85, 15 June 1943, _TP_ IV 2; Wavell, _Journal_, 5 July 1943, 9–10; Bevin to Amery, 24 Nov 1943, _TP_ IV 239; Bullock, _Bevin: Minister of Labour_, 278–80.
[42] Bevin, 'First Draft of a paper for the War Cabinet', 21 June 1943, Bevin Papers, BEVN 2/4/35; Alan Lascelles, Diary, 20 Aug 1943, Bevin Papers, BEVN 9/3.

and the modern device of the public corporation'. Direct taxes on landowners, the encouragement of saving, and a Development Fund provided by the British Government would pay for it.[43] Herbert Morrison too, meeting Wavell before his departure, urged him to 'encourage the masses against the classes by factory legislation, spread of education and mechanisation of farming on the Soviet model'. Wavell was unimpressed. Morrison, he wrote, 'had little idea of the problem, and thought "the depressed classes" and "untouchables" were merely another name for the poor'.[44]

Although one of his first moves was to expand the Viceroy's committees to plan for post-war reconstruction, of whose proceedings Bevin and Cripps were kept informed, Wavell was well aware that extensive British-led intervention in Indian social and economic life was impractical.[45] The structure of the *raj* did not permit British-led development on this scale.[46] Political and administrative necessity had long ago dictated the free market model of economic development favoured by the Government of India. Intervention of the type Cripps suggested was hazardous because the isolated alien bureaucracy of the *raj* in wartime lacked the local knowledge or popular base to justify the sacrifices that its economic policies would make necessary.[47] With nationalist politicians refusing to participate in government, and the *raj*'s own allies with most to lose through reform, there were few mediatory institutions capable or willing to explain British intentions. Cripps and Bevin's plans—if introduced—would have done most for the very least well-off, and this, though admirable in its way, would have done little to weaken Congress. Moreover, as other Fabians realised, too much power had already been delegated in India. It now seemed to Beatrice Webb, in the past herself an enthusiast for developing India, too corrupted by the growth of classes and private interests to be viable for socialism. At the start of the Quit India movement in August 1942, she wrote that the

India conquered by Great Britain is an impossible unit for a sovereign state, with its powerful eighty million Mohammedan population, its Princely provinces, its discordant religious sects and castes. Even within the Congress there is no common living philosophy—Nehru is a Communist, Gandhi is a visionary of

---

[43] Cripps to Amery, 15 Dec 1942.   [44] Wavell, *Journal*, 5 July 1943, 9–10.
[45] Amery to Bevin and Cripps, 21 Jan 1944, *TP* IV 336–7.
[46] Note of an interview with Dalal, 10 Aug 1944, *TP* IV 638.
[47] Tomlinson, *Political Economy*, 102–3, 142.

a fantastic type, the majority being just ordinary profit-making businessmen, or rent-receiving landlords, with a medley of inexperienced reformers of the democratic brand, and a smattering of orthodox and pious Hindus... who would be dead against democratic government, political and industrial, liberal or socialist.[48]

For Attlee, the events of 1942 had revealed a 'degree of totalitarianism in the Congress Party', and the power of Gandhi to act, on occasions, as its dictator.[49] In a series of speeches, he questioned the right of Congress to inherit the *raj*. He continued to defend the post-war provisions of the Cripps Offer as 'the only practicable proposal... whereby all sections of Indian opinion will be able to act together and form their own constitution'.[50] But the Cripps negotiations had shown that Muslim fears of Congress *raj* were genuine, and sparked in Attlee a new sense of the impossibility of reconciling India's communal rivalries.[51] 'We have taught the Indians to desire democracy', Attlee argued, and 'in the Indian provinces... you have Cabinet government and Parliamentary institutions functioning very much as they do here.' But the 'essential thing about democracy' was 'not just its form but its spirit'. For democracy to be introduced successfully in India, '[y]ou must have a willingness to work a democratic system'.[52] The Indians had not learned 'the lesson which we have learned in these islands': tolerance and civic virtue. Without these, it would be 'as useless to expect successful democratic government as it would be to anticipate a fine crop from a field which had never been tilled or tended'. Until it was possible to instil proper democratic values into India's political classes, 'we ought to stand firm where we are'.[53] Attlee also continued to express doubts over the social representativeness of Congress, arguing that in granting self-government to dependent territories, 'all thoughtful people' should be wary of 'handing over those who trust us to be exploited by sectional interests'.[54] Thus, according to Amery, Churchill came to regard Attlee as 'steady and fairly sound' on the Indian issue.[55] Indeed,

[48] Beatrice Webb, *Diary*, 11 Aug 1942.
[49] *Hansard*, 5th ser., v.383, cols.1447–57, 8 Oct 1942; *Hansard*, 5th ser., v.388, cols.136–7, 30 March 1943.
[50] Ibid. v.388, col.138, 30 March 1943.
[51] Ibid. v.383, cols.1447–57, 8 Oct 1942.
[52] Ibid. v.388, cols.136–137, 30 March 1943.
[53] Ibid. v.388, col.136, 30 March 1943.
[54] Attlee, Speech at Carmarthen, 3 Sept 1943, Attlee Papers (Bodleian), dep.10/12.
[55] Amery to Wavell, 15 March 1945, *TP* V 318.

Amery himself was sufficiently impressed by Attlee to recommend him to Churchill as the next Viceroy. Attlee, he wrote, knew the Indian problem and had 'no sentimental illusions as to any dramatic short cut to its solution'.[56]

Attlee refused the offer, but in September 1943, Wavell, the Viceroy-designate, threw a 'spanner in the works' by reviving the idea of bringing Indian politicians on to his Executive.[57] Churchill predictably insisted that victory was 'the best foundation for great constitutional departures'.[58] But Attlee too lined up with the diehard elements, rather than with Halifax and Amery who supported Wavell's plan. He told his colleagues that he 'agreed with the difficulty of having any dealings with Gandhi'. Indeed, 'he was not very keen on having negotiations with the leaders of the political Parties. We were more likely to make a successful approach to the matter if the Centre was built up out of elements drawn from the Provinces and the Indian States, rather than the political Parties.'[59] When Wavell's proposal reached the War Cabinet in October 1943, other Labour ministers agreed. 'Morrison and Bevin were frightened over the Gandhi bogey and talked vaguely of social progress and setting the poor against the rich', wrote Wavell.[60] Attlee and his colleagues 'professed anxiety to give India self-government', but would 'take no risk to make it possible'.[61]

In December 1944, Wavell suggested he should return home to discuss his plan again.[62] Amery told him that in considering the timing of his visit, the 'consideration which weighs most heavily with me is the desirability of Attlee being here'. 'If we have got Attlee', he said, 'we have the strongest possible card to play with Winston.'[63] But again Attlee was unhelpful. He and Morrison did their best to block or postpone Wavell's visit.[64] When Wavell insisted on returning to London in April

[56] Amery to Churchill, 13 Nov 1942, *TP* III 172. Attlee's reaction to the suggestion was 'God forbid'. Churchill thought Attlee was too important to be spared for India, and did not relish losing his support in the War Cabinet. Amery, *Diary*, 14 Oct 1942, 9 Nov 1942, 18 Nov 1942, 839, 841, 844.

[57] Wavell, *Journal*, 10 Sept 1943, 17.

[58] Churchill, 'Indian Policy', 6 Oct 1943, *TP* IV 165.

[59] India Committee, 17 Sept 1943, *TP* IV 120; 29 Sept 1943, *TP* IV 152.

[60] Wavell, *Journal*, 7 Oct 1943, 22–3.

[61] Ibid. 29 Sept 1943, 20; Wavell to Amery, 28 Aug 1944, *TP* IV 674.

[62] Wavell to Amery, 27 Dec *TP* V 164.

[63] Amery to Wavell, 14 and 15 March 1945, *TP* V 314, 318.

[64] Amery to Attlee, 2 Dec 1944, *TP* V 125; Amery to Attlee, 1 Jan 1945, *TP* V 175; Attlee to Amery, 13 March 1945, *TP* V 311; Amery, *Diary*, 5 Feb 1945, 1028.

1945, he found Attlee openly hostile.[65] Amery was puzzled by his Labour colleague's change of attitude. He 'could not understand why the [India] Committee, seeing how far they had been prepared to go in 1942 . . . should now hesitate'.[66] The main reason was Attlee's renewed distaste for the Congress leadership. He told Wavell and Amery that he was 'frankly horrified at the thought of the substitution for the present government of a brown oligarchy subject to no control either from Parliament or electorate'. What really mattered was 'the welfare of the great mass of the people'. He was 'dismayed at the risk that we should hand over the people of India to a few very rich individuals' who could control the political caucuses without responsibility to anyone. The new members would 'owe allegiance to an outside body and not to the Viceroy, who would be forced more and more into the position of a Dominion Governor-General'. Effective control, Attlee feared, 'would pass to an Executive Council responsible only to party caucuses'.[67] Thus when Anderson proposed that Wavell should fill his Executive not with party leaders, but with the nominees of the provincial and central legislatures, Attlee was delighted. The scheme avoided the swamping of the Viceroy's Executive by party caucuses, and 'rested ultimately on election'.[68] It would take longer, but it was to be preferred to the 'reckless' character of Wavell's scheme.[69] Attlee's attitude, Amery wrote angrily, 'really hardly differs from that taken by Winston 10 years ago, namely that we cannot hand India over to Indian capitalists and exploiters'.[70]

Attlee's protests, Cripps' and Bevin's plans and the support of the RDP do not show that Labour had abandoned belief in Indian freedom, but they share a perception that something had gone wrong with Indian nationalism, and a concern to divert it from the sterile oppositional tactics of the Gandhian Congress towards the more constructive channels of nation-building. In defining such constructive work, the Labour leaders fell back upon the paths which had brought their own party

[65] Attlee to Amery, 28 Dec 1944, *TP* V 169; Amery, *Diary*, 18 April 1945, 1037; India Committee, 18 April 1945, *TP* V 396.

[66] India Committee, 10 April 1945, *TP* V 382.

[67] India Committee, 27 March 1945, 5 and 10 April 1945, *TP* V 345, 375, 382.

[68] India Committee, 29 March 1945, *TP* V 348; India Committee, 3 April 1945, *TP* V 369; India Committee, 5 April 1945, *TP* V 375; Wavell, *Journal*, 29 March 1945, 4 April 1945, 120–2.

[69] India Committee, 10 April 1945, *TP* V 382.

[70] Amery, *Diary*, 10 April 1945, 1035–6.

to prominence: local government, labour organisation, and practical social and economic reform, reinvigorated by new wartime impulses and commitments to planning and collectivism. It was these ideals which Bevin articulated to the Party Conference just before the 1945 Election. Indian leaders must be gradually given more responsibility, but not through constitutional change, on which agreement with Congress lawyers was impossible to achieve, but through schemes of reform under the *existing* constitution, with 'some of our own personnel' sent out to help them. 'They [are] fine agitators,' he said of Congress, 'but they jib responsibility.'[71]

Fairly soon after Labour took office, these schemes were forcibly abandoned. Labour's first move was to call fresh elections in India. These took place on the limited electoral rolls then available, though Cripps pressed for the release of the Congress Socialists still in detention, to ensure that progressive parties stood a fair chance of beating the Congress right.[72] Attlee, still doubtful of the representativeness of Congress, also favoured elections, as they would allow 'the newly elected representatives of the people and not merely the party leaders' to be involved in constitution-making. Indeed, he was in favour of ignoring the party leaders altogether, and summoning all 1,500 provincial legislators to a meeting to discuss the best method of advance.[73] When Wavell warned the Cabinet that Congress might launch a fresh Quit India campaign if independence were not granted immediately after the elections, the old instincts of the Labour ministers still twitched.[74] Bevin wanted to 'press on with the economic and social development of India' and called for the Government of India to 'put themselves forward as the champion of the poorer classes'. Cripps lamented that his and Bevin's 1942 plans had been 'frustrated by I[ndia] O[ffice] and G[overnment of] India obscurantism'.[75] 'Let the trouble be between the masses & Indian capitalists . . . [instead of] Indians v[ersus the] B[ritish] Gov[ernmen]'t',

---

[71] Labour Party, *Report of Annual Conference*, 1945, 117–18.

[72] Cripps to Pethick-Lawrence, 22 and 25 Oct, 2 Nov 1945, *TP* VI 155, 170, 182.

[73] IB Committee, IB(45)3, 4 Sept 1945, *TP* VI 92.

[74] Wavell to Pethick-Lawrence, 7 Nov 1945, *TP* VI 194; IB Committee IB(45)7, 19 Nov 1945, *TP* VI 217.

[75] Cabinet CM(45)56, 27 Nov 1945, *TP* VI 244; CSN, 27 Nov 1945, CAB 195/3, NA.

Morrison told the Cabinet.[76] He wanted improved publicity to allow Labour to 'reach the peasant over the head of the anti-British vested interests' and thought the Government of India should set itself up as 'the poor man's protector and friend', since 'the leaders of the anti-British movement were all from the exploiting professional and money-lender classes whose policies did not serve the real interests of the masses'.[77]

However, the elections put paid to these ideas. They confirmed the strength both of Congress, which won over 90 per cent of the vote in the non-Muslim electorates and the Muslim League, which won 89 per cent of the Muslim vote, and all the Muslim seats in the Assembly.[78] All but one of the RDP's candidates were defeated, effectively ruling it out of consideration as an alternative to Congress. Although the RDP continued to lobby Labour, the Cabinet Mission to India in 1946 did not propose to see its leaders at all unless they requested a meeting. When they did, making their usual demands for power, the Viceroy noted that '[t]hey did not expect this to be taken seriously . . . [N]or did anyone else.'[79] With Congress provincial governments in place, it was clear that it was now too late to introduce any socio-economic projects for its reform. When Aneurin Bevan suggested that the Cabinet Mission take out trade unionists and economists to 'distract fr[om] morbid concentr[atio]n on [the] constit[utiona]l problem', Attlee told him, 'you can't divert to economics people who want to talk of politics'.[80] 'Everything in India' Cripps commented, 'must be political now.'[81] Though Bevin continued to hope that an appeal over the heads of Congress to the Indian villages could be made, the Cabinet was advised that anything emanating from British sources was now suspect.[82]

In 1924 and again in 1929, Labour's freedom of manoeuvre had been restricted by inherited structures and procedures, notably official suspicion in the India Office, the binding policy commitments made by

[76] CSN, 27 Nov 1945, CAB 195/3, NA.
[77] Notes of a Meeting at Chequers, 23 Nov 1945, PREM 8/58, NA.
[78] Moore, *Escape*, 65, 79–80.
[79] Pethick-Lawrence to Wavell, 27 Feb 1946, *TP* VI 471; RDP Meeting with Cabinet Mission, *TP* VII 87; Wavell, *Journal*, 11 April 1946, 243.
[80] CSN, 22 Jan 1946, CAB 195/3, NA.
[81] CSN, 21 Feb 1946, CAB 195/4, NA.
[82] CSN, 5 June 1946, CAB 195/4, NA.

previous administrations, and the necessity of developing and imple-
menting policy through a semi-autonomous structure 6,000 miles away,
headed by the irremovable Viceroy. Labour ministers who wished to
diverge from the policy direction indicated by these arrangements had
soon worked out that, in the absence of a like-minded Viceroy, it was
necessary to break these official monopolies by building a parallel structure of shared information and private agreement with Congress. Since
the Attlee Government secured the passage of the Indian Independence
Act in 1947, it is tempting to conclude that the mechanisms of imperial
governance must, in this third period of government, have been firmly
in the grip of Labour ministers. Indeed, much *had* changed. This time,
Labour had a secure parliamentary majority and significant wartime
governing experience. The coincidence of its electoral victory with the
end of the war and the resumption of normal politics in India meant
that few prior policy commitments stood in the way of a fresh start.
Indeed, the Cripps Offer, for all the fact of its rejection and the efforts
of the Conservatives to rescind it, still stood as an irrevocable guarantee
of a constituent assembly and dominion status: this time it was Labour's
parliamentary opponents who were bound.

Nonetheless, some aspects of the structure were familiar. At the India
Office, the Permanent Under-Secretary was now Sir David Monteath,
who had served as Hirtzel's Private Secretary in 1924, and Benn's in
1929–31. The Labour Party had fired a shot across his bows before the
election, when Bevin told the Party Conference that one of Labour's
first actions would be to abolish the India Office and merge its work
into the Dominions Office.[83] This proposal was suspended until a
political settlement was made, but Bevin still held that the India Office
was 'steeped in the old traditions' and called for the transfer of the
constitutional problem to a wholly new set of officials.[84] Attlee too
thought the India Office was 'reactionary and out of touch' and Cripps
remained convinced that it knew little of 'the real India'.[85] Between the
Cabinet and the Indian people, Cripps complained in November 1945,
there was a 'g[rea]t block of inflexibility', consisting of the Viceroy and

---

[83] Labour Party, *Report of Annual Conference*, 1945, 117–18.

[84] Monteath to Jenkins, 4 Aug 1945, MSS/Eur/D714/66, OIOC; Pethick-Lawrence
to Wavell, 27 Aug 1945, *TP* VI 73; Cripps to Pethick-Lawrence, 30 Dec 1945, *TP* VI
319; CSN, 27 Nov 1945, CAB 195/3, NA.

[85] Attlee, Minute on India, 12 Dec 1945, *TP* VI 284; Cripps to Pethick-Lawrence, 3
Dec and undated, *TP* VI 261–2.

the India Office. He wanted special advisers, such as Carl Heath of the ICG, appointed to leaven it.[86]

Though Monteath did not share Hirtzel's hostility to political progress, he did share his sense of the intractability of the problem. He thought Labour had not 'learned caution', and were too keen, as they had been in 1929, to 'plunge into Indian politics on purely *a priori* grounds' and try to ' "settle it" without further ado'.[87] Even more problematic was the relationship with the Viceroy. The India League and its enlarged cohort of new Labour MPs had demanded that the new Secretary of State, Pethick-Lawrence, summon the Viceroy and issue him with fresh instructions,[88] but Pethick-Lawrence, doubtless to the pleasure of the India Office, told them that in his first few days he had learned that 'the Viceroy is not simply another civil servant'.[89] This was also Wavell's view of the relationship. In his first letter home to the new Government, he loftily gave Pethick-Lawrence permission to visit India, provided he announced publicly before arriving that he had no policy objective in view.[90] Like Monteath, Wavell was worried about Labour, believing its majority was too large and the ministers ignorant and hasty in their approach to India.[91]

The Attlee Government made several innovations to ensure that its own direction of policy was not restricted by the 'block of inflexibility'. Attlee decided not to place a powerful minister at the India Office, choosing the ineffectual but amiable seventy-four year old Frederick Pethick-Lawrence, whom he had ruled out of consideration for government in 1940 because of his age.[92] Instead, the powerhouse of Attlee's Indian policy was the Cabinet's India and Burma Committee, chaired by

[86] Cabinet 27 Nov 1945, CSN, CAB 195/3, NA; Cripps to Pethick-Lawrence, 22 Oct 1945, *TP* VI 154.

[87] Monteath to Abell, 20 Aug 1945, *TP* VI 45; Monteath to Cunningham, 25 Aug 1945, MSS/Eur/D714/70 OIOC.

[88] Menon to Pethick-Lawrence, 6 Sept 1945, L/PJ/8/530, OIOC; 'Gathering of MPs interested in Indian Freedom', 21 Aug 1945, KMP, 11/4/7; Dobbie *et al.* to newspaper editors, 6 Sept 1945, *TP* VI 97; Note of meeting between Pethick-Lawrence and Deputation of Labour MPs, 17 Sept 1945, *TP* VI 111; Notes for Meeting, undated, KMP 11/16/B; *Daily Herald*, 25 Sept 1945.

[89] Note of meeting, 17 Sept 1945; Pethick-Lawrence to Wavell, 21 Sept 1945, *TP* VI 120.

[90] Wavell to Pethick-Lawrence, 5 Aug 1945, *TP* VI 4.

[91] Wavell, *Journal*, 26 July, 6 Aug, 3, 4 and 11 Sept 1945, 159, 161, 169–71.

[92] Paul Addison, *The Road to 1945: British Politics in the Second World War* (London, 1975), 113.

the Prime Minister himself, and comprising Cripps, Pethick-Lawrence, Benn (now Lord Stansgate), Ellen Wilkinson and the Earl of Listowel, with Dalton attending for financial questions. A. V. Alexander, the Minister of Defence, and Viscount Addison, the Secretary of State for the Dominions, were added in the summer of 1946. Besides Attlee, it was Cripps who dominated its proceedings. It was he, rather than Pethick-Lawrence, who chaired the Committee in Attlee's absence.[93] The India and Burma Committee was the source of all the significant policy initiatives, and, on constitutional questions, the India Office became little more than a post office through which Cabinet and Viceregal exchanges passed on their way.

Attlee and Cripps also decided early on that the Viceroy would not do. Cripps thought that he was in the hands of 'anti-Congress' officials and did not have the political skills to secure a settlement on his own; Attlee believed that he lacked what he termed the 'suppleness of mind' or 'political *nous*' necessary for the detailed negotiations with Indian leaders.[94] They repeatedly attempted to press 'political advisors' on the soldier-Viceroy, telling him that '[p]olitics has its own technique which can only be acquired by practice and not from text-books'.[95] Having summoned him home and found he did not share their sense of urgency, Attlee and Cripps decided that ministerial authority needed to be strengthened through direct negotiations between the Cabinet and Indian leaders.[96] Attlee suggested the dispatch of a single minister to India as a plenipotentiary empowered to make a settlement without reference home at all.[97] Such a figure would be 'divorced from the machine of Indian administration'.[98] No one in the Cabinet really wanted Wavell involved at all, but they feared that to exclude him might precipitate his resignation, which would be worse. The Cabinet therefore decided on a three-man team comprising the Secretary of State, Cripps and Alexander

[93] Peter Clarke, *The Cripps Version: The Life of Sir Stafford Cripps, 1885–1952* (London, 2002), 393–476.

[94] Attlee to Pethick-Lawrence, 22 Dec 1945, *TP* XII A1 (Supplementary Documentation), doc.4; Pethick-Lawrence to Attlee, 26 Dec 1945, *TP* XII A1 doc.5.

[95] Attlee to Wavell, 22 July 1946, *TP* VIII 64; Wavell, *Journal*, 4 May 1946, 257; Cabinet CM(45)56, 27 Nov 1945, *TP* VI 244.

[96] Cripps to Pethick-Lawrence, 22 Oct 1945, *TP* VI 155; IB Committee IB(45)8, 28 Nov 1945, *TP* VI 247; Cripps to Pethick-Lawrence, undated but prob. written 4 Dec 1945, *TP* VI 262; Cripps to Pethick-Lawrence, 19 Dec 1945, Pethick-Lawrence Papers 5/63.

[97] Attlee to Pethick-Lawrence, 22 Dec 1945.

[98] Pethick-Lawrence to Attlee, 26 Dec 1945.

to 'outweigh' Wavell.[99] This time, in contrast to previous Labour Governments, the Ministers would be the 'men on the spot', able to invoke Cabinet authority through the provision, at Cripps' insistence, of rapid teleprinter communication with London, unavailable in 1942.[100] Once in India, Cripps frequently bypassed the officials and the Viceroy in a strenuous parallel diplomacy made up of private chats, personal appeals and secret meetings, assisted by a team of informal emissaries, including Woodrow Wyatt, Major 'Billy' Short, Agatha Harrison and Horace Alexander of the ICG, as well as an Indian, Sudhir Ghosh. These intermediaries were able to convey informally the views and concerns of the various parties, independently of officialdom, thereby building trust. The India Office staff and ICS were, Cripps told Wyatt, irrelevant: 'Quite frankly it doesn't matter what they say because . . . *we* are really doing the negotiations and keeping them out of it.'[101]

The personal connections established between Cripps and Congress in 1946, in defiance of Wavell and the ICS, came close to achieving the parallel structure that had eluded previous Labour Governments. The Government had realised early on that personal diplomacy would be needed to repair the bridges broken in 1942.[102] It had dispatched a ten-strong Parliamentary delegation to develop connections between the new Parliament and India, including outright opponents of the *raj* such as Sorensen, whose inclusion would have been inconceivable ten years earlier.[103] Cripps had also moved quickly to establish an independent channel of communication by private correspondence with India and especially with Nehru. Some of his Indian correspondence was shared with the India Office, but other letters were sent to Pethick-Lawrence marked 'not for circulation in your Dept!'.[104] Not even

[99] CSN, 22 Jan 1946, CAB 195/3, NA.   [100] Clarke, *Cripps Version*, 308.

[101] Woodrow Wyatt, *Confessions of an Optimist* (London, 1985), 140.

[102] Attlee's Report to Cabinet, 9 Sept 1945, CP(45)155, *TP* VI 100; IB Committee, 19 Nov 1945, TP VI 217; Cripps to Nehru, 12 Dec 1945, CAB127/143, NA; Pethick-Lawrence to Attlee, 17 April 1946, Attlee Papers (Bodleian), dep.35.

[103] Turnbull to Pethick-Lawrence, 28 Sept 1945, *TP* VI 124; Pethick-Lawrence to Attlee, 4 Oct 1945, *TP* VI 129; Pethick-Lawrence to Wavell, 9 Oct 1945, TP VI 136; Wavell to Pethick-Lawrence, 19 Oct 1945, *TP* VI 151; Pethick-Lawrence to Attlee, 13 Dec 1945, *TP* VI 286; 'Rough notes of points made by various Members of the Parliamentary Delegation at the meeting at No. 10 Downing Street', 13 Feb 1946, *TP* VI 426; Reginald Sorensen, 'The Parliamentary Delegation to India, Jan 1946' in C. H. Philips and M. Doreen Wainwright (eds.), *The Partition of India: Policies and Perspectives, 1935–1947* (London, 1970), 535–45.

[104] Cripps to Pethick-Lawrence, 19 Dec 1945, Pethick-Lawrence Papers, 5/63.

Pethick-Lawrence was allowed to see what Cripps wrote in reply. 'I am rather alarmed at S.C.'s regular correspondence with Congress people', Pethick-Lawrence told Attlee. 'He frequently shows me their letters to him but I never know what he writes to them.'[105] Rebuilding links was not easy, however, for the Congress leaders had emerged from prison distrustful of Labour and Cripps in particular.[106] 'I have not yet got over Stafford Cripps' behaviour just after his visit to Delhi in 1942', Nehru told Menon on his release. '[It] created a greater gulf between India and England than the action or inaction of any other individual in recent years.'[107] From India, Agatha Harrison told Cripps himself that his actions in 1942 had 'shattered badly' the faith of all the Congress leaders: 'It was one of the first things Nehru raised when we talked. He said he could not understand *how* you could have said what you did . . . It has left a deep mark. On average, every day I have been here, someone has raised this matter . . .'[108]

Nehru's own response to Cripps' approaches provided a clue to what was needed. 'I can have faith in an individual but not in a machine', Nehru told him.[109] Cripps' solution was therefore to work independently of the official machinery to build a direct alliance with Congress. This could be counterposed to the official preference for the British Government to stand above the conflict between Congress and the Muslim League, remaining neutral between them, a passive stance which Cripps was sure would guarantee a breakdown. '[W]e must at all costs come to an accomodation with Congress', he wrote, 'We can get through . . . without the League if we have Congress, but not without Congress even if we have the League.'[110] In India, he exhibited a personal solicitousness to Congress leaders, fetching glasses of water for Gandhi, participating in Gandhi's meetings in the *harijan* quarter and, probably for the first time for a British Cabinet

---

[105] Pethick-Lawrence to Attlee, 28 Nov 1945, Attlee Papers (Bodleian), dep.27/253–5.

[106] Government of India, Information and Broadcasting Department to Secretary of State, 1 Aug 1945, *TP* VI 1; G. B. Pant to Nehru, 15 Aug 1945, JNC, v.79; Shiva Rao to Cripps, 15 Oct 1945, CAB127/147, NA; Richard Symonds, 'Note of Conversation with Mr. Gandhi 30 Oct 1945', Symonds Papers, MSS/Photo Eur/347/13, OIOC.

[107] Nehru, 'Prison Diary', 17 Dec 1943, *SWJN*, xiii, 311; Nehru to Menon, 3 Sept 1945, *SWJN*, xiv, 80–84.

[108] Harrison to Cripps, 27 Feb 1946, CAB127/132, NA.

[109] Nehru to Cripps, 3 Dec 1945, CAB127/143, NA.

[110] Cripps Mission Diary, 14 May 1946, Cripps Papers (Bodleian), uncat.

Minister, apologising for British imperialism.[111] '[I]t's not your fault', Jayaprakash Narayan told him, '[I]t's just history'.[112] Wavell completely misunderstood the reasoning for this, deploring Cripps' 'slumming with Gandhi', and 'continuous courting, flattery and appeasement of Congress'.[113]

In May 1946, the Cabinet Mission managed to get the agreement of both Congress and the Muslim League to a three tier federation, in which the provinces should concede such powers as they wished to sub-federal governments, while foreign affairs, defence, communications, and finance would be reserved to a federal centre.[114] However, Jinnah had been assured that constitution-making would be carried out by provinces meeting in sections which could only be altered by the consent of both parties. Congress, which disliked the prospect of the non-League provinces of NWFP and Assam, and the Sikhs in the Punjab, having constitutions forced on them by majority vote of the Muslim League provinces, had accepted Cripps' plan on the understanding that provinces would have the right to opt out of their allotted sections. When Jinnah called for the rejection of the Congress interpretation, the Mission prevaricated, anxious to avoid a breach with Congress. Failing to gain satisfaction, and convinced that Congress was determined to collapse the three tier system into a centralised two tier system, Jinnah withdrew the League's acceptance of the plan and the League resolved to resort to direct action to achieve Pakistan.[115] Matters were made worse at the end of August when Nehru was invited to join an Interim Government which was composed according to a formula which allowed Congress to nominate a Muslim. Further negotiations brought the League into the Interim Government in late October, but this was largely in order to continue the struggle for Pakistan from a

[111] Wavell, *Journal*, 3 April 1946, 236.

[112] Cripps Mission Diary, 15 April 1946.

[113] Wavell, *Journal*, 1 and 24 April 1946, 12 and 14 May 1946, 3 June 1946, 233, 251, 267, 269, 287; 'Retrospect of Mission', 1 July 1946, 310–11; Wavell to Attlee, 1 Aug 1946, *TP* VIII 102; Attlee to Wavell, 20 Aug 1946, *TP* VIII 184; Wavell to Attlee, 28 Aug 1946 and draft replies by Attlee, *TP* VIII 212.

[114] Cripps' first draft of an Award, dated 18 April 1946, is in *TP* VII 126. After discussion and amendment, a draft was sent to Attlee on 30 April, and is in *TP* VII 173. Subsequent drafts and amendments dated from 5 to 8 May are in *TP* VII 193, 198, 214. The final version dated 12–13 May is in *TP* VII 268, and the Award itself, published on 16 May 1946, is in *TP* VII 303.

[115] Pethick-Lawrence and Alexander felt sufficiently guilty about the way in which he had been treated to apologise privately. Jinnah to Pethick-Lawrence, 11 Sept 1946, Pethick-Lawrence Papers 5/72.

position of influence. Wavell insisted that the only way to reconcile the League was to press Congress to provide a guarantee that it work the Constituent Assembly according to the grouping procedure. But Labour ministers feared that Wavell would push Congress too far, and precipitate a breakdown of the whole procedure. At a meeting of ministers on 23 September, it was privately agreed that if a final attempt at persuading Jinnah—to be made not by Wavell but under Labour's own auspices in the calmer atmosphere of London—failed to bring the League Muslims into the Assembly, its work must go ahead without them.[116] To placate Jinnah, the Labour ministers were prepared to accept Jinnah's interpretation of grouping, now backed by the legal opinion of the Lord Chancellor, and to tell Nehru that if the Muslims failed to join the Assembly, then the constitution it produced could be applied only to those parts of India it represented, and that 'some other means of ascertaining the wishes of the Muslim Provinces' would have to be found.[117] At the Conference in London it was agreed that the Federal Court should adjudicate in matters concerning the Statement of 16 May, and even though it was likely that the Court would favour the League's interpretation of the provisions for grouping, Nehru attempted to persuade his colleagues to accept the compromise.[118] But their eventual agreement was as cagey as the Congress' acceptance of the Mission Plan.[119] For his part, Jinnah remained unprepared to cooperate with the distrusted Constituent Assembly, and stated his intention to work for 'Pakistan, within the British Commonwealth'.[120]

In September 1946, Wavell told the Cabinet that he could not expect to maintain control of India for more than eighteen months. He feared that Congress, now cooperating in the Interim Government, would under threat of resignation, force him to acquiesce in the suppression of Muslim agitation. He therefore recommended resort to a Breakdown Plan by which Britain would attempt to force the issue to a conclusion. The Viceroy would declare Britain's intention to quit no later than March 1948. Meanwhile, power would be transferred immediately in the Hindu provinces, and Britain would retreat to the disputed Muslim territory in the hope of securing a settlement. The Cabinet rejected

---

[116] Meeting of Ministers, 23 Sept 1946, *TP* VIII 354; Pethick-Lawrence to Attlee, 24 Sept 1946, *TP* VIII 361.

[117] Meeting of Ministers, 4 Dec 1946, *TP* IX 153.

[118] HMG Statement at conclusion of Indian Conference in London, 6 Dec 1946, *TP* IX 166; Cabinet CM(46)104, 10 Dec 1946, *TP* IX 181.

[119] Moore, *Escape*, 180–1.   [120] Meeting of Ministers, 4 Dec 1946, *TP* IX 153.

this plan but was forced to accept Wavell's recommendation that only the announcement of a date for British withdrawal would break the Indian impasse. Even if no agreed constitution emerged, power would be transferred to 'responsible Indian hands' no later than June 1948.[121]

The Cabinet had been uneasy about setting a date for withdrawal from India. In May 1946, Cripps' suggestion that, in the event of a breakdown of negotiations, Britain should simply 'announce. . . [her] departure in a year's time' had been dismissed by his Cabinet colleagues as 'not a practical policy', for it would fail to secure 'our main objective of averting administrative chaos'.[122] In August 1946, Attlee himself had told the new Governor of Burma that there was 'no advantage in setting paper dates'.[123] Several Ministers had expressed 'grave objections' to the proposal when it had been made by Wavell.[124] At Cabinet on 31 December, Attlee's proposals were very widely criticised.[125] In mid-1946, Bevin, Morrison, Shinwell and Ellen Wilkinson had all favoured staying in India, using arrests and force against Congress if necessary, despite the view of the Cabinet Mission and the Viceroy that repression was not feasible.[126] Bevin had wanted the Ministry of Labour to ask demobilised men if they would contemplate military service in India.[127] Now he led an attack on the decision to agree a date for departure: 'We are throwing away the Empire because of one man's pessimism', he told the Cabinet. He doubted the capacity of Indians for self-government, and opposed 'scuttle. . . without dignity or plan'. 'We knuckle under', Bevin wrote, 'at the first blow'.[128] 'I am not defeatist but realist', Attlee replied. 'If you disagree with what is proposed, you must offer a practical alternative.'[129] After a private meeting with Bevin and Alexander, the

---

[121] IB Committee, IB(46)13, 20 Dec 1946, *TP* IX 213.

[122] Meeting of Cabinet Delegation and Wavell, 15 May 1946, *TP* VII 289; Cabinet CM(46)55, 5 June 1946, *TP* VII 455; Alexander Diary, A. V. Alexander Papers, 34.

[123] Directive to the new Governor, 29 Aug 1946, in Hugh Tinker (ed.), *Burma: The Struggle for Independence 1944–48* vol.1 *From Military Occupation to Civil Government* (London, 1983), 678.

[124] IB Committee IB(46)8, 11 Dec 1946, *TP* IX 186; IB Committee Paper IB(46)52 by Addison, 18 Dec 1946, *TP* IX 206.

[125] Cabinet CM(46)108, 31 Dec 1946, *TP* IX 235.

[126] CSN, 5 June 1946, CAB 195/4, NA.

[127] CSN, 6 June 1946, CAB 195/4, NA.

[128] CSN, 31 Dec 1946, CAB 195/4, NA; Bevin to Attlee, 1 Jan 1947, *TP* IX 236.

[129] Attlee to Bevin, 2 Jan 1947, TP IX 243.

Viceroy noted that the Labour ministers 'were in reality imperialists and dislike any idea of leaving India'.[130]

To coincide with the announcement, Wavell was to be replaced by Mountbatten. Labour had been reluctant to sack Wavell, partly because they feared it would be used by the Conservatives against them, and partly because he had support in the ICS, whose sagging morale was a danger to the extrication of British interests from India. Instead they had marginalised him, a humiliating position, but one which reflected their inability to work with him or get rid of him. Mountbatten's instructions also reflected Labour's distrust of the inflexible officials of the ICS. He was allowed to appoint his own staff and superimpose them upon the officials of Government House, and in a secret codicil to his instructions, permitted to remove any member of the ICS who obstructed him.[131] Cripps also tried to get the Viceroy's Private Secretary replaced.[132] Listowel, who replaced Pethick-Lawrence as Secretary of State in April 1947, claimed later that the India Office was not even told of the full extent of Mountbatten's powers.[133] When Mountbatten seemed briefly to have lost the chance of an agreement with Congress, Attlee toyed again with the idea of replacing Mountbatten with a minister with full powers and the minimum of reference home.[134]

Mountbatten's first attempt at a solution was aptly named 'Plan Balkan'. Power would be transferred to provinces, or in the case of Bengal, Assam and the Punjab, sub-provinces, which would then be free to join a Hindustan Group, a Pakistan Group, or remain independent. Congress, frightened by the collapse of ordered government in the disputed provinces, seemed at first willing to accept it, but later, complaining that the Plan presented a 'picture of fragmentation and conflict and disorder' which threatened to make India 'a thing of shreds and patches', rejected it. Mountbatten rapidly shifted to a new plan

---

[130] Wavell, *Journal*, 24 Dec 1946, 399.

[131] Attlee to Mountbatten, 8 Feb 1947, *TP* IX 365; Mountbatten to Attlee, 11 Feb 1947, *TP* IX 376.

[132] For Cripps' attempt to have Abell, the Viceroy's Private Secretary, replaced, see Mountbatten to Attlee, 11 Feb 1947, *TP* IX 377.

[133] Lord Listowel, 'The Whitehall Dimension of the Transfer of Power', *Indo-British Review*, 7/3–4 (1978), 23–4.

[134] Rowan to Attlee, 14 May 1947, *TP* X 435.

for partition into two dominions. This gave provinces a simple choice: they could join the existing Constituent Assembly, or join together in a new one. They could not stand out for separate independence. The Cabinet had reservations about this solution, but it was at least an agreed one. Communal rioting was the effective solvent of the parties' incompatible demands: Congress, keen to inherit the *raj* before its own authority was irretrievably broken, had come to accept the need for rapid partition, and Jinnah was by now the prisoner of the Pakistan demand, from which there could be no retreat. On 15 August 1947, India and Pakistan achieved independence. 'If you are in a place where you are not wanted, and where you have not the force, or perhaps the will, to squash those who don't want you', Hugh Dalton had written earlier in the year, 'the only thing to do is to come out'.[135]

Labour's private feelings at the achievement of Indian independence were mixed ones. 'To me the solution falls far short of what I should have liked to see', wrote Pethick-Lawrence, '[and] yet it is far better than at one time I dared to hope.'[136] Labour had honoured its commitment to ending British rule and had also achieved an agreed departure, managing to avoid the humiliation of a scuttle like that from Palestine in 1948, which almost totally spared British lives and property. Had Britain not quit, Attlee wrote, the violence would have been 'infinitely worse & would have extended to all India & our people would have been the first victims'.[137] At the same time, it was wishful thinking to pretend that the coming of Indian independence amounted to anything less than a defeat for most of the Party's other pre-war objectives. Violent partition, even if chosen by the principal Indian parties, had always been considered by Labour to be an illogical and damaging solution. While diehards might console themselves with the reassurance that India had never really been a single nation, such thoughts were alien to Labour's conception of Indian unity. Labour hopes of reforming Indian nationalism in more socially and politically progressive directions were also stillborn. Power was transferred to parties whose claims to the allegiance of the Indian masses had never been tested by elections on the basis of universal suffrage. The Indian electorate remained largely

---

[135] Hugh Dalton, *High Tide and After* (London, 1962), 211.
[136] Pethick-Lawrence to Nehru, 26 Aug 1947, Pethick-Lawrence Papers 5/75.
[137] Attlee to Ammon, 12 Sept 1947, Ammon Papers, 1/7.

illiterate and impoverished, and vulnerable to the types of communally-driven, caste-ridden or corrupt electoral politics that Attlee deplored. The worsened rioting that followed the announcement of the decisions of the Radcliffe Boundary Commission seemed to offer little more than the prospect of the fragmentation of India under communal pressures from the minorities, or of the growth of authoritarian one-party rule from the centre. 'I doubt if things will go awfully easily now as the Indian leaders know little of administration', Attlee wrote privately.[138] Although Nehru's address to the Constituent Assembly had promised that democracy and socialism would be at the heart of the new India, there was no guarantee that India would follow his preferred path rather than that of Patel. Indeed, the history of the pre-war Congress suggested that land redistribution or public ownership would either be voted down by Congress leaders attentive to the interests of Indian industrialists, rural landowners and the richer farmers, or dropped at the behest of Gandhians anxious to avoid dividing the traditional rural order.

However, by the end of the 1950s, many of Nehru's social democratic promises had been unexpectedly realised, not wholly or in full measure, but very substantially. The reasons for this were complex: the deaths of Gandhi and Patel left Nehru free to establish a powerful planning bureaucracy, and the electoral hegemony of the Congress Party, of which Nehru regained the leadership in 1951, helped him to break some of the resistance of the local Congress parties, and establish the basic principles and commitments of what has come to be known as the Nehruvian state: the erosion of communal identities and caste discrimination through secularisation, representative democracy based on universal suffrage, and state-led industrial planning in a mixed, though largely state-built, economy.[139] This programme, with its astonishing closeness to Labour's own ideals, naturally earned the latter's approval, though what was being admired was as much Labour's reflection as India. Approval of this kind had always been easy to give. Labour's Indian dilemma, chewed over since Keir Hardie and Ramsay MacDonald, had been a question of reconciling familiarity and authenticity: what was familiar turned out not to be authentic and *vice versa*. For all his radicalism, Nehru had proved a much more digestible nationalist than Tilak or Gandhi, because he had satisfactorily resolved this dilemma:

[138] Attlee to Tom Attlee, 18 Aug 1947, Attlee Papers (Bodleian), MSS Eng c.4792/66.
[139] Kaviraj, 'Introduction', *Politics in India*, 14.

India was, it turned out, set on the same historical path to modernity as everyone else, and the authenticity of this orientation was guaranteed by Nehru's discovery of India and earning, through the independence struggle and election, the right to speak for it.[140] The anomalies and inauthenticities which in the past had complicated this view of India were still there, not least among the large numbers of Indians for whom Nehruvian politics remained unintelligible, but they had been buried for the time being, and they did not trouble Labour. Indeed, for those of the 1930s and 1940s generation that knew Krishna Menon and Nehru best, faith in the Nehruvian state would extend to the defence of his daughter Indira Gandhi's Emergency in 1975–7, on the grounds that it was necessary to protect the gains for the poor that the Nehrus had made.[141]

Labour's preferred schemes for India had thus first been set aside in the interests of a quick political solution, rather than abandoned through reflection, and then strangely validated by the successes of the Nehruvian state. Labour was able to decolonise without needing fully to abandon its traditionally-held criteria of fitness for self-government. This is clear not just from the twitchings of Bevin, Morrison and others over India, but also from the more considered policies adopted by Labour in other colonial settings where time seemed less pressing. In Africa and the Middle East, Labour wanted to ensure that anti-colonial nationalism was not permitted to sour through concentration on anti-British struggle, as it had in India, but was channelled into healthy nation-building activities, not so much in order to delay self-government, but to normalise politics before it came. The ideas that had been ditched in India were still thought useful. Attlee continued to see municipal government as a solvent of anti-British feeling and a means of developing constructive work. Cripps and Bevin continued to view colonial economic development, now in Africa and the Middle East, as the means of arresting anti-British sentiment and of building the foundations of social democracy.[142] Their Indian experience suggested

---

[140] For this view of Nehru, see Chatterjee, *Nationalist Thought and the Colonial World.*

[141] Jennie Lee to Indira Gandhi, 2 and 19 July, and 4 Dec 1978; Lee to Djilas, 8 Oct 1975, Lee to Reuther, 21 Jan 1977, Lee to Aiyar, 7 Oct 1977, Jennie Lee Papers (uncat.), Open University.

[142] Ronald Hyam (ed.), *The Labour Government and the End of Empire 1945–1951* (London, 1992), esp. Cripps, Speech to African Governors' Conference, 12 Nov 1947, doc.66; Comments by Ivor Thomas at conference on overseas territories, 26 June 1948,

that western ideas needed to be implanted early and vigorously, and by cooperation with nationalists rather than by the colonial state.

What such a perspective missed were the many ways that Indian democracy had been deepened and enhanced not so much by copying the British, as by fighting them. Legislative work, for example, which for Attlee was a necessary apprenticeship for Indian politicians, turned out to be less important than the techniques of popular mobilisation and group empowerment developed by Gandhi, which Attlee had generally regarded as undisciplined and infantile.[143] Labour undervalued these products of the independence struggle, in part because it undervalued the struggle itself, with what Orwell termed its 'endless changes of front, line-ups, *démarches*, denunciations, protests and gestures'.[144] The British left's continued sounding of the colonies according to its own ideals produced much effective anti-imperialism, to the degree that anti-colonial movements could plausibly be presented as socially progressive and modernising, but was for this reason, as it had been in India, vulnerable to the boom and bust of artificially inflated expectation and subsequent disappointment.

The unanswered proposal was that of Gandhi. This had been hard to miss, for Gandhi was more open than many Indian nationalists to cross-cultural exchange, especially with those on the dissenting margins of their own societies. But it had also been hard to hear, since Gandhi only once after 1920 came to Britain to plead for it. As we have seen, too, he refused to authorise an organisation to do so either, or imposed exacting conditions for such an organisation which proved impossible to meet. As a result, Gandhi was well known in Britain, but not well understood. He was valued but only once translated. Many of those who tried to understand him effectively remoulded him in their own image, as (western) pacifist, social radical, or humanitarian. This

doc.179; Attlee, Memorandum on Cyprus, 22 Dec 1947, doc 236; Attlee, Comments at Commonwealth affairs Committee, 19 Jan 1949, doc 406. For the planning of the new African policy, see John Kent, 'Bevin's Imperialism and the Idea of Euro-Africa', in Michael Dockrill and John W. Young (eds.), *British Foreign Policy, 1945–56* (Basingstoke, 1989). For the Middle East, see Nicholas Owen, 'Labour and the New Empire in the Middle East', in Martin Kolinsky and Michael Cohen (eds.), *The Demise of the British Empire in the Middle East, 1943–55* (London, 1997).

[143] For explorations of the roots of Indian democracy, see Rajni Kothari, *Politics in India* (New Delhi, 1970); Atul Kohli (ed.), *India's Democracy* (Princeton, 1990) and *The Success of India's Democracy* (Cambridge, 2001).

[144] Orwell, *Wartime Diary*, 29 April 1942, in Orwell and Angus, *Collected Essays*, ii, 479.

was not always ineffective: it brought Gandhi to British audiences in a comprehensible way, though it was also susceptible to misunderstanding and disenchantment. It also stopped short of what Gandhi offered in place of the status which metropolitan anti-imperialists had generally enjoyed: a combined, experimental search for truth, on equal terms, based on mutual respect and openness to the possibility of learning about politics from unfamiliar sources. But outside the small circle of British Gandhians and Theosophists, hardly any of the metropolitan anti-imperialists really believed that Indians had anything to teach them about politics. The Gandhian dialogue would have required them not merely to learn, which they were not always unwilling to do, but also to unlearn much of what they thought they already knew.

Bibliography

1. UNPUBLISHED SOURCES

National Archives, Kew

Cabinet (CAB)
Records of the Central Criminal Court (CRIM)
Ministry of Information (INF)
Foreign Office (FO)
Metropolitan Police (MEPO)
Prime Minister's Office (PREM)
Security Services (KV, HW)
Home Office (HO)
Cripps Papers (CAB 127)
MacDonald Papers (PRO 30/69)

Labour History Archives and Study Centre, Manchester

Communist Party of Great Britain
   Minutes of the Central Committee (CP/CENT)
   Minutes of the Politburo (CP/CENT/PC)
   Organization Department (CP/ORG)
   Individual Collections (CP/IND)
     Ben Bradley Papers
     Rajani Palme Dutt Papers
Labour Party
   Minutes of the National Executive Committee
   Minutes of the International Sub-Committee of the NEC
   Minutes of the Advisory Committee on International Questions
   Minutes of the Advisory Committee on Imperial Questions
   Minutes of the Commonwealth Committee
   Archives of the Parliamentary Labour Party
   Records of the International Department; William Gillies Correspondence
     and Denis Healey Correspondence

General Secretary's Records; Morgan Phillips Papers
Brailsford Papers
Laski Papers

Oriental and India Office Collections, British Library

India Office Records
  Council of India (C)
  Economic Department (L/E)
  Information Department (L/I)
  Private Office (L/PO)
  Public and Judicial Department (L/PJ)
  Political and Secret Department (L/PS)
  Record Department: Native Newspaper Reports (L/R)
  Proceedings (P)
  Indian States Residencies Records (R)
European Manuscripts
  Anderson Collection (F207)
  Andrews Papers (D1113)
  Besant Correspondence (C888)
  Montagu Butler Collection (F225)
  R. G. Casey Diary (Photo Eur 48)
  Chelmsford Collection (E264)
  Cotton Collection (D1202, F82)
  Cunningham Collection (D670)
  Digby Collection (D767)
  Dunlop-Smith Collection (F166)
  Elwin Collection (D950)
  Hailey Collection (E220)
  Halifax Collection (C152)
  Hirtzel Diary (D1090)
  Lansdowne Collection (D558)
  Linlithgow Collection (F125)
  Maynard Papers (F224)
  Montagu Collection (D523)
  Morley Collection (D573)
  Polak Papers (D1238)
  Pole Papers (F264)
  Permanent Under Secretaries Collection (D714)
  Reading Collections, Viceregal and Private (E238, F118)
  Saklatvala Papers (D1173)
  P. B. Seal Papers (Photo Eur 446)

Seton Collection (E267)
Simon Collection (F77)
Stewart Collection (D890)
Stopford Collection (E346)
Sykes Collection (F150)
Templewood Collection (E240)
Zetland Collection (D609)
Microfilm
Gokhale Microfilm
Sapru Microfilm

National Archives of India, New Delhi

Home (Political) Series
Jayakar Collection
Khaparde Collection and Diary
Polak Collection
Prasad Collection
Sastri Collection
Tilak Collection

Nehru Memorial Museum and Library, New Delhi

All-India Congress Committee
All-India Trades Union Congress
Horace Alexander Papers
Sudhir Ghosh Papers
India League Papers
N. M. Joshi Papers
Syed Mahmud Papers
V. K. Krishna Menon Papers
Dadabhai Naoroji Papers
Natesan Papers
Motilal Nehru Papers
Jawaharlal Nehru Papers
Oral History Collection
B. Shiva Rao Papers
M. N. Roy Papers

Rossiiskii gosudarstvennyi arkhiv sotsial'no-politicheskoi istorii (RGASPI), Moscow

Communist International
Papers relating to the Communist Party of India (495/68)

Papers relating to the Communist Party of Great Britain (495/100)
INCOMKA Comintern Records Project

Bodleian Library, Oxford

Independent Labour Party (microfilm)
Attlee Papers
Addison Papers
Bradlaugh Papers (microfilm)
Cripps Papers
Dawson Papers
Fisher Papers
Gorell Papers and Diary
Francis Johnson Collection (microfilm)
Nevinson Diary
Sankey Papers
Schuster Papers
Simon Papers
Rennie Smith Papers
Richard Stokes Papers
Edward Thompson Papers

British Library, Manuscripts Department

James Chuter Ede Diary
Rajani Palme Dutt Papers

British Library of Political and Economic Science, London

Hugh Dalton Collection
George Lansbury Collection
Passfield Collection and Beatrice Webb Diary

Bromsgrove Public Library

Laurence Housman Correspondence

Cambridge University Library

Crewe Papers
Hardinge Papers

Centre for South Asian Studies, Cambridge

V. K. Krishna Menon Microfilm

Churchill College, Cambridge

A. V. Alexander Papers
Attlee Papers
Bevin Papers
Brockway Papers
Gordon Walker Papers
Noel-Baker Papers

Friends House, London

India Conciliation Group Archive
Agatha Harrison Collection
Horace Alexander Collection
Reginald Reynolds Collection

Gandhi Smarak Sangrahalaya, New Delhi

Gandhi Papers

Brynmor Jones Library, University of Hull

Ammon Papers
Bridgeman Papers
Laski Papers
League Against Imperialism Papers

International Institute of Social History, Amsterdam

League Against Imperialism Archive
Labour and Socialist International Archive

House of Lords Library

Stansgate Papers
Reginald Sorensen Papers.

McMaster University, Hamilton, Ontario

George Catlin Collection
Bertrand Russell Collection

John Rylands Library, University of Manchester

Manchester Guardian Archive
J. R. MacDonald Papers

National Library of Scotland
Elibank Papers
J. Keir Hardie Papers
Minto Papers

University of Newcastle
C. P. Trevelyan Papers

Nuffield College, Oxford
Fabian Society Papers

Open University
Jennie Lee Papers

Rhodes House, Oxford
Polak Papers

Sardar Patel Memorial Trust Library, New Delhi
Minute Books of the British Committee of the Indian National Congress

Private collections
Leo Amery Papers (in possession of Lord Amery)

Ruskin College, Oxford
Middleton Papers

Trinity College, Cambridge
R. A. Butler Papers
Pethick-Lawrence Papers
Montagu Papers

Rhodes House Library, Oxford
C. R. Buxton Papers
Coupland Papers
Arthur Creech Jones Papers

Royal Archives, Windsor
Papers of George V

University of Keele
Josiah Wedgwood Papers

University of Liverpool

J. Bruce Glasier Papers

University of Sussex

Kingsley Martin Papers
Leonard Woolf Papers

Archives of the Theosophical Society, Madras

Besant Papers

University of Warwick Modern Records Centre

Trades Union Congress
  Papers of the General Council of the Trades Union Congress
  Papers of the National Council of Labour

Borthwick Institute, University of York

Pole Papers

2. PUBLISHED SOURCES

Official Records

Houses of Parliament, *Official Report* ('Hansard'), 4th and 5th series
Royal Commission upon Decentralization in India, Cd 4360 (1908)
Indian Agitators Abroad: containing short accounts of the more important Indian political agitators who have visited Europe and America in recent years, and their sympathisers (Government of India, Criminal Intelligence Office, Simla, 1911)
Report of the Operations of the Currency Department (Government of India, 1913-14–1922-3), *Report of the Controller of Currency* (1923-4–1934-5) and Reserve Bank of India, *Report on Currency and Finance* (1935-36–1947-48)
Royal Commission on the Public Services in India: Report of the Commissioners, v.1, Cd 8382 (1916)
India Office, *Report of Indian Students Committee (Lytton Report)* (1922)
Communist Papers: Documents selected from those obtained on the arrest of the Communist leaders on the 14th and 21st October, 1925, Cmd. 2682 (1926)
Report of the Indian Statutory Commission, Cmnd. 3568–9 (1930)
Indian Round Table Conference, Proceedings, 12 November 1930–19 January 1931, Cmnd.3778 (1931)
Indian Round Table Conference, Proceedings, 7 September–1 December 1931, Cmnd.3997 (1932)
Indian Round Table Conference, Proceedings, 17 November–24 December 1932, Cmnd.4238 (1933)

Joint Committee on Indian Constitutional Reform, Proceedings, Session 1933–4 (H.C.5 (I Part II)) (1934)
Congress Responsibility for the Disturbances, Cmnd.6340 (1943)
India: The Transfer of Power, 1942–7 (12v., London, 1970–83)

Organisational Records

Independent Labour Party, *Reports of Annual Conferences*
Labour Party, *Reports of Annual Conferences*
Theosophical Society, *General Report of the Year's Work of the Theosophical Society in England & Wales*
Trades Union Congress, *Reports of Annual Conferences*

PUBLISHED SOURCES

Books and Articles

Abbasi, Muhammad Yusuf, *London Muslim League (1908–1928): An Historical Study* (Islamabad, 1988).
Acharya, M. P. T., *Reminiscences of an Indian Revolutionary* (New Delhi, 1991).
Addison, Paul, *The Road to 1945: British Politics in the Second World War* (London, 1975).
Ahmad, Aijaz, *In Theory: Classes, Nations, Literatures* (London, 1992).
Ahmed, M., *The British Labour Party and the Indian Independence Movement* (New Delhi, 1987).
Ali, Mohamed, *My Life: A Fragment* (Lahore, 1942).
Anand, M. R., *Letters on India* (London, 1942).
—— *Conversations in Bloomsbury* (New Delhi, 1981).
—— *The Bubble* (Delhi, 1984).
Anderson, Benedict, *Imagined Communities: Reflections on the Origins and Spread of Nationalism* (London, 1991).
Argov, Daniel, *Moderates and Extremists in the Indian Nationalist Movement* (Bombay, 1967).
Armitage, David, *The Ideological Origins of the British Empire* (Cambridge, 2000).
Arnold, David, *Police Power and Colonial Control: Madras 1859–1947* (Oxford, 1986).
Attlee, C. R., *The Labour Party in Perspective* (London, 1937).
—— *Empire Into Commonwealth: The Chichele Lectures* (Oxford, 1961).
Azad, A. K., *India Wins Freedom: An Autobiographical Narrative* (Bombay, 1959).
Baker, Christopher, 'Non-cooperation in South India' in Christopher Baker and D. A. Washbrook (eds.), *South India: Political Institutions and Political Change, 1880–1940* (Delhi, 1975).

Balachandran, Gopalan, 'Circulation Through Seafaring: Indian Seamen, 1890–1945', in Claude Markovits et al. (eds.), *Society and Circulation: Mobile People and Itinerant Cultures in South Asia, 1750–1950* (New Delhi, 2003).

Ball, Stuart, *Baldwin and the Conservative Party: The Crisis of 1929–1931* (New Haven, 1988).

Bapat, S. V. (ed.), *Reminiscences and Anecdotes about Lokamanya Tilak* (Poona, 1928).

Barnes, John and Nicholson, David (eds.), *The Empire At Bay: The Leo Amery Diary 1929–1945 Vol.2* (London, 1988).

Barnes, Leonard, *The Duty of Empire* (London, 1935).

—— *Empire or Democracy* (London, 1939).

Barooah, Nirode K., *Chatto: The Life and Times of an Indian Anti-imperialist in Europe* (Delhi, 2004).

Barrier, N. Gerald, 'The Arya Samaj and Congress Politics in the Punjab, 1894–1908', *Journal of Asian Studies*, 26/3 (1967), 363–79.

—— *Banned: Controversial Literature and Political Control in British India 1907–1947* (New York, 1974).

Barrow, Logie, *Independent Spirits: Spiritualism and English Plebeians, 1850–1910* (London, 1986).

—— and Bullock, Ian, *Democratic Ideas and the British Labour Movement, 1880–1914* (Cambridge, 1996).

Basu, Jyoti, *Memoirs: A Political Autobiography* (Calcutta, 1999).

Bellamy, Joyce M. and Saville, John (eds.), *Dictionary of Labour Biography* (13v., London, 1972-).

Berger, Stefan and Smith, Angel (eds.), *Nationalism, Labour and Ethnicity, 1870–1939* (Manchester, 1999).

Bevir, Mark, 'In Opposition to the Raj: Annie Besant and the Dialectic of Empire', *History of Political Thought*, 19/1 (1998), 61–77.

—— 'Theosophy as a Political Movement' in Antony Copley (ed.), *Gurus and Their Followers: New Religious Reform Movements in Colonial India* (Oxford, 2000).

Bhabha, Homi, *The Location of Culture* (London, 1994).

Blaxland, Gregory, *J. H. Thomas: A Life for Unity* (London, 1964).

Blazaar, David, *The Popular Front and the Progressive Tradition: Socialists, Liberals, and the Quest for Unity, 1884–1939* (Cambridge, 1992).

Blunt, Wilfrid Scawen, *My Diaries: A Personal Narrative of Events, 1888–1914* (2v., London, 1919–2).

Boehmer, Elleke, *Empire, the National and the Postcolonial, 1890–1920: Resistance in Interaction* (Oxford, 2002).

Bonnett, Alastair, *Idea of the West: Culture, Politics and History* (London, 2004).

Bor, Michael, *The Socialist League in the 1930s* (London, 2005).

Bose, Arun Coomer, *Indian Revolutionaries Abroad, 1905–1922: In the Background of International Developments* (Patna, 1971).

Bose, Sisir Kumar and Bose, Sugata (eds.), *Netaji: Collected Works of Subhas Chandra Bose* (10v., Calcutta, 1980-).

Bottomley, Arthur, *Commonwealth, Comrades and Friends* (Bombay, 1985).

Brailsford, H. N., *Rebel India* (London, 1931).

—— *India in Chains* (London, 1935).

—— *Subject India* (London, 1943).

Branson, Clive, *British Soldier in India: The Letters of Clive Branson* (London, 1944).

Branson, Noreen, *George Lansbury and the Councillors' Revolt: Poplarism, 1919–25* (London, 1979).

Brasted, H. V. and Douds, G., 'Passages to India: Peripatetic MPs on the Grand Indian Tour 1870–1940', *South Asia*, 2/1–2 (1979), 91–111.

Bridge, Carl, 'Conservatism and Indian Reform (1929–39): Towards a Pre-Requisites Model of Imperial Constitution-making', *Journal of Imperial and Commonwealth History*, 4/1 (1976), 176–93.

—— 'Churchill, Hoare, Derby and the Committee of Privileges, April to June 1934', *Historical Journal*, 22/1 (1979), 215–27.

—— 'The Impact of India on British High Politics in the 1930s: The Limits of Cowlingism', *South Asia*, vol.V, no.2 (1982), 13–23.

—— *Holding India to the Empire: The British Conservative Party and the 1935 Constitution* (New Delhi, 1986).

—— and Brasted, H. V., 'Labour and the Transfer of Power in India: A Case for Reappraisal?', *Indo-British Review*, 14/2 (1987), 70–90.

—— 'The British Labour Party and Indian Nationalism, 1940–1947', *South Asia*, 11/2 (1988), 69–99.

—— 'The British Labour Party "Nabobs" and Indian Reform, 1924–1931', *Journal of Imperial and Commonwealth History*, 17/3 (1989), 396–412.

—— '15 August 1947: Labour's Parting Gift to India' in Jim Masselos (ed.) *India: Creating a Modern Nation* (New Delhi 1990).

Vera Brittain: Wartime Diary ed. Bennett, Aleksandra, and Bishop, Alan (London, 1989).

Brockway, A. Fenner, *A Week in India (And Three Months in an Indian Hospital)* (London, 1928).

—— *The Indian Crisis* (London, 1930).

Brooke, Stephen, *Labour's War: The Labour Party during the Second World War* (Oxford, 1992).

Brown, Emily C., *Har Dayal: Hindu Revolutionary and Rationalist* (Tucson, Ariz., 1975).

Brown, Judith M., *Gandhi's Rise to Power: Indian Politics, 1915–1922* (Cambridge, 1972).

—— *Gandhi and Civil Disobedience: The Mahatma in Indian Politics, 1928–34* (Cambridge, 1977).

—— *Modern India: The Origins of an Asian Democracy* (Oxford, 1985).

—— 'The Mahatma in Old Age: Gandhi's Role in Indian Political Life, 1935–1942', in Richard Sisson and Stanley Wolpert (eds.), *Congress and Indian Nationalism: The Pre-Independence Phase* (Delhi, 1988).

—— *Gandhi: Prisoner of Hope* (New Haven, 1989).

—— *Nehru: A Political Life* (New Haven, 2003)

Bullock, Alan, *The Life and Times of Ernest Bevin: Trade Union Leader, 1881–1940* (London, 1960).

—— *Ernest Bevin: Minister of Labour, 1940–1945* (London, 1967).

—— *Ernest Bevin: Foreign Secretary, 1945–1951* (Oxford, 1983).

Burton, Antoinette, *Burdens of History: British Feminists, Indian Women and Imperial Culture, 1865–1915* (Chapel Hill, NC, 1994).

Bush, Barbara, *Imperialism, Race and Resistance: Africa and Britain, 1919–1945* (London, 1999).

Cain, P. J. and Hopkins, A. G., *British Imperialism*, vol.1, *Innovation and Expansion, 1688–1914* and vol.2 *Crisis and Deconstruction, 1914–1990* (London, 1993).

Callaghan, John, 'Jawaharlal Nehru and the Communist Party', *Journal of Communist Studies*, 7/3 (1991), 357–66.

—— *Rajani Palme Dutt: A Study in British Stalinism* (London, 1993).

—— 'The Communists and the Colonies: Anti-imperialism between the Wars', in Geoff Andrews et al., (eds.), *Opening the Books: Essays on the Social and Cultural History of the British Communist Party* (London, 1995).

—— 'Colonies, Racism, the CPGB and the Comintern in the Inter-War Years', *Science and Society*, 61/4 (1997–98), 513–25.

Cannadine, David, *Ornamentalism: How the British saw their Empire* (London, 2001).

Carrier, N. H., and Jeffery, J. R., *External Migration: A Study of the Available Statistics, 1815–1950* (London, 1953).

Carritt, Michael, *Mole in the Crown: Memoirs of a British Official in India who worked with the Communist Underground in the 1930s* (Calcutta, 1986).

Cashman, Richard, *The Myth of the Lokamanya: Tilak and Mass Politics in Maharashtra* (Berkeley and Los Angeles, 1975).

Catlin, George, *In the Path of Mahatma Gandhi* (London, 1948).

Ceadel, Martin, *Pacifism in Britain, 1914–1945: The Defining of a Faith* (Oxford, 1980).

Ceadel, Martin, 'A Legitimate Peace Movement: The Case of Britain, 1918–1945', in Peter Brock et al. (eds.), *Challenge to Mars: Essays on Pacifism from 1918 to 1945* (London, 1999).

Cell, John W., 'On the Eve of Decolonization: The Colonial Office's Plans for the Transfer of Power in Africa, 1947', *Journal of Imperial and Commonwealth History*, 8/3 (1980), 235–57.

Chakrabarty, Bidyut, 'Jawaharlal Nehru and Planning, 1938–41: India at the Crossroads', *Modern Asian Studies*, 26/2 (1992), 275–87.

Chakrabarty, Dipesh, 'Conditions for Knowledge of Working-Class Conditions: Employers, Government and the Jute Workers of Calcutta, 1890–1940', in Ranajit Guha (ed.), *Subaltern Studies II* (Oxford, 1983).

—— 'Trade Unions in a Hierarchical Culture: The Jute Workers of Calcutta, 1920–50' in Ranajit Guha (ed.), *Subaltern Studies III* (Oxford, 1984).

—— *Rethinking Working–Class History: Bengal 1890–1940* (Princeton, 1989).

—— 'Marx after Marxism: History, Subalternity and Difference', in Saree Makdisi, Cesare Casarino, and Rebecca E. Karl (eds.), *Marxism Beyond Marxism* (New York, 1996).

—— *Provincializing Europe: Postcolonial Thought and Historical Difference* (Princeton, 2000).

Chakravarty, Suhash, *V. K. Krishna Menon and the India League, 1925–47* (2v., Delhi, 1997).

—— *Crusader Extraordinary : Krishna Menon and the India League 1932–36* (Delhi, 2005).

Chandavarkar, Rajnarayan, *The Origins of Industrial Capitalism in India: Business Strategies and the Working Classes in Bombay, 1900–1940* (Cambridge, 1994).

—— *Imperial Power and Popular Politics: Class, Resistance and the State in India, 1850–1950* (Cambridge, 1998).

Chandra, Bipan, *Rise and Growth of Economic Nationalism in India: Economic Policies of National Leadership 1881–1915* (Delhi, 1966).

Chatterjee, Partha, *Nationalist Thought and the Colonial World* (London, 1986).

—— *The Nation and Its Fragments: Colonial and Postcolonial Histories* (Princeton, 1993).

Chatterji, B., 'Business and Politics in the 1930s: Lancashire and the Making of the Indo-British Trade Agreement, 1939', *Modern Asian Studies*, 15/3 (1981), 527–77.

Chaudhuri, Nupur, and Strobel, Margaret, *Western Women and Imperialism* (Bloomington, Ind., 1992).

Chirol, Valentine, *Indian Unrest* (London, 1910).

Choudhary, Valmiki (ed.), *Dr. Rajendra Prasad: Correspondence and Select Documents* (16v., New Delhi, 1984-).

Clarke, Peter, *The Cripps Version: The Life of Sir Stafford Cripps, 1885–1952* (London, 2002).

Cline, Catherine A., *Recruits to Labour: The British Labour Party, 1914–31* (Syracuse, NY, 1963).

Cotton, Sir Henry, *New India; or India in Transition* (London, 1885).

——, *Indian & Home Memories* (London, 1911).

Coupland, R. G., *Report on the Constitutional Problem in India* (3 vs., Oxford, 1942).

—— *The Cripps Mission* (Oxford, 1942).

Cowling, Maurice, *The Impact of Labour, 1920–1924: The Beginning of Modern British Politics* (Cambridge, 1971).

Crawley, W. F., 'Kisan Sabhas and Agrarian Revolt in the United Provinces', *Modern Asian Studies*, 5/2 (1971), 95–109.

Cumpston, Mary, 'Some Early Indian Nationalists and Their Allies in the British Parliament, 1851–1906', *English Historical Review*, 76 (1961), 279–97.

Dalton, Dennis, *Mahatma Gandhi: Non-Violent Power in* Action (New York, 1993).

Dalton, Hugh, *Practical Socialism for Britain* (London, 1935).

—— *Call Back Yesterday: Memoirs, 1887–1931* (London, 1953).

—— *The Fateful Years: Memoirs, 1931–1945* (London, 1957).

—— *High Tide and After: Memoirs, 1945–1960* (London, 1962).

Dar, Bishen Narayan (ed.), *India in England* (2v., Lucknow, 1889–90).

Darnton, Robert, 'Literary Surveillance in the British Raj: The Contradictions of Liberal Imperialism', *Book History*, 4 (2001), 133–76.

Darwin, John, 'British Decolonization since 1945: A Pattern or a Puzzle?', *Journal of Imperial and Commonwealth History*, 12/2 (1984), 187–209.

—— 'The Fear of Falling: British Politics and Imperial Decline', in *Transactions of the Royal Historical Society*, 5th series, 36, 1986, 27–44.

—— *Britain and Decolonisation* (Basingstoke, 1988).

—— *The End of the British Empire: The Historical Debate* (Oxford, 1991).

Das, Durga (ed.), *Sardar Patel's Correspondence, 1945–50* (10v., Ahmedabad, 1971–4).

Datta, V. N., *Madan Lal Dhingra and the Revolutionary Movement* (New Delhi, 1978).

Datta Gupta, Sobhanlal, *Comintern and the Destiny of Communism in India, 1919–1943* (Calcutta, 2006).

Davies, Ioan, 'The Labour Commonwealth', *New Left Review*, 22 (1963), 75–94.

Davis, Lance E. and Huttenback, Robert A, with the assistance of Susan Gray Davis, *Mammon and the Pursuit of Empire: The Political Economy of British Imperialism, 1860–1912* (Cambridge, 1986).

Davison, Peter (ed.), *The Complete Works of George Orwell* (20v., London, 1986–98).

Degras, Jane (ed.), *The Communist International 1919–1943: Documents* (3v., New York, 1956–65).

Desai, Mahadev, *Day to Day with Gandhi* (9v., Varanasi, 1968–72).

Dewey, Clive, *Anglo-Indian Attitudes: The Mind of the Indian Civil Service* (London, 1993).

Dhanki, Joginder Singh (ed.), *Perspectives on Indian National Movement: Selected Correspondence of Lala Lajpat Rai* (New Delhi, 1998).

Digby, William, *Condemned Unheard: The Government of India and H.H. the Maharaja of Kashmir* (London, 1890).

—— *Indian Politics in England: The Story of an Indian Reform Bill in Parliament Told Week by Week with other matters of interest to Indian reformers* (Lucknow, 1890).

Dikshit, Sheila (ed.), *Jawaharlal Nehru: Centenary Volume* (Delhi, 1989).

Divekar, V. D. (ed.), *Lokmanya Tilak in England, 1918–19: Diary and Documents* (Pune, 1997).

Dixon, Joy, *Divine Feminine: Theosophy and Feminism in England* (Baltimore, 2001).

Douds, Gerald, 'Tom Johnston in India', *Journal of Scottish Labour History*, 19 (1984), 6–21.

Dowse, R. E., *Left in the Centre: The Independent Labour Party, 1893–1940* (London, 1966).

Dummett, Raymond E. (ed.), *Gentlemanly Capitalism and British Imperialism: The New Debate on Empire* (London, 1999).

Dutt, Paramananda (ed.), *Memoirs of Moti Lal Ghose* (Calcutta, 1935).

Dutt, Rajani Palme, *Modern India* (London, 1927).

—— *India Today* (London, 1940).

Dwarkadas, Jamnadas, *Political Memoirs* (Madras, 1969).

Dwarkadas, Kanji *India's Fight for Freedom 1913–1937: An Eye-Witness Story* (Bombay, 1966).

Eisenstadt, S. N., 'Multiple Modernities', *Daedalus*, 129/1 (2000), 1–29.

Etherington, Norman, 'Hyndman, the Social Democratic Federation and Imperialism', *Historical Studies*, 16 (1974), 89–103.

Evans, Neil, 'The South Wales race riots of 1919', *Llafur, the Journal of Welsh Labour History*, 3/1 (1980), 5–29.

Fasana, Enrico, 'Deshabhakta: The Leaders of the Italian Independence Movement in the Eyes of Marathi Nationalists', *Asian and African Studies*, 3/2 (1994), 152–75.

Federowich, Kent, *Unfit for Heroes: Reconstruction and Soldier Settlement in the Empire Between the Wars* (Manchester, 1995).

Feuer, L. S., *Imperialism and the Anti-Imperialist Mind* (New York, 1978).

Fieldhouse, D.K. 'The Labour Governments and the Empire-Commonwealth', in Ritchie Ovendale (ed.), *The Foreign Policy of the British Labour Governments, 1945–1951* (Leicester, 1984).

Fischer, Georges, *Le Parti Travailliste et la décolonisation de l'Inde* (Paris, 1966).

Flint, John, 'Planned Decolonization and its Failure in British Africa', *African Affairs*, 82, 328 (1983), 389–411.

Foot, Michael, *Aneurin Bevan: A Biography* (2 vols., 1962–1973).

Fox, Richard G., *Gandhian Utopia: Experiments with Culture* (Boston, 1989).

Frykenberg, R. K., 'The Last Emergency of the Raj', in H. C. Hart (ed.), *Indira Gandhi's India* (Boulder, Colo., 1976), 37–66.

Gallagher, John, *The Decline, Revival and Fall of the British Empire: The Ford Lectures and Other Essays* (Cambridge, 1982).

—— Johnson, Gordon, and Seal, Anil (eds.), *Locality, Province and Nation: Essays on Indian Politics, 1870–1940* (Cambridge, 1973).

Gandhi, Leela, *Affective Communities: Anticolonial Thought, Fin-de-siècle Radicalism and the Politics of Friendship* (Durham, NC, 2006).

Gandhi, M. K., *The Collected Works of Mahatma Gandhi* (printed edition, 100v., 1958–88, and e-book edition, 2000).

Gandhi, Sonia, (ed.), *Freedom's Daughter: Letters Between Indira Gandhi and Jawaharlal Nehru, 1922–39* (London, 1989).

—— *Two Alone, Two Together: Letters Between Indira Gandhi and Jawaharlal Nehru, 1940–1964* (London, 1992).

Garnett, David, *The Golden Echo* (3v., 1953–62).

Garratt, G. T., *An Indian Commentary* (London, 1928).

—— *The Mugwumps and the Labour Party* (London, 1932).

Ghose, Aurobindo (ed.), *Speeches of B. G. Tilak* (Madras, n.d.).

Ghosh, P. C., *The Development of the Indian National Congress, 1892–1909* (Calcutta, 1960).

Ghosh, Sudhir, *Gandhi's Emissary* (Boston, 1967).

Gilbert, Martin, (ed.), *Plough My Own Furrow: The Story of Lord Allen of Hurtwood as told through his Writings and Correspondence* (London, 1965).

—— *Winston S. Churchill, 1874–1965* (8v., 1966–88).

Gilroy, Paul, et al. (eds.), *Without Guarantees: In Honour of Stuart Hall* (2000).

Golant, W., 'C. R. Attlee in the First and Second Labour Governments', *Parliamentary Affairs*, 26 (1973), 318–35.

Goldsmith, Raymond W., *The Financial Development of India, 1860–1977* (New Haven, 1983).

Goldsworthy, David, *Colonial Issues in British Politics, 1945–1961* (Oxford, 1971).

Gooch, G. P., *Frederic Mackarness: A Brief Memoir* (London, 1922).

Gopal, Sarvepelli (ed.), *Selected Works of Jawaharlal Nehru* First Series (15v., New Delhi, 1972–82); Second Series (33v., New Delhi, 1984-).

Grover, B. L. (ed.), *Curzon and Congress: Curzonian Policies and the Great Debate (January 1899–March 1902)* (New Delhi, 1995).

Guha, Ranajit, 'Discipline and Mobilize', *Subaltern Studies VII* (Oxford, 1992).

—— *Dominance without Hegemony: History and Power in Colonial India* (Cambridge, Mass., 1997).

Gupta, Nirmal Sen, *The Influence of Communism among Indian Students in London* (Calcutta, 1989).

Gupta, Partha Sarathi, 'British Labour and the Indian Left, 1919–1939', in Nanda, B.R. (ed.), *Socialism in India* (New Delhi, 1972).

—— *Imperialism and the British Labour Movement, 1918–1964* (London, 1975).

—— 'Imperialism and the Labour Government of 1945–51', in Jay Winter (ed.), *The Working Class in Modern British History: Essays in Honour of Henry Pelling* (Cambridge, 1983).

—— 'Imperial Strategy and the Transfer of Power, 1939–51', in A. K. Gupta (ed.), *Myth and Reality: The Indian Freedom Movement 1945–47* (New Delhi, 1987).

Gwyer. M., and Appadorai, A., (eds.), *Speeches and Documents on the Indian Constitution, 1921–47* (Bombay, 1957).

Haden Guest, L., *The Labour Party and the Empire* (London, 1926).

Haikal, Mustafa, 'Willi Munzenberg und die "Liga gegen Imperialismus und fur nationale Unabhangigkeit', in Tania Schlie et al., (eds.), *Willi Munzenberg (1889–1940): Ein Deutscher Kommunist in Spannungsfeld Zwischen Stalinismus und Antifachismus* (Frankfurt-am-Main, 1995).

Haithcox, John P., *Communism and Nationalism in India: M. N. Roy and Comintern Policy, 1920–1939* (Princeton, 1971).

Hamilton, M. A., *Remembering My Good Friends* (London, 1944).

Hardie, J. Keir, *India: Impressions and Suggestions* (London, 1909).

Hardiman, David, *Peasant Nationalists in Gujarat: Kheda District, 1917–1934* (Delhi, 1981).

—— *Peasant Resistance in India, 1858–1914* (Delhi, 1992).

Harnetty, Peter, 'The Indian Cotton Duties Controversy, 1894–96', *English Historical Review*, 77 (1962), 684–702.

Harris, Kenneth, *Attlee* (London, 1982).

Harrison, Irene, *Agatha Harrison: An Impression by her Sister* (London, 1956).

Haynes, Douglas et al., *Contesting Power: Resistance and Everyday Social Relations in South Asia* (Delhi, 1991).

Heehs, Peter, *The Bomb in Bengal: The Rise of Revolutionary Terrorism in India, 1900–1910* (New Delhi, 1994).

Henningham, Stephen, *Peasant Movements in India: North Bihar, 1917–1942* (Canberra, 1982).

—— 'The Contribution of "Limited Violence" to the Bihar Civil Disobedience Movement', *South Asia*, 2/1–2 (1979), 60–77.

—— 'Quit India in Bihar and the Eastern United Provinces: The Dual Revolt', in Ranajit Guha (ed.), *Subaltern Studies II* (Oxford, 1983).

Hobsbawm, Eric, *Labouring Men: Studies in the History of Labour* (London, 1964).

—— *Interesting Times: A Twentieth-Century Life* (London, 2002).

Hollis, Patricia, *Jennie Lee: A Life* (Oxford, 1997).

de Howe, M. Wolfe (ed.), *The Holmes-Laski Letters* (2v., London, 1953).

Howe, Stephen, 'Labour Patriotism, 1939–83', in Raphael Samuel (ed.), *Patriotism: The Making and Unmaking of British National Identity, vol.1 History and Politics* (London, 1989).

—— *Anticolonialism in British Politics: The Left and the End of Empire, 1918–1964* (Oxford, 1993).

Howell, David, *MacDonald's Party: Labour Identities and Crisis, 1922–31* (Oxford, 2002).

Hoy, David Couzens, *Critical Resistance: From Poststructuralism to Post-Critique* (Cambridge, Mass., 2004).

Hume, A. O., *The Old Man's Hope: A Tract for the Times* (Calcutta, 1886).

Hunt, James D., *Gandhi in London* (New Delhi, 1978).

Hutchins, F. G., *Spontaneous Revolution: Gandhi and the Quit India Movement* (Cambridge, Mass., 1973).

Hyam, Ronald, 'Africa and the Labour Government 1945–51', *Journal of Imperial and Commonwealth History*, 16/3, (1988), 148–72.

—— (ed.), *The Labour Government and the End of Empire 1945–1951* (4v., London, 1992).

Hyndman, H. M., *England for All* (London, 1881).

—— *The Bankruptcy of India* (London, 1886).

—— *The Ruin of India by British Rule, being the Report of the Social Democratic Federation to the International Socialist Congress at Stuttgart* (London, 1907).

Inden, Ronald, *Imagining India* (Oxford, 1990).

India League, *The Condition of India: Being the Report of the Delegation Sent to India by the India League in 1932* (London, 1933).

Iqbal, Afzar (ed.), *Select Writings & Speeches of Mohamed Ali* (2v., Lahore, 1963).

Israel, Milton, *Communications and Power: Propaganda and Press in the Indian Nationalist Struggle, 1920–1947* (Cambridge, 1994).

Jaffrelot, Christophe, *The Hindu Nationalist Movement in India* (New York, 1996).

Jagadisan, T. N. (ed.), *Letters of the Rt. Hon V. S. Srinivasa Sastri* (Bombay, 1963).

Jahn, Beate, 'Barbarian Thoughts: Imperialism in the Philosophy of John Stuart Mill, *Review of International Studies*, 31 (2005), 599–618.

Jalal, Ayesha, *The Sole Spokesman: Jinnah, the Muslim League and the Demand for Pakistan* (Cambridge, 1985).

Jayakar, M. R., *The Story of My Life* (2v., Bombay, 1958).

Jayal, Niraja Gopal (ed.), *Sidney and Beatrice Webb: Indian Diary* (Oxford, 1987).

Jefferys, Kevin, (ed.), *Labour and the Wartime Coalition: From the Diary of James Chuter Ede, 1941–1945* (London, 1987).

—— *The Churchill Coalition and Wartime Politics 1940–1945* (Manchester, 1991).

John, Angela, *War, Journalism and the Shaping of the Twentieth Century: The Life and Times of Henry W. Nevinson* (London, 2006).

Johnson, Gordon, *Provincial Politics and Indian Nationalism: Bombay and the Indian National Congress, 1880–1915* (Cambridge, 1973).

—— 'Partition, Agitation and Congress: Bengal 1904 to 1908', *Modern Asian Studies*, 7/3 (1973), 533–88.

Johnston, Thomas, *Memories* (London, 1952).

—— and Sime, J. F., *Exploitation in India* (Dundee, 1926).

Jones, Jean, *Ben Bradley* (London, 1994).

—— *The League Against Imperialism* (London, 1996).

Jones, K. W., *Arya Dharm: Hindu Consciousness in 19th-Century Punjab* (Delhi, 1976).

Joshi, V. C. (ed.), *Lala Lajpat Rai: Writings and Speeches* (2v., Delhi, 1966).

Juergensmeyer, Mark, 'Saint Gandhi', in J. S. Hawley (ed.), *Saints and Virtues* (Berkeley and Los Angeles, 1987).

Kahler, Miles, *Decolonization in Britain and France: The Domestic Consequences of International Relations* (Princeton, 1984).

Kaminsky, Arnold P., *The India Office, 1880–1910* (London, 1986).

Kanungo, Hema Candra, *Bamlaya Biplaba Praceshta* (Calcutta, 1928).

Karnik, V. B., *The New India: A Short Account of the Radical Democratic Party, Its Programme and Policy* (London, 1944).

—— *M. N. Roy: a Political Biography* (Bombay, 1978).

Kaushik, Harish P., *Indian National Congress in England* (Delhi, 1991).

Kaviraj, Sudipta, 'On State, Society and Discourse in India' in James Manor (ed.), *Rethinking Third World Politics* (London, 1991).

—— (ed.), *Politics in India* (Delhi, 1997).

—— 'Modernity and Politics in India', *Daedalus*, 129/1 (2000), 137–62.

—— and Khilnani, Sunil, *Civil Society: History and Possibilities* (Cambridge, 2001).

Kaye, Sir Cecil, *Communism in India 1919–1924* (reprinted, Calcutta 1971).

Keer, Dhananjay, *Veer Savarkar* (2nd ed., Bombay 1966).

Kelkar, N. C., *Speeches and Addresses* (Pune, n.d.).

Kennedy, W. P., *Industrial Structure, Capital Markets and the Origins of British Economic Decline* (Cambridge, 1987).

Kent, John, 'Bevin's Imperialism and the Idea of Euro-Africa', in Michael Dockrill and John W. Young (eds.), *British Foreign Policy, 1945–56* (Basingstoke, 1989).

Ker, J. C., *Political Trouble in India, 1907–1917*, (reprinted, Calcutta, 1973).

Khilnani, Sunil, *The Idea of India* (London, 1997).

—— 'Gandhi and Nehru: The Uses of English', in Arvind Krishna Mehrotra (ed.), *A History of Indian Literature in English* (London, 2003).

Kiernan, V. G. 'India and the Labour Party', *New Left Review*, 42 (1967), 44–55.

—— 'The British Labour Movement and Imperialism', *Bulletin of Society for the Study of Labour History*, 31 (1975), 96–101.

King, Francis and Matthews George (eds.), *About Turn : The British Communist Party and the Second World War : The Verbatim Record of the Central Committee Meetings of 25 September and 2–3 October 1939* (London, 1990).

Knowles, Caroline, *Race, Discourse and Labourism* (London, 1992).

Koch, Stephen, *Double Lives: Stalin, Willi Munzenberg and the Seduction of the Intellectuals* (London, 1994).

Kohli, Atul, *India's Democracy* (Princeton, 1991).

—— *The Success of India's Democracy* (Cambridge, 2001).

Kohn, Margaret, and O'Neill, Daniel I., 'A Tale of Two Indias: Burke and Mill on Empire and Slavery in the West Indies and America', *Political Theory*, 32/4 (2005), 1–37.

Koss, Stephen E., *John Morley at the India Office, 1905–1910* (New Haven, 1969).

Kothari, Rajni, *Politics in India* (New Delhi, 1970).

Kramnick, Issac and Sheerman, Barry, *Harold Laski: A Life on the Left* (London, 1993).

Krishna, Gopal, 'The Development of the Indian National Congress as a Mass Organization, 1918–1923', *Journal of Asian Studies*, 25/3 (1966), 413–30.

Krishnan, N. K., *Testament of Faith: Memoirs of a Communist* (New Delhi, 1990).

Kumar, Ravinder et al. (eds.), *Selected Works of Motilal Nehru* (7v., New Delhi, 1982–95).

Kumar, Ravindra (ed.), *Selected Documents of Lala Lajpat Rai, 1906–1928* (5v., New Delhi, 1993).

Kunte, B. G. (ed.), *Source Material for a History of the Freedom Movement*, vol. VII (Bombay, 1978).

Kutty, Madhavan, *V. K. Krishna Menon* (Delhi, 1988).

Lansbury, George, *My Life* (London, 1928).

—— *Labour's Way with the Commonwealth* (London, 1935).

Lee, Francis, *Fabianism and Colonialism: The Life and Political Thought of Lord Sydney Olivier* (London, 1988).

Lee, J. M., *Colonial Development and Good Government: A Study of the Ideas Expressed by the British Official Classes in Planning Decolonisation, 1939–1964* (Oxford, 1967).

Lenin, V. I., *Collected Works* (4th edition, Moscow, 1965).

Listowel, Lord, 'The Whitehall Dimension of the Transfer of Power', *Indo-British Review*, 7/3–4 (1978), 22–31.

—— 'The British Partner in the Transfer of Power', in John Grigg (ed.), *Nehru Memorial Lectures 1966–1991* (Oxford, 1992).

Louis, Wm. Roger, *Imperialism at Bay: The United States and the Decolonization of the British Empire* (Oxford, 1977).

—— *The British Empire in the Middle East, 1945–1951: Arab Nationalism, the United States and Postwar Imperialism* (Oxford, 1984).

—— *In the Name of God, Go! Leo Amery and the British Empire in the Age of Churchill* (New York, 1992).

Low, D. A., 'The Government of India and the First Non Co-operation Movement, 1920–22', in Ravinder Kumar (ed.), *Essays on Gandhian Politics: The Rowlatt Satyagraha of 1919* (Oxford, 1971).

—— *Congress and the Raj: Facets of the Indian Struggle, 1917–1947* (London, 1977).

—— 'The Mediator's Moment: Sir Tej Bahadur Sapru and the Antecedents to the Cripps Mission to India, 1940–42', in R. F. Holland and Gowher Rizvi (eds.), *Perspectives on Imperialism and Decolonization: Essays in Honour of A. F. Madden* (London, 1984).

—— *Eclipse of Empire* (Cambridge, 1991).

—— *Rearguard Action: Selected Essays on Late Colonial Indian History* (New Delhi, 1996).

—— *Britain and Indian Nationalism: The Imprint of Ambiguity* (Cambridge, 1997).

Lutyens, Emily, *Candles in the Sun* (London, 1957).

MacDonald, J. Ramsay, *The Awakening of India* (London, 1910).

—— *The Government of India* (London, 1919).

MacIntyre, Stuart, *Imperialism and the British Labour Movement in the 1920s: An Examination of Marxist Theory* (London, 1975).

MacEwen, Malcolm, *The Greening of a Red* (London, 1991).

McKean, Lise, *Divine Enterprise: Gurus and the Hindu Nationalist Movement* (Chicago, 1996).

McKibbin, Ross, *The Evolution of the Labour Party 1910–1924* (Oxford, 1974).

—— 'Why was there no Marxism in Great Britain?' *The English Historical Review*, 391 (1984), 297–331.

McLane, J. R., *Indian Nationalism and the Early Congress* (Princeton, 1977).

Maclean, Iain, *Keir Hardie* (London, 1975).

McLeod, John, *Postcolonial London: Rewriting the Metropolis* (2004).

McMeekin, Sean, *The Red Millionaire: A Political Biography of Willi Munzenberg* (New Haven, 2003).

Manley, John, 'Moscow Rules? 'Red' Unionism and 'Class Against Class' in Britain, Canada, and the United States, 1928–1935', *Labour/Le Travail*, 56 (2005), 9–50.

Markovits, Claude, *The UnGandhian Gandhi: The Life and Afterlife of the Mahatma* (London, 2004).

Marquand, David, *Ramsay MacDonald* (London, 1977).

—— *The Progressive Dilemma: From Lloyd George to Kinnock* (London, 1991).

Marsh, Arthur and Ryan, Victoria, *The Seamen: A History of the National Union of Seamen 1887–1987* (Oxford, 1989).

Martin, Briton, *New India, 1885* (Berkeley and Los Angeles, 1969).

Masani, Minoo, *Bliss Was It in that Dawn to be Alive: A Political Memoir up to Independence* (New Delhi, 1977).

Masani, R. P., *Dadabhai Naoroji: The Grand Old Man of India* (London, 1939).

Matthai, John, *Village Government in British India* (London, 1915).

Mehrotra, S. R., 'Imperial Federation and India, 1868–1917', *Journal of Commonwealth Political Studies*, 1/1 (1961), 29–40.

—— *The Emergence of the Indian National Congress* (Delhi, 1971).

—— *A History of the Indian National Congress, volume 1* (New Delhi, 1995).

Mehta, Uday Singh, *Liberalism and Empire: A Study in Nineteenth Century British Liberal Thought* (Chicago, 1999).

Menon, V. K. Krishna, *India Faces Peril* (London 1942).

Middlemas, Keith (ed.), *Thomas Jones: Whitehall Diary* (3.v, London, 1969–71).

Miliband, Ralph, *Parliamentary Socialism* (London, 1961).

Moir, Martin, Peers, Douglas, and Zastoupil, Lynn (eds.), *J. S. Mill's Encounter With India* (Toronto, 1999).

Mommsen, Wolfgang and Osterhammel, Jürgen (eds.), *Imperialism and After: Continuities and Discontinuities* (London, 1986).

Mookerj, Radhakumud, *The Fundamental Unity of India* (London, 1913).

Moon, Penderel (ed.), *Wavell: The Viceroy's Journal* (London, 1973).

Moore, R. J., 'John Morley's Acid Test: India, 1906–1910, *Pacific Affairs*, 40/3–4 (Autumn 1967–Winter 1967–8), 333–40.

—— *Liberalism and Indian Politics 1872–1922* (London, 1966).

—— 'The Mystery of the Cripps Mission', *Journal of Commonwealth Political Studies*, 11 (1973), 195–213.

—— *The Crisis of Indian Unity, 1917–1940* (Oxford, 1974).

—— *Churchill, Cripps and India, 1939–1945* (Oxford, 1979).

—— *Escape From Empire: The Attlee Government and the Indian Problem* (Oxford, 1983).

—— *Making the New Commonwealth* (Oxford, 1987).

—— *Endgames of Empire: Studies of Britain's Indian Problem* (Delhi, 1988).

Morefield, Jeanne, *Covenants without Swords: Idealist Liberalism and the Spirit of Empire* (Princeton, 2004).

Morgan, D. J., *The Official History of Colonial Development*, vol.1 *The Origins of British Aid Policy, 1924–1945* (London, 1980).

Morgan, Kenneth O., *Keir Hardie: Radical and Socialist* (London, 1975).

Morgan, Kenneth O., *Labour in Power, 1945–1951* (Oxford, 1984).

—— *Labour People: Leaders and Lieutenants, Hardie to Kinnock* (Oxford, 1987).

Morgan, Kevin, *Against Fascism and War: Ruptures and Continuities in British Communist Politics, 1935–1941* (Manchester, 1989).

Morley, John, 'British Democracy and Indian Government', *Nineteenth Century and After,* April 1911, 69/408, 189–209.

W. H. Morris-Jones '"If It Be Real, What Does It Mean?" Some British Perceptions of the Indian National Congress', in Richard Sisson and Stanley Wolpert (eds.), *Congress and Indian Nationalism: The Pre-Independence Phase* (Delhi, 1988).

—— and Fischer, Georges (eds.), *Decolonisation and After: The British and French Experience* (London, 1980).

Moulton, Edward C., 'British Radicals and India in the Early Twentieth Century', in A. J. Morris (ed.), *Edwardian Radicalism* (London, 1974).

—— 'Early Indian Nationalism: Henry Cotton and the British Positivist and Radical Connection, 1870–1915', *Journal of Indian History,* 60 (1982), 25–59.

—— 'William Wedderburn and Early Indian Nationalism', in Kenneth Ballhatchet et al. (eds.), *Changing South Asia: Politics and Government* (Hong Kong, 1984).

—— 'The Early Congress and the British Radical Connection', in D. A. Low (ed.), *The Indian National Congress: Centenary Hindsights* (Oxford, 1988).

Mukerjee, Haridas and Uma, *Bipin Chandra Pal and India's Struggle for Swaraj* (Calcutta, 1958).

Mukherji, Haridas and Uma, *Sri Aurobindo and the New Thought in Indian Politics* (Calcutta, 1964).

Muthu, Sankar, *Enlightenment Against Empire* (Princeton, 2003).

Nanda, B. R. (ed.), *Socialism in India* (New Delhi, 1972).

—— *Gokhale: The Indian Moderates and the British Raj* (Princeton, 1977).

—— B. R. Nanda (ed.), *Essays in Modern Indian History* (Delhi, 1980).

—— 'The Swarajist Interlude', in Indian National Congress, *A Centenary History of the Indian National Congress* (5v., New Delhi, 1985), v.2, 113–60.

—— (ed.), *Selected Works of Govind Ballabh Pant* (17v., Oxford, 1993-)

—— (ed.), *Collected Works of Lala Lajpat Rai* (4v., New Delhi, 2003-)

Nandurkar, G. M. (ed.), *Sardar's Letters—Mostly Unknown* (5v., Ahmedabad, 1974–8).

Nandy, Ashis, *The Intimate Enemy: Loss and Recovery of Self under Colonialism* (Delhi, 1983).

—— *Traditions, Tyranny and Utopias: Essays in the Politics of Awareness* (New Delhi, 1987).

Nehru, Jawaharlal, *A Bunch of Old Letters: Written Mostly to Jawaharlal Nehru and Some Written by Him* (Delhi, 1960).

—— *An Autobiography* (London, 1936).

—— *The Discovery of India* (London, 1946).

Nethercot, Arthur H., *The Last Four Lives of Annie Besant* (London, 1963).

Nevinson, H. W., *The New Spirit in India* (London, 1908).

—— *More Changes, More Chances* (London, 1925).

Newman, Michael, *Harold Laski: A Political Biography* (Basingstoke, 1993).

Nicholson, Marjorie, *The TUC Overseas: The Roots of Policy* (London, 1986).

Normanton, Helena, *India in England* (Delhi, 1921).

O'Brien, Nick, '"Something Older than Law Itself", Sir Henry Maine, Niebuhr and "the Path not Chosen"', *Journal of Legal History*, 26/3 (2005), 229–51.

O'Brien, Patrick K., 'The Costs and Benefits of British Imperialism 1846–1914', *Past and Present*, 120 (1988), 163–200.

Olivier, Margaret (ed.), *Sydney Olivier: Letters and Selected Writings* (London, 1948).

Olson, Mancur, *The Logic of Collective Action: Public Goods and the Theory of Groups* (Cambridge, Mass., 1965).

Orwell, Sonia and Angus, Ian (eds.), *The Collected Essays, Journalism and Letters of George Orwell* (4v., Harmondsworth, 1970).

Ovendale, Ritchie, (ed.), *The Foreign Policy of the British Labour Governments, 1945–1951* (Leicester, 1984).

Overstreet, Gene D. and Windmiller, Marshall, *Communism in India* (Berkeley and Los Angeles, 1959).

Owen, Hugh F., 'Towards Nationwide Agitation and Organisation: The Home Rule Leagues, 1915–18', in D. A. Low (ed.), *Soundings in Modern South Asian History* (London, 1968).

—— 'Mrs. Annie Besant and the Rise of Political Activity in South India, 1914–1919' in *The Indian Nationalist Movement, c.1912–22: Leadership, Organisation and Philosophy* (New Delhi, 1990).

Owen, Nicholas, 'Responsibility Without Power: The Attlee Governments and the End of British Rule in India', in Nick Tiratsoo (ed.), *The Attlee Years* (London, 1989).

—— 'India and Britain in the Second World War', in Brian Brivati and Harriet Jones (eds.), *What Difference Did the War Make?* (London, 1993).

—— '"More Than a Transfer of Power": Independence Day Ceremonies in India, 15 August 1947' *Contemporary Record*, 6/3 (1992), 415–51.

—— 'Labour and the New Empire in the Middle East', in Martin Kolinsky and Michael Cohen (eds.), *The Demise of the British Empire in the Middle East, 1943–55* (London, 1997).

—— 'Critics of Empire in Britain', in Judith M. Brown and Wm. Roger Louis (eds.), *The Oxford History of the British Empire, vol.IV, The Twentieth Century* (Oxford, 1999).

—— 'The Cripps Mission: A Reinterpretation', *Journal of Imperial and Commonwealth History*, 30/1 (2002), 61–98.

Owen, Roger and Sutcliffe, Bob (eds.), *Studies in the Theory of Imperialism* (London, 1972).

Pal, Bipin Chandra, *Nationality and Empire: A Running Study of some Current Indian Problems* (Calcutta, 1916).

—— *The New Economic Menace to India* (Madras, 1920).

Pandey, Gyanendra, *The Ascendancy of the Congress in Uttar Pradesh, 1926–1934: A Study in Imperfect Mobilization* (Delhi, 1978).

—— 'Congress and the Nation, 1917–1947', in Richard Sisson and Stanley Wolpert (eds.), *Congress and Indian Nationalism: The Pre-Independence Phase* (Delhi, 1988).

Pandit, Viyajayalakshmi, *The Scope of Happiness* (London, 1979).

Paranjape, Makarand (ed.), *Sarojini Naidu: Selected Letters, 1890s to 1940s* (Delhi, 1996).

Parekh, Bhikhu, *Colonialism, Tradition and Reform: An Analysis of Gandhi's Political Discourse* (New Delhi, 1989).

—— 'Decolonizing Liberalism', in Alexandras Shtromas (ed.), *The End of 'Isms'? Reflections on the Fate of Ideological Politics* (Oxford, 1994).

—— 'Liberalism and Colonialism: A Critique of Locke and Mill', in Jan N. Pieterse and Bhikhu Parekh (eds.), *The Decolonization of Imagination: Culture, Knowledge and Power* (London, 1995).

Parel, Anthony J. (ed.), *M. K. Gandhi: Hind Swaraj and other Writings* (Cambridge, 1997).

Parry, Benita, *Postcolonial Studies: A Materialist Critique* (London, 2004).

Patel, Gordharibhai, *Vithalbhai Patel* (2v., Bombay, 1950).

Patwardhan, R. P. (ed.), *Dadabhai Naoroji Correspondence* (2v., Bombay, 1977).

Pearce, Robert, *Turning Point in Africa: British Colonial Policy, 1938–1948* (London, 1982).

—— (ed.), *Patrick Gordon Walker: Political Diaries 1932–1971* (London, 1991).

—— R. D. Pearce, 'The Colonial Office in 1947 and the Transfer of Power in Africa: An Addendum to John Cell', *Journal of Imperial and Commonwealth History*, 10/2 (1982), 211–15.

—— 'The Colonial Office and Planned Decolonization in Africa', *African Affairs*, vol.83, no.330 (January 1984), 77–93.

Pedersen, Susan, *Eleanor Rathbone and the Politics of Conscience* (New Haven, 2004).

Peele, G. R., 'A Note on the Irwin Declaration', *Journal of Imperial and Commonwealth History*, 1/3 (1973), 331–8.

Petrie, Sir David, *Communism in India 1924–1927* (reprinted Calcutta, 1972).

Phadke, Y. D., *Portrait of a Revolutionary: Senapati Bapat* (Ahmedabad, 1981).

Philips, C. H., and Wainwright, M. Doreen (eds.), *The Partition of India: Policies and Perspectives, 1935–1947* (London, 1970).

Pimlott, Ben, *Labour and the Left in the 1930s* (London, 1977).
—— (ed.), *Fabian Essays in Socialist Thought* (London, 1984).
—— (ed.), *The Political Diary of Hugh Dalton* (London, 1986).
—— (ed.), *The Second World War Diary of Hugh Dalton* (London, 1986).
—— *Hugh Dalton* (London, 1986).
Pitts, Jennifer, *A Turn to Empire: The Rise of Imperial Liberalism in Britain and France* (Princeton, 2005).
Polak, H. S. L. et al., *Mahatma Gandhi* (London, 1949).
Pollard, Sidney, 'Capital Exports, 1870–1914: Harmful or Beneficial?', *Economic History Review*, 38/4 (1985), 489–514.
—— *Britain's Prime and Britain's Decline: The British Economy, 1870–1914* (London, 1989).
Popplewell, Richard J., *Intelligence and Imperial Defence: British Intelligence and the Defence of the Indian Empire, 1904–1924* (London, 1995).
Porter, Bernard, *Critics of Empire: British Radical Attitudes to Colonialism in Africa, 1895–1914* (London, 1968).
—— *The Lion's Share* (London, 1975).
—— 'Fabians, Imperialists and the International Order', in Ben Pimlott (ed.), *Fabian Essays in Socialist Thought* (London, 1984).
—— *The Absent-Minded Imperialists: Empire, Society, and Culture in Britain* (Oxford, 2004).
Postgate, Raymond, *The Life of George Lansbury* (London, 1951), 58, 142.
Prakash, Gyan (ed.), *After Colonialism: Imperial Histories and Postcolonial Displacements* (Princeton, 1995).
—— *Another Reason: Science and the Imagination of Modern India* (Princeton, 1995).
Prasad, Amba, *The Indian Revolt of 1942* (Delhi, 1958).
Purcell, A. A. and Hallsworth, J., *Report on Labour Conditions in India* (London, 1928).
Raghavan, G. N. S. (ed.), *M. Asaf Ali's Memoirs: The Emergence of Modern India* (Delhi, 1994).
Rajagopalachar, C., and Kumarappa, J. C. (eds.), *The Nation's Voice: Being a Collection of Gandhiji's Speeches in England and Sjt. Mahadev Desai's Account of the Sojourn (September to December 1931)* (Ahmedabad, 1932)
Rajan, T. S. S., *Ninaivu Alaikal* (Madras, 1947).
Ram, Janaki, *V. K. Krishna Menon: A Personal Memoir* (Delhi, 1997).
Ramusack, Barbara N., 'Catalysts or Helpers? British Feminists, Indian Women's Rights and Indian Independence', in Gail Minault (ed.), *The Extended Family: Women and Political Participation in India and Pakistan* (Delhi, 1981).
—— 'Cultural Missionaries, Maternal Imperialists, Feminist Allies: British Women Activists in India, 1865–1945', *Women's Studies International Forum*, 13/4 (1990), 309–21.

Ratcliffe, S. K., *Sir William Wedderburn and the Indian Reform Movement* (London, 1923).

Ray, Rajat Kanta, 'Moderates, Extremists, and Revolutionaries: Bengal, 1900–1908', in Richard Sisson and Stanley Wolpert (eds.), *Congress and Indian Nationalism: The Pre-Independence Phase* (Delhi, 1988).

Ray, Sibnarayan (ed.), *Selected Works of M. N. Roy* (3v., Oxford, 1987–90).

—— *M. N. Roy, In Freedom's Quest: A Study of the Life and Works of M. N. Roy, 1887–1954* (3v., Delhi, 1998–2005).

Raychaudhuri, Tapan, 'Indian Nationalism as Animal Politics', *Historical Journal*, 22 (1979), 747–63.

Redfern, Neil, *Class or Nation: Communists, Imperialism and Two World Wars* (London, 2005).

Reynolds, Reginald, *India, Gandhi and World Peace* (London, 1931).

—— *To Live in Mankind: A Quest for Gandhi* (London, 1951).

—— *My Life and Crimes* (London, 1956).

Rich, Paul B., *Race and Empire in British Politics* (Cambridge, 1986).

Riddell, John (ed.), *Lenin's Struggle for a Revolutionary International: Documents, 1907–1916* (New York, 1984).

—— *Workers of the World and Oppressed Peoples, Unite! Proceedings and Documents of the Second Congress of the Communist International, 1920* (2v., New York, 1991).

Risseuw, Carla, 'Thinking Culture Through Counter-Culture: The Case of Theosophists in India and Ceylon and their Ideas on Race and Hierarchy', in Antony Copley (ed.), *Gurus and Their Followers: New Religious Reform Movements in Colonial India* (Oxford, 2000).

Rizvi, Gowher, *Linlithgow and India* (London, 1978).

—— 'Transfer of Power in India: A "Re-Statement" of an Alternative Approach', in R. F. Holland and Gowher Rizvi (eds.), *Perspectives on Imperialism and Decolonization: Essays in Honour of A. F. Madden* (London, 1984), 127–44.

Robb, P. G., *The Government of India and Reform* (Oxford, 1976).

—— *The Evolution of British Policy Towards Indian Politics, 1880–1920* (New Delhi, 1992).

Robinson, Francis, and Brass, Paul R., *The Indian National Congress and Indian Society, 1885–1985: Ideology, Structure and Political Discourse* (Delhi, 1987).

Roy, Asim, 'The High Politics of India's Partition: The Revisionist Perspective', *Modern Asian Studies*, 24/2, (1990), 385–415.

Roy, M. N., *Memoirs* (Bombay, 1964).

—— *Postwar Perspectives: A Peep into the Future* (London, 1945).

Roy, Purabi et al. (eds.), *Indo-Russian Relations, 1917–1947: Select Documents from the Archives of the Russian Federation* (2v., Calcutta, 2000).

Roy, Subodh (ed.), *Communism in India: Unpublished Documents from National Archives of India* (Calcutta, 1971).

Ryan, P. A., ' "Poplarism", 1894–1930' in Pat Thane (ed.), *Origins of British Social Policy* (London, 1978).

Said, Edward, *Orientalism* (London, 1978).

—— 'Travelling Theory', *Raritan*, 1/3 (1982) 41–67.

—— 'Orientalism Reconsidered', in Francis Barker et al., *Europe and its Others*, v.1 (Colchester, 1985).

—— 'Third World Intellectuals and Metropolitan Culture', *Raritan*, 9/3 (1990), 27–50.

—— *Culture and Imperialism* (London, 1993).

Saklatvala, Sehri, *The Fifth Commandment: Biography of Shapurji Saklatvala* (Salford, 1991).

Samanta, Amiya K. (ed.), *Terrorism in Bengal : A Collection of Documents on Terrorist Activities from 1905 to 1939* (6v., Calcutta, 1995).

Samuel, Raphael, *The Lost World of British Communism* (London, 2006).

Sareen, Tilak Raj, *Indian Revolutionary Movement Abroad (1905–1921)* (New Delhi, 1979).

Sarkar, Sumit, *The Swadeshi Movement in Bengal, 1903–8* (New Delhi, 1973).

—— *Modern India, 1885–1947* (Basingstoke, 1983).

Savarkar, V. D., *The Indian War of Independence (National Rising of 1857)* (4th ed., Bombay, 1946).

—— *Samagra Savakara Vanmaya* (8v., Pune, 1963–5).

—— *Satrucya Sibiranta* (Mumbai, 1965).

Saville, John, 'Reginald O. Bridgeman', 'The League Against Imperialism', and 'The Meerut Trial, 1929–33', in Joyce M. Bellamy and John Saville (eds.), *Dictionary of Labour Biography*, vii (London, 1984).

Sayer, Derek, 'British Reaction to the Amritsar Massacre 1919–1920', *Past and Present*, 131 (May 1991), 130–64.

Schneer, Jonathan, *Labour's Conscience: The Labour Left, 1945–51* (Boston, 1988).

—— *George Lansbury* (Manchester, 1990).

—— *London 1900: The Imperial Metropolis* (New Haven, 1989).

Schuster, George, *Private Work and Public Causes: A Personal Record, 1881–1978* (Cowbridge, 1979).

Scott, David, *Conscripts of Modernity: The Tragedy of Colonial Enlightenment* (Durham, NC, 2004).

Scott, Michael, *A Time to Speak* (London, 1958).

Seal, Anil, *The Emergence of Indian Nationalism: Competition and Collaboration in the Later Nineteenth Century* (Cambridge, 1968).

Sehavanis, Chinmohan, 'Communism at Oxford in the Mid-Twenties', in Barun De (eds.), *Essays in Honour of Prof. S. C. Sarkar* (New Delhi, 1976).

Sen, Mohit, *A Traveller and the Road: The Journey of an Indian Communist* (New Delhi, 2003).

Sherwood, Marika, 'The Comintern, the CPGB, the Colonies and Black Britons', *Science and Society*, 60/2 (1996), 137–63.

Silverman, Julius, 'The India League' in Indian National Congress, *A Centenary History of the Indian National Congress* (5v., New Delhi, 1985), v.3, 844–71.

Singer, Wendy, 'Peasants and Peoples of the East: Indians and the Rhetoric of the Comintern', in Tim Rees and Andrew Thorpe (eds.), *International Communism and the Communist International, 1919–43* (Manchester, 1998).

Singh, Anita Inder, *The Origins of the Partition of India 1936–1947* (Oxford, 1987).

—— 'Labour Party and the Partition', *Indo-British Review*, 17/1–2 (1989), 214–17.

Sinha, L. P., *The Left-Wing in India, 1919–47* (Muzaffarpur, 1965).

Sinha, Mrinalini, 'The Lineage of the "Indian" Modern: Rhetoric, Agency and the Sarda Act in Late Colonial India', in Antoinette Burton (ed.), *Gender, Sexuality and Colonial Modernities* (London, 1999).

—— *Specters of Mother India: The Global Restructuring of an Empire* (Duke, NC, 2006).

Sisson, Richard and Wolpert, Stanley (eds.), *Congress and Indian Nationalism: The Pre-Independence Phase* (Delhi, 1988).

Sitaramayya, B. P., *History of the Indian National Congress Volume I (1885–1935)* (reprinted New Delhi, 1969).

Slade, Madeline, *The Spirit's Pilgrimage* (London, 1960).

Spivak, Gayatri Chakravorty ' "Can the Subaltern Speak?" ' in Cary Nelson and Lawrence Grossberg (eds.), *Marxism & The Interpretation of Culture* (Basingstoke, 1988).

—— *The Post-colonial Critic: Interviews, Strategies, Dialogues* (New York, 1990).

Spratt, Philip, *Blowing Up India: Reminiscences and Reflections of a Former Comintern Emissary* (Calcutta, 1955).

Squires, Mike, *Saklatvala: A Political Biography* (London, 1990).

Srivastava, Gita, 'Savarkar and Mazzini', *Rassegna Storica del Risorgimento*, 71/3 (1984), 259–64.

Srivastava, Harindra, *Five Stormy Years: Savarkar in London, June 1906–June 1911, a Centenary Salute to Swatantrayaveer Vinayak Damodar Savarkar* (New Delhi, 1983).

Stewart, Gordon T., *Jute and Empire : The Calcutta Jute Wallahs and the Landscapes of Empire* (Manchester, 1998).

Stokes, Eric, *The English Utilitarians and India* (Oxford, 1959).

Stoler, Ann Laura, 'Cultivating Bourgeois Bodies and Racial Selves', in Catherine Hall (ed.), *Cultures of Empire: Colonizers in Britain and the Empire in the Nineteenth and Twentieth Centuries: A Reader* (Manchester, 2000).

Studdert-Kennedy, Gerald, *British Christians, Indian Nationalists and the Raj* (Delhi, 1991).

—— *Providence and the Raj* (New Delhi, 1998).

Subramanyam, C. S., *M. P. T. Acharya: His Life and Times* (Madras, 1995).

Sundararajan, Saroja, *Saytamurti: A Political Biography* (New Delhi, 1983).

Tabili, Laura, '*We Ask for British Justice': Workers and Racial Difference in Late Imperial Britain* (Ithaca, NY, 1994).

Taylor, A. J. P., *The Trouble Makers: Dissent over British Foreign Policy, 1792–1939* (London, 1957).

Taylor, Anne, *Annie Besant: A Biography* (Oxford, 1992).

Taylor, Charles, 'Modernity and Difference' in Paul Gilroy et al., (eds.), *Without Guarantees: In Honour of Stuart Hall* (London, 2000).

Taylor, Miles, ' "Imperium et Libertas?" Rethinking the Radical Critique of Imperialism in the Nineteenth Century', *Journal of Imperial and Commonwealth History*, 19 (1991), 1–23.

Thompson, Andrew S., *Imperial Britain: The Empire in British Politics, c.1880–1932* (Harlow, 2000).

—— *The Empire Strikes Back? The Impact of Imperialism on Britain from the Mid-Nineteenth Century* (Harlow, 2005).

Thompson, Edward, *The Reconstruction of India* (London, 1930).

—— A *Letter from India* (London, 1932).

—— *Enlist India for Freedom!* (London, 1940).

Thompson, E. P., 'The Nehru Tradition', in his *Writing by Candlelight* (London, 1980).

—— *Alien Homage: Edward Thompson and Rabrindranath Tagore* (New Delhi, 1998).

Thornton, A. P., *The Imperial Idea and Its Enemies* (London, 1959).

Thorpe, Andrew, *The British General Election of 1931* (Oxford, 1991).

—— *The British Communist Party and Moscow, 1920–43* (Manchester, 2000).

Tilak, B. G., *Samagra Lokmanya Tilaka* (7v., Pune, 1974–6).

Tinker, Hugh, *The Ordeal of Love: C. F. Andrews and India* (Delhi, 1979).

—— 'The India Conciliation Group, 1931–1950: Dilemmas of the Mediator', *Journal of Commonwealth and Comparative Politics*, 14 (1976), 224–41.

—— (ed.), *Burma: The Struggle for Independence 1944–48* vol. 1 *From Military Occupation to Civil Government* (London, 1983).

—— 'British Liberalism and India, 1917–1945', in J. M. W. Bean (ed.), *The Political Culture of Modern Britain: Studies in Memory of Stephen Koss* (London, 1987).

Tomlinson, B. R., *The Indian National Congress and the Raj, 1929–1942: The Penultimate Phase* (London, 1976).

—— *The Political Economy of the Raj, 1914–1947: The Economics of Decolonization in India* (London, 1979).

—— *The Economy of Modern India, 1860–1970* (Cambridge, 1993).

Tripathi, Amales, *The Extremist Challenge: India Between 1890 and 1910* (New Delhi, 1967).

Trivedi, Harish, *Colonial Transactions: English Literature and India* (Calcutta, 1993).

Tsuzuki, Chushichi, *H. M. Hyndman and British Socialism* (London, 1961).

Van der Veer, Peter, *Imperial Encounters: Religions and Modernity in India and Britain* (Princeton, 2001).

Vickers, Rhiannon, *The Labour Party and the World, vol.1, The Evolution of Labour's Foreign Policy, 1900–51* (Manchester, 2003).

Vidwans, H. D. (ed.), *Letters of Lokamanya Tilak* (Poona, 1966).

Visram, Rozina, *Asians in Britain: 400 Years of History* (London, 2002).

Viswanathan, Gauri, *Outside the Fold: Conversion, Modernity and Belief* (Princeton, 1998).

—— 'The Ordinary Business of Occultism', *Critical Inquiry*, 27/1 (Autumn 2000), 1–20.

Voigt, Johannes H., *India in the Second World War* (Delhi, 1987).

Waley, S. D., *Edwin Montagu: A Memoir and an Account of his Visits to India* (London, 1964).

Walker, Graham, *Tom Johnston* (Manchester, 1988).

Walker, William, *Juteopolis: Dundee and its Textile Workers, 1885–1923* (Edinburgh, 1979).

Ward, Paul, *Red Flag and Union Jack: Englishness, Patriotism and the British Left, 1881–1924* (Woodbridge, 1998).

Weber, Thomas, *Gandhi as Disciple and Mentor* (Cambridge, 2004).

Wedderburn, Sir William, *Allan Octavian Hume, C.B.* (London, 1913).

Wedgwood, C. V., *The Last of the Radicals: Josiah Wedgwood M.P.* (London, 1951).

Wedgwood, J. C., *Essays and Adventures of a Labour M.P.* (London, 1924).

—— *Memoirs of a Fighting Life* (London, 1940).

Wellock, Wilfred, *India's Awakening* (London, 1922).

Williams, Donovan, *The India Office, 1858–1869* (Hoshiapur, 1983).

Williams, Keith, '"A Way Out of our Troubles": The Politics of Empire Settlement, 1900–22' in Stephen Constantine (ed.), *Emigrants and Empire: British Settlement in the Dominions Between the Wars* (Manchester, 1990).

Williams, Raymond, 'The Bloomsbury Fraction' in his *Problems in Materialism and Culture* (London, 1980).

—— *The Politics of Modernism: Against the New Conformists* (London, 1989).

Williamson, Philip, '"Party first and India second": The Appointment of the Viceroy of India in 1930', *Bulletin of the Institute of Historical Research*, 55 (1983), 86–101.

—— *National Crisis and National Government: British Politics, the Economy and Empire, 1926–1932* (Cambridge, 1992).

Winter, J. M., 'The Webbs and the Non-white World: A Case of Socialist Racialism', *Journal of Contemporary History*, 9/1 (1974), 181–92.

Wolpert, Stanley A., *Tilak and Gokhale: Revolution and Reform in the Making of Modern India* (Berkeley and Los Angeles, 1962).
—— *Morley and India, 1906–1910* (Berkeley and Los Angeles, 1967).
—— *Nehru: A Tryst with Destiny* (New York, 1996).
Woods, Philip, 'The Montagu–Chelmsford Reforms (1919): A Reassessment', *South Asia*, 17/1 (1994), 25–42.
Woolf, Leonard (ed.), *A Writer's Diary: Being Extracts from The Diary of Virginia Woolf* (New York, 1954).
—— *Beginning Again: An Autobiography of the Years 1911–1918* (London, 1964).
—— *Downhill All The Way: An Autobiography of the Years 1919–1939* (London, 1967).
—— *The Journey Not the Arrival Matters: An Autobiography of the Years 1939–1969* (London, 1969).
Worley, Matthew (ed.), *In Search of Revolution: International Communist Parties in the Third Period* (London, 2004).
Wrench, J. E. L., *Geoffrey Dawson and Our Times* (London, 1955).
Wyatt, Woodrow, *Confessions of an Optimist* (London, 1985).
Yajnik, Indulal, *Shyamji Krishnavarma: Life and Times of an Indian Revolutionary* (Bombay, 1950).
Young, Robert, *Postcolonialism: An Historical Introduction* (Oxford, 2001).
Zaidi, A. M. (ed.), *Encyclopaedia of the Indian National* Congress (28v., New Delhi, 1976–94).
—— *Congress Presidential Addresses* (5v., New Delhi, 1985–9).
—— *The Glorious Tradition: Texts of the Resolutions Passed by the INC, the AICC, and the CWC* (5v., New Delhi, 1987–9)
—— *The Story of Congress Pilgrimage* (7v., New Delhi, 1990).
Zastoupil, Lynn, *John Stuart Mill and India* (Stanford, Calif., 1994).
Ziegler, Philip, *Mountbatten* (London, 1985).

Newspapers

Amrita Bazar Patrika
Bala-Bharata
Bande Mataram
Bengalee
Colonial Information Bulletin
Commonweal
The Communist Review
Daily Herald
Daily News
Daily Worker
Forward

The Friend
Hind
The Hindu
Hindustan Review
India
India and England
India Bulletin
Indian Annual Review
Indian News
Indian Opinion
Indian Quarterly Review
The Indian Review
Indian Sociologist
Indian Spectator
Indus
International Press Correspondence
Justice
Karmayogin
Labour Monthly
Lansbury's Labour Weekly
Leicester Daily Post
The Listener
Mahratta
Manchester Guardian
The Modern Review
The Nation
New International
New Leader
New Statesman and Nation
News Chronicle
NewsIndia
The Other India
The Panjabee
Peace News
Political Quarterly
Reynolds News
The Seaman
Servant of India
The Spectator
Svaraj
Theosophy

The Times
Tribune
United India
Workers' International News
World News and Views

Unpublished theses and conference papers

Arora, K. C., 'The India League and the India Conciliation Group as factors in Indo-British Relations 1930–49' (London, Ph.D., 1989).

Calder, Angus, 'The Common Wealth Party, 1942–1945' (Sussex, Ph.D., 1967).

Golant, W., 'The Political Development of C. R. Attlee to 1935' (Oxford, B.Litt., 1967).

Howe, Stephen, 'Anti-Colonialism in British Politics: the Left and the End of Empire' (Oxford, D.Phil., 1981).

Husain, Syed Anwar, 'The Organisation and Administration of the India Office, 1910–1924' (London, Ph.D., 1978).

Jones, Jean, 'The Anti-Colonial Politics and Policies of the Communist Party of Great Britain, 1920–1951' (Wolverhampton, Ph.D., 1997).

Matikkala, Mira, 'William Digby and the British Radical debate on India from the 1880s to the 1890s' (Cambridge, M.Phil., 2004).

Morrow, Margot, 'Origin and Early Years of the British Committee of the Indian Nationalist Congress, 1885–1907' (London, Ph.D., 1977).

Owen, Nicholas, 'The Confusions of an Imperialist Inheritance: The British Labour Party and the Indian Problem, 1940–47' (Oxford, D.Phil., 1993).

—— 'Reporting the Indian Civil Disobedience Movement in Britain, 1930–32', unpublished paper (2006).

Puri, Madan Mohan, 'British Labour and India, 1927–1947: A Study of the Policy Formulation Process in the British Labour Party on the Indian Question' (Cologne, Dr.rev.pol. thesis, 1961).

Thompson, Andrew S., '"Thinking Imperially?": Imperial Pressure Groups and the Idea of Empire in Late-Victorian and Edwardian Britain' (Oxford, D.Phil., 1994).

Index

Lightning Source UK Ltd.
Milton Keynes UK
UKOW050833200612

194735UK00001B/5/P